Legal Maxims in Islamic Criminal Law: Theory and Applications

Brill's Arab and Islamic Laws Series

Edited by

Dr. Khaled Abou El Fadl
University of California, Los Angeles, School of Law

VOLUME 9

The titles published in this series are listed at *brill.com/bail*

Legal Maxims in Islamic Criminal Law: Theory and Applications

By

Luqman Zakariyah

BRILL
NIJHOFF

LEIDEN | BOSTON

Library of Congress Cataloging-in-Publication Data

Zakariyah, Luqman, author.
Legal maxims in Islamic criminal law : theory and applications / By Luqman Zakariyah.
pages cm. — (Brill's Arab and Islamic laws series ; 9)
Includes bibliographical references and index.
ISBN 978-90-04-25836-5 (hardback : alk. paper) — ISBN 978-90-04-30487-1 (e-book)
1. Legal maxims (Islamic law) 2. Criminal law (Islamic law) I. Title.

KBP40.2.Z35 2015
345'.167—dc23

2015029278

This publication has been typeset in the multilingual "Brill" typeface. With over 5,100 characters covering Latin, IPA, Greek, and Cyrillic, this typeface is especially suitable for use in the humanities.
For more information, please see www.brill.com/brill-typeface.

ISSN 1871-2894
ISBN 978-90-04-25836-5 (hardback)
ISBN 978-90-04-30487-1 (e-book)

This book is printed on acid-free paper.

Printed by Printforce, the Netherlands

Dedication

To the memory of my beloved mother, Sabitiyu Abike

To my dearest wife Ruqayatu Omowunmi

To those who are victims of the misinterpretation of Shariah in Northern Nigeria

To those who are implementing the law of Allah with sincerity and wisdom

Contents

Table of Statutes

Table of Cases

Acknowledgement

This book is based on my PhD thesis submitted to the University of Wales, Lampeter, UK in 2009. First and foremost, I give sincere thanks to Almighty Allah for giving me the ability to complete the work despite all the stumbling blocks on my way during the academic journey. Without Him, (Subhanahu Wataʿala), I would not have been able to accomplish this work. For the six years I have worked on this thesis, I found Allah on my side to break through.

Many people have directly and indirectly contributed to this achievement. I sincerely appreciate the invaluable contribution of my supervisor, Dr. Dawoud El-Alami. It has been my humble privilege to complete this work under his supervision. His advice on how to frame the final topic of my thesis deserves much praise. Special thanks to my former supervisor, Dr Zaki Badawi, (the former director and founder of The Muslim College London). It was under his supervision this work started before he answered the call of his Lord.

My humble appreciation goes to Professor Mashood A. Baderin of the School of Oriental and African Studies (SOAS), University of London who was the external examiner of my thesis. His critical evaluation and suggestions to improve this work to the stage of publication is substantially invaluable. Not only that, he has been a wonderful mentor for me since I have started my academic career. I also appreciate the thorough reading and professional input of Dr. Rob Warner, head of the department of theology and religious studies, University of Wales, Lampeter, who was the internal examiner. I would also like to thank all members of staff at the University of Wales, Lampeter and the Muslim College London for their cooperation and understanding of the nature of my works and the resilient supports given to me during the course of my study.

My sincere thanks to my name sake, Dr. Shaykh Luqman Jimoh of the Kwara State University, Malete; Brother Abdul Basit Mukhtar of OIC Jeddah; Dr. Ishaq Olatunbosun of The American University Sharjah, UAE; Dr Abdul Waheed Adebisi and Dr Ahmad Agbaje of the University of Ilorin; Dr Abdul Lateef Adetona of Lagos State University, and host of others who had contributed to this achievement in one way or the other.

I am also indebted to some governmental and academic institutions, both in Britain and in Nigeria. In Britain, I would like to thank the staff members of the University of Birmingham Library; the University of Edinburgh Library; the University of Wales Lampeter; the British National Library, London and the Scottish National Library, Edinburgh for giving me access to their precious recourses and for helping me in acquiring other materials which are not available in their libraries. In Nigeria, I would like to thank the ministries of justice, Kano State and Zamfara State; Sharia Courts in Zamfara, Kano, Kastina and Kwara States; Faculties of Laws at the Usmanu Danfodiyo University, Sokoto; Ahmad Bello University, Zaria and Bayero University Kano Librarians for giving permission to me to access some relevant cases and materials for this work. I appreciate the help of Dr Tawfiq Ladan of the Faculty of Law, Ahmadu Bello University, Dr. Mansur and Dr. S.O. Rabiu of the Faculty of Law, Usmanu Danfodiyo University, Sokoto.

I am grossly indebted to my beloved family for the love and encouragements given to me during my lengthy period of study. Special thanks to my wife, Ruqayatu Omowunmi who was the backbone of this achievement, Hikmat Abike and Ummulkhayr Omolabake who have sacrificed their parental rights for the sake of my academic achievement.

I give my highest degree of thanks and prayers to my parents for their sincere prayers for me and my siblings while they were alive. I pray to Allah (SWT) to make their souls perfect in the grave and to reward them with paradise on the day of resurrection.

Luqman Zakariyah
KIRKH, IIUM
Kuala Lumpur, Malaysia
2015

CHAPTER 1

Introduction

An Overview of Islamic Law

Concept of Islamic Law

The concept of Islamic Law has not been precisely defined, as some authors use the term to reference the Sharīʿa while others use it to refer to *fiqh* (jurisprudence).[1]

Scholars have explored various approaches in classical and modern literature to explain the concept of Sharīʿa and its principles. A number of approaches meant to juxtapose the Sharīʿa and its values with other concepts tend to suggest a clash between civilizations while advocating the superiority of one legal system over another, thus resonating with a sense of egoism and incompatibility.[2] Other approaches portray the Sharīʿa as a restricted corpus of rules—of do's and don'ts—that result in severe punishments and barbaric discipline when violated. However, such descriptions subjugate the Sharīʿa to "obscurantist confinement, medieval stubbornness, and fanaticism".[3] While there is no doubt that it indeed embodies rules and regulations, such aspects, however, only form the strictly legalistic notion of the Sharīʿa but do not exhaust its holistic and comprehensive nature, as will be discussed below.

Although the most common English translation for Sharīʿa is 'Islamic Law', many Muslim scholars demur, as this suggests a narrow legalistic interpretation.[4] The term Sharīʿa originates from the triliteral Arabic root (*shīn-rāʾ-ʿayn*) of the verb *sharaʿa* (to legislate). However, as a noun, Sharīʿa literally

1 See Mashood A. Baderin, *International Human Rights and Islamic Law* (Oxford: Oxford University Press, 2005) 32–40. The conclusion of the author is that Sharīʿa is the source of the law while *fiqh* is the method "by which the law is derived and applied" (p. 33). See also Luqman Zakariyah, "Sharīʿah Values for Modern Societies: Analysis of Contents and Contexts", in *The Routledge International Handbook of Education, Religion and Values*, eds. James Arthur and Terence Lovat (New York: Routledge, 2013), 373–375.

2 Michael J. Kelly, "Islam and International Law: A Brief (In)Compatibility Study", *Pace International Law Review Online Companion* (1 March 2010): 1–31. See also, Abdullahi Ahmed an-Naʿim, *Islam and the Secular State* (Cambridge, MA: Harvard University Press, 2008).

3 Tariq Ramadan, *Islam, the West and the Challenges of Modernity* (Leicester: The Islamic Foundation, 2001), 47.

4 Baderin; see also an-Naʿim, *Islam*.

 | DOI 10.1163/9789004304871_002

means "a path to be followed",[5] or "the way which leads to a source".[6] The traditionalist approach to the Sharīʿa defines it as "the command of God revealed to Prophet Muḥammad"[7] (Peace be upon Him: PBUB).[8]

From the latter definition, different interpretations have emerged. For classical scholars, as well as several contemporary authors, the Sharīʿa embodies revelation, an association that regards the Sharīʿa as the source of Islamic Law.[9] Mawdūdī suggests that the Sharīʿa comprises the substance of God's commandments gradually revealed to His prophets at different points in time, applicably amended to each particular era, and thereafter completed upon the advent of Prophet Muḥammad.[10] Mawdūdī considers the Sharīʿa to be the "detailed codes of conduct" or "canons of law" that include "modes of worship, standards of morals and life and laws".[11] Ramadan's contemporary definition[12] is somewhat generic, with a demarcation between acts of worship (*ʿibāda*) and social affairs (*muʿāmalāt*); while rules regarding the former are permanently coded and fixed, those regarding the latter are open to interpretation. According to Ramadan, if a proper procedure is followed for interpreting the sources, in order to legislate on social affairs, then a derived rule can be regarded as part of the Sharīʿa, although its implementation may differ as a result of individual reflection on the law based on the circumstances and context in which the rule of law is debated and implemented. Hence, one might encounter at diverse locations "different legislations" adopted for an issue that both can be considered "Islamic".[13]

Technically the problem of rendering interpretations of the Sharīʿa lies in the fact that some Muslim scholars tend to mix that which is immutable and that which is changeable and can be adapted. In his locution, al-Shaltūt is quoted in al-Ashqar to have asserted that the Sharīʿa is deemed immutable:

---

5 Abdur Rahman I. Doi, *Sharīʿah: Islamic Law* (London: Ta-Ha Publishers, 1987), 2.

6 Ramadan, *Islam*, 48.

7 Muḥammad Muslehuddin, *Islamic Jurisprudence and the Rule of Necessity and Need* (Islamabad: Islamic Research Institute, 1980), 55.

8 The phrase "Peace Be Upon Him", at times abbreviated as 'PBUH', will not be repeated as required by Islam but rather implied whenever Prophet Muḥammad is mentioned.

9 Baderin, 33; Jørgen S. Nielsen, "Introduction", in Jørgen S. Nielsen and Christoffersen Lisbet (eds.), *Sharīʿa as Discourse: Legal Traditions and the Encounter with Europe*, (Farnham, UK: Ashgate, 2010), 4.

10 Abū al-Aʿlā Mawdūdī, *Towards Understanding Islam* (Indianapolis: Islamic Teaching Center, 1970), 143.

11 *Ibid.*

12 Ramadan, *Islam*, 48.

13 *Ibid.*

> [t]here is no other code which deserves to be called law except the Sharīʿa because it originates from the Lord of Mankind who alone reserves the right to legislate for man [...] All man-made laws are false because they are enacted by those who have no right to make them.[14]

However, such a statement invokes a misconception with regard to what is divine and immutable and what is changeable and adaptable in the Sharīʿa. The interpretations given by Ramadan[15] and Baderin[16] suggest the presence of two elements of law in the Sharīʿa: *i.e.*, the source of law (revelation) and the law itself.[17] The former aspect is what many traditional Muslims refer to as immutable and unchangeable, while the latter aspect refers to (i) the fundamental essence of the law directly and explicitly expressed in the sources and (ii) derivative rules that emerge from human understanding and interpretation of the source of law and, in some cases, application of these derivative rules, *i.e.*, *fiqh* or jurisprudence.[18]

Indeed, adherence to the strict traditionalist interpretation of the Sharīʿa as 'Islamic Law' will erect a barrier to accessing the Sharīʿa's overall objectives (*maqāṣid ash-sharīʿa*). While it is unanimously agreed upon that the Sharīʿa is immutable, one's understanding might differ depending on the concept and content to which a rule is applied. One way to make Islamic Law more universal and dynamic would be to consider both components when applying any rule (*ḥukm*) of Islamic Law. Thus, in this book, the term 'Islamic Law' will be used often to refer to *fiqh* or the jurisprudential aspect of the Sharīʿa unless stated otherwise. One must remember that the origin of *fiqh* derives partly from the sources of the Sharīʿa and partly from human interpretation based on independent reasoning or personal exertion (*ijtihād*). The ultimate aim of this book is to discuss and demonstrate how Muslim jurists appear to interpret the

---

14 al-Ashqar, ʿUmar Sulaymān, *al-Sharīʿa l-Ilāhiyya lā l-Qawānīn al-Jāhiliyya* (Kuwait: Dār al-Daʿwa, 1983), 24. Schacht alludes to this fact saying that "the *Sharīʿah* is the most typical manifestation of the Islamic way of life [...] the core and kernel of Islam itself" (see Joseph Schacht, *An Introduction to Islamic Law* (Oxford: Oxford University Press, 1964), 1), while Anderson also observes that Sharīʿa is "explicit and assured in its enunciation of the quality of life which God requires of man and woman" (see J.N.D. Anderson, "The Legal Tradition", in James Kritzeck and William H. Lewis (eds.), *Islam in Africa*, (New York: Van Nostrand Reinhold, 1969), 35.

15 Ramadan, *Islam*, 48.

16 Baderin, 34.

17 See Nielsen, 4.

18 Baderin, 32–34.

Sharīʿa and how it ought to be interpreted and implemented, especially in our contemporary era.

Scope of Islamic Law

Broadly speaking, Islamic Law is wide in scope, rigid in principle and dynamic in application. The scope of Islamic Law is largely divided into two parts: (1) rules that guide religious rites (*ukhrāwiyya*, otherwise called *ʿibādāt*) and (2) laws that guide mankind in his ordinary day-to-day activities (*dunyāwiyya*). While *ukhrāwiyya* refers to rules pertaining to religious observances, such as beliefs, prayers, almsgiving, fasting and pilgrimage, *dunyāwiyya* refers to laws governing the affairs of this world that can be sub-divided into criminal law, family law, transaction law, as well as political and international laws.[19]

The fundamental value of all aspects of the law is to fulfill the purpose of our earthly existence, which is to serve God, and to realize the benefits of this life and the life hereafter.[20] Thus, all aspects of the law intertwine to accomplish this purpose. Attempting to attain our spiritual goals will ultimately help us realize other Sharīʿa principles. The relationship between the Sharīʿa, religion (*dīn*), and Islam resonates first and foremost in a Muslim's acts of devotion (worship and spirituality, when correctly performed) from which social, political and economical values can be derived and fully realized.[21] Through intertextualization of the sources of the Sharīʿa, it becomes possible to appreciate the interconnection between all its dimensions and their associated values.

The importance of the aspect of 'political will' in Islamic Law rests on the fact that, historically, Muslim rulers have enjoyed the privilege of being God's

---

19 Ṣubḥī R. Maḥmaṣṣānī, *Falsafat at-Tashrīʿ fī l-Islām* (*The Philosophy of Jurisprudence in Islam*), trans. Farhat J. Ziadeh (Kuala Lumpur: The Open Press, 2/000), 10; Sayed H.A. Malik, "Shariʿah: A Legal System and a Way of Life", in Abdul-Rahmon M. Oloyede (ed.), *Perspectives in Islamic Law and Jurisprudence*, (Ibadan: National Association for Muslim Law Students, 2001), 25–26. See also Christopher G. Weeramantry, *Islamic Jurisprudence: An International Perspective*, 2nd edn. (Kuala Lumpur: The Other Press, 2001); Luqman Zakariyah, "Sharīʿah Values for Modern Societies: Analysis of Contents and Contexts", in James Arthur and Terence Lovat (eds.), *The Routledge International Handbook of Education, Religion and Values*, (New York: Routledge, 2013), 376–381.

20 The purpose of creation is mentioned in the Qurʾānic verse 51:56: "And I [Allāh] created not the jinns and humans except they should worship Me [Alone]". Reference is also made in the Qurʾānic verse 28:77 to the benefit of creatures on the earth. Further, Qurʾānic verse 49:13 explains the purpose of creating mankind in different clans, tribes, and races. Human beings cannot conclusively say categorically that these reasons are the only purposes of God in creation.

21 Zakariyah, "Sharīʿah Values", 376.

vicegerents on earth, acting in accordance to their understanding of Divine Law (Sharīʿa) and dispensing justice as they deemed fit. In so doing, they sometimes infringed upon certain aspects of human rights. In a number of Muslim countries, the violation of human rights makes clearly evident a discrepancy between the existence of principles embedded in the Sharīʿa and their lack of implementation through the just rule of law. Baderin observes that a "static and immoderate application of some of the traditional interpretations of the Sharīʿah can however constrain the scope of Islamic Law for present times".[22] This stagnation and imbalance in application of Islamic Law could lead to concealment of the legacy left by the earliest great Islamic jurists. He further observes that most of the articles in the International Covenant on Civil and Political Rights (ICCPR) are compatible with the Sharīʿa:[23] whenever discrepancies occur, mutual understanding can be sought through appreciation of the Sharīʿa's objectives. Similarly, Doi elucidates Sharīʿa's stand on the protection of the rights of non-Muslims in an Islamic state, such as the right to own property, to enjoy privacy and security, to have religious freedom to practice their beliefs as they see fit.[24] As proof that such rights were objectively honored during the early years of the Islamic civilization, it is worth noting that non-Muslims at that times preferred to be judged under Islamic Law rather than by their own religious codes, as evidenced by the assertion: "we prefer your government and its keen sense of justice to the cruelty and injustice of our co-religionists".[25]

In the Sharīʿa, the fundamental principle of justice, the most basic guideline inspiring universal human rights, is free "from time-space elements".[26] It is neither confined to a particular gender, to a certain group of people, race or tribe, to affiliates of a political party or religious sect. Sharīʿa's notion of justice means justice for all mankind, as stated unequivocally in the Qurʾān.[27] However, not all aspects of the Sharīʿa are so easily applicable in contemporary

22 Baderin, 40.

23 Such as the prohibition of torture in the Sharīʿa and in Article 7 of the ICCPR; see Baderin, 75.

24 Abdur Rahman I. Doi, *Non-Muslims Under Shariʿah* (*Islamic Law*), (London: Ta-Ha Publishers, 1983/1997), 120.

25 *Ibid.*

26 Abdul Hamid Abu Sulayman, *Towards an Islamic Theory of International Relations: New Directions for Islamic Methodology and Thought* (Herndon, VA: International Institute of Islamic Thought, 1993), 140.

27 "O you who believe! Be steadfast witnesses for Allāh in equality, and let not hatred of any people seduce you into dealing unjustly. Deal justly, that is nearer to your duty, Observe your duty to Allāh. Lo! Allāh is informed of all that you do" (Q. 5:8; *cf.*, Q. 16:90; Q. 57:25; Q. 7:29; Q. 4:48).

time, and some are even radically disputed. Apart from issues raised against the inadequate application of some aspects (*e.g.*, social affairs) of Islamic Law, such as the allegation of inequality in Islamic family law and political injustice, the most controversial aspect of the Sharīʿa is criminal law.[28]

Islamic Criminal Law

Islamic criminal law, often perceived in the West as a 'barbaric' infliction of unnecessary harm, is one of the most contestable aspects of Islamic Law in modern societies. Islamic criminal law consists of three categories: (1) *ḥudūd* or predetermined, mandatory penalties prescribed for certain *ḥudūd* crimes; (2) *qiṣāṣ* or retributive penalties prescribed for offences resulting in bodily injury; and (3) *taʿzīr* or discretionary penalties prescribed for offences that do not fall within the previous categories.[29]

The term *ḥadd* (pl. *ḥudūd*) means boundary, standard, penalty, prevention and inhibition.[30] *Ḥadd* penalties share three distinctive features. First, they are injunctions commanded by God to serve social justice. Second, the magnitude of these pre-determined penalties can neither be limited or reduced nor increased or made more severe. Third, *ḥadd* punishments are mandatory and must be administered to the accused once the crime has been reported to the authorities and sufficient proof of guilt established.[31] Pardon (*ʿafw*) is not an option.[32] Remarking on the reflective purpose of punishment in Islam to the linguistic meaning (*lughawiyya*) of *ḥadd*, Abdul Rahman Doi says that punishment is called *ḥadd* because it is "a restrictive and preventive ordinance, or

---

28 See Zakariyah, "Sharīʿah Values", 373–384.

29 For general overviews on Islamic criminal law, see ʿAbd al-Qadir ʿAwda, *at-Tashrīʿ al-Jināʾī l-Islāmī Muqāranan bi-l-Qānūn al-Waḍaʿī* (Beirut: Muʾassasat ar-Risāla, 1995); Muhammad S. el-Awa, *Punishment in Islamic Law* (Plainfield, IL: American Trust Publications, 1982); Rudolph Peters, *Crime and Punishment in Islamic Law: Theory and Practice from the Sixteenth to the Twenty-First Century* (Cambridge: Cambridge University Press, 2006); Mohammad Shabbir, *Outlines of Criminal Law and Justice in Islam* (Selangor, Malaysia: International Law Book Services, 2002); Muhammad Iqbal Siddiqi, *The Penal Law of Islam* (New Delhi: International Islamic Publishers, 1994); M.M. Khan, *Islamic Law and Criminology* (New Delhi: Discovery Publishing House, 2011). Some authors deal with the subject of Islamic criminal law in a more critical manner such as Baderin (pp. 78–85).

30 Munīr al-Dīn Baʿalbakkī, *al-Mawrid: A Modern Arabic-English Dictionary*. 8th edn. (Beirut: Dār al-ʿIlm li-l-Malayin, 1997), 455–456; and Muḥammad b. Makram Ibn Manẓūr, *Lisān al-ʿArab*, edited by Amin Muhammad ʿAbd al-Wahhab and Muḥammad Sadiq al-ʿUbayd, (Beirut: Dār Iḥyāʾ at-Turāth al-ʿArabī and Muʾassasat al-Ṭārikh al-ʿArabī, 1997), 4:93.

31 El-Awa, 1–2.

32 See Peters, *Crime and Punishment*, 53–65; Baderin, 78–85.

statute of God concerning things [that are] lawful (*ḥalāl*) and things [that are] unlawful (*ḥarām*)".[33]

Technically, Islamic scholars view the term *ḥadd* from two somewhat different perspectives. First, some Islamic scholars take into consideration whose rights have been violated and find a limited number of *ḥudūd* crimes with fixed, or pre-established, immutable punishments mentioned in the Holy Qur'ān or referred to by the Sunna of the Prophet. Moreover, from their point of view, *qiṣāṣ* crimes, involving the right to retaliate in kind, could also be classified as *ḥudūd* crimes rather than as a separate category, because they also have distinct characteristics and predetermined punishments set forth in the Qur'ān or mentioned in the Prophet's Sunna. Less serious *taʿzīr* crimes are awarded variable penalties dependant on the discretion of the judge (*qāḍī*) or ruler (*ḥākim*).[34] Generally, Muslim jurists have unanimously agreed on six types of *ḥudūd* crimes: namely, (1) *sariqa* (theft: amputation of a hand); (2) *zinā* (adultery/fornication or illicit sexual relations: stoning to death (*rajm*) for a married person, and flogging (*jald*): 100 lashes for an unmarried person); (3) *qadhf* (defamation/slanderous accusations: 80 lashes); (4) *ridda* (apostasy: death); (5) *shurb al-khamr* (alcohol consumption/inebriation: 80 lashes); and (6) *ḥirāba* (banditry/brigandage: death, cutting off an opposite leg and arm, or exile (*nafī*), according to the severity of the crime).[35] Islamic literature also speaks about *baghy* (treason against a just leader).[36] This enumeration is compatible with the definition of crimes provided by al-Māwardī (d. 450/1058), and in line with the majority of classical jurists, including the Mālikīs, Shāfiʿīs and Ḥanbalīs. However, the Ḥanafīs exclude inebriation and robbery from their list of *ḥudūd* crimes.[37]

Second, other Islamic scholars hold the view that *ḥadd* penalties are prescribed as the absolute right of God (*ḥaqq Allāh*)[38] and therefore are not

---

33 Doi, *Sharīʿah*, 221; Peters, *Crime and Punishment*, 53–65; Baderin, 78–85.

34 *Ibid.*

35 *Ibid.*

36 ʿAwda, *at-Tashrīʿ*, 2:343–345; Sayyid Sābiq, *Fiqh as-Sunnah*, (Cairo: Dār al-Fath li-l-ʿIlām al-Arabī, 2004/1425), 689.

37 ʿAlī b. Muḥammad al-Māwardī, *al-Aḥkām as-Sulṭāniyya wa-l-Wilāya ad-Dīniyya* (Beirut: Dār al-Kutub al-ʿIlmiyya, n.d.), 218–223; Muḥammad b. Aḥmad Ibn Rushd, *Bidāyat al-Mujtahid wa-Nihāyat al-Muqtaṣid* (Beirut: Dār al-Fikr, n.d.), 2:424–449; al-Shirazī, Abū Isḥāq Ibrāhīm b. ʿAlī al-Shirazī, *al-Muhadhdhab* (Beirut: Dār al-Fikr, n.d.), 2:266–289; ʿAwda, 2:345, 1:105–107; and Aʿlā l-Dīn Abī Bakr b. Masʿūd al-Kāsānī, *Badāʾiʿ aṣ-Ṣanāʾiʿ fī Tartīb ash-Sharāʾiʿ* (Beirut: Dār al-Kutub al-ʿIlmiyya, 1997), 7:33–97.

38 This is in terms of the punishment when an accused is convicted. A punishment allocated and fixed by God can neither be reduced nor increased nor can an accused be pardoned

applicable for murder, manslaughter or bodily injury, on the grounds that the penalties for such crimes are retaliatory (*qiṣāṣ*) or restitutive (*diya*) and considered the right of man (*ḥaqq al-ādamī*). Accordingly, murder and manslaughter are excluded because, in such cases, restitution by paying blood money (*diya*) can be sought by the victim's relatives in lieu of retaliation (*qawad*) in kind.[39] Some scholars argue in response that the opportunity to exchange *qawad* for *diya* also constitutes a predetermined *ḥadd* penalty stipulated by God. Several contemporary scholars who endorse this point of view include Abū Zahra and ʿAbd al-Qādir ʿAwda, who argue that, in contrast to *qiṣāṣ, diya*, and *taʿzīr* penalties, the distinctive feature of *ḥadd* punishments is that they are sanctioned primarily to honor the absolute right of God and maintain social justice.

One should note that even crimes that call for a *ḥadd* punishment, such as slander (*qadhf*) and theft (*sariqa*), can be pardoned by the victims prior to the crime being reported. However, to define *ḥudūd* crimes as a violation of the absolute right of God will be to exclude many crimes mentioned in the *ḥudūd* category as explained above. In other words, only a few crimes, such as apostasy (*ridda*), illicit sexual intercourse (*zinā*), and consumption of alcohol (*shurb al-khamr*), can be classified as a violation of the absolute right of God, and even punishment for the latter is not predetermined in the Qur'ān nor its status consistent in the Sunna.

Some of the salient issues in *ḥadd* punishments resonate in the requirements set out to establish whether such a crime has taken place. As will be explained later, it is often said that it is prudent to conceal (*satara*) rather than report (*shahida*) certain *ḥudūd* crimes, such as illicit sexual intercourse and alcohol consumption, especially if punishment is the absolute right of God. This reasoning gains support from the Ḥadīth reported by ʿĀ'isha (one of the Prophet's wives). The Prophet said:

---

by the authorities. See Abū Zahra, Muḥammad, *al-Jarima wa l-ʿUquba fī l-Fiqh al-Islāmī*, (Cairo: Dār al-Fikr al-ʿArabī, 1998), 49–52.

39 As mentioned in Qur'ānic verse 4:92: "And never is it for a believer to kill a believer except by mistake. And whoever kills a believer by mistake—then the freeing of a believing slave and a compensation payment presented to the deceased's family [is required] unless they give [up their right as] charity. But if the deceased was from a people at war with you and he was a believer—then [only] the freeing of a believing slave; and if he was from a people with whom you have a treaty—then a compensation payment presented to his family and the freeing of a believing slave. And whoever does not find [one or cannot afford to buy one]—then [instead], a fast for two months consecutively, [seeking] acceptance of repentance from Allāh. And Allāh is ever Knowing and Wise".

> Avoid *ḥudūd* crimes involving Muslims to the extent possible; if there is an exculpating cause [for the accused], then release him, as it is better that the Imām make a mistake in pardoning than in punishing.
>
> (*idraʾū l-ḥudūd ʿan al-muslimīn mā staṭaʿtum fa-in kāna lah makhrajan fa-khallū sabīlah fa-inna l-imām an yukhṭi fī l-ʿafw khayr min an yukhṭi fī l-ʿuqūba*)[40]

This Ḥadīth as well as many actions of the Prophet and practices of his Companions (*ṣaḥāba*) illustrate that penalties are meant to be symbolic deterrents (*zajr*) rather than to inflict harm on the masses. Thus, many penalties are variable rather that pre-established, depending on the "discretion of the victim of the offence (or the heirs)"[41] in the case of *qiṣāṣ* and on the gravity of the offence in the case of *taʿzīr*. Far from being a mere list of prescribed punishments for specific crimes, the function of Islamic penal law is both preventive and curative, meant to curb further aggression and to purify the souls of transgressors in Muslim societies.[42] Although wrongdoers must be punished because "justice cannot be achieved without punishing the culprit",[43] and because every person "is obligated to pay the penalty or the injustices that [s]he may commit",[44] many Qurʾānic verses also show clemency.[45] Thorough study of Islamic texts indicates that "while punishments attempt to protect the fundamental values of the victims, implementation of these punishments is meant to protect the accused persons".[46] Therefore, although penal

40 The Ḥadīth is reported by al-Tirmidhī, and al-Albani described it as a weak (*ḍaʿīf*) Ḥadīth. See Muḥammad b. ʿĪsā al-Tirmidhī, *Sunān al-Tirmidhī*, edited by Bashashar ʿAwad Maʿruf, (Beirut: Dār al-Gharb al-Islāmī, 1998), 3:85. Intisar Rabb has traced the authenticity of the Ḥadīth in different books of Ḥadīths and made some significant comments on the issue. See Intisar Rabb, *Doubt's Benefit: Legal Maxims in Islamic Law 7th–16th Centuries*, Ph.D. Dissertation (Princeton: Princeton University Press, 2009), 93–101. The English translation is from the latter author.

41 Baderin, 78–79.

42 Saeed Hassan Ibrahim and Nasir b. Ibrahim Mehemeed, "Basic Principles of Criminal Procedure Under Islamic Shariʿah", in Muhammad Abdel Haleem, Adel Omar Sharif, and Kate Daniels (eds.), *Criminal Justice in Islam: Judicial Procedure in the Shariʿa*, (London: I.B. Tauris, 2003), 31.

43 *Ibid.*

44 Majid Khadduri, *The Islamic Conception of Justice* (Baltimore: John Hopkins University Press, 1984), 160.

45 Such as Qurʾānic verses 2:178 and 5:33–34.

46 Zakariyah, "Sharīʿah Values", 379.

Qur'ānic verses clearly instruct values, application of punishments endorsed in these verses is open to interpretation.

Evolution of Islamic Law

Substantive and Interpretative Sources

Generally the sources of Islamic Law are classified as either primary or secondary. The four primary sources of Islamic Law are the Holy Qur'ān (revealed to Prophet Muḥammad), Sunna (sayings, traditions and tacit approvals of the Prophet collections called Ḥadīths), scholarly consensus (*ijmāʿ*) and analogical deduction (*qiyās*), although some Schools of Islamic Jurisprudence (*madhhab*, pl. *madhāhib*) attached restrictions on the use of the latter two sources.[47] The Qur'ān and Sunna are textual and regarded as divine by orthodox scholars, predominantly those from the Sunni Schools. Although *ijmāʿ* and *qiyās* are not textual, Muslim scholars have agreed upon their incorporation as sources of Islamic Law; while not divine in nature, *ijmāʿ* is meant to be infallible due to the fact that the Prophet exonerated the Muslim nation from having agreed in error.[48]

As a religion, Islam offers insight into the needs of human beings through the global perspectives of the Qur'ān and Sunna.[49] The Holy Qur'ān and collections of prophetic Ḥadīths stand as an encyclopedia of Islamic knowledge, and upon these sources Islamic Law was established at the time of Prophet Muḥammad. In other words, during this particular period, the Qur'ān and Ḥadīths were unanimously accepted as the only sources of Islamic Law, which expounded the fundamental principles of life.[50] Later as these deeds, sayings

---

47 All scholars agree with this assertion. Some have accepted only the Qur'ān and Ḥadīth as primary sources of Islamic Law while others hold that *ijmāʿ* and *qiyās* are secondary sources. The truth of the matter is that when considering the textual sources of Islamic Law, indeed, the Qur'ān and Ḥadīth are primary while other sources are secondary. However, if reference is to agreed-upon sources, then the Qur'ān, Ḥadīth, *ijmāʿ* and *qiyās* are the primary sources. See Muhammad Hashim Kamali, *Principles of Islamic Jurisprudence* (Kuala Lumpur: Ilmiah Publishers, 2000).

48 Doi, *Sharīʿah*, 65–84. The four Sunni Schools of Thought are the Ḥanafī, Mālikī, Shāfiʿī and Ḥanbalī (see text below for the details about the schools); Hossein M. Tabatabai, *An Introduction to Shiʿi Law: A Bibliographical Study* (London: Ithaca Press, 1984), 3. Although it can be found in the early works of Shīʿite legal study, *qiyās* was not actually mentioned as a source of law, as noted by Tabatabai in a footnote of the above book.

49 The Holy Qur'ān is the divine book revealed to Prophet Muḥammad. Ḥadīths are collections of the sayings, deeds and tacit approvals of the Prophet. Ḥadīths stand as a practical explanatory source for the Qur'ān.

50 Muslehuddin, *Islamic Jurisprudence*, 67–68.

and teachings were collected and compiled into books of Ḥadīths that also served to explain and complement the Holy Book.

When the Prophet or his Companions applied personal reasoning to interpret and clarify issues, their explanations were corroborated against main textual sources. If the Qur'ān authenticated the Prophet's rationale, then that source of law established by virtue of his effort would be the Qur'ān. When Prophet Muḥammad's rationale derived from inspiration, it would constitute his Sunna[51] and become an independent source of Islamic Law. However, his Companions' efforts were embedded as tacit approval in the Prophet's Sunna.

As Messenger of God, two of the Prophet's duties were to explain God's commands to the people and, through his personal endeavors, to act in accordance with the aims of His commands. The Prophet's Sunna is meant to reiterate in a simple way God's commandments, to explain the general principles embedded in the Qur'ānic text, to clarify ambiguous textual passages, and, at times, to set rules not derived through revelation but rather through independent reasoning.[52]

With the demise of the Prophet, Islamic Law entered its second period of development, which would last until the beginning of the ʿAbbāsid era (132 AH/750 AD). However, between the Prophet's death (11 AH/632 AD) and establishment of the Umayyad Dynasty (41–132 AH/661–750 AD), the Muslim community was ruled by four orthodox or 'rightly guided' caliphs who had known and supported the Prophet: Abū Bakr, ʿUmar, ʿUthmān, and ʿAlī. During the rule of the orthodox caliphs (11–40 AH/632–661 AD), lawmakers resorted to scholarly consensus (*ijmāʿ*) and analogical reasoning (*qiyās*) to address newly occurring issues that resulted from the rapid expansion of Islam beyond the Arabian Peninsula to other cultures, races and nationalities. This expansion inevitably created jurisprudential problems about which neither of the two divine sources made any explicit statement. The use of scholarly consensus, which is "the unanimous agreement of the Mujtahidun [the learned Muslims Jurisconsults] of the Muslim community of any period following the demise of the Prophet Muhammad on any matter",[53] substantiated the authority of

51 Sunna is the practice of the Prophet which excludes his practices before he became a prophet. The terms 'Sunna' and 'Ḥadīth' are used interchangeably in most Islamic literature but differ in terms of their application. 'Hadith' is more general and includes all the Prophet's Sunna. See Muhammad Hashim Kamali, *Principles of Islamic Jurisprudence* (Kuala Lumpur: Ilmiah Publishers, 2000), 48–62.

52 Kamali, *Ibid.*, p. 248.

53 *Ibid.*, 156. For conflicts in the use of *ijmāʿ*, see Iysa A. Bello, *The Medieval Islamic Controversy Between Philosophy and Orthodoxy*: Ijmāʿ *and* Taʾwīl *in the Conflict Between al-Ghazālī and Ibn Rushd.* (Leiden/New York: Brill, 1989).

the Prophet who was no longer alive.[54] The validity of consensus was based on the Prophet's saying: "My community shall never agree on an error",[55] while analogical deduction (*qiyās*), which is "the extension of a Sharīʿa value from an original case [*aṣl*] to a new case, because the latter has the same effective cause as the former"[56] was intended to meet the demands of novel jurisprudential dilemmas. It is important to state here that the relationship between the secondary sources, consensus (*ijmāʿ*) and analogy (*qiyās*), derives from independent legal reasoning (*ijtihād*) through the personal efforts of qualified scholars (*fuqahāʾ*) of Islamic Law. *Qiyās* can become *ijmāʿ* if supported by general agreement between versed scholars.[57] It is worth noting that both *ijmāʿ* and *qiyās* are products of *ijtihād* and can never be achieved without the means of independent legal reasoning.

During the Umayyad era, all four sources were accepted foundations for Islamic Law, although scholars were criticized for providing inadequate reasoning on a number of issues. Thus, it was said at the time that Divine Law was being subjected to reason "which served to deform and distort it".[58] After the fall of the Umayyad Dynasty when the ʿAbbāsids seized power, Islamic history entered what is known as the third period or 'Golden Age' of Islamic culture (132–656 AH/750–1258 AD). During this third period, the development of Islamic Law reach great heights as a number of Schools of Islamic Jurisprudence began to evolve. Today the four most notable surviving eponymous Sunni Schools are the Ḥanafī, Mālikī, Shāfiʿī and Ḥanbalī, as well as the Ẓāhirī and Shīʿite Schools. Other Schools of Islamic Jurisprudence, however, have since faded into extinction. During this period, the traditions of the Prophet and his Companions were being collected and commentaries on the Qurʾān put to writing. In addition, academic as well as other source

---

54 Ahmad Hasan, *The Early Development of Islamic Jurisprudence*, (Islamabad: Islamic Research Institute, 1970), 156–157; Iyas A. Bello, "The development of *Ijmaʿ* in Islamic Jurisprudence", in M. Oloyede Abdul-Rahmon (ed.), *Perspectives in Islamic Law and Jurisprudence*, (Ibadan: National Association of Muslim Law Students, 2001), 162; for variations in the use of *ijmāʿ* during the later development of Islamic Law, see also Schacht, *Introduction*, 30, 61–68.

55 Muḥammad b. Yazīd Ibn Mājah, *as-Sunān*, edited by Muḥammad Fu'ad ʿAbd al-Baqī, (Beirut: Dār al-Fikr, n.d.), Ḥadīth No. 3950.

56 Kamali, *Principles*, 167.

57 Muslehuddin, *Islamic Jurisprudence*, 69.

58 *Ibid.*, 73; Noel J. Coulson, *History of Islamic Law* (Edinburgh: Edinburgh University Press, 1964), 30–31.

materials were compiled and methodologies employed to give rulings on Islamic issues; however, opinions differed on how rulings should be applied.[59]

The first recognized School of Islamic Jurisprudence was founded by Abū Ḥanīfa an-Nuʿman Ibn Thābit (d. 150/767),[60] who relied extensively on rationalization and the theory of *raʾy* (personal opinion). He is also accredited with formulating the theory called *istiḥsān* (juristic preference).[61]

The second School was named after the great scholar from Medina, Imām Mālik Ibn Anas al-Asbahī (d. 179/795).[62] Mālikī scholars (*ahl al-ḥadīth*) can be distinguished from Iraqi Ḥanafī scholars (*ahl al-raʾy*) by their strict adherence to prophetic tradition or Ḥadīth. Imām Mālik placed emphasis on the unrestricted or public interest (*maṣāliḥ al-mursala*) as source of law, which relied upon the customs, practices and indigenous traditions (*ʿurf / ʿamal / ʿāda*) of the people of Medina on the presumption that these were precedents set by the Prophet and transmitted down through the ages.[63]

The third School, founded by Imām Muḥammad Ibn Idrīs al-Shāfiʿī (d. 204/820), the erudite scholar of *uṣūl al-fiqh* (principles of Islamic jurisprudence), struck a balance between the emphasis placed by the Ḥanafīs on *raʾy* and by the Mālikīs on the use of prophetic tradition or Ḥadīth. Al-Shāfiʿī's book *Treatise on the Principles of Islamic Jurisprudence* (*ar-Risāla*)[64] is a monumental work that illustrates his vision and vast legal knowledge.[65] He developed a methodology for the study of jurisprudence "to a degree of competence and mastery which had never been achieved before and was hardly equaled and never surpassed after him".[66]

The fourth surviving Sunni School was founded by Imām Aḥmad Ibn Ḥanbal (d. 241 /855).[67] The Ḥanbalī School, known to adhere to tradition, was averse to *raʾy*. Ibn Ḥanbal believed that the proven Divine Law should be restricted to the textual sources; namely, the Holy Qurʾān and Ḥadīths. For this reason he undertook a journey throughout all the Muslim territories in quest of prophetic Ḥadīths which he complied in his collection entitled *Musnad*, for which the authoritative chain (*isnād*) of narration derived continuously (*muttaṣil*)

59 Maḥmaṣṣānī, *Falsafat at-Tashrīʿ fī l-Islām*, 17; Muslehuddin, *Islamic Jurisprudence*, 74.

60 Anwar A. Qadir, *Islamic Jurisprudence in the Modern World* (Delhi: Taj Company, 1986), 91.

61 Muslehuddin, *Islamic Jurisprudence*, 74.

62 Qadir, 91.

63 Muslehuddin, *Islamic Jurisprudence*, 75.

64 Supposedly the first book to be written on *uṣūl al-fiqh*.

65 *Ibid.*, 76.

66 Joseph Schacht, *The Origin of Muhammadan Jurisprudence* (Oxford: Oxford University Press, 1950), 12.

67 Maḥmaṣṣānī, 30.

from the Prophet himself. He acknowledged five sources: (1) the Holy Qur'ān, (2) Ḥadīth texts, (3) religious verdicts (*fatwās*) definitely consistent with and not in contradiction to Qur'ānic or sound Ḥadīth texts (*ṣaḥīḥ* or direct chain of transmission), (4) texts from the *mursal* tradition (intermittent or broken chain of authoritative transmitters), (5) texts resulting from analogy (*qiyās*) when necessary.[68]

Other Sunni Schools, now extinct, followed the guidance of such scholars as Imām 'Abd al-Raḥman al-Awzā'ī (d. 157/774), Dāwūd ibn Khalaf al-Ẓāhirī (d. 270/884) and Abū Ja'far Muḥammad ibn Jarīr al-Ṭabarī (d. 310/922).[69] These Schools of Islamic Jurisprudence (*madhāhib*) artificially coded the term *fiqh* (jurisprudence) to differentiate their thinking from dialectical schools of thought (*madrasāt ahl al-kalām*). The term *fiqh* (jurisprudence) or knowledge of *aḥkām ash-shar'* (legal rulings pertaining to conduct that has been derived from specific evidence)[70] originally included all the Sharī'a sciences, namely the theological, spiritual, ethical and jurisprudential sciences.[71] Later, during the time of the 'Abbāsid Caliph al-Mā'mūn (d. 218/833), the denotation of *fiqh* was restricted to practical matters or problems relating to legal matters.[72] Hereafter, the term assumed a technical connotation and the scope was distinguished from dialectical theology.

Legal Methodology

Consequently, a new subject termed the principles of jurisprudence (*uṣūl al-fiqh*) emerged to regulate the deduction of rules from the concept of *fiqh*. As stated above, Imām al-Shāfi'ī is accredited with this endeavor in his book *ar-Risāla*.[73] Although *uṣūl al-fiqh* has been shown to be invaluable, most relevant literature written on this subject is in Arabic. More recently, following

68 Muḥammad Ibn Abī Bakr Ibn al-Qayyim al-Jawziyya, *I'lām al-Muwaqqi'īn 'an Rabb al-'Ālamīn* (Beirut: Dār al-Jil, 1973), 23–26.

69 Maḥmaṣṣānī, 33–34; Muslehuddin, *Islamic Jurisprudence*, 80–81.

70 Muhammad Hashim Kamali, *An Introduction to Shariah* (Kuala Lumpur: Ilmiah Publishers, 2006), 35. Schacht refers to it as "science of shariah" (see Schacht, *Introduction*, 1), which to me is not a comprehensive meaning. *Fiqh*, can be described as the human understanding and interpretation of the Divine law derived from the Qur'ān and the Ḥadīth. See also Baderin, *International Human Rights and Islamic Law*, 33–34.

71 Baderin, *Ibid.*, 34; Qadir, 16.

72 Baderin, *Ibid.*

73 See al-Shāfi'ī, Muḥammad b. Idrīs, *ar-Risāla fī Uṣūl al-Fiqh* (*Treatise on the Foundations of Islamic Jurisprudence*), trans. Majid Khadduri, 2nd edn. (Cambridge, UK: Islamic Texts Society, 1987).

the examples of Neil J. Coulson[74] and Joseph Schacht,[75] additional painstaking efforts have been undertaken to study the discipline of *uṣūl al-fiqh*. As Nabil rightly noted on the meticulous nature of this subject: "this may be due to the complexity of... [it], a subject that concerns itself not only with the law proper, but also with questions of linguistics, logic, methodology, epistemology, and theology".[76] Despite this complexity, no scholar grounded in Islamic jurisprudence will ignore the essential nature of the subject. Nabil further observes:

> The usefulness of *uṣūl al-fiqh* lies primarily in its being an indispensable source for understanding the views of a large and important segment of Muslim thinkers who used the subject as a vehicle for their opinions on the various topics mentioned above.[77]

From the late 20th century onwards, *uṣūl al-fiqh* has been dealt with extensively by both English- and Arabic-language scholars. Credit is due to Kamali, Ahmad Hasan, George Makdisi, Wael B. Hallaq, Joseph Lowry, Nabil Shehaby, as well as a host of other scholars for their invaluable contributions in addressing the subject in English.[78] Discussions on *uṣūl al-fiqh* include a range of issues such

---

74 See Neil J. Coulson, *Succession in the Muslim Family* (Cambridge: Cambridge University Press, 1971), a book on Islamic family law which touches upon some aspects of Islamic legal theory, including *uṣūl al-fiqh*.

75 See Schacht, *Introduction*.

76 Nabil Shehaby, "*ʿIlla* and *Qiyās* in Early Islamic Theory", *Journal of the American Oriental Society*, 102/1 (1982): 27.

77 *Ibid.*, 27.

78 See Kamali, *Principles*; Ahmad Hasan, *The Doctrine of Ijmāʿ in Islam* (Islamabad: Islamic Research Institute, 1978); George Makdisi, "The Juridical Theology of Shāfiʿī Origins and Significance of *Uṣūl al-Fiqh*", *Studia Islamica* 59 (1984): 5–47; Wael B. Hallaq, "The Logic of Legal Reasoning in Religious and Non-Religious Cultures: The Case of Islamic Law and the Common Law", *Cleveland State Law* Review 34 (1985–1986): 94–95; Wael B. Hallaq, "Was al-Shāfiʿī the Architect of Islamic Jurisprudence?", *International Journal of Middle East Studies*, 25/4 (Nov. 1993): 587–605; Wael B. Hallaq, *A History of Islamic Legal Theories: An Introduction to Sunnī* Uṣūl al-Fiqh (Cambridge: Cambridge University Press, 1997); Wael B. Hallaq, *Sharīʿa: Theory, Practice, Transformations* (Cambridge: Cambridge University Press, 2009); and Joseph E. Lowry, "The Reception of al-Shāfiʿī's Concept of *Amr* and *Nahy* in the Thought of His Student al-Muzani", in Joseph E. Lowry, Devin Stewart, and Shawkat M. Toorawa (eds.), *Law and Education in Medieval Islam: Studies in Memory of Professor George Makdisi*, (Cambridge, UK: Gibb Memorial Trust, 2004).

as abrogation (*naskh*),[79] consensus (*ijmāʿ*),[80] analogy (*qiyās*),[81] juristic preference (*istiḥsān*),[82] public interest (*maṣlaḥa*),[83] and custom (*ʿurf*).[84]

Legal rulings formulated in *uṣūl al-fiqh* are categorized as obligatory (*wājib*), prophetic tradition (*sunna*), desirable (*mustaḥabb*), detestable (*makrūh*), prohibited (*ḥarām*), and permissible (*mubāḥ*). Such a schema helps jurists examine the legal consequences of any deed, decide whether it is punishable or merits reward, and determine if it is lawful or illegal.[85]

Development continued until the Schools of Islamic Jurisprudence reached their peak. It is pertinent to mention here that during this Golden Era, there were considerable achievements in the sciences of law and jurisprudence. However, this rapid progress came to a standstill and took a downward turn at the end of the ʿAbbāsid era. For fear of persecution, a number of Sunni jurists campaigned to close the door to *ijtihād* after the fall of Baghdad at the hands of the Mongol Hulagu Khan in the middle of the 7th century Hijra (1258 AD). They also claimed that four Sunni Schools were sufficient to cater to the needs

---

79 Amin M. Sallam al-Manasyeh al-Btoush, *The Question of Abrogation* (Naskh) *in the Qur'ān* (Karak: Deanship of Research and Graduate Studies, Mu'tah University, 1994); John Burton, *The Sources of Islamic Law: Islamic Theories of Abrogation* (Edinburgh: Edinburgh University Press, 1990).

80 Iysa A. Bello, *The Medieval Islamic Controversy Between Philosophy and Orthodoxy*: Ijmāʿ *and* Ta'wīl *in the Conflict Between al-Ghazali and Ibn Rushd* (Leiden/New York: Brill, 1989); Kemal A. Faruki, Ijmaʿ *and the Gate of* Ijtihād (Karachi: Gateway Publications, 1954); Hasan, *Doctrine*.

81 Ahmad Hasan, *Analogical Reasoning in Islamic Jurisprudence: A Study of the Juridical Principle of* Qiyās (Islamabad: Islamic Research Institute, 1986).

82 Muhammad Hashim Kamali, Istiḥsān*: (Juristic Preference) and its Application to Contemporary Issues* (Jeddah: Islamic Research and Training Institute, Islamic Development Bank, 1997); Muhammad Hashim Kamali, "*Istiḥsān* and the Renewal of Islamic Law", *Islamic Studies*, 43/4 (2004): 561–581; Saim Kayadibi, *Doctrine of* Istiḥsān *(Juristic Preference) in Islamic Law*, Ph.D. Dissertation (Durham, UK: University of Durham Press, 2007).

83 For historical accounts and contemporary use of the term *maṣlaḥa*, see Felicitas Opwis, Maṣlaḥa *and the Purpose of the Law: Islamic Discourse on Legal Change from the 4th/10th to 8th/14th Century* (Leiden: Brill, 2010).

84 For elucidation of the controversy surrounding the right of application of the theory of custom in Islamic Law from medieval times to date, see Ayman Shabana, *Custom in Islamic Law and Legal Theory* (New York: Palgrave Macmillan, 2010). See also Luqman Zakariyah, "Custom and Society in Islamic Criminal Law: A Critical Appraisal of the Maxim '*al-Ādah Muhakkamah*' (Custom is Authoritative) and its Sisters in Islamic Legal Procedures", *Arab Law Quarterly*, 26/1 (2012): 75–97.

85 Kamali, *Principles*, 280–290.

of all Muslims.[86] Thus people resorted to blind imitation or dogmatic adherence (*taqlīd*) to a particular School of Jurisprudence without investigating the sources of its opinions.[87] This trend persisted until the onset of the 19th century when many reformers emerged throughout the Muslim territories, most especially when Islam began spreading to countries in the West. Thus, the eclectic approach undertaken to construct new codes of law for solving particular problems resulted in the emergence of two new disciplines as a replacement for *taqlīd*: namely, *takhayyur* (eclectic choice and synthesis of rules from different Schools) and *talfīq* (piecing together or amalgamating doctrines from various Schools).[88]

Some achievements resulting from this transformation were to simplify the understanding of Islamic jurisprudence, to unify differences in thought, and to broaden the scope of Islamic Law on the identical *modus operandi* by introducing new disciplines, such as the study of the objectives of Islamic Law (*maqāṣid ash-sharīʿa*),[89] and the science of Islamic legal maxims (*al-qawāʿid al-fiqhiyya*). The discipline *maqāṣid ash-sharīʿa* tends to concentrate on God's intention behind His revelation of law to mankind and on the goals and objectives these laws are expected to bring about for mankind. The discipline *al-qawāʿid al-fiqhiyya*, which is the focus of this book, is aimed at harmonizing the opinions of scholars in particular cases through principles laid down in order to depict the aims and objectives of the Sharīʿa.

Aims and Scope of this Book

This book attempts to analyze the five major Islamic legal maxims (*al-qawāʿid al-fiqhiyya al-kulliyya*) and their applications in Islamic criminal law. In doing so, a number of related maxims will be examined if their applications have distinctive features requiring elucidation. The focus in analyzing and applying these maxims is to demonstrate the purpose of Islamic Law in prescribing penalties for particular crimes.

---

86 Maḥmaṣṣānī, 93.

87 Muslehuddin, *Islamic Jurisprudence*, 81.

88 Maḥmaṣṣānī, 93; Muslehuddin, *Islamic Jurisprudence*, 81.

89 See Kamali, *Introduction*, 115–131. Much literature has flooded libraries on the theory of *maqāṣid ash-sharīʿa* that ranges between objectivity and subjectivity in applications of this theory, which remains of indubitable importance to the dynamic nature of Islamic Law.

Where relevant and available, cases and issues regarding contemporary application of Islamic criminal law are examined to show the extent to which contemporary Muslim jurists are aware of the importance of these legal maxims in delivering justice in Islamic criminal cases. When analyzing the legal maxims, prominence will be given to the four Sunni Schools because the cases referred to originate in countries that have adopted their laws from among these schools.

Literature Review

The study of, and explication on, the subject *al-qawāʿid al-fiqhiyya* is said to have begun quite late due to the fact that, during the lifetime of the Prophet and his Companions, no additional sources were needed to facilitate one's reliance on the Sharīʿa. Even at the beginning of the 4th century Hijra, Islamic legal maxims were still hardly noticeable, although this does not imply that elements of legal maxims were not used in scholarly writing and expressions at that time. *The Book of Tax and Revenue* (*Kitāb al-Kharāj*) by Qāḍī Abū Yūsuf (d. 182/798) stands as a landmark among the writings on Islamic legal maxims and contains evidence that early Islamic scholars were acquainted with the subject matter. Similarly, discussion on the rules for prescribing discretionary penalties and the rights of leaders to confiscate their subjects' properties can be found in *The Book of Tax and Revenue*.[90] Another notable piece of literature written at that time is the book entitled *The Book of Fundamental Principles* (*Kitāb al-Aṣl*) by Muḥammad Ibn al-Ḥasan al-Shaybānī (d. 189/804).[91]

The most reliable pieces of literature on Islamic legal maxims written between the 4th and 10th centuries Hijra are the two tomes entitled *Similitudes and Resemblance* (*al-Ashbāh wa-n-Naẓāʾir*) written by al-Suyūṭī (d. 911/1504) as well as by Ibn Nujaym, *The Scattered* [*Issues*] *in Legal Maxims* (*al-Manthūr fī l-Qawāʿid*) written by al-Zarkashī, and *Legal Maxims* (*al-Qawāʿid*) written by

90 In *Kitāb al-Kharāj*, the Qāḍī Abū Yūsuf states many Islamic legal maxims, among which are: "It is left to the leader/judge to decide an appropriate discretionary punishment considering the proportionate [nature] of the offence" (*at-taʿzīr ilā l-imām ʿalā qadr ʿaẓam al-jurm wa-ṣigharihi*), and "It is not the right of the leader to take away someone's property without an established and well-known right" (*laysa li-l-imām an yakhruj shayʾan min yadd aḥadin illā ʿalā bi-ḥaqqin thābit maʿrūf*). See Abū Yūsuf Yaʿqub Ibn Ibrāhīm, *Kitāb al-Kharāj*, 6th edn. (Cairo: al-Maṭbaʿat as-Salafiyya wa-Maktabatuhā, 1397/1976) 180 and 71, respectively.

91 Muḥammad b. Ḥasan al-Shaybānī, *Kitāb al-Aṣl*, edited by Abū al-Wafaʾ al-Afghani, (Hyderabad: Maṭbaʿat Dār al-Maʿarif al-ʿUthmāniyya, n.d.), 3:45.

Ibn Rajab. Although these books formed the basis of the science, and are generally very useful in enumerating Islamic legal maxims, they are lacking in detail on how to apply legal maxims to various fields of Islamic jurisprudence. Take for instance the two books written by al-Suyūṭī and Ibn Nujaym, with identical titles and arrangements. While they enumerate the first five Islamic legal maxims agreed upon among Islamic scholars at that time, and succinctly mention their application to different fields of Islamic jurisprudence, they neglect to mention either their application to Islamic criminal law or provide examples of any controversial issues regarding the maxims. The same holds for the books by al-Zarkashī and Ibn Rajab.

From the 13th/18th century onwards, many resources address different dimensions of Islamic legal maxims.[92] The most popular and widespread publication on *al-qawāʿid al-fiqhiyya* dating from the 19th century is the Ottoman *Civil Code* (*Majalla al-Aḥkām al-ʿAdliyya*), hereafter referred to as the '*Majalla*'.[93] This *Civil Code* holds specific significance when studying Islamic legal maxims, not because it is comprehensive in nature but because it represents the hallmark of official legal codification in Islamic history. The *Majalla* contains 99 substantial codified legal rules followed by numerous explanations. The majority of these codifications are meant to address issues related to Islamic transactional law.

Aḥmad al-Zarqāʾ (d. 1938 AD) and his son Muṣṭafa al-Zarqāʾ (d. 1999 AD) each produced a commentary on the *Majalla*, the significance of which lies in their further exegeses of maxims featured in the *Majalla* as well as their addition of new maxims.[94] Al-Burnu is another contemporary Islamic scholar who has studied Islamic legal maxims from an academic perspective. His two books, *A Concise Book on the Explanation of Islamic Legal Maxims* (*al-Wajīz fī Īḍāḥ al-Qawāʿid al-Fiqhiyya al-Kulliyya*) and *Encyclopedia of Islamic Legal Maxims* (*Mawsūʿat al-Qawāʿid al-Fiqhiyya*) are invaluable sources for research.[95] The significance of al-Burnu's contribution to scholarship on Islamic legal maxims is characterized in his second encyclopedic book on the subject in question, in which he includes all the legal maxims extracted from various books pertaining to the different Schools of Islamic Jurisprudence. A similar contribution can also be ascribed to ʿAlī al-Nadawī.[96] The approach of both authors is

---

92 Rashed Saud al-Amiri, *Legal Maxims in Islamic Jurisprudence: Their History, Character and Significance*, Ph.D. Dissertation (UK: Birmingham University, 2003), 158.

93 The full account of the book can be found in Ch. 2, pp. 46–48.

94 See for more details, Section 'Stage of Maturity'.

95 See for the description of his book, Section 'Stage of Maturity' and note 186.

96 See for more details, Section 'Stage of Maturity'.

theoretical and offers a useful point of departure when studying the subject of Islamic legal maxims.

Other dimensions of inquiry have been explored in contemporary writings on *al-qawāʿid al-fiqhiyya* and include the following:

1. researching a single book, wherein a particular work by one jurist is studied in such a way that all the maxims mentioned therein are extracted and thoroughly explained, such as in al-Nadawī's Ph.D. Thesis, *Legal Maxims and Principles Extracted from the Book at-Taḥrīr* (*al-Qawāʿid wa-Ḍawābiṭ al-Mustakhlaṣ min at-Taḥrīr*), submitted to the Umm al-Qura University, Makkah, Saudi Arabia. Here the researcher has extracted all the maxims that Maḥmūd al-Ḥaṣīrī (d. 1239/1823) has cited in his book *at-Taḥrīr*;[97]
2. researching all the books by one particular jurist and collecting all the legal maxims mentioned therein on a specific *fiqh* theme, as in al-Ḥusayyin's *Legal Maxims and Principles Related to Islamic Transaction Law According to Ibn Taymiyya* (*al-Qawāʿid wa-ḍ-Ḍawābiṭ li-l-Muʿāmalāt al-Māliyya ʿinda Ibn Taymiyya*) and al-Sawwat's *Legal Maxims and Principles of Islamic Family Law According to Ibn Taymiyya* (*al-Qawāʿid wa-ḍ-Ḍawābiṭ ʿinda Ibn Taymiyya fī Fiqh al-ʿUsra*);[98] and
3. researching a single Islamic legal maxim through the application of thorough and extensive examination and explication, and subjecting that particular maxim to the method adopted by Ṣāliḥ al-Yūsuf in his work *Hardship Begets Ease: A Theoretical and Empirical Study* (*al-Mashaqqa Tajlib at-Taysīr: Dirāsa Naẓariyya wa-Taṭbīqiyya*), and also by Maḥmūd Armush in his work *Legal Maxim: A Word Should be Construed as Having Some Meaning, Rather Than Disregarded* (*al-Qāʿida l-Kulliyya: Iʿmāl al-Kalām aw-lā min Ihmālih*), submitted as Masters Theses at Imām Ibn Saud University, Riyadh, Saudi Arabia.[99]

It is pertinent to say that comprehensive narrations on this subject in the English language are very rare indeed. Schacht did not regard Islamic legal maxims as a science. In spite of having published books and articles on Islamic Law, he only allotted several pages to the summary of *al-qawāʿid al-fiqhiyya*

---

97 al-Amiri, *Legal Maxims in Islamic Jurisprudence*, 165.

98 Both books are Masters Theses presented by the authors, al-Ḥusayyin and al-Sawwat, at the Imām Ibn Saud University, Riyadh, Saudi Arabia.

99 al-Amiri, *Legal Maxims in Islamic Jurisprudence*, 166.

without reflecting on the term as concept or its importance in Islamic Law.[100] A number of writers in English have included witty sections on legal maxims in their works, but these, at best, are only an introduction to the subject. Thus, a huge vacuum still waits to be filled by intensive, in-depth studies of the science in English.[101] Recently, more attention has been given to the importance of this science and research in English is surfacing in academic circles. Some of the research that has been carried out to date on the science of Islamic legal maxims can be attributed to S.O. Rabiu and Rashed al-Amiri Saud.[102] The former maintains a somewhat practical approach, while the latter adopts a purely theoretical approach to the subject and does little more than translate previous works.[103] More recently, Elgariani[104] has taken a step further by applying legal maxims to contemporary medical issues, thus demonstrating the outstanding applicability of the science in today's world.

Hence, the aim of this book is to focus on how legal maxims can be applied to Islamic criminal law and how they can be used to extrapolate the overall objectives of Islamic criminal law in protecting human rights in this contemporary age. To make this subject matter more interactive and empirical, several criminal cases from Northern Nigeria have been perused to examine the extent to which the courts have complied to Sharīʿa objectives in those states with such an Islamic judicial apparatus.[105]

---

100 Schacht, *Origin*, 180–188; and Schacht, *Introduction*, 40.

101 Such as Muhammad Hashim Kamali, "*Qawāʾid al-Fiqh*: The Legal Maxims of Islamic Law", *Journal of the Association of Muslim Lawyers*, 3/2 (1998); http://www.aml.org.uk/cms/assets/Uploads/journals/3.2/Kamali-Qawaid-al-Fiqh.pdf (21 June 2006); Mawil Izzi Dien, *Islamic Law: From Historical Foundations to Contemporary Practice* (Notre Dame: University of Notre Dame Press, 2004).

102 Sulaiman O. Rabiu is a senior lecturer in the Department of Shariʿah, Uthman dan Fodio University, Sokoto, Nigeria, and Rashed Saud al-Amiri was a Ph.D. student in the department of Theology and Religion, University of Birmingham, UK.

103 Rabiu's work is somewhat empirical as it uses several court cases to illustrate the maxims, although the maxims treated are restricted to the five major ones. By contrast, Rashed's work is purely theoretical, as it only gives us the historical development of the subject, without providing any analysis or practical illustration of the maxims. In other words, it is more a translation of the works written in Arabic on the subject.

104 Fawzy Shaban Elgariani, Al-Qawāʿid al-Fiqhiyyah (*Islamic Legal Maxims*): *Concepts, Functions, History, Classifications and Application to Contemporary Medical Issues*, Ph.D. Dissertation (Exeter, UK: University of Exeter, 2012).

105 I chose Northern Nigerian criminal cases because of many questions raised in the wake of applications of Islamic criminal law in the region, a practice which began in 1999. Sometimes I also look into cases from other Muslim countries where judgments complied with Islamic Law.

Research Methodology

This book adopts both descriptive and prescriptive approaches. It starts by looking at the concept of legal maxims and outlines the five basic legal maxims in Islamic criminal law. In addition to citing historical examples of how the maxims were applied by past Islamic jurists from the four Sunni Schools of Islamic Jurisprudence, the discussion examines the empirical application of Islamic legal maxims in several pronouncements of Sharīʿa courts in Northern Nigeria in particular and in Muslim countries in general to demonstrate further the originality of this research. This study is quite atypical from cases described in local, national and international law reports as this investigation focuses on cases that have generated heated argument and controversy among scholars both within and outside Muslim countries.

The principal reason for adhering to the four Sunni Schools cited above is that the laws of many Muslim countries whose criminal cases are cited herein derive from these Schools. In arguing for or against the way a case is adjudicated, our analysis relies on the theory of *talfīq* (piecing together or amalgamating doctrines from various Schools) as opposed to *taqlīd* (dogmatic adherence to one specific School), as the latter approach might result in rigidity in the application of aspects of Islamic criminal law. Observations regarding these cases include suggestions and recommendations with a view to avoiding lapses in legal rigor and to improving the application of Islamic legal maxims in the future.

Structure of this Book

This book comprises seven chapters with a general conclusion and recommendations. As we have seen, Chapter 1 provides an introduction to and an overview of Islamic Law as well as explains ambiguities in rendering the Arabic term 'Sharīʿa' into English. The difference between an immutable Sharīʿa and fluctuating *fiqh*, resulting from man's interpretation of the Sharīʿa, is also explained while touching on the necessity for and level of usefulness of secondary sources to supplement the primary sources of Islamic Law. The chapter also deals with different aspects of Islamic Law while focusing on components of criminal law in particular; it traces how different sciences, subjects and terminologies relating to Islamic Law have emerged historically; it discusses the appearance of different Schools of Islamic Jurisprudence and the roles these schools have played in the development of this science; and it tracts the systematic evolution of methodologies such as *uṣūl al-fiqh* and *al-qawāʿid al-fiqhiyya*.

Chapter 2 focuses on the concept of Islamic legal maxims (*al-qawāʿid al-fiqhiyya*), their historical development, categories, and roles they play in the Islamic legal system.

Chapter 3 examines the legal maxim "Matters shall be judged by their objectives" (*al-umūr bi-maqāṣidihā*), with regard to intention (*niyya*), action (*umūr*) and their functions in Islamic criminal law, especially when determining the guilt or innocence of an accused individual.

Chapter 4 critically examines the position of the legal maxim "Certainty cannot be overruled by doubt" (*al-yaqīn lā yazūl bi-sh-shakk*) in Islamic criminal procedures. Here, the legal maxim is analyzed alongside other related maxims subsumed under this basic principle.

Chapter 5 discusses the legal maxim "Hardship begets facility" (*al-mashaqqa tajlib at-taysīr*) and the facilities or easements provided by Islamic Law in the face of hardship. This legal maxim is examined alongside other related maxims.

Chapter 6 discusses the legal maxim "No harm shall be inflicted or reciprocated" (*lā ḍarar wa-lā ḍirār*) as well as Islam's stance on the elimination of harm, whether aggressively inflicted or reciprocated. Focus will also elucidate other related maxims.

Chapter 7 examines extensively the legal maxim "Custom is authoritative" (*al-ʿāda muḥakkama*) and delves into the function of custom in Islamic criminal law. Here the terms for custom, practice or indigenous tradition (*ʿurf* and *ʿāda*) are defined concisely to remove any lingering ambiguity surrounding their use. The effect of *ʿurf* in Islamic criminal law will be emphasized while also debating whether rules of law can be modified as time and circumstances change.

The subsequent concluding remarks summarize the text, offer recommendations for improving the application of *al-qawāʿid al-fiqhiyya*, and make suggestions for areas of further research on the vast topic of Islamic legal maxims.

CHAPTER 2

Islamic Legal Maxims (*al-Qawāʿid al-Fiqhiyya*): Historical Development, Concepts and Content

Introduction

Chapter 2 examines the concept of legal maxims (*al-qawāʿid al-fiqhiyya*) and provides a literal definition while tracing their historical development and emergence as an independent subject in Islamic jurisprudence. Here we will attempt to distinguish between the characteristics of *al-qawāʿid al-fiqhiyya* and those features and terminologies of other subjects in Islamic Law. To some extent, this endeavor should remove any speculation on the ability of *al-qawāʿid al-fiqhiyya* to function as an independent source upon which legal verdicts can be based. Because numerous legal maxims have been articulated in classical books on Islamic jurisprudence, Chapter 2 explains their hierarchy and justifies why certain maxims should also be granted a general status alongside the five famous maxims agreed upon by classical Islamic scholars.

Historical Development of *al-Qawāʿid al-Fiqhiyya*

During the modern age of Islamic scholarship, many subjects have undergone rearrangement and been given a separate status to facilitate learning. Historically, as a result of divergent opinions asserted by a number of classical Islamic scholars writing on the subject, misconceptions have arisen about whether *al-qawāʿid al-fiqhiyya* constitute an independent discipline or rather are part and parcel of the principles of Islamic jurisprudence (*uṣūl al-fiqh*). For example, in the book *al-Majmūʿ* by Imām al-ʿAllaʾī (d. 761/1359), the works by Imām Ibn al-Wakīl (d. 716/1316) and Ibn Subkī (d. 771/1370) and the two books entitled *Similitudes and Resemblances* (*al-Ashbāh wa-n-Naẓāʾir*) by al-Suyūṭī (d. 911/1505) and by Ibn Nujaym (d. 970/1562), the two subjects are conflated into a composite whole.[1] Because of this misconception, it is difficult to give precise dates for the emergence of these concise adages as

1 ʿAlī Aḥmad al-Nadawī, *al-Qawāʿid al-Fiqhiyya: Mafhūmuhā, Nashʾatuhā, Taṭawwuruhā, Dirāsatuhā, Muʾallafātuhā, Adillatuhā, Muhimmatuhā, Taṭbīquhā*, 2nd edn. (Damascus: Dār al-Qalam, 1998), 39–40.

 | DOI 10.1163/9789004304871_003

a separate subject in Islamic jurisprudence. However, we have observed that *al-qawāʿid al-fiqhiyya* have undergone three stages of development: *i.e.*, primitive, florescence and mature.

The Primitive Stage

The first stage in the emergence of Islamic legal maxims or *al-qawāʿid al-fiqhiyya* can be traced back to the era of the Prophet and to the early period of his Companions (*ṣaḥāba*, pl. *aṣḥāb*).[2] The Prophet was endowed with the use of precise yet comprehensive and inclusive expressions (*jawāmiʿ al-kalim*), and prophetic Ḥadīths are full of such adages and sayings. In spite of the status of these prophetic traditions as one of the sources of Islamic Law, they also form an integral part of the formulation of Islamic legal maxims. For instance, "Revenue and responsibility go together" (*al-kharāj bi-ḍ-ḍamān*), *i.e.*, a government that taxes its subjects must guarantee their safety,[3] "No harm shall be inflicted or reciprocated" (*lā ḍarar wa-lā ḍirār*),[4] "Any substance whose large quantity intoxicates is also prohibited in a small quantity" (*mā askara kathīruhu, fa-qalīluhu ḥarām*),[5] and "The burden of proof is on the claimant and the oath is on the one who denies" (*al-bayyina ʿalā l-muddaʿī wa-l-yamīn ʿalā man ankar*)[6] are but a few of those prophetic expressions that emerged as legal maxims. Remarking on the nature of the statement regarding the prohibition of small quantities of intoxicating substances, al-Nadawī observes that the Ḥadīth is a maxim laid down by the Prophet for the prohibition of any intoxicating substance.[7] Of course, this prophetic axiom can be used to determine the legal status of a number of contemporary substances that contain intoxicating ingredients, once the cause (*ʿilla*) of prohibition has been found in such a substance. al-Bukhārī also reports on different occasions that the Prophet said: "Indeed, the owner of the right has a say" (*inna li-ṣāḥib al-ḥaqq maqāl*).[8] This Ḥadīth, as precise as it is, makes a huge contribution to the law of claim and legal procedure. Many other examples of prophetic Ḥadīths stand,

2 Muḥammad Siddiq Aḥmad al-Burnu, *Mawsūʿat al-Qawāʿid al-Fiqhiyya* (n.p., 2003), 12.

3 Ibn Mājah, Ḥadīth No. 2243, 3:753.

4 al-Nadawī, 90.

5 Muḥammad ʿAbd al-Raʾuf al-Munāwī, *Fayḍ al-Qadīr Sharḥ al-Jāmiʿ aṣ-Ṣaghīr*, 2nd edn. (Beirut: Dār al-Maʿrifa li-t-Tibaʿ, 1972/1391), 5:420. See also Muḥammad b. ʿĪsā al-Tirmidhī, *Sunān al-Tirmidhī* or *al-Jāmiʿ aṣ-Ṣaghīr*, edited by Hisham al-Bukhārī, (Beirut: Dār Iḥyāʾ at-Turāth al-ʿArabī, 1995), especially the chapter "*Bāb ash-Shurba*".

6 Aḥmad b. ʿAlī b. Ḥajar al-ʿAsqalānī, *Bulūgh al-Marām* with translation (Riyadh: Dār as-Salaam Publications, 1996), Ḥadīth No. 1210, 498.

7 al-Nadawī, 90.

8 al-Bukhārī, Ḥadīth No. 2183.

without any refinement or rewording, as legal maxims and are applicable to various issues in this contemporary age.

After the demise of Prophet Muḥammad, during the generation of his Companions *Ṣaḥāba* and their Followers (*tābiʿūn*), more legal maxims surfaced. It was reported that ʿAbdullāh Ibn ʿAbbās said: "In the Qurʾān, every injunction in which many things are joined together with the conjunctive particle 'or' [Arabic: *aw*] is an indication that a free choice is allowed among these things" (*kullu shayʾin fī-l-qurʾān aw, aw, fa-huwa mukhayyar*).[9] It is also reported that ʿAlī Ibn Abī Ṭālib said: "A profit shareholder is not held responsible for loss" (*man qāsam ar-ribḥ fa-lā ḍamān ʿalayhi*).[10] The former statement stands for the maxim of atonement in Islamic jurisprudence, while the latter stands for the maxim of partnership in Islamic transactions.[11]

Subsequently, during the era of the Followers, Imām Qāḍī Shuraih Ibn al-Ḥārith al-Kindī (d. 76/695) demonstrated his juristic talent with statements that were recognized as maxims in the judicial arm of government. He said: "He who willingly gives a condition binding himself without compulsion shall be held responsible for it" (*man sharaṭ ʿalā nafsihi ṭāʾiʿan ghayr mukrah fa-huwa ʿalayhi*),[12] and "The producer [of something] is more entitled to its profit than the claimant [of the ownership]" (*an-nātij aw-lā min al-ʿārif*).[13] The first maxim (*qāʿida*) denotes agreement so that if someone willingly signs an agreement to supply goods at a specified time and fails to do so without genuine reason, he shall be held responsible for any damage caused by the breach. The second *qāʿida* stresses making a claim for ownership.

During the 2nd century Hijra, tremendous efforts were made by leading Islamic jurists. This period was a landmark in the emergence of Islamic jurisprudence, as many legal maxims can be traced to their authors. One of the early works on Islamic legal maxims during that period is *The Book of Tax and Revenue* (*Kitāb al-Kharāj*) by the Qāḍī Abū Yūsuf (d. 182/798). In his discourse he alludes to legal maxims on the rule of discretionary punishment and on the divergent opinions held within the Ḥanafī School of Jurisprudence. He states:

---

9 ʿAbd al-Razzāq b. Humām al-Ṣanʿānī, *Muṣannaf ʿAbd ar-Razzāq*, edited by Ḥabīb al-Raḥman al-Aʿzamī, (Beirut: Maṭbaʿat Dār al-Qalam, n.d.), 4:395. This maxim is inferred from Qurʾānic verse 2:196.

10 *Ibid.*, 8:253.

11 al-Nadawī, 92.

12 al-Bukhārī, with explanation by al-Karmānī in the chapter on the condition for a dowry in marriage contracts, 19:111.

13 al-Ṣanʿānī, ʿAbd al-Razzāq, 8:277.

"It is left to the leader/judge to decide an appropriate discretionary penalty considering the proportionate [nature] of the offence" (*at-taʿzīr ilā l-imām ʿalā qadr ʿaẓam al-jurm wa-ṣigharih*).[14] Without doubt, this pronouncement establishes a unique maxim that can be used to determine which discretionary penalty should be awarded for a *taʿzīr* crime as well as who should make such a decision. In the same book, the Qāḍī Abū Yūsuf also addresses the statement that establishes the legitimate authority of leaders over their subjects. He says: "It is not the right of the leader/judge to take away someone's property without an established and well-known right" (*laysa li-l-imām an yakhruj shay'an min yaddi aḥadin illā bi-ḥaqqin thābit maʿarūf*).[15] This statement has been refined to conform with the conventional norm of coding maxims, thus: "Nothing should be stripped from someone without a legal right" (*lā yunzaʿ shay'un min yaddi aḥadin illā bi-ḥaqq thābit maʿrūf*).[16] The latter is more general than the former as it includes guardians, legal representatives, judges and leaders.

Another work that has contributed to the development of Islamic legal maxims is *The Book of Fundamental Principles* (*Kitāb al-Aṣl*) written by Muḥammad Ibn al-Ḥasan al-Shaybānī (d. 189/804). In his book, al-Shaybānī made many statements that later formed the basis for legal maxims in Islamic jurisprudence. He says, for example, "Wage and responsibility cannot be combined" (*lā yujmaʿ al-ajr wa-ḍ-ḍamān*).[17] This statement formed a maxim in the *Majalla*, but with a little rearrangement.[18] It reads thus: "Wage and responsibility cannot be combined" (*al-ajr wa-ḍ-ḍamān lā yajtamiʿān*).

The books, *al-Risāla* and *al-Umm*, written by Imām al-Shāfiʿī (d. 204/820) are also recognized as sources for the formulations of legal maxims. Among many of Imām al-Shāfiʿī's sayings are: "Facilities should not be taken beyond their premises" (*ar-rukhaṣ lā yutaʿaddā mawāḍiʿihā*),[19] and "No statement or action should be imputed to someone who is silent, but a statement and action should be imputed to the one who made the statement or carried out the action" (*lā yunsab ilā sākit qawlu qā'il wa-lā ʿamal ʿāmil, innamā yunsab ilā kullin qawluhu wa-ʿamaluh*).[20] Many other maxims remain which could be retrieved from

14 Ibn Ibrāhīm, 180.

15 *Ibid.*, 71.

16 Muṣṭafā Aḥmad al-Zarqā', *al-Madkhal al-Fiqhī l-ʿĀmm* (Damascus: Maṭbaʿat al-Jamiʿa, 1983), 2:982.

17 al-Shaybānī, *Kitāb al-Aṣl*, 45.

18 See *Majalla*, Article 86.

19 Muḥammad b. Idrīs al-Shāfiʿī, *Kitāb al-Umm* (Beirut: Dār al-Maʿrifa, 1381/1961), 1:80, quoted in al-Nadawi, 100.

20 al-Shāfiʿī, *Ibid* quoted in al-Nadawi, 101.

books written during this period of development but the examples given here should suffice.[21]

The extent of the development of *al-qawāʿid al-fiqhiyya* during its primitive stage can be summarized as follows:

1. The terms *qāʿida* (sg.) or *qawāʿid* (pl.) were neither specifically mentioned in the expressions of the Prophet, nor in those of his Companions and scholars during the early period.
2. Islamic legal maxims were scattered throughout various works written by the early Islamic scholars, and no book exists that was written purely on the subject of Islamic maxims.
3. The majority of maxims were memorized by heart and called upon when needed.
4. Some maxims are lengthy and do not conform to the general principles of maxim codification.

The Florescence Stage

As explained in the previous section, a separate book dedicated purely to the study of legal maxims (*al-qawāʿid al-fiqhiyya*) was never written during the first stage of their development, partly due to the lack of necessity, since Schools of Islamic Jurisprudence were still nonexistent during the Prophet's lifetime and that of his Companions. However, when they did begin to emerge and flourish, scholars were extremely well versed, knowledgeable, and able to conduct *ijtihād* or independent legal reasoning based on sound sources such as the Qurʾān and Ḥadīth texts. During this vigorous period of enquiry, blind imitation or dogma (*taqlīd*) was unnecessary.

From the middle of the 4th/10th century, *al-qawāʿid al-fiqhiyya* began to gain popularity when it became recognized as a discipline separate from legal theory or *uṣūl al-fiqh*. The reason for its advancement was that the spirit of independent legal reasoning was on the brink of extinction, *i.e.*, the so-called "closing of the gate" of *ijtihād*, as some scholars began blindly to imitate the opinions held by the Schools with which they were affiliated.[22] A number of Islamic jurists became concerned as to how they should harmonize the various issues discussed in books that shared similar views on the topic. They were also

21 For the comprehensive notes, see al-Nadawī, 90–132.

22 This is the prevailing view, at least in a general sense. However, some Islamic scholars maintained the status of *ijtihād* during that period, such as Abū Jaʿfar, Muḥammad b. Jarīr al-Ṭabarī (d. 310/922), al-Ṭaḥāwī (d. 321/933), and a host of others. See al-Nadawī, 133, note 1.

concerned with clarifying the issue of differing opinions expressed in scholarly writing.[23]

Without prejudice, contemporary Islamic scholars are in agreement that the early generation of Ḥanafī jurists held precedence in the field of *al-qawāʿid al-fiqhiyya*.[24] One of the first recognized works on legal maxims is *Karkhī's Principles* (*Uṣūl al-Karkhī*) written by the Ḥanafī scholar, Abū al-Ḥasan al-Karkhī (d. 340/951).[25] It is claimed apocryphally, however, that al-Karkhī's work was simply an expansion of the collection of Abū Ṭāhir al-Dabbās, who lived between the 3rd and 4th centuries Hijra. It is reported that al-Dabbās, a Ḥanafī scholar and contemporary of al-Karkhī, compiled 17 legal maxims, including the five major maxims from the Ḥanafī School of Jurisprudence. Later, al-Karkhī expanded that number to 39 and compiled them in the form of a book. However, as there is no real evidence suggesting the precedence of al-Dabbās over al-Karkhī, Abū al-Ḥasan al-Karkhī is assumed to be the first scholar to have written an independent book on Islamic legal maxims.[26]

Even so, the contributions of jurists from other Schools of Islamic Jurisprudence during this period are of immeasurable significance. Muḥammad Ibn al-Ḥārith al-Khushnī (d. 361/971), a Mālikī scholar, wrote a valuable book entitled *Principles on Giving Fatwās* (*Uṣūl al-Futyā*), in which he discussed many *fiqh* maxims.[27] During the 5th century Hijra, Abū Zayd al-Dabūsī (d. 430/1038) further developed the work of al-Karkhī in his book *Establishing Inquiry* (*Taʾsīs an-Naẓar*). One important point to note is that, during this century, the term *qawāʿid* was not used in scholarly writings. Instead, the terms *aṣl* or *uṣūl* were employed as seen in a phrase in *Taʾsīs an-Naẓar*: "The principle according to Abū Ḥanīfa is ..." (*al-aṣl ʿinda Abī Ḥanīfa*).[28]

During the 7th to 9th centuries Hijra, an incredible number of works emerged on Islamic legal maxims. Unfortunately, these cannot be enumerated here due to the constraints of space. Among these were the works by al-Sahlakī (d. 613/1216) and ʿIzz al-Dīn Ibn ʿAbd al-Salām (d. 660/1261), both from the

---

23 Muḥammad Siddiq Aḥmad al-Burnu, *al-Wajīz fī Īḍāḥ Qawāʿid al-Fiqhiyya l-Kulliyya*, 5th edn. (Beirut: Mu'assasat ar-Risāla, 2002), 59; and al-Nadawī, 133.

24 al-Nadawī, 135.

25 *Ibid.*, 136; and Muhammad Khaleel, "The Islamic Law Maxims", *Journal of Islamic Studies*, 44/2 (2005).

26 al-Suyūṭī, *al-Ashbāh wa-n-Naẓāʾir fī an-Naḥw*, edited by Ṭāhā ʿAbd al-Raʾuf, (Cairo: Sharkat at-Tibaʿa l-Faniyya al-Muttaḥida, 1975), 7; Zayn al-ʿĀbidīn Ibn Ibrāhīm Ibn Nujaym, *al-Ashbāh wa-n-Naẓāʾir ʿalā Madhhab Abī Ḥanīfa al-Nuʿmān* (Beirut: Dār al-Kutub al-ʿIlmiyya, 1993), 10–11.

27 al-Nadawī, 136.

28 Abū Zayd al-Dabūsī, *Taʾsīs an-Naẓar* (Cairo: Maṭbaʿat al-Imām, n.d.), 21.

Shāfiʿī School. Al-Sahlakī's book is exclusively concerned with the Shāfiʿī School, while that of ʿIzz al-Dīn Ibn ʿAbd al-Salām is a general work on Islamic jurisprudence.[29] Another relevant author is al-Bakrī al-Qafsī (d. 680/1281), who wrote a book on Islamic legal maxims from the Mālikī point of view.[30]

Moreover, during the 8th to 10th centuries Hijra, many books appeared with differing titles by notable scholars from various Schools of Islamic Jurisprudence. Among those Islamic scholars who contributed to the development of *al-qawāʿid al-fiqhiyya* during this period were Ibn al-Wakīl (d. 716/1316), al-Maqqarī al-Mālik (d. 758/1356), al-Aʿlaʾī al-Shāfiʿī (d. 761/1359), Tāj al-Dīn al-Subkī (d. 771/1370), al-Isnawī (d. 772/1371), al-Zarkashī (d. 794/1391), Ibn Rajab al-Ḥanbalī (d. 795/1392), al-Ghazzī (d. 799/1396), Ibn al-Mulaqqin (d. 804/1401), al-Zubayrī (d. 808/1405), al-Maqdisī (d. 815/1412), al-Ḥisnī (d. 829/1425), al-Suyūṭī (d. 910/1504), al-Tujībī al-Mālikī (d. 912/1506), and Ibn Nujaym al-Ḥanafī (d. 970/1562).[31]

It is worth noting that numerous other famous scholars did not write specific books on this subject, although they contributed to its development. Many expressions relating to *al-qawāʿid al-fiqhiyya* are found in the works of Islamic jurists such as al-Qarāfī (d. 684/1285), Ibn Taymiyya (d. 728/1327), and Ibn Qayyim al-Jawziyya (d. 751/1350). Al-Qarāfī, in one of his discussions on cleanliness, states: "The principle is that rules should only be based on real knowledge" (*al-aṣl allā yubnā l-aḥkām illā ʿalā l-ʿilm*).[32] This expression formed the maxim of 'certainty' and gave it preference over 'doubt'. Ibn Taymiyya was accustomed to explore maxims in support of his arguments. On one occasion he states: "A rule that is established by virtue of cause [*ʿilla*] shall expire when the cause expires" (*al-ḥukm idhā thabata bi-ʿilla zāla bi-zawālihā*).[33] Ibn al-Qayyim also says: "Among the general legal maxims [of Islamic Law is that] there is no obligation in the face of incapability and there is no prohibition in the face of necessity" (*min qawāʿid ash-shariʿa l-kulliyya annahu lā wājib maʿa ʿajz wa-lā ḥarām maʿa ḍarūra*).[34] That is to say, when a Muslim is faced with

29 al-Sahlakī entitled his book *al-Qawāʿid fī Furūʿ al-Shāfiʿī* while Izz al-Dīn named his *Qawāʿid al-Aḥkām fī Maṣāliḥ al-Anām*.

30 al-Nadawī, 138.

31 The names of these contributors are briefly and chronologically mentioned because of their lesser significance to this project.

32 Aḥmad b. Idrīs al-Qarāfī, *adh-Dhakhīra*, edited by Muḥammad Ḥājjī (ed.), (Beirut: Dār al-Gharb al-Islāmī, 1994), 1:212–213.

33 Aḥmad b. ʿAbd al-Ḥalīm al-Ḥarrānī Ibn Taymiyya, *Majmūʿ al-Fatāwā* (Medina: Mujammaʿ al-Mālik Fahd li-t-Tabaʿ al-Maṣḥaf al-Sharīf, 1995), 21:312–313.

34 Ibn al-Qayyim al-Jawziyya, *Iʿlām al-Muwaqqiʿīn*, 2:48.

constraint to perform an obligatory duty or an act according to the dictates of the law, he will be temporarily exempted from performing this obligation.

Some of the features of *al-qawāʿid al-fiqhiyya* during their second stage of development are as follows:

1. The term *qawāʿid* was prevalent in most titles: *e.g.*, *General Legal Maxims* (*al-Qawāʿid al-Aḥkām fī masāliḥ al-Anām*) by ʿIzz al-Dīn; *Book of Legal Maxims* (*Kitāb al-Qawāʿid*) by al-Maqqari; *The Scattered* [*Issues*] *in Legal Maxims* (*al-Manthūr fī l-Qawāʿid*) by al-Zarkashī; and *Legal Maxims* (*al-Qawāʿid al-Fiqhiyya*) by Ibn Rajab.
2. Other terms such as *ashbāh* (similitude) and *naẓāʾir* (resemblance) were used in place of *qawāʿid* as seen in the phrase "*ash-ashbāh wa-n-naẓāʾir*" found in the titles of books by al-Subkī, al-Isnawī, al-Suyūṭī and Ibn Nujaym.
3. During this period, some scholars were concerned with writing legal maxims expressing the singular opinion held by their particular School, without taking into consideration those opinions held by other Schools of Islamic Jurisprudence: *e.g.*, *Clarification of Pathways to the Legal Maxims of Imām Mālik* (*Īḍāḥ al-Masālik ilā Qawāʿid al-Imām Mālik*) by al-Wansharīsī (d. 914/1508) and *Attractive Collection of Legal Maxims of the* [*Mālikī*] *School* (*al-Majmūʿ al-Mudhhab fī Qawāʿid al-Madhhab*) by al-ʿAlāʾī (d. 761/1360).
4. It has been observed that, during this stage of development, many works were either repetitions, expansions or interpretations of works from the first stage, as in *Maxims* (*al-Qawāʿid*) by Ibn al-Mulaqqin, and *Similitudes* (*ash-Ashbāh*) by Ibn Nujaym. Both were extracted from the works of Ibn Subkī and others.[35] Al-Suyūṭī extracted a number of maxims from al-ʿAlāʾī, al-Subkī and al-Zarkashī to include in his book *Similitudes* (*ash-Ashbāh*), while al-Tujībī (d. 912/1506) compiled his book on *al-qawāʿid al-fiqhiyya* from various books by Imām Mālik.[36]
5. At the beginning of this stage, some of the *qawāʿid* were rendered in excessively long sentences. For example, in *The Principles* (*al-Uṣūl*), al-Karkhī states: "The fundamental principle is that a man will be held responsible for what he confessed to in a matter related to his right and he shall not be believed [in his confession] on the nullification of the right of another person or on the imposition of a right on another person" (*al-aṣl anna l-marʾ yuʿāmil fī ḥaqq nafsihi ka-mā aqarr bi-hi, wa-lā*

35 al-Nadawī, 139.

36 *Ibid.*, 140.

yuṣaddaq ʿalā ibṭāl ḥaqq al-ghayr aw ilzām al-ghayr ḥaqqan).[37] However, this maxim was later reconstructed in this more concise form: "Confession [of guilt] is binding proof only on the confessor" (*al-iqrār ḥujja qāṣira*).[38]

6. In many cases, *al-qawāʿid al-fiqhiyya* were often confused with *al-qawāʿid al-uṣūliyya*.
7. Scholars were allowed freedom of expression and codification to reframe or rearrange what they saw as inconsistent in earlier works on the subject.

Stage of Maturity

The stage of maturity or last thrust in the development of *al-qawāʿid al-fiqhiyya* began around the 13th/18th century. One distinctive feature of this stage is that the study of maxims is established as a separate discipline in Islamic jurisprudence. Another feature is the simultaneous standardization of formulae for their codification. Just as Ḥanafīs were instrumental in the development of *qawāʿid*, they were also pioneers during this last stage of development. The first treatises written on *al-qawāʿid al-fiqhiyya* were by Ḥanafī scholars. Muḥammad al-Khadimī (d. 1762) wrote *Conclaves of Facts* (*Majāmiʿ al-Ḥaqāʾiq*) in which 154 maxims were appended, and Muṣṭafā al-Kuzilhisarī (d. 1800) ran commentaries on the book by al-Khadimī entitled *Accurate Benefits in Annotation of Conclaves of Facts* (*Manāfiʿ ad-Daqāʾiq fī Sharḥ Majāmiʿ al-Ḥaqāʾiq*). Sulaymān al-Qarqaghajī (d. 1870) and Muṣṭafā Hāshim also followed suit in writing commentaries on the *Majāmiʿ*, but their respective works, believed to have been published in 1822 and 1878 AD, have not been found in circulation.[39] The work of Maḥmūd Ibn Hamza (d. 1304/1887), then-Muftī of Damascus and a Ḥanafī scholar, is also notable. The title of his work is *al-Farāʾid al-Bahiyya fī l-Qawāʿid wa-l-Fawānid al-Fiqhiyya*.[40]

The most popular work on Islamic legal maxims during the 19th century was the Ottoman *Civil Code* (*al-Majalla al-Aḥkām al-ʿAdliyya*). The *Majalla* was presented by a seven-man committee named the "*Majalla* Commission" during the era of Sultan al-Ghazi ʿAbd al-Azeez of the Ottoman Empire.[41] This commission was chaired by the then-Minister of Justice, Ahmed Cevedah

---

37 ʿUbaydallah b. al-Ḥusayn al-Karkhī, *Usūl al-Karkhī, maʿa Tasis an-Naẓar* (Cairo: Maṭbaʿat al-Imām, n.d.), 112.

38 *Majalla*, Article 78.

39 al-Burnu, *al-Wajīz*, 104.

40 al-Amiri, *Legal Maxims*, 158.

41 al-Nadawī, 178–179.

(d. 1895).[42] The aim of the Commission was to codify civil rules consistent with Islamic jurisprudence in accordance with the Ḥanafī School. Under royal decree, the book was entitled *The Corpus of Juridical Rules* (*Ahkame Adliyah*). The *Majalla* Commission explained the reasoning behind the book in these words:

> Lawyers who have studied jurisprudence (*fiqh*) have converted its propositions into a number of universal rules. Each of these, while embracing and containing many propositions, is taken as evidence for the proof of these propositions being from the admitted truths in the sacred law books. And, in the first place, the understanding of these rules gives familiarity with the propositions in mind. Therefore, ninety-nine rules of jurisprudence have been collected, and brought forward to form the second part of the preface.[43]

Despite its shortcomings, the *Majalla* has filled many gaps in the field of Islamic jurisprudence and has functioned as a very useful resource book for scholarly research. However, the book is rather one-sided, as the maxims and the opinions illustrated therein are from the Ḥanafī point of view only. Moreover, the majority of the maxims stated in the book are related only to the field of transactions (*muʿāmalāt*), which is only one field in Islamic jurisprudence.[44]

After the *Majalla*, many commentaries emerged from both Muslim and non-Muslim jurists. Salim Baz (d. 1920), a Christian lawyer from Lebanon, wrote a commentary on the *Majalla* entitled *Annotation of the Majalla* (*Sharḥ al-Majalla*). Another commentary, written in Turkish by Ali Haydar, and translated into Arabic by Fahmī al-Ḥusainī, also appeared. However, the most popular and widespread commentary is the work by Aḥmad al-Zarqāʾ, which has gained credibility through its well-arranged and extensive explanations; it also contains maxims additional to those included in the *Majalla*.[45] Muṣṭafā al-Zarqāʾ also followed his father's example. In his work, he observes that the *Majalla*'s maxims are not consistent and that many of them focusing on one topic are scattered throughout the book. He therefore rearranged these maxims by sub-dividing them into two groups: basic universal maxims, of

42 Maḥmaṣṣānī, 42–43.

43 *Majalla*, Article 1.

44 Khaleel, 197; and al-Nadawī, 156.

45 See Aḥmad b. Muḥammad al-Zarqāʾ, *Sharḥ al-Qawāʿid al-Fiqhiyya*, 4th edn. (Damascus: Dār al-Qalam, 1996), 102, 267.

which there are 40 in number, and subsidiary legal maxims, of which there are 59.[46]

However, due to the shortcomings of the *Majalla* mentioned above, as well as the fact that the majority of books written on legal maxims from their earliest conception failed to adopt an academic approach, there still exists a vacuum that must be filled. Al-Burnu was one of the first contemporary Islamic scholars to direct his attention to the study of Islamic legal maxims. When the Sharīʿa Faculty at Imām Ibn Saud University first introduced the subject of *al-qawāʿid al-fiqhiyya* into its curriculum, al-Burnu was chosen to design a program with which to teach this subject matter. However, he was unsuccessful in his search for a suitable publication to be used as an academic handbook. This prompted him to write his book entitled *A Concise Book on the Explanation of the Basic General Islamic Legal Maxims* (*al-Wajīz fī Īḍāḥ al-Qawāʿid al-Fiqhiyya al-Kulliyya*).[47] The majority of the maxims included in his book are from the *Majalla*, while others are taken from various books written on the subject that emanate from various Schools of Islamic Jurisprudence. He too divided legal maxims into two categories.[48]

Another authority in the field of legal maxims is ʿAlī al-Nadawī, who has published two books on the subject. His first book, entitled *Islamic Legal Maxims, Their Concept, Emergence, Development, and Study of Their Treaties, Evidence, Importance and Applications* (*al-Qawāʿid al-Fiqhiyyya, Mafhūmuhā, Nashʾatuhā, Taṭawwuruhā, Dirāsatuhā, Muʿallafātuhā, Adillatuhā, Muhimmatuhā, wa-Taṭbīqātuhā*),[49] al-Nadawī approaches the historical development of *al-qawāʿid al-fiqhiyya* more or less theoretically.[50] For his second book, entitled *An Encyclopedia of Islamic Legal Maxims and Principles*

46 M. al-Zarqā, *al-Madkhal*, 2:977–979.

47 al-Burnu, *al-Wajīz*, 7–9. The approach of the author in this book is unique and unprecedented. In it, a maxim is mentioned and traced according to its evidence, importance and application. Occasionally, the maxim's anomaly is mentioned and reasons for it given.

48 In his book, al-Burnu divides Islamic legal maxims into two units, the first unit consisting of six maxims. Al-Burnu describes these six maxims as general grand legal maxims, including the five agreed upon among all scholars. The additional maxim is "a word should be construed as having some meaning rather than disregarded" (*Majalla*, Article 60). However, inclusion of this sixth maxim amongst the general grand ones has been proved by the author. Al-Burnu's second unit consists of 25 maxims: "general legal maxims lesser than the former".

49 This book was originally a dissertation presented by the author for his Masters Degree at Umm al-Qura University, Makkah, Saudi Arabia.

50 For the first book, see the author's introduction and his objectives (25–34). The second book is published by the same author and makes clear that the author's focus is on Islamic

Governing Monetary Transactions in Islamic Jurisprudence (*Mawsūʿat al-Qawāʿid wa-Ḍawābiṭ al-Fiqhiyya al-Ḥākima li-l-Muʿāmalāt al-Māliyya fī l-Fiqh al-Islāmī*), he collected 3,107 legal maxims on transactions. Another substantial work on *al-qawāʿid al-fiqhiyya* is the ongoing project initiated in 1995 by the Islamic Fiqh Academy, a subsidiary of the Organization of Islamic Conference (OIC).[51] The aim of the project is to collect legal maxims from various books on Islamic jurisprudence. Other dimensions have emerged in contemporary writing on Islamic legal maxims as detailed in the previous chapter.[52]

Some of the distinctive features of this third stage in the development of *al-qawāʿid al-fiqhiyya* as a subject can be summarized as follows:

1. Most of the expressions prevalent during the first two stages have been re-arranged and reconstructed.
2. The *qawāʿid* can be easily memorized because their wording is now concise and precise.
3. Some scholars have chosen to research particular maxims in a practical manner, in contrast to the prevailing norm of covering as much general ground as possible.

Concepts of *al-Qawāʿid al-Fiqhiyya*

Definition of al-Qawāʿid al-Fiqhiyya

Literal Meaning of *al-Qawāʿid al-Fiqhiyya*

The term Islamic legal maxims or *al-qawāʿid al-fiqhiyya*[53] refers to a particular science in Islamic jurisprudence and denotes a certain discipline in Islamic

business transactions. This, and al-Sawwat's work on Islamic family law aspects of legal maxims, prompted me to look into the criminal aspects of the subject.

51 This project is entitled *Maʿlama al-Qawāʿid al-Fiqhiyya*. See al-Amiri, 163–164.

52 See Ch. 1, note 104.

53 The translation of *al-qawāʿid al-fiqhiyya* as 'Islamic legal maxim' has almost become conventional in the writings of contemporary scholars, although some scholars simply translated it as 'legal maxims' to form a parallel meaning with the term used by Western scholars. However, the latter approach will undermine the value of Islamic maxims since, in the Islamic domain, they cannot merely be called legal maxims, in the Western sense. This important difference will be explained in due course when discussing the importance and role of legal maxims. It is worth noting that the translation of this subject matter in my Masters Thesis was 'Islamic juristic maxim', a rendering I still maintain. This is because the word 'juristic' is wider than the word 'legal'. Of course, these maxims are useful not only to law practitioners but also to individuals who issue religious verdicts

studies. One cannot accurately define the subject matter of *al-qawāʿid al-fiqhiyya* until first clarifying the two components that form the term. *Qawāʿid* (pl. of *qāʿida*) is derived from the triliteral root (*qāf-ʿayn-dāl*) for the verb *qaʿada*, which has many lexical meanings in the Arabic language that denote, *e.g*., stability, constancy and foundation.[54] In general terms, *qāʿida* synonymously means "base, principle, rudiment, maxim and precept".[55] Thus, *qāʿida* can also refer to a religious, philosophical, political or legal basis or foundation.[56] For example, in Arabic the word *muqʿad* (sick person) refers to someone unable to move from one place to another because of his constancy in one location. A married woman is sometimes referred to as *qaʿīdat ar-rajul* (pillar of man)[57] just as *qāʿidat al-bayt* means the foundation of a house. Several Qur'ānic verses refer to the latter meaning: *e.g*., where God says: "And [remember] when Abraham and Ismail were raising the foundations of the house" (*wa-idh yarfaʿu Ibrāhīm al-qawāʿid min al-bayt wa-Ismāʿīl*).[58]

Technical Meaning of *Qawāʿid*

A general definition explains that a maxim (*qāʿida*) is either "a general theorem which applies to all of its related particulars" (*qaḍiyya kulliyya munṭabiq ʿalā jamīʿ juzʾiyyātihā*),[59] or "a general rule which applies to its particulars in order to deduce rules from it" (*ḥukmun kullī yanṭabiq ʿalā juzʾiyyātih li-yataʿarraf aḥkāmuhā minhi*).[60] The distinctive feature of both definitions lies in the fact that the former is ascribed to scholars of logic (*manṭiq*), while the latter is ascribed to scholars of jurisprudence (*fiqh*), all of whom agree on the generality of *qāʿida*. For a *qāʿida* to be universally accepted, it must be general, *i.e*., no exceptions should be encountered when applying it to its particulars.[61] However, both definitions have one important linguistic difference: *i.e*., the

---

(*muftī*). However, I prefer to adopt the current translation here because the term 'legal maxim' is well understood to both Islamic modern scholars and Western lawyers, and because the area to which I want to relate the maxims is purely legal.

54 Ibn Manẓūr, s.v. "*ʿAyn*"; and *al-Muʿjam al-Wāsiṭ*, s.v. "*ʿAyn*".

55 Baʿalbakkī, 844.

56 al-Nadawī, 39.

57 *Ibid*., s.v. "*ʿAyn*".

58 Q. 2:127.

59 ʿAlī b. Muḥammad al-Jurjānī, *Kitāb at-Taʿrīfāt* (Beirut: Dār al-Kutub al-ʿIlmiyya, 1983), 171.

60 al-Nadawī, 40.

61 Muḥammad b. Aḥmad al-Futūḥī Ibn al-Najjār, *Sharḥ al-Kawkab al-Munīr*, edited by Muḥammad al-Zuhaylī and Dr. Nazih Hummad, (Riyadh: Maktabat al-ʿUbaykan, 1997), 1:45.

term 'maxim' is specified as either *qaḍiyya* (proposition) or *ḥukm* (measure for extracting a ruling, which is the term used by *uṣūl* scholars (or *uṣūl*-ists).

Islamic jurists are split down the middle with regard to how *qāʿida* should be defined. One group of scholars perceives no difference in the way in which linguists or jurists define what constitutes a maxim. Thus, to them the definitions for *qāʿida* are one and the same whether expressed by linguists, logicians or *uṣūl*-ists.[62] In contrast, another group discerns a number of differences regarding the linguistic and juristic definitions.[63] On one hand, some scholars assert that a *qāʿida* is a general rule (*ḥukm kullī*) that relates to juristic norms but differs in usage from the *uṣūl* and *manṭiq*. This view is expressed by al-Maqarī (d. 758/1356), who says: "What we mean by *qāʿida* is any general [rule] which is more specific than *uṣūl* and other general rationale" (*naʿnī bi-l-qawāʿid kull kullī huwa akhaṣ min al-uṣūl wa-sāʾir al-maʿānī l-ʿaqliyya l-ʿāmma*).[64] On the other hand, al-Ḥamawī holds that a *qāʿida* is a 'preponderant rule' (*ḥukm aghlabī*) when he states: "The term *qāʿida*, from the perspective of the jurists, differs from its meaning from the perspective of the linguists and *uṣul*-ists. From the jurists' view, it is a preponderant, not general, rule, which applies to many of its particulars from which they deduce their rules" (*inna l-qāʿida ʿinda l-fuqahāʾ ghayrhā ʿinda n-nuḥāh wa-l-uṣūliyyīn, idh ʿinda l-fuqahāʾ ḥukm aktharī lā kullī yanṭabiq ʿalā akthar juzʾiyyātih li-yutaʿarraf aḥakāmuhu*).[65]

The reason that Islamic jurists hold such divergent points of view regarding the nature of *qāʿida* stems from the fact that a *qāʿida*—from its origination—is general (*kulliyya*). However, in some exceptionally rare cases, a number of scholars have expressed reservations regarding its generality. Nonetheless, it is safe to say that the application of *al-qāʿida al-fiqhiyya* is general, regardless of any exclusion that may occur for the following reasons. First, to say that *qāʿida* is general (*kulliyya*) conforms to its original usage. Second, the fact that there are exceptions in some cases is not sufficient to impact greatly the generality of the term because no formula is without some exception to its rules or applications. Third, it has been well established in Islamic jurisprudence, and is an acceptable rule, that any preponderant majority rule (*ḥukm ghālib aktharī*)

62 Such as Tāj al-Dīn al-Subkī, *al-Ashbāh wa-n-Naẓāʾir*; see al-Nadawī, 41.

63 Muḥammad b. ʿAbdullāh al-Sawwat, *al-Qawāʿid wa-ḍ-Ḍawābiṭ al-Fiqhiyya ʿind Ibn Taymiyya fī Fiqh al-Usra* (Taʾif: Dār al-Bayān al-Ḥadītha, 2001), 1:88.

64 al-Nadawī, 41. 2nd edn. Damascus: Dār al-Qalam, 1998.

65 Aḥmad b. Muḥammad al-Ḥamawī, *Ghamz ʿUyūn al-Baṣāʾir Sharḥ al-Ashbāh wa-n-Naẓāʾir* (Beirut: Dār al-Kutub al-ʿIlmiyya, 1985/1405), 1:22.

is regarded as a consistent general rule (*ḥukm kullī muṭṭarid*) as al-Shāṭibī (d. 790/1388) observes:

> Even those *qawāʿid* assumed to be less general might be 'general and consistent' in another way which we do not perceive, or, albeit, may not be maxims on their own because of insufficient conditions qualifying them to be called *qawāʿid*.[66]

Of course, one of the accepted principles is that what is preponderant should be given the status of generality, in as much as it is consistent in many cases and is of common occurrence, and the rule and effect are given to what is regular and universally prevailing.[67]

Having discussed the term *qāʿida*, the overall definition of *al-qawāʿid al-fiqhiyya* should now be broached. It is pertinent to briefly define *fiqh*, to which *qawāʿid* are attributed. The word *fiqh* derives from the triliteral Arabic root (*fāʾ-qāf-hāʾ*) for the verb *faqiha* (to know, understand, grasp and comprehend).[68] In this context, the word '*fiqhiyya*' is an adjective used to qualify *qawāʿid*. Moreover, in Islamic studies, *fiqh* has been defined in different ways. The *Majalla*, among others, defines it as "the knowledge of a practical legal question",[69] but this definition does not make clear the complete nature of the term. The general definition of *fiqh*, however, states that it "is the science of the derived legal rules as required from their particular sources".[70]

---

66 Abū Isḥāq Ibrāhīm b. Mūsā al-Shāṭibī, *al-Muwāfaqāt fī Uṣūl ash-Sharīʿa*, edited by ʿAbdullāh Darraz, (Beirut: Dār al-Maʿrifa, 1975), 2:53.

67 *Majalla*, Articles 40–41.

68 Aḥmad b. Muḥammad al-Fayumī, *al-Miṣbāḥ al-Munīr fī Gharīb ash-Sharḥ al-Kabīr* (Beirut: Maktabat Lubnān, 1987), 248.

69 *Majalla*, Article 1.

70 Qadir; 91; and Maḥmaṣṣānī, 8. Several Islamic scholars have developed a modern theory in which *fiqh* is deemed to be the method by which Islamic Law is derived and applied. This attempt seeks to distinguish the terms 'Sharīʿa' and '*fiqh*', but there is confusion in rendering the translation of the two terms into the English language. In many cases both terms are translated as 'Islamic Law', yet as Baderin asserts, the two terms are not technically synonymous (see Baderin, *International Human Rights*, 33). It seems that the phrase 'Islamic Law' cannot be isolated from the two terms because the understating of Islamic Law (*fiqh*) cannot be drawn without recourse to the divine and quasi-divine revelation (Sharīʿa). However, it is safe to say that everything termed Sharīʿa can be called 'Islamic Law' (in terms of its immutability), but not vice versa. See also Said Ramadan, *Islamic Law: Its Scope and Equity* (London: Macmillan, 1970), 33–36.

It should be noted, however, that in most medieval and contemporary works *al-qawāʿid al-fiqhiyya* has only been defined as a term but not subject matter. As already stated above, the majority of medieval writers considered *qawāʿid* to be a specific terminology in Islamic jurisprudence and thus, for them, its function was defined. Many contemporary scholars also reiterate this approach. Ṣubḥī Maḥmaṣṣānī renders the definition of 'maxim' as "a general rule that applies to all its particulars".[71] This dogmatic approach does not facilitate comprehension of the extreme nature of this subject matter. Failure to incorporate many features of the science has created a vacuum that must be filled. Mawil Izzi Dien, another contemporary writer, defines 'maxims' as "principles and concepts that could be applied to a wide variety of cases".[72] While this definition sounds attractive, it could be taken to task for its failure to recognize the cognizance of *al-qawāʿid al-fiqhiyya*, as opposed to any other *qawāʿid*. Another interesting definition is that of Muhammad Hashim Kamali[73] who defines *al-qawāʿid al-fiqhiyya* as "statements of principles that are derived from the detailed reading of the rules of *fiqh* on various themes".[74] This definition, although credible because it recognizes some of the features of the *fiqh* maxim, fails to address its essence. Of course, maxims are said to be products of extensive perusal of the rules of *fiqh*, but the essence of this extrapolation is to apply this product to other cases that fall under their subject.

A more comprehensive definition of *al-qawāʿid al-fiqhiyya* has been given by both Muṣṭafā al-Zarqā[75] and Muḥammad Ibn ʿAbdullāh al-Sawwat.[76] While M. al-Zarqāʾ says that Islamic legal maxims "are universal *fiqh* principles, expressed in legal, concise statements, that encompass general rulings in cases that fall under their subject",[77] al-Sawwat defines *al-qawāʿid al-fiqhiyya* as "a study of the science of practical legal Islamic universal theorems and how they are applicable to their particulars".[78]

Comparison of the leading definitions reveals two observations. First, both definitions agree on the universality and generality of Islamic legal maxims. This conforms to the opinion of al-Shāṭibī mentioned above. Second, the former regards *al-qawāʿid al-fiqhiyya* to be 'rules or principles' (*aḥkām aw uṣūl*)

---

71 Maḥmaṣṣānī, *Ibid.*, 151; Izzi Dien, 113–114.

72 Izzi Dien, *Ibid.*

73 Kamali, *Qawāʿid al-Fiqh*, 1.

74 *Ibid.*

75 M. al-Zarqāʾ, *al-Madkhal*, 2:933.

76 al-Sawwat.

77 M. al-Zarqāʾ, *al-Madkhal.*

78 al-Sawwat.

while the latter views them as theorem (*qaḍiyya*). By and large, one important aspect has been left unaddressed in the aforementioned definitions: namely, the end objectives of the legal maxims. This issue has been raised by both Kamali and Izzi Dien.[79] Kamali observes that one of the functions of Islamic legal maxims is to depict the "general picture of the nature, goals and objectives of the Sharīʿah … [and this is why many scholars have] … treated them as a branch of *maqāṣid* (goals and objectives literature)".[80] In light of this, I, the author, submit that legal maxims are as follows:

> They are legal rules, the majority of which are universal, expressed in concise phraseology, depicting the nature and objectives of Islamic Law and encompassing general rules in cases that fall under their subject matter.
>
> (*hiya aḥkām fiqhiyya aktharuhā kulliyya maṣūgha bi-uslūbin muʾjaz tuʿabbir ʿan maqāṣid ash-sharīʿa wa-tataḍamman aḥkām tashrīʿiyya ʿāmma fī l-ḥawādith allatī tadkhul taḥtahā*)[81]

By examining the words *aḥkām* and *fiqhiyya*, the definition distinguishes the subject matter from other maxims as well as preserves the importance of conciseness in formulating legal maxims. This is essential because using lengthy and inarticulate phrases will render the nature of the maxims unattractive for use. Also, there is a sense of belonging that Islamic legal maxims are formulated to express the nature and value of the Sharīʿa that will guide the application of the maxims in accordance with the spirit of Islamic Law.

Differences between al-Qawāʿid al-Fiqhiyya *and Other Related Concepts*

al-Qawāʿid al-Fiqhiyya and *al-Qawāʿid al-Uṣūliyya*

The science of *al-qawāʿid al-fiqhiyya* is not identical to *uṣūl al-fiqh* and its *qawāʿid*. *Al-qawāʿid al-uṣūliyya* are assumed to be the same as the science of *uṣūl*. This is clearly indicated by Ibn al-Ḥājib (d. 646/1248) when he defined *uṣūl al-fiqh* as: "knowledge of *qawāʿid* which could be used to infer branches of legal rulings from their general sources through the means of deduction".[82]

---

79 Kamali, *Qawāʾid al-Fiqh*; and Izzi Dien, 113.

80 Kamali, *Ibid.*

81 This definition is based on, and formulated from, various opinions, to include the ultimate goal of the subject.

82 See al-Sawwat, 1:101.

Thus, it is possible to infer from the above definition that no independent science has been established for *al-qawāʿid al-uṣūliyya* as the science of *uṣūl al-fiqh* is *qāʿida* on its own.[83] This opinion is not well supported by the majority of scholars. However, the sciences of *fiqh* and *uṣūl* clearly differ despite the fact that some legal maxims "are often cross-referenced and sectioned with those relating to *uṣūl al-fiqh*".[84] Al-Ghazālī maintains that the science of *fiqh* focuses on the action of the individual in relation to legal orders, while the science of *uṣūl* focuses on the study of the meaning of words and definitions in order to deduce legal orders.[85] Moreover, each of these sciences has its own independent *qawāʿid*, as indicated above. However, *al-qawāʿid al-uṣūliyya* have never been separated from their source, in contrast to *al-qawāʿid al-fiqhiyya*, which have been treated as an independent discipline.

An in-depth study of these two sciences shows that there are similarities and differences between both subjects and their maxims. The similarities are as follows:

1. The maxims of both sciences are general principles that apply to many branches of *fiqh*.
2. Some maxims are interwoven between *uṣūl* and *fiqh*, such as the maxim of custom (*ʿurf*). If regarded as legal evidence from the viewpoint of its topic, it is deemed an *uṣūl* maxim, but if considered an act of a person of sound mind (*mukallaf*), it is deemed a *fiqh* maxim.[86]

The differences can be summarized as follows:

1. Legal maxims are extended products of the legal sources, or extrapolations of legal issues similar to each other. However, *al-qawāʿid al-uṣūliyya* are derived from the same source as the science of *uṣūl*, which consists of Arabic linguistics, principles of religion, etc.[87]

---

83 *Ibid.*, 1:151.

84 Izzi Dien, 114.

85 Abū Ḥāmid Muḥammad al-Ghazālī, *al-Mustaṣfā min ʿIlm al-Uṣūl*, 3rd edn. (Beirut: Dār Iḥyāʾ at-Turāth al-ʿArabī and Muʾassasat at-Tarikh al-ʿArabī, 1993), 1:5.

86 al-Nadawī, 70.

87 The derivation of *uṣūl* from those sources is mentioned by many scholars. See al-Jurjānī, *al-Burhān*, 1:47; ʿAlī Ibn Muḥammad al-Amidi, *al-Iḥkām fī Uṣūl al-Aḥkām*, edited by Sayyid al-Jumayli, 2nd edn. (Beirut: Dār al-Kitāb al-ʿArabī, 1986), 1:78; Muḥammad Ibn Bahāʾ al-Dīn al-Zarkashī, *al-Baḥr al-Muḥīṭ fī Uṣūl al-Fiqh* (Beirut: Dār al-Kutub al-ʿIlmiyya, 2000), 1:28; Ibn al-Najjār, 1:48; and al-Sawwat, 1:102.

2. Legal maxims are based on *fiqh* itself, while *uṣūl* and its maxims are concerned with legal reasoning, the applied meaning of commands, and prohibitions.[88]
3. Legal maxims can be used directly to derive legal rulings, as opposed to *al-qawāʿid al-uṣūliyya*, which can only be used to derive rulings through the source of Islamic Law. To illustrate this difference, the maxims "Imperative implies obligation" (*al-amr yaqtaḍī l-wujūb*), and "Matters shall be judged by their objectives" (*al-umūr bi-maqāṣidihā*) are apt examples. The former is a *al-qawāʿid al-uṣūliyya*, which implies that prayer is an obligatory duty but that implied meaning cannot be directly and clearly understood without imploring the interpretation of Qurʾānic verses such as: "... and observe prayer" (*wa-aqīmū aṣ-ṣalāt*, Q. 2:43). It is from the imperative form of the verse that the obligatory status of prayer is derived. However, the latter expression, being a legal maxim, can supply the obligation of intention in all human acts.[89]
4. Legal maxims are concerned with acts of a person of sound mind (*mukallaf*), while *al-qawāʿid al-uṣūliyya* are concerned with legal sources. For example, the legal maxim "Certainty cannot be overruled by doubt" (*al-yaqīn lā yazūl bi-sh-shakk*) gives a ruling on the certainty of the act of a *mukallaf*, while the maxim "Imperative implies obligation" (*al-amr yaqtaḍī l-wujūb*) is about any obligatory legal rule.[90]
5. Legal maxims are not always general and occasionally have exceptions to the rule, in contrast to *al-qawāʿid al-uṣūliyya* that are always general and without exceptions.[91]

al-Qawāʿid al-Fiqhiyya and *aḍ-Ḍawābiṭ al-Fiqhiyya*

The terms *ḍawābiṭ and qawāʿid* are occasionally used interchangeably. *Ḍawābiṭ* (pl. of *ḍābiṭ*) literally means a 'regulator' or 'controller'.[92] This verbal noun derives from the triliteral root (*ḍād-bāʾ-ṭāʾ*) for the verb *ḍabaṭa* (to tie or control something). In general, the term *ḍābiṭ* differs somewhat from *qāʿida* because the scope of each term is quite distinctive. However, from the perspective of

---

88 Kamali, *Qawāʿid al-Fiqh*, 1; al-Sawwat, 1:102–103; and Khaleel, 194.

89 ʿAbd al-Karīm Zaydān, *al-Wajīz fī Sharḥ al-Qawāʿid al-Fiqhiyya fī sh-Sharīʿa l-Islāmiyya* (Beirut: Muʾassasat ar-Risāla, 1997), 188; Khaleel, 194; and al-Sawwat, 1:103.

90 al-Sawwat, 1:102.

91 al-Nadawī, 68.

92 Baʿalbakkī, 706. The term *ḍābiṭ* can also be translated into 'regulator' because it also regulates an issue discussed from various points of view in particular topics of Islamic jurisprudence.

an Islamic jurist, there are two opinions regarding their usage. A number of classical as well as contemporary scholars regard the term *ḍābiṭ* as a 'sister' of *qāʿida*. In effect, they perceive no difference between the two terms.[93] In sharp contrast, other scholars hold the opinion that both terms are distinctly different.[94] The distinct factor that sets these two terms apart only comes to light when seen within the sphere in which these terms operate. The scope of *ḍābiṭ* is limited to a particular subject or chapter of Islamic jurisprudence and, as such, encounters very limited exceptions. By contrast, *qāʿida* is not confined to a particular theme or subject matter in jurisprudence. This dissimilarity is clarified by the Hāshiyat al-Bannānī: "a legal maxim, unlike *ḍābiṭ*, is not peculiar to a subject".[95] Moreover, al-Suyūṭī emphasizes the fundamental principle that *qāʿida* encompasses branches of various chapters of *fiqh* while *ḍābiṭ* is confined to individual chapters,[96] such as those on cleanliness (*ṭahāra*) and marriage (*nikāḥ*). Two examples can illustrate this argument. An example of *ḍābiṭ* is the following statement by jurists: "When water reaches two feet, it does not carry dirt". An example of *al-qawāʿid al-fiqhiyya* is the statement: "The affairs of the Imām concerning his people are judged by reference to *maṣlaḥa* [benefit]".[97] The *ḍābiṭ*'s range covers one topic exclusively, namely cleanliness, while that of the more general legal maxim is wider in scope and non-specific with regard to one's personal affairs, be they transactional, administrational, or spiritual.

From the foregoing discussion, one can reliably define *ḍābiṭ* from the viewpoint of scholars who distinguish between this term and *qāʿida*: namely, that *ḍābiṭ* is "a general rule that applies to branches of a particular theme".[98] In this way, a new term is established that allows knowledge to evolve even further: "Establishing a new norm is better than emphasizing an existing one" (*at-taʾsīs aw-lā min at-taʾkīd*).[99] However, one cannot rule out the possible

---

93 Such as Ibn Umam (d. 861 AH); *cf.*, *at-Tahrīr* with its *Sharh ʿalā Taqrīr wa-Tahrīr* by Ibn Amīr al-Ḥājj 1:29. Among the contemporary scholars who see no differences between the two terms is Wahba Muṣṭafā al-Zuhaylī. See Aḥmad Fahmī Abū Sanna, *al-Naẓariyya al-ʿĀmma li-l-Muʿāmalāt fī sh-Sharīʿa l-Islāmiyya* (Cairo: Dār at-Taʾlīf, 1965), 199.

94 al-Suyūṭī, *al-Ashbāh … fī l-Naḥw*, 1:9; Zayn al-ʿĀbidīn Ibn Ibrāhīm Ibn Nujaym, *al-Ashbāh wa-n-Naẓāʾir ʿalā Madhhab Abī Ḥanīfa l-Nuʿmān* (Beirut: Dār al-Kutub al-ʿIlmiyya, 1993), 197; and al-Burnu, *al-Wajīz*, 47.

95 ʿAbd al-Raḥman b. Jad Allāh al-Bannānī, *Hāshiyat al-Bannānī ʿalā Sharḥ al-Jalāl al-Muhallā ʿalā Jamʿ al-Jawāmiʿ* (Cairo: ʿĪsā al-Bāb al-Ḥalabī, n.d.), 2:290. See also al-Nadawī, 46.

96 al-Suyūṭī, *al-Ashbāh*, 1:7; and Ibn Nujaym, *al-Ashbāh wa-n-Naẓāʾir*, 192.

97 Kamali, *Qawāʿid al-Fiqh*, 1.

98 Ibn Nujaym, *al-Ashbāh wa-n-Naẓāʾir*, 192; and al-Sawwat, 1:96.

99 al-Sawwat, 1:96.

existence of a corollary between both terms, each of which, having been defined as a general legal ruling (*ḥukmun kullī fiqhī*) are applicable to issues within the Islamic legal framework. In his writings al-Subkī illustrates that both terms can be referred to as *qāʿida*, although each is defined by different adjectives. Therefore, we can refer to maxims having a wider scope 'general legal maxims' (*al-qawāʿid al-ʿāmma*) and those having a narrower scope 'specific legal maxims' (*qawāʿid al-khāṣṣa*).[100]

In sum, opinions diverge on the use of the term *ḍābiṭ* to mean *qāʿida*. However, as shown above, providing the *ḍābiṭ* with a separate meaning establishes a new term, without necessarily making it synonymous with *qāʿida*.

al-Qawāʿid al-Fiqhiyya and *an-Naẓariyyat al-Fiqhiyya*

Having distinguished between the terms *qawāʿid* and *ḍawābiṭ*, we must now shed light on a newly developed term in Islamic jurisprudence, namely *an-naẓariyyat al-fiqhiyya* (legal theory). The use of this modern term is aimed at covering a particularly important area of Islamic Law in order to create a thematic and comprehensive framework for it. Two examples are *naẓariyyat al-ʿaqd* (theory of transaction) and *naẓariyyat al-ithbāt* (theory of evidence). The theoretical nature of this term serves as an important landmark and point of departure from the old style of writing on Islamic jurisprudence whereby topics were not well articulated in a suitably formulaic way.[101]

The word *naẓariyya* is derived from the triliteral Arabic root (*nūn-ẓāʾ-rāʾ*) for the verbal noun *naẓar* (an in-depth look into what is visible, or thought, observation and reasoning).[102] According to *uṣūl*-ists, the term *naẓar* refers to reasoning aimed at attaining particular knowledge.[103] We can assume that the term *naẓariyya*, as well as its style of writing, were borrowed from Western scholarship by modern Islamic writers who, in one way or another, have had contact with a Western orientation to legal studies.[104] As such, a number of scholars are cynical about its use in Islamic jurisprudence because, as al-Burnu notes, theory (*naẓariyya*) springs from human reasoning that is not infallible,

---

100 al-Nadawī, 51, quoting al-Shubkī from his book *al-Ashbāh wa-n-Naẓāʾir*, Part 3, under the discussion of *qawāʿid al-khāṣṣa* (specific legal maxims).

101 Kamali, *Qawāʿid al-Fiqh*, 5.

102 Ibn Manẓūr, 5:215.

103 al-Amidi, 1:10; al-Zarkashī, *al-Baḥr al-Muḥīṭ*, 1:42; and Muḥammad b. ʿAlī al-Shawkānī, *Irshād al-Fuḥūl ilā Taḥqīq al-Ḥaqq min ʿIlm al-Uṣūl*, edited by Muḥammad Saʿīd al-Badrī, (Beirut: Dār al-Fikr, 1992), 20.

104 al-Nadawī, 63.

while the primary textual sources of Islamic Law are divine.[105] However, al-Sawwat has remarked that use of the term is justified, regardless of its derivation, if the nature of the issues dealt with under *al-naẓariyyat al-fiqhiyya* mirrors the nature of *ijtihād* (personal legal reasoning).[106] Of course, this opinion is based on the viewpoint that knowledge is knowledge and should be admired regardless of its origin, as long as such knowledge neither contradicts nor devalues Islamic morals.

However, the term *naẓariyya* contributes philosophically to knowledge and deserves its own in-depth examination. It is defined as a theory of a "number of topics of Islamic jurisprudence which contain legal issues based on rules and conditions and bound together under a subject unit".[107] Therefore, one apt example might be a collection of thoughts on one particular branch of jurisprudence where its sub-sections are inter-related, such as the theories of ownership and contract. This newly formulated terminology is employed in the contemporary style of *fiqh* writing, exemplified by Abū Sanna in his *The General Theory of Transactions in Islamic Law* (*an-Naẓariyyat al-ʿĀmma li-l-Muʿāmalāt fī sh-Sharīʿa al-Islāmiyya*).[108] However, during the development and incorporation of this term into Islamic jurisprudential terminology, a number of scholars assumed that it was equivalent to the term *qawāʿid*. One modern scholar inclined to make that assumption is Abū Zahara who says: "it is important to distinguish between the knowledge of *uṣūl al-fiqh* and *qawāʿid*, which embodies branches of legal rules. Here *qawāʿid* are best called general theories (*an-naẓariyyāt al-ʿāmma*) such as maxims of ownership (*qawāʿid al-milkiyya*)".[109] This view is antithetical to the prevailing opinion of the majority of Islamic writers.[110] *Qawāʿid* are said to belong to a separate discipline while *naẓariyya* is a separate style.

However, the ways in which both terms function show traces of similarity. For instance, fragments of *qawāʿid* and *ḍawābiṭ*, which form *naẓariyya*, can be found in maxims related to custom (*ʿurf*): namely, "Custom is authoritative" (*al-ʿāda muḥakkama*), "People's practice is authoritative and should be reckoned with" (*istiʿmāl an-nās ḥujja yajib al-ʿamal bi-hā*), "It is undeniable

---

105 al-Burnu, *Mawsūʿat al-Qawāʿid*, 1:96–102.

106 al-Sawwat, 106 (footnote).

107 al-Nadawī, 63.

108 Abū Sanna, *an-Naẓariyya l-ʿĀmma*, 44.

109 Muḥammad Abū Zahra, *Uṣūl al-Fiqh* (Cairo: Dār al-Fikr al-ʿArabī, n.d.), 10. The same view is emphasized by Abū Ṭāhir Aḥmad al-Khatabī, in his introduction to the edition of *Īḍāḥ al-Masālik* by al-Wanshirīsī, 111.

110 Such as M. al-Zarqā', *al-Madkhal*, 1:235.

that rules [based on *ʿurf*] change with time" (*lā yunkar taghayur al-aḥkām bi-taghayur al-azmān*), "Custom is considered only when it is regularly occurring and prevailing" (*innamā tuʿtabar al-ʿāda idhā iṭṭaradat aw ghalabat*).[111] These and other related maxims can be called theories on custom/tradition (*naẓariyyāt al-ʿurf*), regardless of their individual details because the prevailing obvious theme of all aforementioned maxims is *ʿurf*.[112] The same methodology can be applied to maxims related to confession (*iqrār*); when treated together they can be called theories on confession (*naẓariyyāt al-iqrār*). This explains why the *Majalla* is perceived to be *naẓariyya* in nature because its predominant focus is on transaction. However, many ways in which the two terms differ significantly are listed below:

1. *an-Naẓariyyāt al-fiqhiyya*, which deal with details of particular themes in Islamic jurisprudence, are lengthy in scope and construction. In contrast *al-qawāʿid al-fiqhiyya* are very precise in wording and style, yet comprehensive in their application to various branches and different topics of *fiqh*. However, the aim of *al-qawāʿid al-fiqhiyya* is not to provide details for all their particulars.[113]
2. *al-Qawāʿid al-fiqhiyya* are not defined using their own basic elements or conditions, in contrast to *naẓariyyāt*, the themes of which must be defined in detail.[114]
3. It is possible to say that *naẓariyyāt* are wider in scope than *qawāʿid*, although a *qāʿida* can serve as *ḍābiṭ* within a *naẓariyya* theme: *e.g.*, "The fundamental principle of contracts is the consent of the two contractual parties" (*al-aṣl fī l-ʿuqūd riḍā l-mutaʿāqidayn*). This maxim forms a *ḍābiṭ* (controller) within a *naẓariyyat al-ʿaqd*, which is uncommon because there are other ways in which *qawāʿid* can be broader in scope than *naẓariyyāt*. The maxim "Matters shall be judged by their objectives" (*al-umūr bi-maqāṣidihā*) is widely applicable, not only in the branch of contract (*ʿaqd*) law but also in all facets of Islamic jurisprudence.[115]

111 *Majalla*, Articles 36, 37, 39 and 41, respectively.

112 al-Nadawī, 65.

113 *Ibid.*, 66.

114 *Ibid.*, 65; and al-Sawwat, 1:108.

115 al-Suyūṭī, *al-Ashbāh wa-n-Naẓāʾir*, 47; and al-Sawwat, 1:108.

Contents of *al-Qawāʿid al-Fiqhiyya*

Sources of al-Qawāʿid al-Fiqhiyya

To justify any thought in Islamic jurisprudence, its source must be traced and its authenticity confirmed. The same applies to *al-qawāʿid al-fiqhiyya*, which are important aspects of Islamic Law. The word 'source' refers to the fount from which *qawāʿid* are formulated. Medieval scholars paid little or no attention in their narrations to the sources underlying any legal maxim because, at that time, this subject matter had not yet become well established. Rather, their practice was to name a maxim and then state whether its roots were in the Qurʾān or Sunna. When maxims were attributed to earlier scholars, frequently the sources from whence they were derived or formulated were not included.[116]

However, this dilemma has prompted contemporary Islamic scholars to adopt a distinctively different approach to the study of legal maxims and their sources: *i.e.*, they could choose to adhere to the medieval method or to provide a separate discussion on the sources of legal maxims and their derivation.[117] The way in which Muslim authors apply the latter method to *al-qawāʿid al-fiqhiyya* is not unique. For example, Rasheed al-Amiri focuses solely on whether the author is an independent or restricted *mujtahid* (scholarly authority permitted to pronounce Islamic verdicts).[118] al-Sawwat asserts that there are six sources of *al-qawāʿid al-fiqhiyya*: (1) Qurʾānic texts (*naṣṣ*); (2) Ḥadīths on the Prophet's Sunna; (3) consensus (*ijmāʿ*); (4) statements by the Prophet's Companions and Followers; (5) pronouncements by the scholarly authorities (*mujtahidūn*); and (6) extrapolation of the branch of legal issues having the same legal consequence.[119]

A general reading of the literature on the science of *al-qawāʿid al-fiqhiyya*, however, provides four main sources from which legal maxims can be derived: namely, the Holy Qurʾān, Ḥadīths, *ijmāʿ* (consensus) and *qiyās* (analogy by *mujtahidūn*).[120]

---

116 *Cf.*, the way in which al-Suyūṭī and Ibn Nujaym approach the sources of Islamic legal maxims in their *al-Ashbāh wa-n-Naẓāʾir*.

117 Such as M. al-Zarqāʾ, *al-Madkhal*, 2:969; and al-Burnu, *al-Wajīz*.

118 al-Sawwat, 1:114–121; *cf.*, al-Amiri, 32–45.

119 al-Sawwat, 1:114–120.

120 It is possible to adopt another way of classifying the sources of Islamic legal maxims since there is no dogma in terminology.

The Holy Qurʾān

The Holy Qurʾān is the source held in highest esteem from which *qawāʿid* are derived because it is the word of God. Legal maxims deduced either directly or indirectly from the Qurʾān are well established, irrefutable and all encompassing. A legal maxim can be derived without effort directly from the Qurʾān, such as when a layman easily understands the obvious correlation between a legal maxim and the Qurʾānic text. One example is the following statement from Qurʾānic verse 2:275: "… and God has permitted trade and forbidden usury" (*wa aḥalla Allāh al-bayʿa wa ḥarrama r-ribā*). This verse, which became a universal maxim guiding the theory of transactions (*muʿāmalāt*), was revealed to teach disputing unbelievers what was or was not legal in trade as well as to refute their claim that "trade and usury are alike".[121] As a principle, this Qurʾānic verse prohibits all unlawful transactions, thus making usury (*ribā*) the main reason for prohibition by taking as yardstick the objectives of Islamic Law (*maqāṣid ash-sharīʿa*).[122]

Qurʾānic verse 7:199 explicitly serves as an Islamic maxim: "Hold for forgiveness, command what is right, and turn away from the ignorant" (*khudh al-ʿafw wa-ʾmur bi-l-ʿurf wa-aʿriḍ ʿan al-jāhilīn*). Al-Qurṭubī (d. 671/1273) deduces three maxims from this verse, saying:

> This verse of three sentences consists of Islamic principles of command and forbiddance, *viz.* "Hold forgiveness" (*khudh al-ʿafw*) is a maxim for having forgiveness, "Command what is right" (*wa-ʾmur bi-l-ʿurf*)… Muslims are to command and enjoin what is right, no matter the condition, "Turn away from the ignorant" (*wa-aʿriḍ ʿan al-jāhilīn*)… no attention should be paid to ignorance.[123]

Qurʾānic verse 9:91 stands as a general legal maxim: "No ground [of complaint] can there be against the good-doers" (*mā ʿalā l-muḥsinīn min sabīl*). Ibn al-ʿArabī comments on this part of the verse when he says: "This is an indisputable general maxim of Sharīʿa which declares that neither complaint nor punishment should be inflicted on a good-doer".[124]

---

121 Q. 2:275.

122 Kamali, *Qawāʿid al-Fiqh*, 3.

123 Muḥammad b. Aḥmad al-Qurṭubī, *al-Jāmʿ li-Aḥkām al-Qurʾān*, 2nd edn. (Cairo: Dār al-Kutub al-Miṣriyya, 1936), 7:344.

124 Abū Bakr Muḥammad b. ʿAbdallah Ibn al-ʿArabī, *Aḥkām al-Qurʾān*, edited by Muḥammad ʿAta, (Lebanon: Dār al-Fikr, n.d.), 2:249.

However, in addition to formulating Islamic legal maxims directly from Qurʾānic text, they can also be deduced indirectly from the Qurʾān by considering the effective cause of the rule (*ḥukm*) with which the text deals. This method is one of the ways in which independent legal reasoning (*ijtihād*) can be used to deduce legal maxims from the Holy Qurʾān. Although commonly employed, before being permitted to deduce legal maxims indirectly, one must be conversant with the context of the Qurʾān, have a superior knowledge of the Arabic language, as well as have achieved a high level of *ijtihād*. The way in which legal maxims are deduced from the Qurʾān is demonstrated in the next section.

The Ḥadīths

Ḥadīths (corpus of narratives about the Prophet's deeds, sayings and teachings) are the second textual source for Islamic legal maxims. As discussed above, the Prophet was endowed with the ability to express himself concisely while also conveying inspirational, all-encompassing, and meaningful wisdom. Legal maxims can also be derived from the Ḥadīth of the Prophet in two forms. Legal maxims have been derived directly from a large number of prophetic expressions, with or without paraphrasing. One maxim derived directly from a prophetic Ḥadīth is: "Any intoxicant is forbidden" (*kullu muskirin ḥarām*).[125] This maxim is a reiteration of the Ḥadīth which states that all substances, whether originating from grapes, dates or other substances, that inebriate are regarded as forbidden (*ḥarām*), since the sole cause for prohibition in this Ḥadīth is inebriety. By analogy, this Ḥadīth also forbids the consumption of cocaine and other similar substances.[126]

Moreover, the Ḥadīth "No harm shall be inflicted or reciprocated" (*lā ḍarar wa-lā ḍirār*)[127] lends support to one of the major maxims in Islamic jurisprudence. According to one interpretation, the prophetic tradition indicates that: "Do not harm anyone and do not reciprocate harm for harm".[128] Another Ḥadīth upholding a legal maxim is the prophetic saying: No right for the sweat of an oppressor (*laysa li-ʿirq ẓālim ḥaqq*).[129] This Ḥadīth is considered to be a general rule for any issue similar to that which prompted the Prophet's response. M. al-Zarqāʾ (d. 1999 AD) remarks that this Ḥadīth is a fundamental

---

125 Ibn Mājah, Ḥadīth No. 3388, 4:68.

126 al-Burnu, *al-Wajīz*, 32.

127 Ibn Mājah, Ḥadīth No. 2340, 3:107.

128 al-Burnu, *al-Wajīz*, 32.

129 Abū Dāwūd Sulaymān b. al-Ashʿath, *as-Sunān* (Cairo: Maṭbaʿat as-Saʿada, 1950), Ḥadīth No. 3594, 4:24.

principle which establishes nullification of the rights of any aggressor, not only in the particular case to which the Ḥadīth refers but also in any case involving usurpation.[130]

An apt example of a legal maxim derived indirectly from the Qur'ān and Ḥadīth are the words "Hardship begets facility" (*al-mashaqqa tajlib at-taysīr*).[131] This aforementioned Islamic legal maxim is coded from intertextualizing concepts from various Qur'ānic verses and prophetic traditions. The maxim is said to have been inferred from the following Qur'ānic verses:

> God intends for you ease, and He does not want to make things difficult for you (Q. 2:185)
> (*yurīd Allāh bi-kum al-yusr wa-lā yurīd bi-kum al-ʿusr*);
>
> God burdens no individual beyond his capacity (Q. 2:286)
> (*lā yukallif Allāh nafsan illā wusʿahā*); and
>
> God wishes to lighten the burden for you. (Q. 4:28)
> (*yurīd Allāh an yukhaffif ʿankum*)

This maxim also refers to the prophetic Ḥadīth: "Make things easy for people, and do not make things difficult for them, and give them good tidings, and do not make them run away" (*yassirū wa-lā tuʿassirū wa-bashshirū wa-lā tunaffirū*).[132] The major connotation inferred from all these quotations is that the tenet of Islamic Law is to provide facility in the face of hardship or difficulty.

By and large, the quantum of legal maxims derived directly or indirectly from the two main sources of Islamic Law cannot be overstressed. Ibn al-Qayyim reflects on the importance of the texts in deriving Islamic legal maxims when he remarks:

> If the followers of the different Schools of Thought [*madhāhib*] have the ability to regulate the opinions of their *madhāhib* by using some general sayings that encompass what is lawful and what is not, in spite of their lack of eloquence compared to God and His messenger, then God and His messenger are more capable of achieving that. This is because the

130 M. al-Zarqā', *al-Madkhal*, 2:1090.

131 Muḥammad Ibn Bahā' al-Dīn al-Zarkashī, *al-Manṯūr fī l-Qawāʿid*, edited by Taysir F.A. Maḥmūd, 2nd edn., (Kuwait: Ministry of Endowment and Islamic Affairs, 1405), 3:169.

132 al-Bukhārī, Ḥadīth No. 69; and Muslim, Ḥadīth No. 1732.

Prophet pronounces a comprehensive statement that is considered as a general principle and a universal proposition that encompasses endless detail.[133]

Consensus

The maxim "A ruling established by means of independent reasoning cannot be reversed by a similar effort" (*al-ijtihād lā yunqaḍ bi-mithlihi*)[134] is said to be attributed to a statement by the Caliph ʿUmar ibn al-Khaṭṭāb and is also supported by consensus (*ijmāʿ*) among the Prophet's Companions.[135] Although maxims that emerged from this type of consensus are very rare, due to the scope of this discussion the analysis and application of the above maxim will be dealt with in due course.

Expressions by Islamic Scholars

Certain maxims have been brought to light by Islamic scholars (*mujtahidūn*) as a result of their thorough, detailed research on the sources of Islamic jurisprudence.[136] Expressions used to formulate Islamic maxims may have originated from the Prophet's Companions (*ṣaḥāba*) or Followers (*tābiʿūn*, those who followed the companions) or from jurists (*fuqahāʾ*) associated with one of the Schools of Islamic Jurisprudence. One of the most famous maxims, abridged from sayings of leading Islamic scholars, is "No statement or action should be imputed to someone who is silent, but a statement and action should be imputed to the one who made the statement or carried out the action" (*Lā yunsab ilā sākit qawlu qāʾil wa-lā ʿamal ʿāmil, innamā yunsab ilā kullin qawlihi wa-ʿamalihi*)[137] is reported to have been coded from the saying of ʿUbaydallah al-Karkhī (d. 340/951) and also "The principle is that a question should be based on how people understand it in their domain" (*al-aṣl ann as-suʾāl yamḍī ʿalā mā taʿārafa kull qawm fī makānihim*).[138]

133 Ibn al-Qayyim al-Jawziyya, *Iʿlām al-Muwaqqiʿīn*, 1:251.

134 al-Suyūṭī, *al-Ashbāh*, 101; Ibn Nujaym, *al-Ashbāh wa-n-Naẓāʾir*, 115; and *Majalla*, Article 16.

135 Kamali, *Qawāʿid al-Fiqh*, 4.

136 A *mujtahid* is one who is capable of giving Islamic verdicts from his personal opinion. He must have attained that status of being capable to do so according to the rules and regulations laid down with regard to the status.

137 *Majalla*, Article 36.

138 al-Burnu, *al-Wajīz*, 84.

Typology of al-Qawāʿid al-Fiqhiyya

During its early stage of development, the notion of categorizing *al-qawāʿid al-fiqhiyya* did not occur. Later, however, a number of Islamic scholars did undertake such efforts in their narrations, and we are indebted to them for facilitating the later classification of *al-qawāʿid al-fiqhiyya* into different categories. In general, legal maxims can be viewed with regard to three issues:

1. their scope and the extent in which they are applied to branches and issues in Islamic jurisprudence;
2. agreement among Islamic scholars as to whether their content demonstrates concurrence;
3. their status as either an independent or subsidiary to a general legal maxim.[139]

The first classification is more relevant to this book because the second and third issues fall under it and because discussions on the application of legal maxims in relation to criminal cases are based on it. The majority of Islamic scholars have divided *qawāʿid* into three categories according to their scope:

1. Maxims that are wider in scope and far more applicable to all branches of *fiqh* are called 'basic general legal maxims' (*al-qawāʿid al-fiqhiyya al-kulliyya*);
2. Maxims that are general and universal in nature, but not applicable to all issues of Islamic jurisprudence, are called 'independent general legal maxims' (*al-qawāʿid al-fiqhiyya al-kulliyya al-mustaqilla*); and
3. Maxims that predominate in a specific chapter of *fiqh* are called 'controllers' (*aḍ-ḍawābiṭ al-fiqhiyya*).[140]

Basic General Legal Maxims

Basic general legal maxims (*al-qawāʿid al-fiqhiyya al-kulliyya*) are those which can be described as comprehensive and which stand as pillars of Islamic

---

139 See al-Burnu, *Mawsūʿat al-Qawāʿid*, 1:32 and al-Sawwat's approaches in this regard.

140 The term *ḍawābiṭ* is used here to encompass those maxims that control peculiar themes in particular as well as different Schools. It is stated that *ḍābiṭ* is assumed to be a principle that controls similar issues in one School. However, in this book, it is meant to be any maxim that controls peculiar themes or subjects in Islamic jurisprudence, regardless of which School adopts the maxim.

jurisprudence. These maxims naturally include numerous sub-maxims.[141] Several distinctive features of basic general legal maxims are the following:[142]

1. They must be acceptable to all Schools of Jurisprudence;
2. They must cover all or most of the scope of *fiqh*;
3. They must contain subsidiary maxims that either function as conditions or restrictions for the major legal maxim; and
4. They must be based on one of the three sources of Islamic Law; namely, the Qur'ān, Sunna, and consensus (*ijmāʿ*).

These basic general legal maxims number between five and seven maxims. Early Islamic scholars unanimously agreed upon five, while the remaining two maxims are presented in *Similitudes and Resemblances* (*al-Ashbāh wa-n-Naẓā'ir*) by al-Suyūṭī's work.[143] The five grand maxims generally agreed upon are the following:

1. "Matters shall be judged by their objectives" (*al-umūr bi-maqāṣidihā*);
2. "Certainty cannot be overruled by doubt" (*al-yaqīn lā yazūl bi-sh-shakk*);
3. "Hardship begets facility" (*al-mashaqqa tajlib at-taysīr*);
4. "Harm should be eliminated" (*aḍ-ḍarar yuzāl*); and
5. "Custom is authoritative" (*al-ʿāda muḥakkama*).[144]

However, al-Burnu contends that the maxim which addresses the effects of the expression, *i.e.*, "A word should be construed as having some meaning, rather than disregarded" (*iʿmāl al-kalām aw-lā min ihmālih*),[145] should be classified among the basic general legal maxims[146] because it shares their features and

141 These sub-maxims can be conditional clauses for major or independent maxims, or exceptions, such as "Necessity should be proportional" (*aḍ-ḍarar tuqaddir bi-qadarihā*), which stands as a condition for the maxim "Hardship should be eliminated" (*aḍ-ḍarar yuzāl*), or "Necessity makes prohibited things permissible" (*aḍ-ḍarūrāt tubīḥ al-maḥẓūrāt*).

142 al-Suyūṭī, *al-Ashbāh*, 6.

143 *Ibid.*, 83; al-Burnu, *al-Wajīz*, 27.

144 al-Suyūṭī, *al-Ashbāh*, 88–196; Ibn Nujaym, *al-Ashbāh wa-n-Naẓā'ir*, 23–89; and al-Nadawī, 351. The exception is al-Burnu who creates a sixth maxim, "A word should be construed as having some meaning, rather than disregarded" (*iʿmāl al-kalām aw-lā min ihmālih*), arguing that the maxim is generally and widely applicable to many subjects and issues in Islamic jurisprudence. See al-Burnu, *al-Wajīz*, 314.

145 al-Suyūṭī, *al-Ashbāh*, 128; and Ibn Nujaym, *al-Ashbah wa-n-Naẓā'ir*, 130.

146 al-Burnu, *al-Wajīz*, 314–315.

will be quite difficult to ignore in books on jurisprudence. In other words, it is comprehensive enough to be elevated to the status of a basic general maxim. Our research will neither consider this legal maxim nor its 'sisters' as one of the *al-qawāʿid al-fiqhiyya al-kulliyya*, not because of any lack of merit as put forward by al-Burnu but because it is already renown in the literature.

Independent General Legal Maxims

Independent general legal maxims (*al-qawāʿid al-fiqhiyya al-kulliyya al-mustaqilla*) do not belong to the above-mentioned category,[147] the differences being that these maxims are accorded more exceptions than those in the previous category. Moreover, their acceptability among the Schools of Islamic Jurisprudence lacks common ground. Two maxims that fall under this category are the following:[148]

1. Governance should be in the public interest (*at-taṣarruf ʿalā r-raʿiyya manūṭ bi-l-maṣlaḥa*);[149] and
2. When its use is forbidden, its possession is also forbidden (*mā ḥaruma istiʿmāluhu ḥaruma ittikhādhuhu*).[150]

Controllers or Topical Maxims

Maxims classified as controllers/regulators or topical maxims (*aḍ-ḍawābiṭ al-fiqhiyya*) are peculiar to certain topics of *fiqh*. For example, different topics are subsumed under the chapter on acts of worship (*ʿibādāt*). The *ḍābiṭ* is meant to regulate, within one School of Islamic Jurisprudence, the divergent opinions among those Islamic scholars on the issue in question. For example, the maxim "Effect is given to purpose and meaning, not to literalness and structure" (*al-ʿibra fī l-ʿuqūd li-l-maqāṣid wa-l-maʿānī lā li-l-alfāẓ wa-l-mabānī*) is peculiar to the theme of contracts in the Ḥanafī School. This is the general opinion on the concept of *ḍawābiṭ*.[151] However, *ḍawābiṭ* are not only maxims that control the rulings of one particular school. Although they attract discussion among the different Schools of Islamic Jurisprudence, they also control

147 They are not up to the general grand maxim but they are also widely applicable to many subjects and issues in Islamic jurisprudence. See al-Burnu, *al-Wajīz*, 330–409; al-Sawwat, 1:109; and al-Nadawī, 351.

148 al-Suyuti, *al-Ashbāh wa-l-Naẓāʾir*, 95 and 103.

149 *Majalla*, Article 58, *cf.*, al-Suyūṭī, *al-Ashbāh*, 21.

150 M. al-Zarqāʾ, *al-Madkhal*, 2:235, al-Nadawī, 64; A. al-Zarqāʾ, *Sharḥ*, 55; and *Majalla*, Article 3.

151 al-Sawwat, 1:110.

particular themes upon which they do not, with regard to authenticity, enjoy agreement. Two examples are "Fixed [*ḥadd*] punishments should be averted in the face of doubt" (*al-ḥudūd tudraʾ bi-sh-shubhāt*),[152] and "It is left to the leader/judge to decide an appropriate discretionary punishment considering the proportionate [nature] of the offence" (*at-taʿzīr ilā l-imām ʿalā qadr ʿaẓam al-jurm wa-ṣigharh*).[153] These two maxims can better be classified as *ḍawābiṭ* of punishment within the theme of criminal law, and yet they are debated within all the Schools of Islamic Jurisprudence.

Importance and Role of al-Qawāʿid al-Fiqhiyya

Importance of *al-Qawāʿid al-Fiqhiyya*

Because life is naturally comprehensive, there must be rules and principles to guide mankind. Law is an essential tool in regulating human life. The importance of *al-qawāʿid al-fiqhiyya* cannot be overemphasized because of its relationship with the Sharīʿa and with the maxim "The branch shares the same rule as the origin" (*al-farʿ lahu ḥukm al-aṣl*). In Western schools of law, legal maxims play a vital role in the judgment process, and their importance has been described as:

> ...a general principle; a leading truth so-called, *quia maxima est ejus dignitas et certissima auctoritas atque quod maxime omnibus probetur*—because its dignity is the greatest and its authority the most certain, and because it is universally approved by all.[154]

In contrast, other modern English jurists who disagree hold the opinion that those legal maxims "... are rather minims than maxims, for they give not a particularly great, but a particularly small, amount of information".[155] They (the Latin maxims) "are almost invariably misleading" and "mostly bad abstract" in law.[156] The cause of this disagreement stems from the fact that most Western legal maxims are based on common sense, and common sense is subject to

---

152 al-Suyūṭī, *al-Ashbāh*, 236; Ibn Nujaym, *al-Ashbāh wa-n-Naẓāʾir*. 142; and al-Zarkashī, *al-Manṯūr*, 2:40 and 225.

153 Ibn Ibrāhīm, *Kitāb al-Kharāj*, 180.

154 Earl Jowitt and Clifford Walsh, *Jowitt's Dictionary of English Law* (London: Sweet and Maxwell, 1977), 2:1164.

155 *Ibid.*, quoting Justice Stephen in *History of Criminal Law*, 94.

156 *Ibid.*

criticism and liable to objection.[157] More importantly, they do not have principal references. This is not to say that those maxims are not useful in the modern era. Indeed, because the realm of law has expanded and become more complex, the usefulness of maxims is increasing and "they bring back the mind to first principles".[158] However, the value of Islamic legal maxims cannot be underestimated because they either directly or indirectly originate from divine sources, namely the Qur'ān and Ḥadīth. It becomes *sine qua non* for any Islamic jurist and judge today to master a certain level of *qawāʿid* in order to be able to dispense Islamic verdicts and to pass accurate judgments. It is also essential to master and memorize large sections of the Qur'ān and Ḥadīth. The rigorous attention that Islamic scholars have paid to this subject since the 3rd century Hijra clearly underscores the importance attached to it. Moreover, the utterances of scholars have demonstrated the significance accredited to the subject. Imām al-Qarāfī (d. 684/1285) affirms thus:

> These maxims are very important in Islamic jurisprudence. By knowing these maxims, the value of a jurist is measured. Through it, the beauty of *fiqh* is shown and known. With it, the methods of verdicts [*fatwā*] are clearly understood. [...] Whoever knows *fiqh* with its maxims [*qawāʿid*] shall be in no need of memorizing most of the subordinate parts "of *fiqh*" because of their inclusion under the general maxims.[159]

Role of *al-Qawāʿid al-Fiqhiyya*

After studying the concepts of *al-qawāʿid al-fiqhiyya* extensively, it becomes possible to highlight their role in Islamic jurisprudence as follows:

1. Because *al-qawāʿid al-fiqhiyya* are generally composed of single, concise expressions, they have been of inestimable value for the vast discipline of Islamic jurisprudence, by helping to bring together related cases and similar issues from among the numerous branches of law. During the development of Islamic jurisprudence or *fiqh*, much of the literature was being written in piecemeal fashion and fragmented styles because the majority of scholars were writing independently. At that time there were

157 David M. Walker, *The Oxford Companion to Law* (Oxford: Oxford University Press, 1980), 181.

158 Lazar Emanuel, *Latin for Lawyers: The Language of the Law* (Larchmont, NY: Emanuel Publishing, 1999).

159 Aḥmad b. Idrīs al-Qarāfī, *Anwār al-Burūq fī Anwāʾ al-Furūq*, edited by Khalīl al-Manṣūr, (Beirut: Dār al-Kutub al-ʿIlmiyya, 1998), 1:3; and al-Nadawī, 326.

no guidelines as to standards, style, or presentation. This factor together with many other reasons may have contributed to the wide diversity of opinions in *fiqh* literature. As their role spread, legal maxims were derived or created as general directives that articulated theoretical abstracts scattered among the various Schools of Islamic Jurisprudence.[160] Remarking on this important role of *al-qawāʿid al-fiqhiyya*, M. al-Zarqāʾ observed that "were it not for the legal maxims, the rules would have remained dispersed without any ideational connection".[161] They have not only enabled jurists to understand *fiqh* rulings with less difficulty but they have also helped judges comprehend the basic tenets of Islamic Law on any contentious issue. For instance, if it is established in the mind of a judge that a (fixed) *ḥadd* punishment should be averted in the face of doubt, this will convey significant merit when identifying the aim of Islamic Law in offences related to *ḥudūd* crimes. Exploring such an opportunity would also enhance the ability of Islamic scholars, judges and jurists to deliver sound and impartial legal judgments.[162]

2. Increased understanding of *qawāʿid* gives a student of *fiqh* the ability to enjoy this concept on intellectual grounds. Al-Zarkashī (d. 794/1392) submits that if detailed issues scattered in the books of Islamic Law are controlled "by the legal maxims", it will facilitate their memorization and comprehension.[163]
3. The generality of legal maxims creates space in which to compare and contrast past and present occurrences. Thus, knowledge of *al-qawāʿid al-fiqhiyya* helps jurists pronounce judgment on present-day cases that could not have occurred in the distant past.[164] For example, the issue of interest is similar to usury (*ribā*). However, the role that interest plays in today's world of finance is different from how *ribā* operated in the past, although the reasons for prohibiting *ribā* still exist in the modern system of banking: "The branch has the same rule as the origin" (*wa-l-farʿ lahu ḥukm al-aṣl*). In a similar way, the maxim "The accessory shares the same rule of the root" (*at-tābiʿ tābiʿ*)[165] justifies the prohibition of cocaine as an intoxicant.

160 Kamali, *Qawāʿid al-Fiqh*, 4.
161 M. al-Zarqāʾ, *al-Madkhal*, 2:935.
162 Izzi Dien, 114; and Kamali, *Qawāʿid al-Fiqh*, 1–2.
163 al-Zarkashī, *al-Manṯūr*, 1:69–70.
164 al-Suyūṭī, *al-Ashbāh*, 31; and al-Sawwat, 1:128.
165 al-Suyūṭī, *Ibid.*, 117; Ibn Nujaym, *al-Ashbāh wa-n-Naẓāʾir*, 120; and *Majalla*, Article 47.

4. Since Islamic scholars concur on the majority of *qawāʿid*, their consensus might provide researchers with a broader knowledge about similar opinions held by leading Schools of Islamic Jurisprudence. Moreover, studying how scholars agree on some matters also helps to pinpoint how they differ: *i.e.*, what was the genesis of their disagreements on issues and what was the rationale behind such differences.
5. As subject matter, the function of *qawāʿid* underscores how far Islam progressed in coding terminologies, principles, rulings and legal techniques before the onset of common law.
6. Last, but not least, exploiting legal maxims, especially those on arbitration and enforcement of custom, will accommodate non-Muslims living in a state governed by Islamic Law. In other words, taking into consideration the maxim of custom, *inter alia*, will emphasize the universality of Islam and the possibility of ruling any society in a just manner.

However, speculation surrounds the extent to which legal maxims are deemed important. The *Majalla* asserts that the essence of legal maxims is to facilitate a better understanding of the Sharīʿa[166] and that a judge may not base a ruling upon a legal maxim unless it is derived from either the Qurʾān or Sunna. To some extent, this assertion is justifiable in that restricting the use of maxims will help curtail any prejudice against the Sharīʿa in cases where maxims are initiated arbitrarily. Nevertheless, this point of view is thought to undermine their general usefulness. In contrast, al-Qarāfī maintains that a judicial decision can be reversed if it contains any violation of a generally accepted maxim.[167] To find a balance between the two views, we submit that there is no doubt that a legal maxim derived directly or indirectly from the texts or by sound consensus or by completed analogy will prove to be a sufficient basis for judgment. However, if a legal maxim is formulated from a mere reading of the details, it must then be endorsed by the leading Schools of Islamic Jurisprudence. Moreover, a legal maxim specific to one School of Jurisprudence, which does not enjoy the support of any other School, is not a sufficiently reliable basis for sound judgment. Therefore, because the majority of these maxims are subject to certain exceptions, it is not totally acceptable for jurists and practitioners of law to depend on such principles as a primary source of evidence or to employ them alone as proofs. Islamic jurists are enjoined first to base their judgments on the primary sources, *i.e.*, the Qurʾān, Ḥadīth, or consensus (*ijmāʿ*), and

166 ʿAlī Haydar, *Durar al-Ḥukkām fī Sharḥ Majallat al-Aḥkām*, edited by Fahmī al-Ḥusaynī, (Beirut: Dār al-Kutub al-ʿIlmiyya, n.d.), 1:10; and M. al-Zarqāʾ, *al-Madkhal*, 2:949.

167 al-Qarāfī, *adh-Dhakhīra*, 4:40.

only then to use *qawāʿid* independently. However, when the primary source is unclear, then *qawāʿid* can still be put to use.[168]

It is worth stating that the codification of Islamic legal maxims, which has continued for generations, is still ongoing. Indeed, legal maxims are coded from time to time or previous expressions are recoded as necessity demands, as demonstrated by the *Majalla*'s codification of several medieval Islamic legal maxims. Today, new or modified legal maxims can be formulated to deal with novel issues, through inter- and hyper-textualization of the concepts and context of Islamic texts to extrapolate the tenets of the overall objectives of Islamic Law.

Conclusion

In summary, Chapter 2 that represents the theoretical section of this book has introduced *al-qawāʿid al-fiqhiyya* as subject matter as well as demonstrated their concepts, historical development, and function. Clearly this subject requires an additional in-depth study of its practical values, a lacuna this text aims to fill in part. This chapter has established systematically the developments which the discipline has undergone. Traditionally scholars agree that there are five basic legal maxims. However, what al-Burnu considers to be the sixth basic maxim, although worthy of further study in an independent investigation, falls outside the scope of this book because it is infamous in itself.

The following chapters will focus on the analysis of the five basic legal maxims agreed upon by Islamic scholars as well as on their application in criminal law. This analysis will make use of information from a number of criminal cases reported in several Muslim countries in general, with special focus on some cases that have occurred in Northern Nigeria.

---

168 al-Nadawī, 323–347.

CHAPTER 3

Legal Maxim of Intention and Action: "Matters Shall Be Judged by Their Objectives" (*al-Umūr bi-Maqāṣidihā*)*

Introduction: Intention and Action in Islamic Criminal Law

In Islamic Law, intention (*niyya*) is an important criterion for determining whether a criminal act is punishable or pardonable, or whether the penalty for such a crime is predetermined (*ḥadd*) or discretionary (*taʿzīr*). No offender can be found guilty until his intention in committing the crime has been taken into consideration. The same is true for Western criminal procedures; *mens rea* (mental element) alone provides insufficient proof to establish the guilt of the accused if it is not accompanied by *actus reus* (physical element).[1] According to Lord Kenyon C.J. in *Flower v. Padget*: "It is a principle of natural justice and of our law, that *actus non facit reum nisi mens sit rea*—the intent and the act must both concur to constitute the crime".[2] The Islamic criminal system examines the action of the accused before considering his intention. However, there is no way a man's intention can be examined without thorough knowledge of the elements by which the crime was committed or the state of mind of the alleged criminal. According to the Islamic legal maxim "Matters shall be judged by their objectives" (*al-umūr bi-maqāṣidihā*), the establishment of intention alongside action is given paramount consideration. In what follows, we shall address those maxims related to this aspect of a criminal offence.

Definition and Interpretation of al-Umūr bi-Maqāṣidihā

"Matters shall be judged by their objectives" (*al-umūr bi-maqāṣidihā*) is one of the five grand general maxims agreed upon by Islamic scholars because of its consistency with, and relevance to, Islamic jurisprudence. It implies that any action or matter (*umūr*), whether physical or verbal, should be considered

* al-Suyūṭī, *al-Ashbāh*, 8; Ibn Nujaym, *al-Ashbāh wa-n-Naẓāʾir*, 27; al-Ḥamawī, 1:37; *Majalla*, Article 2; Haydar, 1:17; and A. al-Zarqā', *Sharḥ*, 47.

1 Maḥmaṣṣānī, 160.

2 James William Cecil Turner and A.L. Armitage, *Cases on Criminal Law*, 3rd edn. (Cambridge: Cambridge University Press, 1964), 1.

 | DOI 10.1163/9789004304871_004

and judged according to the intentions (*niyya*) of the (wrong) doer. In fact, the whole sphere of *fiqh* is concerned with rules or judgments on matters.[3] The appropriate interpretation of this maxim should therefore be that any rulings made for or against a case should be in conformity with the intention of the offender(s) involved in the case.[4] Every branch of *fiqh* will take under consideration the intention or motive behind an act, a *sine qua non* for the validity of any action. Indeed, intention is a fundamental concept existent throughout the entire Islamic Religious Law. It significantly figures "in Muslim approaches to acts in general, and to religious acts in particular".[5]

Two distinctive words constitute the elements of this maxim: matters (*umūr*) and objectives (*maqāṣid*). Without considering both elements, criminal justice cannot be carried out. The first word, which is *umūr* (pl. of *amr*), is literally translated as a matter, issue, or act, whether physical or verbal.[6] According to al-Aṣfahānī, the word *amr* encompasses both actions and utterances, as stated in Qur'ānic verse 11:97: "The command of the Pharaoh was not the right guide" (*wa-mā amr fir'awn bi-rashīd*). This refers to his utterances and actions.[7] The second word is *maqāṣid* (pl. of *maqṣad*), which literally means 'will' or the determination to do something for a purpose.[8] The term is also synonymous for intention (*niyya*).[9] The maxim simply means that rulings on all physical or verbal actions of a person of sound mind (*mukallaf*) shall be determined in accordance with the intent and objectives of the person who carried out the action.[10] Thus, an action can be described as culpable and punishable only when the motive of the perpetrator has been brought to light.

---

3 A. al-Zarqā', *Sharḥ*, 47.

4 *Ibid.*

5 Brinkley Messick, "Indexing the Self: Intent and Expression in Islamic Legal acts", in David S. Powers (ed.), *Islamic Law and Society*, (Leiden: Brill, 2001), 8:153.

6 Ibn Manẓūr, 1:96; see also Rāghib al-Aṣfahānī, *al-Mufradāt fī Gharīb al-Qur'ān*, edited by Muḥammad Sayyid Kaylani, (Lebanon: Dār al-Ma'rifa, n.d.), for explanation of the meaning of *amr* in Qur'ānic verses 11:97 and 3:123, 154. See also al-Burnu, *Mawsū'at al-Qawā'id*, 1:133.

7 al-Aṣfahānī, *Rāghib, al-Mufradāt fī Gharīb al-Qur'ān*, edited by Muḥammad Sayyid Kaylani (Lebanon: Dār al-Ma'rifa, n.d.) 24–25.

8 Ibn Manẓūr, 1:96.

9 Aḥmad b. Faris al-Rāzī, *Mu'jam Maqāyīs al-Lugha*, edited by 'Abd al-Salam M. Harun, (Beirut: Dār Iḥyā' al-Kutub al-'Arabiyya, n.d.), s.v. "*nawā*".

10 Khalid al-Atāsī and Muḥammad Ṭāhir al-Atāsī, *Sharḥ Majallat al-Aḥkām al-'Adliyya* (Damascus: Hams Press, 1349/1930), 1:13; and al-Burnu, *Mawsū'at al-Qawā'id*, 1:124.

Sources of the Maxim *al-Umūr bi-Maqāṣidihā*

Islamic jurists have evoked much textual evidence to justify the legality of this maxim. The most authentic and direct evidence is the Ḥadīth reported by many traditionalists, but particularly by al-Bukhārī and Muslim, the two most authoritative compilers of books on Ḥadīths, in which the Prophet is reported to have said: "Actions are judged according to intentions" (*innamā l-aʿmāl bi-n-niyyāt*).[11] Many other Qurʾānic verses and prophetic Ḥadīths also emphasize the need for sincerity in the endeavors of all Muslims, although most of these texts refer to rewards for acts that are in accordance with sincere intention in the Hereafter.[12] This is not to say that the Ḥadīth is not useful in determining the penalties for criminal acts concordant with *mens rea*. On the contrary, the Ḥadīth has implications for any action, whether devotional, social, political, or commercial.[13] For many interpreters, the Ḥadīth on intention (*niyya*) cannot be undermined as it is said to represent one-third of Islamic knowledge.[14]

Corroboration of Action with Intention in Islamic Criminal Law

The use of the maxim "Matters shall be judged by their objectives" (*al-umūr bi-maqāṣidihā*) relates to matters where the legal ruling is based on both action (*ʿamal*) and intention (*niyya*). Conversely, in the Islamic legal framework a number of rulings can be established on the basis of intention alone, such as having the intention to commit apostasy (*ridda*) or the willingness to perform religious duties (*ʿibāda* or *ukhrāwiyya*). For instance, if someone dies while intending to commit apostasy, or actually fails to perform those ritual duties, reward would be based on his/her intention, even when the intention was not overtly expressed. In fact, this implies that intention can be considered without the involvement of action. However, in most cases, or as a fundamental principle (*aṣl*), the essence of intention is ostensibly effective when coupled with

11 al-Bukhārī, Ḥadīth No. 1; and Muslim, Ḥadīth No. 1599.

12 al-Burnu, *Mawsūʿat al-Qawāʿid*, 1:133; Q. 4:100, 134; Q. 17:19; and Q. 30:39; and al-Bukhārī, Ḥadīths No. 1356 and No. 1737.

13 ʿAbd al-Raḥman b. Shihab al-Dīn Ibn Rajab, *Jāmiʿ al-ʿUlūm wa-l-Ḥikam*, edited by Shuʿayb al-Arnaʾut and Ibrāhīm Bajis, 2nd edn., (Beirut: Muʾassasat ar-Risāla, 1997), 5.

14 See al-Suyūṭī, *al-Ashbāh*,; Ibn Nujaym, *al-Ashbāh wa-n-Naẓāʾir*; M. al-Zarqāʾ, *al-Madkhal*, 96; al-Burnu, *al-Wajīz*, 122–125; Aḥmad b. ʿAlī b. Ḥajar al-ʿAsqalānī, *Fatḥ al-Bārī Sharḥ Ṣaḥīḥ al-Bukhārī*, edited by Muḥbib al-Dīn al-Khaṭīb, (Beirut: Dār al-Maʿrifa, n.d.), 1:11–13; and Yaḥyā b. Sharif al-Nawawī, *Sharḥ Ṣaḥīḥ Muslim*, 2nd edn. (Beirut: Dār Iḥyāʾ at-Turāth al-ʿArabī, 1392/1972).

action. Al-Sarakhsī (d. 490/1096) emphasizes that "Fundamentally, there is no effect [in worldly matters] on intention devoid of act" (*al-aṣl ʿanna n-niyya idhā tajarrad ʿan al-ʿamal lā takun muʾaththira* [*fī l-umūr ad-dunyāwiyya*]).[15] This is because intention is not being overtly or physically expressed and is only applicable to mundane matters.[16] Thus, when a link can be drawn between one's action (*ʿamal*) and intention (*niyya*), that act will be judged according to intention. From an Islamic theological point of view, if someone intends to commit apostasy, then it is said that the person has become apostate.[17] However, no worldly punishment will be inflicted since the intention was neither voiced nor acted upon.

In contrast, some rulings can be established by action alone. Such is the case for defamation (*qadhf*), where the utterance is sufficient to prosecute the defamer if what was said is deemed defamation without interpretation. This is because *qadhf* involves the right of man. However, in other cases, legal rulings rely heavily on both action and intention before judgment can be reached. Generally speaking, in criminal cases, there can be no doubt, and it is of utmost importance, that a person's intention and his/her action must concur. Therefore, in most cases, an act cannot be justifiably established as criminal without first considering the intent of the accused. Take, for example, the following classical case: when someone takes property in the public domain that does not belong to him, one cannot conclude that theft has occurred until the perpetrator's intention has been clarified. He might have been acting as trustee to save the rightful owner's property, or he might have been committing an act of thievery.[18] In Western criminal terminology, *actus reus* (guilty act) is a physical act (or unlawful omission) by the defendant.[19] It is a collective rather than mental element, while *mens rea* (guilty mind) is the state of mind or intent of the individual defendant at the time of his act.[20] Before someone can be charged as having committed a crime, there must be concurrence: namely, the physical act and mental state of the offender must have occurred simultaneously.

In Islamic Law, *mens rea* (*ʿamd* or *qaṣd jināʾī*) works differently depending on the nature of the alleged crime. In *ḥudūd* crimes, *mens rea* (*qaṣd jināʾī*) must

---

15 Muḥammad b. Aḥmad al-Sarakhsī, *al-Mabsūṭ* (Beirut: Dār al-Maʿrifa, 1986), 1:239.

16 al-Burnu, *Mawsūʿat al-Qawāʿid*, 1:159.

17 Ibn Nujaym, *al-Ashbāh wa-n-Naẓāʾir*, 15–21.

18 *Majalla*, Article 769; A. al-Zarqāʾ, *Sharḥ*, 49; and Maḥmaṣṣānī, 160.

19 Imran A. Khan Nyazee, *General Principles of Criminal Law: Islamic and Western* (Islamabad: International Islamic Univerisity, Shari'ah Academy, 2007), 80.

20 *Ibid.*

concur with *actus reus* (*fi'l jināʾī*) before one can be found guilty of the crime especially in crimes that are classified as *ḥaqq Allāh*, such as adultery (*zinā*) and consumption of alcohol (*shrub al-khamr*). For example, if someone stands firmly by the fact that he has actually committed a murder, then the act itself overrides his intention.[21] However, while intention is considered to have an impact on the validity and gravity of any action, "weighing intentions would be a system of strict liability."[22] Strict liability in Islamic criminal law subsumes what is termed as quasi-intentional and unintentional bodily injuries which incur *diya*.[23]

Correlation between Action and Intention in Islamic Criminal Law

In the case of murder, for example, a defendant's intention (*ʿamd*) must concur with the act that constitutes the crime in question before he can be convicted for murder. One must first tackle two crucial conditions when considering the concurrence of *mens rea* and *actus reus*. (1) Intention must be the motivating factor behind the act. Consider the following example: A intends to kill B by gunshot but first locks B in a stuffy room while he fetches the gun; however, B dies before A's return. It cannot be said that a causal relationship exists between A's intention and B's death, which may have resulted from A's recklessness or negligence. As such, A will still be liable for manslaughter. (2) If the criminal act (*actus reus*) was continuous, then the presence of a guilty mind (*mens rea*) during that act, but not necessarily at the point of completion of the act, will be sufficient proof. Take, for example, the following case: A intends to kill B by poisoning, but the poison does not work immediately and B is rushed to hospital. Upon arrival, there is no space available for admission, and delayed death from poisoning occurs. It can be said that, although the poison did not act instantaneously, it is the *actus reus* which eventually caused death.[24]

In Islamic criminal law, the actual instrument employed in a homicide is the external standard upon which to focus to determine whether an offender's act and intention concur. Investigating the inner state or intention of an offender is not only challenging, but can actually be prohibited in some cases.[25] Thus,

21 *Ibid.*

22 Paul R. Powers, *Intent in Islamic Law, Motive and Meaning in Medieval Sunni Fiqh*, (Leiden – Boston: Brill, 2006), p. 173.

23 *Ibid.*

24 *Ibid.*, 97. This theory will be expanded in the discussion on direct and indirect causation.

25 Especially in matters related to *ḥudūd* (in which the crime is solely the right of God).

the only prudent measure is to focus on the instrument with which the crime was committed. This standard approach has no direct point of reference in Islamic texts but rather has been derived by text-based deduction. Islamic criminal law differentiates between intentional criminal acts and errors resulting in crimes that relate to retaliation (*qawad*) in kind: namely, intentional (*ʿamd*), unintentional (*khaṭaʾ*), and quasi-intentional (*shibh ʿamd*). The prophetic tradition states: "Retaliation should be by sword" (*al-qawad bi-s-sayf*).[26] This statement can be interpreted in two ways: (1) when an offender deserves a *qiṣāṣ* punishment, execution must be by sword, and (2) any homicidal crime by a sword invites retaliation (*qawd*) in kind.[27] The use of a sword in homicides, as interpreted herein, suffices as an external criterion with which to determine a perpetrator's intention. To be sure, because a sword is an instrument for killing, one can infer from the nature of the instrument that the perpetrator indeed intended to commit the crime of homicide. From this tradition, Islamic jurists established a criterion for intentional homicide.[28] According to the Ḥanafīs, "*mens rea* of murder is found when the offender uses an instrument designed for killing".[29] This covers the use of swords, guns, knives, arrows, poison and lethal weapons of all kinds.[30] However, according to Abū Ḥanīfa, the use of a blunt instrument, such as a wooden club, can only lead to conviction for a quasi-intentional (*shibh ʿamd*) rather than murderous (*qatl ʿamd*) act.[31] Thus, when Islamic jurists rule that whoever kills with a stick must pay blood money (*diya*) of 100 camels, they are providing apt evidence to infer that its use indicates the intention to inflict "grievous injury"[32] rather than murder. Although striking with an ordinary stick is not meant to cause death, when it does then the act can be presumed to be an unintentional error (*khaṭaʾ*).

The pertinent question we must pose here is: Can we apply only the standards affirmed by the traditions to establish an external criterion for determining *mens rea*? It is a well-established principle that Islamic Law is universal and applicable for any generation or norm. However, it is necessary to prove universality in light of modern technology. Thus, when someone uses chemical

26 ʿAlī b. ʿUmar al-Daraquṭnī, *as-Sunān*, edited by Sayyid ʿAbdullāh Ḥāshim al-Madanī, (Beirut: Dār al-Maʿrifa, 1966), Ḥadīth No. 89, 3:107; Abū Muḥammad ʿAlī b. Aḥmad Ibn Ḥazm, *al-Muḥallā bi-l-Āthār* (Beirut: Dār al-Afāq al-Jadīda, n.d.), 10:372; and Aḥmad al-ʿAynī, *ʿUmdat al-Qārī* (Beirut: Dār Iḥyāʾ at-Turāth al-ʿArabī, n.d.), 24:39.

27 Nyazee, *General Principles of Criminal Law*, 104,

28 Al-Zuḥaylī, Wahbah, *al-Fiqh al-Islāmī*, vol. 7, p. 5658; Awdah, al-Tashrī al-jināʾī, vol. 2, p. 32.

29 al-Sarakhsī, 26:104; Aḥmad b. ʿAlī al-Jaṣṣāṣ, *Aḥkām al-Qurʾān*, edited by Muḥammad Sadiq al-Qamhawi, (Beirut: Dār Iḥyāʾ at-Turāth al-ʿArabī, 1985), 3:199–2001.

30 Nyazee, 99.

31 *Ibid.*

32 *Ibid.*, 98.

weapons to target individual(s), which results in the victim(s)' death, then the perpetrator will be charged for his murderous act even when no external force necessitated the action. Obviously there will be no explicit mention of modern lethal weapons in classical Islamic texts; nevertheless the purpose (*maqāṣid*) expressed in such texts can still be inferred by means of analogy (*qiyās*).

In contrast, to maintain justice, if someone is killed by mistake, then the killer will not be given a *qiṣāṣ* penalty because of the absence of intention to kill. However, the instrument used to commit the act must first be examined before designating the act an error. In recognizing the quasi-intentionality of a homicide, the instrument used to commit the crime stands as a measure for determining the allegation. An accidental blow to the body that results in death will be considered quasi-intentional (*shibh ʿamd*). As the Prophet was reported to have said: "Lo, the quasi-intentional killing is what occurred by strip, stone and wood".[33] However, this does not imply the absence of criminal liability. In cases of quasi-intentionality, for example, the perpetrator would be liable to pay extra blood money (*diya mughallaẓa*), according to part of the Ḥadīth mentioned above.[34]

Similarly, if while practicing his profession a medical doctor commits an error resulting in the death or injury of his patient, he will not be given a *qiṣāṣ* penalty because of the absence of criminal intent.[35] Rather, the victim or his/her heir will receive retribution through the payment of blood money (*diya*) by the government's treasury or his employer or other means of compensation prearranged for such occurrence. However, this does not apply to non-professional medical doctors who unwittingly cause injury or death.[36] They would be penalized by having to pay a heavy financial penalty (*diya mughallaẓa*). As the Prophet was reported to have said: "Whoever practices surgery without the proper knowledge will be liable for compensation".[37] Such cases refer to death or injury due to carelessness and inexcusable negligence, although intent to kill may not be concluded except if established by other means.

---

33 al-Ashʿath, Ḥadīth No. 4588; Ibn Mājah, *Kitāb ad-Diyāt*, Ḥadīth No. 2627.

34 At the end, it is mentioned that, when the case of homicide is quasi-intentional, the penalty will be heavily imposed. See Ḥadīths in Note 33.

35 ʿAwda, 1:521.

36 *Ibid.*, 522.

37 Ibn Mājah, *Kitāb ad-Diyāt*, Ḥadīth No. 4586; and Aḥmad Ibn Shuʿayb al-Nasaʾī, *as-Sunān*, "*Bāb Shibh al-ʿAmd*" in *Kitāb al-Qasāma*, edited by ʿAbd al-Ghaffar Sulaymān and Sayyid Kasrawi, (Beirut: Dār al-Kutub al-ʿIlmiyya, 1991).

Contradiction between Intention and Action

Whether physical or verbal, acts themselves generally provide sufficient evidence to reach a verdict in criminal cases related to the rights of humans, as explained above. In contrast, acts of devotion, where an action performed without intention (*niyya*) is invalid, are a different matter. Before an act itself can serve as the basis for a verdict in a criminal act, one must have achieved a degree of clarity and sense of coherence, so as to leave no further doubt, about the perpetrator's intention. For example, if an individual ties up and then knives his victim—and his action cannot be attributed to an external force such as a legal impediment, insanity or coercion—then it is sufficient to rule that the act was deliberate murder. In some cases, however, the perpetrator's possible intention and his action are contradictory. For example, if a parent strikes his child with a stick—which normally does not lead to death—and the child eventually dies, the parent's action resulting in death cannot be called intentional murder since the tool used does not ordinarily cause death. Convicting the parent without first considering his intention would lead to injustice and also, from an Islamic criminal law point of view, parents are not suspected of having any intention of killing their children.[38] Thus, it is necessary to investigate the offender's intention in such cases.

Factors Rendering Actions Non-Concurrent with Intention

Muslim jurists, when considering the effect of intention on one's action, also discuss factors that render the action inconsistent with intention. In effect, the ability to reach a verdict may be impeded by the interference of such factors, some of which will be discussed below: namely, ignorance (*jahl*), coercion (*ikrāh*), error (*khaṭaʾ*) and puberty (*bulūgh*).

---

38 Awda, *al-Tashrīʿ al-Jināʾī*, 7:117; al-Zuhayli, *al-Fiqh al-Islāmī*, 7:5668. This may not be the case in some parts of the world including the Muslim countries where it could be easy for parents to commit criminal acts against their wards. See for general reference CL Mayer, M. Oberman and K. White, *Mothers who kill their children: Understanding the acts of Moms from Susan Smith to the "Prom Mom"*, New York, New York University Press, 2001; Lita Linzer Schwarz and Natalie K. Isser, *Child Homicide: Parents Who Kill*, USA, Taylor & Francis Group, 2006.

Ignorance

Muslim jurists have discussed extensively the effect of ignorance (*jahl*) of the law or fact of the law in determining the criminal intent of the accused.[39] In a strictly legal sense, ignorance cannot provide an excuse for committing any crime.[40] Due to the nature of Islamic criminal law, and the severity of its punishments in some cases, Muslim jurists differ on the degree in which ignorance can be admitted as an excuse for conviction of any *ḥudūd* crime. Ibn Qudāma unequivocally states: "there is no predetermined [*ḥadd*] penalty applied to one who does not know that adultery/fornication [*zinā*] is forbidden".[41] He ascribes this view to 'Uthmān ibn 'Affān, 'Alī ibn Khaṭṭāb (among the Prophet's Companions) and all men of learning in Islamic jurisprudence.[42] Several other Schools of Islamic Jurisprudence do not accept the mere claim of ignorance as an excuse.[43] This inconsistency necessitates critical evaluation regarding the degree by which ignorance can be accepted as an excuse in Islamic Law and, in particular, in criminal law.

Close reading of the literature on Islamic criminal law shows that ignorance (*jahl*), in contrast to negligence (*ihmāl*), is sometimes accepted in *ḥudūd* crimes where the accused is genuinely ignorant of the law or fact of the law. Authorities have rightly observed that the reason for giving ignorance *locus standi* in Islamic Law to allow for leniency in meting out *ḥadd* punishments is consistent "with a prevalent attitude in the texts, a reluctance to apply the *ḥadd* penalties"[44] due to their severe nature. Hence, a number of Muslim jurists insist on the admissibility of ignorance as an excuse for not imposing a *ḥadd* punishment on an accused who claims ignorance of the law or fact of the law. Apt examples might be someone who, upon regaining consciousness, discovers that he has committed a *ḥudūd* crime,[45] or a new convert to Islam living in a non-Muslim country, as opposed to someone living in Muslim-majority land who has had a

---

39 For a general understanding of the discussion on the sensitivity of this issue, see Paul R. Powers, in Ruud Peters and Bernard Weiss (eds.), *Intent in Islamic Law: Motive and Meaning in Medieval Sunnī Fiqh, Studies in Islamic Law and Society* (Leiden: Brill, 2006), 25: 169–199. See also 'Awda, 1:430–431 and 2:375; Manṣūr Muḥammad Manṣūr al-Hafnāwī, *al-Shubhāt wa-Aṭharuhā fī l-'Uqūbat al-Jinā'iyya fī l-Fiqh al-Islāmī Muqāranan bi-l-Qānūn* (Cairo: Maṭba'at al-Amana, 1986), 346–363; and Nyazee, 144–148.

40 Nyazee, 145; and 'Awda, 1:430.

41 'Abdullāh b. Aḥmad Ibn Qudāma, *al-Mughnī*, edited by 'Abdullāh al-Turki and 'Abd al-Fattah al-Hilu, (Riyadh: Dār 'Alam al-Kutub, 1999), 9:58.

42 *Ibid.*

43 Imran Ahsan Nyazee, *General Principles of Criminal Law* (*Islamic and Western*), (Islamabad: Shari'ah Academy, International Islamic University Islamabad, 2007), 144–147.

44 Paul R. Powers, *Intent in Islamic Law*, 195.

45 'Awda, 2:375.

long affiliation with Islam.[46] However, ignorance of the fact of the law can be claimed in all *ḥudūd* crimes where scholars differ in their interpretations and particularities.[47] In *qiṣāṣ* crimes involving bodily injury, ignorance of the law is not an excuse, as we all know intrinsically that taking a life is inherently wrong. However, ignorance of what might lead to killing may be admitted based on the judge's assessment. In this scenario, such cases will be treated as unintentional killing, whereby financial restitution (*diya*) will be incurred.

In recognition of the detriment of ignorance, Muslim jurists have invoked the tradition of the Prophet in which he is reported to have said: "Recording of deeds is closed for a sleeping person until he wakes up, an infant until he attains the age of puberty, and an insane person until he regains his senses".[48] Take, for example, the following situation when applying this tradition. If, while asleep, someone rolls over onto another sleeper and thus causes that individual's death, the act will not be considered intentional murder (*qatl ʿamd*) because one cannot assume that the act was committed on purpose. Any criminal act committed while asleep (*nawm*), insane (*junūn*) or before adolescence (*bulūgh*) shall be deemed unintentional because of the absence of criminal intent.[49] It is reported that after ʿUbaid Allāh, the son of ʿUmar, committed adultery while the woman slept, he as offender was punished but the woman was acquitted.[50]

However, common knowledge of material fact proves the intentionality of criminal acts, unless other evidence makes it ineffective. For example, if a person knows that adultery or fornication (*zinā*) is a crime that necessitates a *ḥadd* punishment, but does not understand the legal definition of *zinā* which is not common knowledge, then that person may not be given a *ḥadd* punishment; instead a discretionary (*taʿzīr*) penalty may be accorded for the crime. The basis for this assertion is the Ḥadīth in which the Prophet apparently casts doubt on the intentionality of Māʾiz in order to avoid punishing him.[51] As we shall learn in the following case, the Zamfara State Penal Code (Zamfara SPCL), Section 64, observes this fact stating: "A person is presumed, unless the contrary is proved, to have knowledge of any material fact if such fact is a matter of common knowledge".[52]

---

46 *Ibid.*, 2:505.

47 al-Hafnāwī, 353.

48 al-Ashʿath, *al-Sunān, Kitāb al-Ḥudūd*, Ḥadīth No. 4398; al-Tirmidhī, Ḥadīth No. 1446; Ibn Mājah, Ḥadīth No. 2041.

49 Doi, *Sharīʿah*, 227.

50 *Ibid.*, 227.

51 *Cf.* Muḥammad al-Amin al-Shinqitī, *Aḍwāʾ al-Bayān* (Beirut: Dār al-Fikr, 1995), 5:386.

52 Sharīʿah Penal Code Law of Zamfara State of Nigeria (Zaria, Nigeria: Gasikiya Corporation Limited, 15 June 2000), vol. 3.

One recent case, relevant to several points of discussion in this book, is that of *Safiyyatu v Sokoto, State of Nigeria*, which was one of the first adultery cases tested under the re-Islamization of criminal law in Northern Nigeria. The accused villager Safiyyatu Hussaini was arraigned before the Upper Sharīʿa Court for allegedly having had illegal sexual intercourse with her former husband, Yakubu Abubakar, who denied the accusation and was acquitted. Safiyyatu was convicted, based on her confession (*iqrār*) and apparent (*ẓāhir*) state of pregnancy, and sentenced to death by stoning (based on Section 128 and 129 of the Sokoto State Sharīʿa Penal Code Law 2000). Safiyyatu, who spoke the native language instead of Arabic, claimed ignorance of the details and charge against her as well as of the legal connotation of *zinā*. She was also ignorant of the fact that her conviction could be dropped or reversed or that she could be awarded a *taʿzīr* (discretionary) rather than *ḥadd* punishment. She appealed and was acquitted on 25 March 2002 on the grounds of legal technicalities.[53]

In contrast to acts committed out of ignorance (*jahl*), any crime resulting from negligence (*ihmāl*) is presumed to be intentional, unless negligence results involuntarily. For instance, a person committing adultery, theft, defamation, or murder when in a state of voluntary intoxication will be presumed to have committed such a crime intentionally. However, if negligence is involuntary, such as when someone who has been plied with an intoxicant thereafter commits a criminal offence in an induced state of inebriation, then that person will not be convicted of the offence because of the absence of intention, in accordance with the Ḥadīth mentioned above. Thus, an inebriated individual who has lost consciousness, by analogy, is like someone who is insane or asleep.

Coercion

Actions committed under duress (*ikrāh*) are considered to be unintentional, based on the prophetic tradition: "My *umma* [nation] will be forgiven for crimes it commits under duress, in error, or as a result of forgetfulness".[54] Thus, if someone is forced to commit any crime, it is generally assumed to be unintentional, and, as such, no legal responsibility shall be inflicted on the perpetrator. However, acts committed under duress can be categorized in two ways: *i.e.*, crimes involving the right of man (*ḥaqq al-ādamī*), and crimes involving the right of God (*ḥaqq Allāh*). With regard to *ḥaqq al-ādamī*, no one should allow himself to be coerced into committing an act, especially one that will terminate a life for no life is more precious than another. However, when an

53 See details of the case of Safiyyatu v. Sokoto State of Nigeria in Note 72 of this chapter.

54 Ibn Mājah, Ḥadīth No. 2045.

act does not involve ending a life, then an individual while under duress can carry out what is demanded of him, especially when his own life is in danger. However, the perpetrator (*mukrah*) or coercer (*mukrih*) or both shall be legally responsible for any damage incurred. The reason why an individual under duress is allowed to act upon the coercer's threat, and then be held partially or completely responsible for damages, is because Islamic jurists recognize two kinds of coercion: compelling (*ikrāh mulji'*) and non-compelling (*ikrāh ghayr mulji'*).

Ikrāh mulji' refers to duress where the individual being coerced has no other option than to act upon the coercer's demand, as failure to do so could endanger his own life; here there is the assurance that a third party's life is not involved. In such cases, if the person being coerced does act, then his action will not be considered intentional and he will be acquitted from any resulting crime, if it is solely the right of God. However, if the right of man is involved, the perpetrator or coercer or both will be responsible for damages, although no *ḥadd* punishment, if demanded by the crime, shall be placed upon the individual being coerced. However, when coercion is non-compelling (*ikrāh ghayr mulji'*), the individual has a choice whether to accept or reject the demands placed upon him. When his life is not in danger, his action will be regarded as intentional if he chooses to succumb to the pressure. In this context, both the perpetrator and coercer will be held equally responsible.[55] In general, debates have questioned whether the claim of such legal impediments can sufficiently render the accused free from punishment. In fact, if any crime is committed and one such impediment is involved, there are two ways to prosecute the offender. First, if the crime involves an absolute right of God, then the claim of ignorance (*jahl*), coercion (*ikrāh*) and forgetfulness (*nisyān*) could at least commute *ḥadd* to a *ta'zīr* (discretionary) penalty. However, if the crime involves the right of man, then compensation may be awarded in order to achieve a balance between two individuals. For example, if a *qiṣāṣ* crime originally calls for retaliation (*qawad*) in kind, after criminal intent has been established, then the penalty may be reduced to payment of *diya*, simply because of the legal impediments.

With regard to intentionality in cases of criminal liability, Zamfara SPCL, Section 63, states: "there shall be no criminal responsibility unless an unlawful act or omission is done intentionally or neglectfully".[56] The words 'intentionally' and 'neglectfully' in that provision have rendered any criminal act, in which the perpetrator's intention (*niyya*) or negligence (*ihmāl*) cannot be established, non-punishable. This includes *ḥudūd, qiṣāṣ* or *ta'zīr* crimes.

---

55 Doi, *Sharī'ah*, 227–228.

56 Sharī'ah Penal Code Law of Zamfara State of Nigeria (SPCL), Vol. 3, Section 64.

However, the provision neither specifies from which criteria intention can be inferred nor names the elements that constitute intention.

Errors

An act resulting from an error or accident (*khaṭaʾ*) also constitutes an assumption of unintentionality, if the offender is thought to have committed the error in all innocence. For example, take the case of a man and woman who have sexual intercourse before a 'proper marriage' has taken place, believing that their parents' consent to their relationship is sufficient proof of the legality of their relationship, despite the fact that they are cognizant of the fact that *zinā* calls for a *ḥadd* punishment. Their deed shall be construed as "a mistake of the fact", according to Zamfara SPCL, Section 66. A "mistake of the fact", but not a "mistake of the law", renders an act inoffensive or innocuous:

> Nothing is an offence that is done by any person who is justified by Law, or who by reason of a mistake of fact, and not by reason of a mistake of law, in good faith believes himself to be justified by law in doing it. (*cf.* Section 69, Zamfara SPCL)

Thus, when someone drinks a substance that he believes to be non-alcoholic, although it is in fact an intoxicant, or when a blind man mistakenly has sexual intercourse with a woman he finds asleep in his bed, neither action would incur a *ḥadd* punishment. In the latter case, however, a fair dower (*mahr al-mithl*) may be demanded because the rights of the woman have been infringed upon. Similarly, if an archer aims his arrow at an animal but accidentally inflicts a fatal wound on someone standing nearby, the archer will not be punished for a *qiṣāṣ* crime as the killing was unintentional. If a patient dies after taking a prescribed drug, then the doctor will not be convicted of murder, if he prescribed the medication properly with caution and in good faith because there was no criminal intent involved.[57]

Puberty

Any criminal act committed by a minor, who has not yet reached puberty (*bulūgh*), is believed to be committed unintentionally, based on the Ḥadīth quoted at the outset of this discussion. However, in *ḥudūd* crimes, if no individual rights are involved, then the accused minor will not receive a *ḥadd* punishment, although a discretionary (*taʿzīr*) penalty may still be adjudicated. However, if the right of man is involved, then restitution (*diya*) in the case

57 *Cf.*, Zamfara Sharīʿah Penal Code Law, Section 69.

of homicide (*qatl*), or an equivalent value of the stolen property in the case of theft (*sariqa*), will be imposed.[58]

Maxims Related to *al-Umūr bi-Maqāṣidihā*

From the grand maxim stated above, scholars have deduced a number of sub-maxims that incorporate intent (*niyya*) in human activities. The sub-maxim most relevant to this research is "Should effect be given to purpose and meanings or the words and forms?" (*hal al-ʿibra li-l-maqāṣid wa-l-maʿānī aw li-l-alfāẓ wa-l-mabānī*).[59] This sub-maxim addresses the effect of connotations (*maʿāni*) and expressions (*alfāẓ*) voiced intentionally in order to make a clear statement before a court of law. What a person utters before a court is assumed to embody his intention for, if not, the illocutionary act of the utterance will be without value. In other words, the utterance made by a litigant while taking an oath (*yamīn*) should mean what is outwardly said according to the understanding of the judge and other litigants whose rights depend upon the outward meaning of the oath. The Prophet said: "An oath must conform to the intention of the party tendering it".[60] Because the law must protect the rights of the other party, whether defendant or offender, and because any means to obstruct the course of justice should be prevented, the litigant is obliged to utter an explicit statement that concurs with its agreed-upon meaning, rather than an implicit statement that hides the meaning and perhaps leads to confusion when pronouncing judgment.[61]

---

58 Zamfara SPCL, Section 71(a) and (b).

59 This maxim is re-coined from the maxim "Effect is given to intents and meaning in contracts, not words and forms" (*al-ʿibra fī l-ʿuqūd bi-l-maqāṣid wa-l-maʿānī lā bi-l-alfāẓ wa-l-mabānī*), as agreed upon by Ḥanafīs and Mālikīs (see Ibn Nujaym, *al-Ashbāh wa-n-Naẓāʾir*, 207; and *Majalla*, Article 3), as opposed to the Shāfiʿī and Ḥanbalī views that give a different opinion, depending on the matter at hand. At times, effect is given to the meaning, while at other times it is given to the word (see Shams al-Dīn Muḥammad al-Ramalī, *Nihāyat al-Muḥtāj ilā Sharḥ al-Minhāj* (Beirut: Dār al-Fikr, 1984), 6:242; and Manṣūr b. Yūnus al-Bahūtī, *Kashshāf al-Qināʿ ʿan Matn al-Iqnāʿ*, edited by Hilāl Musilihi Hilāl, (Beirut: Dār al-Fikr, 1982), 3:446). I incline to the opinion of separation between one issue and another in the application of this maxim since there is no uniqueness in the forms that different issues take.

60 Muslim, Ḥadīth No. 1653.

61 Maḥmaṣṣānī, 161; and al-Nawawī, *Sharḥ Ṣaḥīḥ Muslim*, 1:117, states that if the oath is taken outside the court or no right of man is attached to it, then the effect will be given to the intention of the one taking the oath, not to the mere word and form of the expression

Fundamentally, scholars are in agreement that the effect of an utterance is based on the speaker's intended meaning in any matter. However, because of the exceptional requirements demanded in a court of law, the majority of Schools of Islamic Jurisprudence, including the Mālikīs and Shāfiʿīs, assert that the effect of an utterance should be based upon the intention of the one who seeks an oath (the judge).[62] However, Ḥanafīs, agree in principle but disagree in practice, as one can also infer from Ḥanbalī thought. Ḥanafīs state that the oath of the plaintiff will be based on his intention, whereas that of the defendant will be based on the judge's intention.[63] For example, according to the Mālikīs, Shāfiʿīs and one rendering of Ḥanbalī thought, when a judge requests that a person takes an oath in a litigation involving a third party, then the statements made under oath must be understood by both the judge and other party involved. As Ibn al-Qayyim has observed, giving illusive, dissimulative expressions in such matters will contradict the rules of Islamic Law aimed at establishing justice and will jeopardize the rights of the litigant parties attached to the oath.[64] However, the Ḥanafīs and Ḥanbalīs opine that the meaning will only be understood according to the status of the one who takes the oath: namely, the meaning of the plaintiff's oath will be based on his intention whereas that of other oaths will be based on the judge's understanding.[65]

The only way to determine whether the meaning of an oath is consistent with the speaker's intention is to refer to its denotative usage in the society where the litigation is being held, where harmony between the connotative

---

uttered. Thus, this indicates that, in the opinion of al-Shāfiʿī, their question mark attached to the maxim is only relevant in issues related to the rights of man. If there is no right of man attached, their view agrees with those of the Ḥanafīs and Mālikīs.

62 Muḥammad b. Muḥammad b. Aḥmad Ibn Juzayy al-Kalbī, *al-Qawānīn al-Fiqhiyya* (Beirut: Dār al-Qalam, 1977), 334; al-Suyūṭī, *al-Ashbāh*, 44; Maḥmaṣṣānī, 161; and al-Burnu, *al-Wajīz*, 158.

63 Ibn Nujaym, *al-Ashbāh wa-n-Naẓāʾir*, 53; al-Hamawi, 81; Ibrāhīm b. Muḥammad Ibn Ḍūyān, *Manār as-Sabīl fī Sharḥ ad-Dalīl*, edited by ʿIsam al-Qalaji, (Riyadh: Maktabat al-Muʿarif, n.d.), 2:440.

64 Ibn al-Qayyim al-Jawziyya, *Iʿlām al-Muwaqqiʿīn ʿan Rabb al-ʿĀlamīn* 3:119.

65 In some aspects, Ḥanafīs do not agree with the opinions of other Schools. In his *ar-Risāla* al-Karkhī clearly states that "fundamental consideration is given to the intention of the two litigants, not their apparent 'expression'" (see A. al-Zarqāʾ, *Sharḥ*, 64; and al-Hamawi, 2:268). From this, it could be inferred that sometimes the opposite may be applied, as in the discussion above. For a general view on this matter, see Ibn Nujaym, *al-Ashbāh wa-n-Naẓāʾir*, 207; al-Zarkashī, *al-Manṯūr*, 2:371; Haydar, 1:18; al-Suyūṭī, *al-Ashbāh*, 166; ʿAbd al-Raḥman Abū al-Faraj b. Shihab al-Dīn Ibn Rajab, *al-Qawāʿid fī l-Fiqh al-Islāmī* (Beirut: Dār al-Kutub al-ʿIlmiyya, 1992), 37; and al-Kāsānī, 4:134.

and denotative meanings of the oath is lacking. To that effect, a sub-maxim is thus coded as a question: "Is oath based on custom?" (*hal al-aymān mabniyya ʿalā l-ʿurf*).[66] If the form used to express an oath (*yamīn*) deviates from a particular form in Islamic legal procedure, then the effect will be based on what is customary (*ʿurf*) because conventional norms of that particular society in question are paramount. In principle, this maxim is generally accepted by all Schools of Islamic Jurisprudence.[67] However, some scholars have approved dissimulation in cases where an oath has been taken under coercion or duress.[68]

As stated earlier, Islamic criminal law designates intention as one of the most important criteria to consider before adjudicating a *qiṣās* crime, as an imprudent ruling could cause irreparable damage to the accused, such as in the case of homicide for which the recommended punishment is so severe. If one cannot establish that the perpetrator acted intentionally, then calling for a punishment that would elicit retaliation in kind would not be an option for the crime of homicide. In such cases, a discretionary (*taʿzīr*) or similar penalty can be awarded.

The concept of intention is of utmost relevance to evince the overall objectives of Islamic Law (*maqāṣid ash-sharīʿa*) in the case of the death penalty (*itlāf nafs*), which many individuals in the Western world perceive as an archaic relic of times past and an attestation that brands Islamic Law as outdated. The fact of the matter is that Islam recognizes that mankind by nature will seek revenge and does not intend to deny men this right. By upholding this approach, Islam legalizes in principle the right of the family of the victim to see revenge while at the same time encouraging victims or their relatives to forgive by opting for compensation, especially when a homicide has been committed unintentionally.[69] Article 6(2) of the ICCPR (International Covenant on Civil and Political Rights) confirms the essence of this recognition by stating that the death penalty "may be imposed only for most serious crimes in accordance with the law in force at the time of the commission of the crime".[70]

---

66 Ibn Rajab, *al-Qawāʿid*, Article 121, 263–267; and Ibn Ḍūyān, 2:442.

67 ʿAbd al-Raḥman b. Muḥammad Shaykhzadah, *Majmaʿ al-Anhar* (Beirut: Dār al-Kutub al-ʿIlmiyya, 1998), 1:548; and ʿAlī b. Sulaymān al-Mirdāwī, *al-Inṣāf fī Maʿrifat ar-Rājiḥ min al-Khilāf*, edited by ʿAbdullāh al-Turkī, (Cairo: Dār Ḥajar, 1995), 2:327.

68 Ibn Nujaym, *al-Ashbāh wa-n-Naẓāʾir*, 21; and Maḥmaṣṣānī, 161.

69 Q. 2:178–179.

70 United Nations General Assembly, "International Covenant on Civil and Political Rights", 16 December 1966; http://www.ohchr.org/en/professionalinterest/pages/ccpr.aspx (accessed: 1 March 2014).

In the case of adultery/fornication (*zinā*), the perpetrator's intention should be ascertained by investigating the facts surrounding the illicit act. If someone claims ignorance (*jahl*) of the punishment for adultery, or is in doubt as to the legality of the act, thereby claiming that the act was unintentional, a severe *ḥadd* punishment may not be inflicted. In this modern society where young Muslims may be ignorant of Islamic Law and its stance regarding fornication, the first course of action in cases involving ignorance is to provide education, as argued in the case of *Amina Lawal v Katsina, State of Nigeria*, which will be discussed later.[71]

In the case of slander (*qadhf*), Abū Ḥanīfa and al-Shāfiʿī opine that one should consider the intention of the perpetrator before conviction. If he denies the charges and claims to have been joking, then a discretionary (*taʿzīr*) penalty will be awarded. However, according to the above opinion, if the perpetrator veils his accusations in metaphorical figures of speech (*majāz*) when blaming someone for promiscuity, immorality or other *qadhf* offences, then his motives or intention must first be unearthed. If the perpetrator is able to clarify what he originally meant from a different perspective, his interpretation should be accepted and a lesser punishment imposed upon the judge's discretion. In stark contrast, Mālik and Ḥanbal hold the view that a mere accusation of defamation of character is sufficient to inflict a *ḥadd* punishment; here no interpretation need be given because the weight of the defendant's right is too important to be trampled upon.

Regarding theft (*sariqa*), the accused should be questioned to discover whether property was actually stolen or temporarily taken to safeguard it for the rightful owner, as explained earlier in the discussion on the effect of intention on one's actions. The treatment of banditry/brigandage (*ḥirāba*) poses quite a different challenge involving multiple consequences of such an act. If a bandit or his gang of thieves only intend to frighten the victim(s), without actually intending to steal or kill, then the plea will be for the lesser punishment of exile (*nafī*). If the bandit, however, commits murder without stealing property—presumably because that was his actual intention—then punishment for homicide will be imposed. However, if the bandit kills as well as steals property, then his punishment will be doubled, *i.e.*, crucifixion with the death penalty. In such cases, the perpetrator's intention will determine the nature of his crime, which in turn establishes the type of punishment awarded.

71 See *Amina Lawal v Kastina State Government* and *Safiyya v Sokoto State Government*, both from Nigeria. Among the reasons for acquitting the two accused women was that they were ignorant of the fact of the law, as will be explained in the discussion of the following grand maxim.

General Application of the Grand Maxim *al-Umūr bi-Maqāṣidihā* and its Subsidiaries in Several Northern Nigerian Sharīʿa Criminal Law Cases

With regard to adultery/fornication (*zinā*), in Northern Nigeria, the following three cases serve as prime illustrations of how the corroboration of intention (*niyya*) with actions, as well as claims of ignorance of the fact of law, among others, can inadvertently result in injustice when legal proceedings derail. The three cases in question, *Amina Lawal v. Katsina, Safiyyatu Husseini v. Sokoto* and *Bariya Magadisu v. Zamfara States of Nigeria*,[72] in which Safiyyatu, Bariya, and Amina were accused of committing the alleged offence of adultery, could be argued on the basis of non-intentionality because the woman lived in a society where "traditional practices, norms and values have significantly intertwined with Islamic legal tenets and produced sometimes legal results which are fundamentally outside Islamic Law".[73] The accused women were villagers and, as such, might not have intended to violate Islamic rules but rather to follow the dictates of the society in which they lived. It is the responsibility of the courts that represent the Government to verify criminal intent, namely this core objective of Islamic Law, before inflicting a *ḥadd* punishment, which could result in dire consequences for these women.[74] Had the criterion 'criminal intent' been investigated properly, Safiyyatu, Bariya, and Amina might not have been convicted; Section 63(2) of the Kastina State Sharīʿa Penal Code Law, 2001, provides that one cannot be found guilty of an offence without criminal intent.

---

72 See *Amina Lawal vs. Kastina State Government*, in Northern Nigeria Law Report, 2003, 496; Human Rights Watch, *Political Shariʿah*, 35. The case *Safaiyyah vs. Sokoto State Government* can also be found in Human Rights Watch, *Ibid.*, 34; also see the full report of the case in Luqman Zakariyah, *Applications of Legal Maxims in Islamic Criminal Law with Special Reference to Shariah Law in Northern Nigeria* (1999–2007), Ph.D. Thesis, (Lampeter, UK: University of Wales, 2009), Appendix 10. See Bariya's case at Human Rights Watch, *Ibid.*, 61, and Zakariyah, *Application of Legal Maxims*, Appendix 9. The first two accused were eventually acquitted while the last accused was flogged in public. Among the reasons for acquitting the two accused women was that they were ignorant of the fact of the law, as will be explained in the following maxim.

73 Aliyu Musa Yawuri, "Issues in Defending Safiyyatu Husaini and Amina Lawal", in Jibrin Ibrahim (ed.), *Sharia Penal and Family Laws in Nigeria and in the Muslim World: Rights Based Approach*, 201.

74 *Ibid.*, 201; for submission of the counsel to Amina Lawal, see NNLR 2003, 496, where it is reported that Amina claimed to have been deceived by her cohabitant. Having claimed deception in committing the alleged act has rendered the action unintentional.

With regard to defamation/slander (*qadhf*), in the case of *Attorney General of Zamfara State* [complainant] *v. Lawal Akwata R/Doruwa* [defendant], the defendant was charged on suspicion of committing defamation against Ibrahim Sabo, which is an offence under Section 323 of the Sharīʿa Penal Code of Zamfara State. During the trial, the court could not ascertain the locutionary act of the defendant because the two witnesses could not establish the abusive phrases. Thus, it remained unclear whether his alleged abuse had been intentional. However, thereafter, the Upper Sharīʿa Court handed its judgment by sentencing the defendant to 6 months imprisonment or the payment of 10,000 Naira.[75] Justification for the questionable conviction is doubtful.[76]

With regard to theft (*sariqa*), Human Rights Watch has reported that dozens of theft-related cases have been adjudicated in some of the Northern States of Nigeria during the period of re-enforcement of the Sharīʿa.[77] According to the Human Rights Watch reports, and a hardcopy of the case obtained by the researcher, Buba Bello Jangebe refused to have a lawyer and adamantly demanded amputation despite all the Governor's efforts to nullify his punishment.[78] From this juncture, one must examine the accused's sanity, which is a criterion often indicative of the intentionality of a criminal act. In Jangebe's case, it is doubtful that anyone would committed a crime punishable by permanent deformation of one's body and then come forward to confess one's guilt. It is also astonishing that the court failed to ascertain the mental state of the[79] accused before handing down its judgment. Because Jangebe's case was one of the first cases tested under the re-enforcement of full Sharīʿa penal law in Northern Nigeria, perhaps the above-mentioned strategies might not yet have been fully functional. In contrast, intentionality was taken into consideration in the case of theft in *Isiya Alh. Aliyu and others v. State* (*Zamfara*). The accused persons were convicted of stealing 3½ sacks of millet from Alhaji Danjimma's house. During the first trial, the Upper Sharīʿa Court Gummi Zamfara State convicted the accused of theft and sentenced them to amputation of their right hands. The accused appealed successfully on many grounds *inter alia* that the prime accused (Isiya) had been given free access to the house from which it was claimed that the property had been stolen. Thus, it was debatable whether the accused perhaps assumed that prior permission

75 Less than US$100 when the case was allegedly committed.

76 See for details of the case, Zakariyah, *Application of Legal Maxims*, Appendix 6.

77 Human Rights Watch, 36.

78 *Ibid.*, 38.

79 However, extreme religiosity could lead one to confess in Islam as demonstrated by Mai'iz and Ghamidi's cases of adultery.

stood as authorization to take his friend's belongings, an assumption that would render his action unintentional.[80]

Conclusion

The role that intention plays in the mind of a wrongdoer is an important factor when determining ways to adjudicate criminal acts. Muslim jurists are in agreement that in criminal cases the perpetrator's intention must be verified, especially in *ḥudūd* crimes where concealment and forgiveness is encouraged during the initial stage of discovery. Some issues that can render the nature of a criminal act flawed or deceptive are coercion, ignorance of the law or fact of the law, error in committing a crime, and legal incapacity. Although such factors may help to exonerate an accused, facilitating justice between the victim and the wrongdoer has been well thought out in Islamic Law. When human rights are involved, even when there is reason to exonerate the accused, the court will resort to compensation in cases of *qiṣāṣ* crimes and to discretionary penalties in cases of *ḥudūd* crimes.

80 See Zakariyah, *Application of Legal Maxims*, Appendix 1.

CHAPTER 4

Legal Maxim regarding Certainty and Doubt: "Certainty Cannot Be Overruled By Doubt" (*al-Yaqīn lā Yazūl bi-sh-Shakk*)*

Certainty and Doubt in Islamic Criminal Law

Certainty (*yaqīn*) and doubt (*shakk*), or uncertainty, play vital roles in Islamic criminal law. The maxims that deal with these terms will help shed light on how criminal justice can be established through the phenomenon of certainty and the elimination of doubt. Here the second basic general legal maxim states: "Certainty cannot be overruled by doubt" (*al-yaqīn lā yazūl bi-sh-shakk*). Islamic scholars have agreed upon this maxim in principle, although they may find discrepancies in the manner in which it is sometimes applied. This maxim reflects the ease and beauty of Islam by creating a conducive atmosphere for Muslims with regard to the implications of their actions.[1] According to A. al-Zarqā', "the importance of this maxim is unlimited because there is no part of *fiqh* to which it is not applicable".[2] The maxim was first credited to al-Karkhī in his *Ta'sīs*, in which he said: "Whatever is established by certainty cannot be removed by doubt" (*mā thabat bi-l-yaqīn lā yazūl bi-sh-shakk*).[3]

Definition and Interpretation of the Legal Maxim al-Yaqīn lā Yazūl bi-sh-Shakk

Two antonyms, certainty (*yaqīn*) and doubt (*shakk*), form the basis for this maxim. Certainty literally means "undoubted knowledge of something that satisfies the soul".[4] However, there is no consensus among scholars on its technical meaning. For scholars of *uṣūl* (*uṣūl*-ists),[5] certainty is a strong conviction that corroborates with virtual occurrence, which implies that

* Ibn Nujaym, *al-Ashbah*, 47; al-Suyuti, al-Ashbah, 55; A. Zarqa, 79; al-Burnu, al-Wajiz, 166.

1 al-Nadawī, 354.

2 A. al-Zarqā', *Sharḥ*, 78–80.

3 al-Dabūsī, 110; and al-Burnu, *al-Wajīz*, 166.

4 Ibn Manẓūr, 13:457; Muḥammad b. Abī Bakr 'Abd al-Qadir al-Rāzī, *Mukhtār aṣ-Ṣiḥāḥ*, edited by Muḥammad Khatir, (Beirut: Maktabat Lubnān, 1995), 6:2219; and al-Jurjānī, 116.

5 The term *uṣūl*-ists here refers to the scholars who are experts in the field of *uṣūl al-fiqh*. It is not necessary that all *uṣūl*-ists are jurists, but it is necessary that all jurists (*fuqahā'*) are *uṣūl*-ists.

 | DOI 10.1163/9789004304871_005

probability (*ẓann*) cannot be regarded as *yaqīn*. From the viewpoint of the jurists (*fuqahā'*), however, apparent probability can be accepted as "*yaqīn*" because in most legal procedures some element must be assumed 'certain' even in light of reasonable doubt. Such is the case when a witness's evidence is taken as substantive proof although, in fact, it may be fictitious. For example, it would be unlikely that the testimonies of all four witnesses to illicit sexual intercourse may not have an element of intrigue, but, as such, one would find it quite difficult to refute such evidence.

Contrary to their definition of *yaqīn*, jurists and *uṣūl*-ists are in agreement that although the sight of an unmarried couple emerging from a room in a state of disarray might suggest that they had shared sexual intimacy, this observation in itself would not be sufficient proof to accuse the man and woman of illicit fornication (*zinā*). Although one might assume that it is highly improbable that the couple were not intimate, the accusation of *zinā* will be regarded as unfounded because no individual's rights were infringed upon.[6] Moreover, because strict standards have been laid down in the Sharī'a regarding accusations involving *ḥadd* crimes, it is unlikely that someone will be convicted on the basis of improbability. However, a *ta'zīr* (discretionary) penalty may be imposed on the accused individuals for misconduct.

In contrast, doubt (*shakk*), which is the opposite of certainty (*yaqīn*), is defined as hesitation regarding a decision between two choices.[7] Although both jurists and *uṣūl*-ists agree on this definition, *uṣūl*-ists assert that if the mind tends to dwell longer on one of the two choices, then it can be said that one's knowledge of the former is probable and of the latter illusionary. Thus, in the Islamic legal system, knowledge is categorized in descriptive terminology: namely, *yaqīn* (certain), *ghalabat aẓ-ẓann* (highly probable), *zann* (probable), *shakk* (doubtful), and *wahm* (illusionary).[8]

6 In some cases, the rights of man can be involved in the case of *zinā* when the husband reports that his wife has been raped or committed adultery. The former case would normally be dealt with by producing four witnesses or by using modern technology to investigate the allegation against the rapist should the husband be unable to find four witnesses (in my opinion, because of the rights of man involved). The latter case would normally be dealt with against his wife if he could produce four witnesses. However, if four witnesses cannot be found, then the case will be resolved with *li'ān* (five oaths taken by both couples to clear the allegation). See Q. 24:6–9; Doi, *Sharī'ah*, 170–171, 189; and Peters, *Crime and Punishment*, 63.

7 Jalāluddīn Muḥammad b. Aḥmad al-Maḥallī, *Sharḥ al-Waraqāt fī Uṣūl al-Fiqh* (Palestine: al-Quds, 1999), 85.

8 Ibn Manẓūr, 13:457; al-Hamawi, 1:84; Muḥammad b. Ḥusayn al-Rāzī, *al-Maḥsūl fī 'Ilm al-Uṣūl*, edited by Ṭāhā J. al-'Alawānī, (Riyadh: Muḥammad Ibn Saud University, 1400/1979), 1:101;

Jurists and *uṣūl*-ists agree that certainty (*yaqīn*) is unreservedly acceptable as the basis for rulings. Probability (*ẓann*) and high probability (*ghalabat aẓ-ẓann*) are most frequently used to adjudicate issues that are apparently or probably certain. However, *shakk* describes a situation in which an individual shows no preference for either of two choices. Some scholars claim that *shakk* and *ẓann* share the same connotation (*maʿnan*) when used by Islamic jurists. However, this claim has been rebutted by al-Zarkashī, who points out "that they [Islamic jurists] do not differentiate between *shakk* and *ẓann* where the subject is impurity, whereas they have distinguished between them in many places".[9] Thus, rulings may not be established on the basis of uncertainty (*shakk*), not to mention illusion (*wahm*), especially in criminal cases.

The importance of this discussion lies in the fact that recourse to probability is inevitable in Islamic Law because it is difficult, if not impossible, to base all rulings on absolute certainty. The Qur'ān even indicates that certainty might also be based on probability. In other words, both degrees of probability (*ẓann* or *ghalabat aẓ-ẓann*) could perhaps be upgraded in the absence of certainty (*yaqīn*). Qur'ānic verse 2:46 states: "Those who are certain that they will meet their Lord . . ." (*Alladhīna yaẓunnūn annahum mulaqū rabbihim . . .*).[10] Although the verb in this Qur'ānic verse is "*ẓanna*" that means "to assume or suppose" which literally implies doubt, one might well apply the verb "*tayaqqana*" that means "to be convinced or know with certainty".[11]

Islamic Law requires that the proof of a crime be sufficiently convincing to establish the guilt of the accused. Because the gravity of crimes varies, the burden of proof for one particular crime may weigh more heavily than in other cases, and the ability to provide evidence for one particular crime will obviously not be the same for other crimes. Cases such as homicide and illicit sexual intercourse entail different requirements before an offender can be justly convicted. Obtaining pertinent evidence is of paramount importance, even when difficult to unearth, because of the harshness of the punishments prescribed for such crimes. In the case of homicide, which involves the rights of an individual, Islamic Law requires that submitted evidence be at least highly probable (*ghalabat aẓ-ẓann*) and that it corroborates any circumstan-

al-Zarkashī, *al-Manṯūr*, 2:255; Yaḥyā b. Sharif al-Nawawī, *al-Majmūʿ Sharḥ al-Muhadhdhab* (Beirut: Dār al-Fikr, 1997), 1:223; and A. al-Zarqāʾ, *Sharḥ*, 80.

9 al-Zarkashī, *al-Manṯūr*, 2:255, Ibn Nujaym, *al-Ashbāh wa-n-Naẓāʾir*, 82; and al-Nawawī, *al-Majmūʿ*, 1:223.

10 Q. 2:46.

11 See Maḥmūd b. ʿUmar al-Zamakhshari, *al-Kashshāf*, edited by ʿAbd al-Razzāq al-Mahdi, (Beirut: Dār Iḥyāʾ al-Turāth al-ʿArabī, n.d.), 1:163.

tial evidence (*bayyina ẓarfīya*). Evidence provided by at least two eyewitnesses (*shāhidayn al-ʿayn*) to murder must also be substantiated by circumstantial evidence such as video recordings or DNA analysis.[12] The accused can only be convicted of murder on the strength of corroborated evidence. However, if evidence is merely probable, then the accusation will remain unfounded until probable and circumstantial evidence concur. Take, for example, the situation where someone is found standing, knife in hand, beside a dead body. While suspicion may be cast upon this bystander, he cannot be accused of being the culprit unless suspicion is strengthened by other evidence.[13]

In contrast, in the case of illicit sexual intercourse, where no right of man is involved, one standard of proof required to establish the guilt of the accused is virtual certainty, involving, *inter alia*, four men who have actually witnessed the act of illicit sexual intercourse. Each eyewitness must submit a detailed, explicit description of the act, and all statements must correspond. Failure to fulfill these requirements will render the accusation unfounded, based on lack of certainty.[14] Therefore, it was rather surprising to discover that, in addition to the aforementioned case of *Safiyyatu v Sokoto, State of Nigeria*, Amina Lawal also found herself arraigned in the Sharīʿa Court of Bakori, charged with adultery. In the case of *Amina v Kastina, State of Nigeria*, Amina and Yahaya Muhammed, who claimed to have plan to marry, had been having illegal sexual intercourse for 11 months and had given birth to a daughter. After denying charges, Yahaya was discharged and Amina sentenced to death by stoning according to Section 124 of the Kastine State Sharīʿa Penal Code Law No. 2 of 2001. After her appeal, Amina was acquitted on 25 September 2003 on grounds of procedural errors, *e.g.*, the legality of her confession. In both cases, Safiyyatu and Amina were neither given the right of retraction nor benefit of doubt, as the Prophet had given Māʾiz. In addition, because both women had been accused by informants, it was suggested that their rights and privacy had been violated and unnecessary harm (defamation) inflicted. In addition, in Amina's case, gnawing doubt and uncertainty about the paternity of her baby cast its shadow

12 DNA is considered circumstantial evidence in Islamic Law. There are divergent opinions among the contemporary scholars on the strength of such evidence. Most Islamic scholars consider any evidence branded as *qarāʾin* (circumstantial) incapable of being used in rulings related to *ḥudūd* and *qiṣāṣ* crimes. See Muḥammad Ibn Maʿjuz, *Wasāʾil al-Ithbāṭ fī l-Fiqh al-Islāmī* (Beirut: Dār al-Bayda, 1984), 13–14; and Sayed Sikandar Shah Haneef, "Modern Means of Proof: Legal Basis for its Accommodation in Islamic Law", in *Arab Law Quarterly* 20/4 (2006): 344–345.

13 Intisar A. Rabb, "Reasonable doubt" in Islamic Law, The Yale Journal of International Law, 2015, vol. 40:41, pp. 42-94.

14 Peters, *Crime and Punishment*, 13; *cf.*, *Ibid.*, 59–62.

upon the credibility of the verdict. Moreover, scholars disagree about the use of apparent pregnancy as evidence.[15]

In large measure, while absolute certainty is required in some cases to prosecute and convict an accused, probable or circumstantial evidence is deemed sufficient in other cases. However, under no condition will *shakk* or uncertainty be acceptable, regardless of whether the right of the individual (*ḥaqq al-ādamī*) or right of God (*ḥaqq Allāh*) is involved.

Thus, according to their general interpretation of the maxim "Certainty cannot be overruled by doubt" (*al-yaqīn lā yazūl bi-sh-shakk*), Islamic jurists have determined that rulings established by virtue of sound, conclusive evidence can only be nullified by equally conclusive or probable evidence because, logically, uncertainty cannot invalidate certainty.[16]

Sources of the Legal Maxim *al-Yaqīn lā Yazūl bi-sh-Shakk*

The maxim *al-yaqīn lā yazūl bi-sh-shakk* is rooted in the Qur'ān and prophetic Ḥadīth. The Qur'ān states: "And most of them follow nothing but conjecture, certainly conjecture can be of no avail against the truth".[17] It is reported that 'Abdullāh bin Yazīd al-Ansarī asked the Prophet about a person whom he thought had passed wind during prayers (*ṣalāt*). The Prophet replied: "He should not leave his *ṣalāt* unless he hears a sound or smells something".[18] Al-Nawawī comments on this Ḥadīth saying that it serves as one of the pillars of Islam and is an important maxim of Islamic jurisprudence which indicates that things remain in their original state unless proven otherwise and that there is no case for accidental doubt.[19]

15 Muhammad Tawfiq Ladan, *A Handbook on Sharia Implementation in Northern Nigeria: Women and Children's Rights Focus* (Kaduna, Nigeria: LEADS-Nigeria, 2005), 107–120.

16 al-Atāsī and al-Atāsī, 1:18; and M. al-Zarqā', *al-Madkhal*, 96.

17 Q. 10:36.

18 al-Bukhārī, *Kitāb al-Wuḍū'*, Ḥadīth No. 137; and Muslim, Ḥadīth No. 362.

19 al-Nawawī, *Sharḥ*, 4:49–50; *cf.*, Ḥadīth Abī Huraira in Muslim 4:51.

Maxims Related to the Legal Maxim *al-Yaqīn lā Yazūl bi-sh-Shakk*

"The Fundamental Principle is Freedom From Liability" (al-aṣl barā'at adh-dhimma)

"The fundamental principle is the non-existence of something" (*al-aṣl al-ʿadam*)[20]

It is a fundamental principle established in Islamic Law that one cannot be held responsible for any claim (*daʿwā*), or said to have any obligation (*wujūb*) to others, until proof is given. In all litigations, there are two sides to an issue: namely, the claimant (*muthbit*) and the one who refutes the claim. Justice is not served merely by accepting the claimant's word without actual proof; thus one must assume that a claim is invalid until proven otherwise, a position that seems to favor the defender. For instance, when someone lays claim to a piece of jewelry in the merchant's possession, it is apparent that the seller holds the fundamental proof of possession while the claimant must argue his case by providing other proof.[21]

Sometimes that which is considered fundamental (*aṣl*) or apparent (*ẓāhir*) proof is contradictory. When this occurs, that which is apparent proof may be taken into consideration because it approximates right intention. Take, for example, an impotent man who claims to have had a sexual affair with an alleged chaste woman, who upon examination is discovered to have lost her virginity. In this case, the man's claim will be taken into consideration. However, his claim regarding the affair is a new fundamental occurrence. Because the woman's alleged state of virginity has changed, that which is apparent (*ẓāhir, i.e.*, the man's claim) must be considered.[22] Similarly, if four witnesses testify that a man has committed illicit sexual intercourse with a virgin, but the woman upon examination is said to be chaste, the testimony that up to that point was regarded as *aṣl* (*i.e.*, the principle of four eyewitnesses in Islamic Law), will then be nullified because it contradicts what is *ẓāhir* (*i.e.*, the woman's apparent state of virginity). Another example is that of an injured person who claims to have sustained a more serious injury than that acknowledged by the perpetrator. In this case, the confession (*iqrār*) of the person responsible for the injury will be upheld as *aṣl* (*i.e.*, certainty of non-existent injury).[23]

---

20 al-Suyūṭī, *al-Ashbāh*, 52–53; Ibn Nujaym, *al-Ashbāh wa-n-Naẓā'ir*, 59; and *Majalla*, Article 8.

21 A. al-Zarqā', *Sharḥ*, 100–107.

22 *Ibid.*, 110.

23 al-Suyūṭī, *al-Ashbāh*, 52.

Several other examples can be drawn from situations involving uncertain evidence in potential cases of adultery (*zinā*). For instance, when four male eyewitnesses claim that a woman has committed adultery, while, at the same time, a number of trustworthy women bear witness to her virginity, neither the accused nor the four male eyewitnesses will receive a *ḥadd* punishment because there is contradiction between the proof of witness and the status of the woman. The accused cannot be convicted in the face of doubt: "*Ḥudūd* punishment shall be averted in the face of doubt" (*al-ḥudūd tudra' bi-sh-shubhāt*). Here the element of doubt derives from the assertion by trustworthy women that the accused is still a virgin. The four male eyewitnesses will not be given a *ḥadd* punishment for defamation (*qadhf*) since they have fulfilled a legal requirement by functioning as four eyewitnesses. This opinion is upheld by the Shāfiʿīs and Ḥanbalīs, as well as other scholars. However, in such cases, Mālikī jurists will reject evidence provided by trustworthy females, claiming that punishment for illicit sexual intercourse should be accorded. Although women are not allowed to give witness in cases involving *ḥudūd* crimes, here a female must be able to testify as Islamic Law only permits women to examine the private areas of another woman's body.[24] Similarly, if four male witnesses testify against a man accused of having committed illicit sexual intercourse, while another group of four male witnesses testify that it was actually the first group of men who fornicated, no *ḥadd* punishment will be imposed on either group because, according to the Ḥanīfī and Ḥanbalī Schools, the reputation of the first group of men has been stained while the second group of men have come under suspicion. As such, the accused persons in this case would be acquitted.[25]

"The Status Quo of Affairs Remains Lawful 'Until Proven Otherwise'" (al-aṣl baqā' mākān 'alā mākān "ḥattā yaqūm ad-dalīl 'alā kilāf")[26]

This maxim emphasizes that a known certainty continues to be recognized until a greater certainty repelling the former comes to light. For instance, when two parties dispute an issue, judgment shall be based on what was already known about the issue before the dispute occurred, until either party produces additional evidence that overrides what was already known. The relevance of this maxim in criminal cases is that one should not be convicted on just any allegation but rather upon sound evidence required by law. However, there are cases where minimum or circumstantial evidence (*bayyina ẓarfīya*) may prove

24 Ibn Qudāma, *al-Mughnī*, 12:274.

25 *Ibid.*, 12:376.

26 al-Suyūṭī, *al-Ashbāh*, 51; Ibn Nujaym, *al-Ashbāh wa-n-Naẓā'ir*, 57; *Majalla*, Article 5; A. al-Zarqā', *Sharḥ*, 87; al-Burnu, *al-Wajīz*, 172; and al-Atāsī and al-Atāsī, 20.

sufficient to establish a person's guilt; *i.e.*, in situations where the right of man is involved which makes it difficult to obtain the necessary substantive evidence (*bayyina*) required by law.

"The Fundamental Principle is to Ascribe an Event to Its Nearest Point in Time" (al-aṣl iḍāfat al-ḥādith ilā aqrab aw-qātih)[27]

This sub-maxim not only sheds light on the previous one, but it also shows that the fundamental status of any occurrence should be ascribed to the nearest point in time, which is certain and can be traced. Thus, when a dispute arises between two parties regarding damage to property, the last party to have had contact with the damaged goods will be held liable[28] because one can ascertain with certainty who last came in contact with the goods. Thus, when an article appears defective or damaged after purchase, but the merchant and buyer are at odds about who is actually responsible, then the last person to have had contact with the goods shall be held accountable: in this case, the buyer. Thus, any defect or damage will be ascribed to the buyer, although the seller will also be required to take an oath that the object(s) sold were in good condition. The buyer cannot legally breach the terms of the agreement unless the seller refuses to take an oath.[29]

Take, for example, the following situation. Someone strikes a pregnant woman who then delivers prematurely, and the baby dies shortly thereafter. In such a case, the offender would not be held responsible for the baby's death that might possibly have been caused by other means. It could be argued that the most current actor in this case is the person who struck the pregnant woman who delivered prematurely. However, because the baby survived the birth, the offender cannot be held accountable for the infant's death. By contrast, if the baby was born without life (dead), then any claim by the offender that the baby could have died in the womb should not be accepted because it is the offender who was most recently implicated as cause of the premature delivery.[30]

---

27 Ibn Nujaym, *al-Ashbāh wa-n-Naẓā'ir*, 64; Haydar, 1:25; and al-Atāsī and al-Atāsī, 1:32.

28 al-Burnu, *al-Wajīz*, 187.

29 *Ibid.*

30 This scenario is somewhat complicated in the modern age, where a premature baby can be kept alive in a Neonatal Intensive Care Unit (NICU). It can be argued that if such a modern facility is available, the offender may not be accused of causing the death of the baby but rather can be accused of causing injury to the mother. However, if there is no NICU in the location of the accident, it can therefore be argued that the offender may be indicted for the act and its consequence. Thanks to Emily Pollokoff for calling my attention to this.

"In the Presence of a Direct and Indirect Actor [in a Criminal Act], the Direct Actor is Therefore Held Responsible" (idhā ijtamaʿ al-mubāshir wa-l-mutasabbib, yuḍāf al-ḥukm ilā l-mubāshir)[31]

On the surface, the maxim of causation represents a characteristic judicial feature in Islamic criminal law. Islamic jurists have studied liability extensively, distinguishing between the consequences of direct and indirect causation, which is inevitable in criminal law that aims to strike a just balance between the perpetrator(s) and victim(s). In turn, agreement has not been unanimous as to whether one individual can be held solely responsible when two or more persons are involved in a murderous act. The reason for disagreement stems from the question whether an indirect perpetrator should be given benefit of the doubt. Those jurists who wish to excuse an indirect offender from liability reason that this step will deter the occurrence of such vile acts; those who opine that liability should be imposed upon both direct (*mubāshir*) and indirect (*mutasabbib*) perpetrators reason that a just balance will be reached between the accused culprits; finally, those who wish to distinguish between the degree of liability wish to seek a fair outcome for the direct or indirect perpetrators.

A criminal act can be committed individually or collectively. Crimes committed by a single agent are all too familiar. However, collective criminal acts are committed by either one or more individuals, known as primary or secondary agents depending on his/her degree of involvement in the crime. Someone accused of being a secondary agent might have simply offered assistance and encouragement, or even become moderately involved in organizing the crime. The primary person who physically commits the crime, for whatever reason, is the *mubāshir*; the person who is indirectly involved is the *mutasabbib*.[32]

For example, if a man digs a well on public land without first obtaining legal permission, he would be committing a *taʿzīr* offense punishable by a discretionary penalty as deemed fitting by the local authorities. If a second man kills someone by shoving him into that well, then in contrast he would be a direct offence tantamount to a *qiṣāṣ* crime since the person died as a result. Here the digger would be the *mutasabbib*. The *mubāshir*, or active agent, would be the man responsible for pushing another individual into the well, and he

31 Ibn Qudāma, *al-Mughnī*, 8:214, 271; *Majalla*, Article 90; Haydar, 1:80; Ghanim b. Muḥammad al-Baghdādī, *Mujmaʿ aḍ-Ḍamānāt* (Beirut: ʿAlam al-Kutub, 1987), 1:405; al-Zarkashī, *al-Manthūr*, 1:136; and al-Hamawī, 1:466.

32 Muḥammad b. ʿAbd al-Bāqī al-Zarqānī, *Sharḥ al-Muwaṭṭaʾ* (Beirut: Dār al-Kutub al-ʿIlmiyya, 1990), 8:10; and ʿAwda, 1:357.

would be held accountable for his actions. In comparison, if someone accidentally topples into an illegally dug well, without being pushed, the tables would be turned legally speaking. In this case, the *mutasabbib* or indirect agent would now be held responsible. Because his digging was not intended to result in anyone's death, his punishment would differ from that assigned to the *mubāshir* in the previous case. Instead of retaliation in kind, blood money (*diya*) would be accorded the victim's heir(s). Note that, had the well been dug legally after receiving permission or on one's own property, then the digger would not be liable for the accident because "Legal permission invalidates liability" (*al-jawāz ash-sharīʿī yunāfī aḍ-ḍamān*).[33]

It remains remarkable in Islamic Law that classical scholars invest so much time and effort in discussing the rules for punishing the *mubāshir*, but place less emphasis on the responsibilities of the *mutasabbib*, as apparently encouraged in the maxim in question. ʿAwda observes that classical scholars have remained too focused on *ḥudūd* and *qiṣās* crimes that are mandatory, predetermined punishments, as opposed to the plethora of crimes requiring discretionary penalties. Moreover, it is an established norm in Islam that fixed punishments can only be inflicted on those individuals who are directly involved in the crime. The majority of scholars, except Abū Ḥanīfa, opine that the co-accused, indirectly involved in crimes involving injuries to life and limb, poses an exception in certain circumstances. This is because the co-accused may also be responsible for the consequences of the act; thus, an act may occur collaboratively between the *mubāshir* and *mutasabbib*.[34]

When scrutinizing issues involving a direct multiple causation, the controversy among Islamic jurists revolves around whether a group of people can be held accountable and punished together for crimes involving killing or bodily injury. According to the majority of Islamic scholars, in crimes involving retaliation in kind or payment of blood money, each perpetrator involved will be held responsible, depending on his/her intention. For example, if every member of a group intentionally sets fire to a house, consequently damaging the property and killing the inhabitants, each arsonist will be held responsible for repaying the value of that house and will be allotted a *qiṣāṣ* penalty. The only exception

33 *Majalla*, Article 91.

34 Abū Ḥanīfa consistently applies this maxim to all criminal acts by ascribing criminal liability to the *mubāshir*. Thus, in Abū Ḥanīfa's view, if there is any crime incurring *ḥudūd* or *qiṣāṣ*, the *mubāshir* will be responsible, as opposed to in the majority view held by Mālik, al-Shāfiʿī and Ibn Ḥanbal. To them, for *qiṣāṣ*-worthy crimes, the *mutasabbib* may be held responsible for a criminal act if the criminal procedure proves his guilt. See ʿAwda, 1:358.

would be in a situation where (referring to the previous example) the perpetrators claim to have been unaware that people were in the house. In that case, the payment of *diya* will be proportionally shared amongst them. This is the opinion held by Mālikīs, based on the statement of ʿUmar Ibn al-Khaṭṭāb who was reported to have said: "If all people of Sanʿa' [Yemen] are involved in killing him, I will kill all of them".[35]

However, other scholars oppose this view on the basis that there is no justice in killing a group of people in retaliation for one death. The law of retaliation is based on equity and equating multiple and singular deaths is antithetical to equity. One point that should be clarified at this juncture is that, although equity is advocated in the law of retaliation, the law is also enacted for other reasons, such as retribution (*qawad*) in kind and deterrent (*zajr*). Some Islamic jurists consider that the types of punishment to be allocated can vary. However, in the situation discussed earlier, where retaliation can be exchanged for the shared payment of blood money, one can assume that doubt (*shubha*) will moderate the punishment. Thus, the latter view agrees with the maxim in principle, but not in practice.

Conversely, all Islamic scholars agree that for a *ḥudūd* crime, such as gang rape, then each perpetrator will receive an apt punishment,[36] except in situations where there is substantial doubt (*shubha*), such as a father's alleged involvement in his daughter's rape, or the absence of a legal definition for a criminal act. With regard to the father's alleged involvement, their familial bond will rescind the call for a *ḥadd* punishment.[37] Moreover, request for a *ḥadd* punishment will be nullified when a criminal act cannot be legally defined, such as when a group of people steal property that they divide amongst themselves, so that the value of each portion no longer equates the required restitution for the crime of theft. However, each offender will be allotted a *taʿzīr* penalty as deemed just by the supervising authority.[38]

However, if causation is involved in a crime committed by a single or multiple perpetrators, and if the nature of the crime is *ḥudūd*, then all Islamic scholars agree that only the primary offender (*mubāshir*) will be held responsible for the consequences of his act, in line with the maxim in question.

---

35 al-Zarqānī, 4:250.

36 ʿAwda, 1:360.

37 *Ibid.*, 1:360, 363–364.

38 Peters, *Crime and Punishment*, 28; ʿAwda, 1:363; al-Ramalī, 7:261, 263; al-Shirazī, *al-Muhadhdhab*, 2:7116; Aḥmad al-Dardir, "*al-Sharḥ al-Kabīr*", in Muḥammad ʿArafa al-Dasūqī, *Ḥāshiyat ad-Dasūqī ʿalā sh-Sharḥ al-Kabīr*, edited by Muḥammad ʿUlaysh, (Beirut: Dār al-Fikr, n.d.), 4:217; and Ibn Qudāma, *al-Mughnī*, 9:366.

For example, if someone commits illicit sexual intercourse involving rape, or if someone breaks into another man's house and steals property while, in both cases, a second individual stood guard, then only the actual rapist or the thief who broke into the house will be considered *mubāshir* deserving a *ḥadd* punishment. However, the guard (*mutasabbib*) in both examples will be awarded a *taʿzīr* penalty for indulging in wrongdoing upon the discretion of the authorities. One case resulting in unclear judgment on this issue occurred in the general court of Riyadh with regard to ʿAbd al-Raḥman Ibn Saeed al-Zahrānī and ʿAbd al-Raḥman Ibn Qassim al-Feefi, the question being whether both were sentenced to death based on the involvement of others in indulging in wrongdoing. It is reported that these two soldiers stopped a 20-year-old expatriate woman driving with her father in Riyadh. One soldier took her to a desert area and raped her while the other soldier stood by her father threatening to kill him. In their case, it will be assumed that one soldier is the direct perpetrator of the rape while the other is *mutasabbib*. By way of the maxim in question, one can assume that the rapist himself should be given the death penalty if it is established that he is married, while the onlooker should be given *taʿzīr*, a lesser discretionary punishment than that for rape. However, the judgment may only be based on banditry (*ḥirāba*) rather than on fornication (*zinā*) and rape (*ightiṣāb*), as stated in the report that the first soldier was convicted on charges of kidnapping and rape and the second soldier was convicted of abetting his colleague and threatening to murder the father.[39]

In contrast, when reflecting upon *qiṣāṣ* crimes, Abū Ḥanīfa maintains that the sole person responsible is the *mubāshir* (direct agent), thus freeing the *mutasabbib* from guilt. However, the majority of Islamic scholars oppose this view, and reason that the *mutasabbib* should be held responsible according to his/her degree of involvement in the crime. We wish to remark that the latter view is more practical for complex criminal cases: *e.g.*, if an incoming car accidentally crashes into a car parked in an unauthorized public place, causing it to roll towards and hit a building, subsequently causing the building to collapse on and kill a passerby. According to the majority of Islamic scholars, the person who parked the car is responsible for illegal parking, while the driver who crashed into the park car is responsible for the building's collapse and passerby's death. Thus both are involved in the subsequent crimes and each should be responsible for their share of the damages caused by their particular action.

---

39 See the full report of the case online at http://www.arabnews.com/node/311158 (last viewed: 31 March 2014).

Conditions for Holding the Active Agent Liable

Jurists agree unanimously that a perpetrator who has committed a homicide and is therefore subject to a *qiṣāṣ* penalty should be sane, have attained puberty, and possess the free will to act independently and without another agent's participation in the act. However, there are cases in which the *mutasabbib* can be held solely or collectively responsible for the act committed by the actual active agent. For example, consider a case in which a minor is handed a knife with which to kill someone. If he carries out the act, he will become the actual active agent (*mubāshir*), although he lacks criminal intent. Here the person who gave the knife to the minor, but who merely acted as a spectator during the actual stabbing, will be held responsible for coercion (*ikrāh*) to kill and be prosecuted as the primary agent (*mubāshir*). The majority of Islamic scholars agree that an individual who commands and/or coerces another individual to commit a criminal offense also carries the burden of *mens rea* (guilty mind). As such, the minor (*bulūgh*) is like a puppet used by the coercer for the purpose of killing.[40] Contrary points of view have been reported by the four leading Sunni Schools on the issue of the person who coerces (*mukrih*) and the person who is coerced (*mukrah*). In one rendition, Mālik and al-Shāfiʿī opine that both deserve a *qiṣāṣ* punishment. In contrast, Abū Ḥanīfa and al-Shāfiʿī both hold the opinion that the primary agent (*mubāshir*) does not merit a retaliatory (*qiṣāṣ*) penalty with regard to complete coercion (*ikrāh tāmm*) because he was like a puppet; instead, such punishment will be imposed on the secondary agent responsible for coercion (*mutasabbib mukrih*) and the actual cause of the crime. Abū Yūsuf from the Ḥanafī School holds that doubt (*shubha*) will nullify *qiṣāṣ* for both of the accused and that payment of *diya* should be their penalty. Ẓufār (d. 158 AH) of the Ḥanafī School asserts that *qiṣāṣ* should be imposed on the primary active agent whether or not coercion was total, based on the maxim in question.[41] Thus, their quandary regarding contradiction arises from the question whether coercion (*ikrāh*) is complete (*tāmm*) or incomplete (*ghayr tāmm*). If coercion is incomplete, the majority of scholars impose punishment on the primary agent (*mubāshir*) because his life is not more valuable than another life; thus his life should not be preserved at the expense of others. In a typical case where someone restrains an individual so that a third party can kill him, the actual killer should be held responsible, according to Abū Ḥanīfa, al-Shāfiʿī and a rendition of Aḥmad's thought. On the other hand, Mālik and Aḥmad (in a different rendition) deem that both

40 Ibn Qudāma, *al-Mughnī*, 9:331; al-Shirazī, *al-Muhadhdhib*, 2:189; al-Dardir, 7:216; and Ibn Rushd, 2:479.

41 al-Kāsānī, 7:178–180.

culprits are the killers responsible for the murder. Their share of involvement is equal in the end result.[42]

In contrast, if an animal damages property or harms an individual, the rule is that the animal cannot be prosecuted based on the fact that it has no sense of self. Neither will the owner be held responsible because he did not directly damage the property or cause bodily harm. The prophetic tradition states that damage caused by an animal is in vain.[43] This can only be construed if the animal is stationary in an authorized location; it is also the norm that people should keep an eye on their property in the daytime, as mentioned in the discussion on *ʿurf* and *ʿāda*.[44] However, if the animal's owner has mounted it or been negligent by leaving it at an unauthorized location, he will then be held responsible for the damage caused by the animal, although he himself is considered *mutasabbib*. He is held responsible for the damage because he is responsible for taking care of his animal while it is in his service.[45]

Complexity of Causation in Islamic Criminal Law

Causation can be a complex issue in many cases. Take, for example, the above-mentioned case of an incoming car that accidentally crashes into a parked car, that subsequently results in a collapsed building and death of a passerby. Who is responsible? According to a fictitious example from the Ḥanafī School, the owner of the oncoming car that hit the illegally parked car will be responsible for all damages, including the passerby's death. The driver is considered the direct cause of the accident; the owner of the illegally parked car, however, may be prosecuted for illegal parking but not for the series of mishaps. In contrast, if we suppose that the illegally parked car began to roll without being pushed—or perhaps set in motion by a severe wind—then the entire responsibility would fall on the car's owner whose negligence caused the accident.

Another problematic issue when determining direct or indirect causation is the following case. Someone is injured so seriously that his wounds prove fatal. If he is taken to a hospital, where all the necessary fees are paid, but dies

42 Zayn al-ʿĀbidīn Ibn Ibrāhīm Ibn Nujaym, *al-Baḥr al-Rāʾiq*, 2nd edn. (Beirut: Dār al-Maʿrifa, n.d.), 8:345; al-Ramalī, 7:244; al-Dardir, *al-Sharḥ al-Kabīr*, 4:217; ʿAwda, *at-Tashriʿ al-Jinai*, 1:373–377; see also Scots Law in Peter W. Ferguson, *Crimes Against the Person* (Edinburgh: Butterworths, 1990), 68. Ferguson states that if A supplies B with a gun with which to shoot and kill C, A is liable for the murder along with B. *Cf., HM Advocate v Lappen 1956*, SLT 109 at 110, per Lord Patrick.

43 al-Bukhārī, Ḥadīth No. 6514.

44 See Ch. 7 in this book.

45 Muḥammad b. Muhammad b. ʿAbd al-Raḥman al-Ḥaṭṭāb, *Mawāhib al-Jalīl fī Sharḥ Mukhtaṣar Khalīl* (Beirut: Dār al-Maʿrifa, 1398/1977), 6:244.

by virtue of medical negligence after surgery, the maxim appears to indicate superficially that the hospital should be held responsible. However, in all fairness, the person who caused the injury must be held responsible for paying *diya* for the injury, while the hospital authority will be held responsible for paying *diya* for the death. However, we must pose the question: If the victim eventually dies although the hospital has not shirked its duties and treated the patient professionally, should the *mutasabbib* be held responsible for the death or just the injury? One can infer from the general rule of direct and indirect causation that, if the *mubāshir* cannot be held responsible, then one can resort to the *mutasabbib*. Although the *mutasabbib* in this case did not intend to kill, his action led to the victim's death, and therefore he will be held liable to pay restitution (diya).

Another example that demonstrates the complexity of causation is the case of a homicide where only one of the killers harbors the intent to kill. There is consensus among Islamic scholars, based on the texts, that a perpetrator (*mukhṭiʾ*) who has committed an error unintentionally should be exempt from *qiṣās*. However, the Ḥanafīs, Shāfiʿīs and a majority of the Ḥanbalī scholars in turn suggest that neither should the intentional perpetrator (*ʿāmid*) be awarded a *qiṣāṣ* punishment because the issue has become complicated and now resembles a quasi-intentional crime for which *qiṣāṣ* does not apply. In contrast, the Mālikīs and a rendition of Aḥmad's thought assert that the intentional perpetrator should be awarded *qiṣāṣ* because he not only intended but was also responsible for his action.[46]

From the foregoing discussion on this sub-maxim, that "In the presence of the direct and indirect actor [in a criminal act], the direct actor is therefore held responsible", one will obviously recognize the *raison d'être* behind the disagreements and inconsistencies Islamic scholars encounter in their deliberations. The fact is that Islamic Law must serve to protect not only the victim(s) but also the accused, and to ensure that justice is achieved for all parties involved. In crimes where the right of man is not involved, the basic rule states that the *mubāshir* will be considered the prime perpetrator and, as such, carry total responsibility for any damage caused by his action. Thus, if the prosecution fails to establish accountability with regard to the prime offender in a criminal case, then no punishment will be awarded. However, if the right of man is involved in a crime, it becomes apparent that restricting responsibility to the *mubāshir* alone could render this right futile. Thus,

46 Ibn Qudāma, *al-Mughnī*, 8:236.

in cases of complete coercion, the majority of Islamic scholars, including Abū Ḥanīfa, extend liability to the *mutasabbib* to ensure that the right of man can be claimed and justice achieved.

Another reason why Islamic scholars differ with regard to this sub-maxim stems from what ʿAwda[47] believes to be the priority of one causation over another, as summarized below:

1. A situation where cause supersedes perpetration, *e.g.*, where false testimony leads to someone's conviction which results in the issuance of a death penalty. Thus the cause of death originates from the false testimony and supersedes the victim's execution. Had there been no false witness given, then the death penalty would not have been imposed. Although the individual providing false testimony has not directly executed the victim, he has certainly contributed greatly to the outcome.[48]
2. A situation where the *mubāshir* supersedes the *mutasabbib: e.g.*, when someone is thrown into a deep well from which he cannot escape without being rescued. Instead of helping the man climb out of the well, a second individual uses a tool to stab him to death. The act of the *mutasabbib*, or person indirectly responsible, might be deemed murderous if the victim were merely left in the well to die. However, because a second individual actually stabbed and killed the victim in the well, responsibility shifts to the last actor based on the maxim: "A matter is attributed to the time closest to the event" (*yuḍāf al-amr ilā aqrab al-waqt*).[49] In a similar example, when someone stabs or cuts another person's hand, while a second individual then stabs the victim in the stomach which kills him, the last perpetrator will be charged for murder, while the former will be charged for grievous bodily injury.[50]
3. A situation where the two offenders are equally involved, such as when someone is coerced to commit murder. Islamic scholars differ in opinion on this issue as explained above.

---

47 ʿAwda, 1:370.

48 al-Ḥaṭṭāb, 6:241.

49 See *Majalla*, Article 10; and al-Burnu, *al-Wajīz*, 187.

50 al-Ḥaṭṭāb, 6:241.

"The Fundamental Principle is that Things are Permissible for Use until Proof of Prohibition Becomes Evident" (al-aṣl fī l-ashyāʾ al-ibāḥa "ḥattā yadull ad-dalīl ʿalā taḥrīmihā")[51]

This sub-maxim is quite important in man's daily life and offers a relief from the burden of doubt [of the unknown] which many people face in their lives. The link between this sub-maxim and the grand maxim is that the fundamental principle (*aṣl*) connotes certainty (*yaqīn*). Islam stipulates that in general things are created for human use, with a few exceptions that are declared unlawful. In three Qurʾānic verses God emphatically states the following:

> It is He who hath created for you all things that are on earth.[52]

> Say: Who hath forbidden the beautiful [gifts] of God which He hath produced for His servants and the things that are clean and pure for sustenance.[53]

> Say: I find not in the message received by me by inspiration any forbidden thing to be eaten by one who wishes to eat it. Unless it be carrion or blood poured.[54]

Al-Shawkānī, in buttressing his support for the sub-maxim, states that: "He [the Exalted] made the fundamental provision to be lawful and exempted some from being unlawful".[55]

There are two other opinions that contradict this principle. The first is ascribed to Abū Ḥanīfa that opposes the general opinion held by the Ḥanafīs and some Ḥanbalīs who opine that the fundamental principle (*aṣl*) refers to those things that are forbidden until otherwise stated.[56] The second opinion

51 al-Suyūṭī, *al-Ashbāh*, 60; Ibn Nujaym, *al-Ashbāh wa-n-Naẓāʾir*, 66; and al-Zarkashī, *al-Manthūr*, 1:176.

52 Q. 2:29.

53 Q. 7:32.

54 Q. 6:145.

55 al-Shawkānī, *Irshād al-Fuḥūl*, 286.

56 al-Suyūṭī ascribes this opinion to Abū Ḥanīfa, while Ibn Qudāma reports that Ibn Ḥāmid (d. 403/1013) and Qāḍī Abū Yaʿlā (d. 458/1066), both Ḥanbalīs, profess the same opinion, although the majority of Ḥanafīs incline to the first opinion. See al-Suyūṭī, *al-Ashbāh*, 60; Ibn Nujaym, *al-Ashbāh wa-n-Naẓāʾir*, 66; ʿAbdullāh b. Aḥmad Ibn Qudāma, *Rawḍat an-Nāẓir wa-Jannat al-Munāẓir*, edited by ʿAbd al-ʿAziz ʿAbd al-Raḥman al-Saʿīd, 2nd edn.,

professes the cessation (*tawaqquf*) of anything until there is evidence to prove whether it is lawful or unlawful.[57] However, every indication suggests that God's creation is meant for the use and benefit of mankind, through His revelation and inspiration regarding their use. Thus, a fundamental principle must exist that generally unites all of mankind in their actions and hence brings favor and facility to all. One way to facilitate this is to uphold what is fundamentally permissible (*mubāḥa*) rather focus on what is prohibited (*maḥẓūra*). It is said that the numbers of things permitted are boundless and unspecified in the Holy Qur'ān and prophetic tradition, while those things that are unlawful are less in number and specific.

The relevance of this sub-maxim in criminal law is that which is clearly stated as permitted in the texts should continue to be accepted as legitimate, while everything described in the texts as illegal should remain as such. Thus, any act that the law stipulates as criminal, *e.g.*, illicit sexual intercourse, alcohol consumption, and unjustifiable killing, remains fundamentally *ḥarām*.

Paradoxically, if the opinions of the majority of scholars who ascertain the legality of all things are loosely construed, one may assume, based on this maxim, that committing other offences not referred to in the texts is legal. However, if by applying analogy (*qiyās*), one can prove that what is stated in the texts and what is deduced by analogy are equivalent, then both would share a similar status. For example, it is possible for jurists to apply the principle of analogy to establish illegality in cases involving intoxicants, homosexuality, murder, etc.; once all the elements of analogy is fulfilled and the crimes established by that analogy are proven to be harmful to mankind.

(Riyadh: Imām Ibn Saud University, 1399/1978), 1:245. Their opinion is based on the Qur'ānic verse 16:116, which prohibits saying something falsely, *e.g.*, that this is lawful and this is unlawful, in order to invent lies against God. But there is no indication that the verse provides clear evidence in support of their claim.

57 This opinion is ascribed to a number of Ḥanafīs as well as Ḥanbalīs (see al-Burnu, *al-Wajīz*, 196).

"Fixed Punishments Should be Averted in the Case of Doubt/ Suspicion" (al-ḥudūd tusqaṭ bi-sh-shubhāt)[58]

The sub-maxim that *ḥudūd* should be averted in the face of doubt is generally accepted among the four Schools of Islamic jurisprudence.[59] It is reported that the Prophet said: "Avert *ḥudūd* [punishment] when there are doubts [*shubhāt*]".[60] There are many instances from the Prophet's Sunna and the sayings, actions and consent of his Companions with which to justify the legality of this maxim. Ibn Humām observes that when Mā'iz[61] confessed the error of adultery, the Prophet replied: "Maybe you kissed [...] touched her".[62] Thus the Prophet's enquiries were nothing but a means to eliminate doubt, as Mā'iz could simply have acknowledged the kissing or touching while leaving other details about his behavior unsaid and beyond doubt.[63] In this way Mā'iz could have retracted his confession (*iqrār*) to avoid conviction. Certainly, the Prophet never suggested to anyone who confessed guilt for failing to repay a debt (namely, an infraction against the right of man to be reimbursed for a loan) that the debt was probably a 'trust' (which would not necessitate repayment, and was therefore not punishable), as he did in this case related to the absolute right of God (*ḥaqq Allāh*). This indicates that caution should be taken

58 al-Suyūṭī, *al-Ashbāh*, 122–123; Ibn Nujaym, *al-Ashbāh wa-n-Naẓā'ir*, 127; al-Hamawi; Haydar; and al-Zarkashī, *al-Manṯūr*, 1:400. Almost all Schools of Islamic Jurisprudence accept the maxim in principle but apply it differently in various locations. The exception is the Ẓāhirī School, whose followers object to it based on their rejection of the Ḥadīth reported in support of the maxim (see Yūsuf Ibn 'Abdullāh Ibn 'Abd al-Barr, *at-Tamhīd li-mā fī l-Muwaṭṭa' min al-Ma'ānī wa-l-Asānīd*, edited by Muṣṭafā Aḥmad al-'Alāwī, (Morocco: Ministry of Endowment and Islamic Affairs, 1967), 15:34; al-Shinqitī, 5:392; al-Sarakhsī, 18:127; Ibn Qudāma, *al-Mughnī*, 9:116–119, 123, 259; and Ibn Ḥazm, *al-Muḥalla*, 11:153–156.

59 The most recent study of juristic debates on the origin of this maxim and its acceptance and application in Islamic Law in general and its criminal law in particular features in Intisar Rabb's Ph.D. Dissertation (Princeton: Princeton University Press, 2009).

60 The Ḥadīth is reported in various ways, although all the chains of its narration have been criticized. According to al-Shawkānī, the Ḥadīth is better considered as *mawqūf* or untraceable (see Muḥammad b. 'Alī al-Shawkānī, *Nayl al-Awṭār* (Beirut: Dār al-Jil, 1973), 7:118). However, it is reported as *marfū'* or traceable is ascending order to the Prophet by Ibn 'Abbās, in *Musnad Abī Huthayfa*, Ḥadīth No. 4, *Kitāb al-Ḥudūd*, 32. According to al-Nadawī, the narration of Ibn 'Abbās is authentic. This clarifies the ambiguity surrounding the acceptability of the Ḥadīth. See al-Nadawī, 278.

61 One of the Companions of the Prophet who committed adultery and voluntarily confessed to the Prophet.

62 al-Bukhārī, Ḥadīth No. 6438.

63 Rabb, *Reasonable doubt*, pp. 52-60

in the execution of *ḥadd* punishments.[64] ʿUmar Ibn al-Khaṭṭāb is reported to have said: "For me to commit an error in averting the punishment of *ḥudūd* is preferable than to execute it in the face of doubts [*shubhāt*]".[65]

Before demonstrating how doubts (*shubhāt*) can thwart the establishment of *ḥudūd* crimes, it is necessary to explain briefly the meanings of the words *ḥadd* and *shubha* as defined by Islamic jurists. As already explained in detail in Chapter 1, Section Islamic Criminal Law, the word *ḥadd* means boundary, standard, penalty, prevention and inhibition,[66] which Doi describes as "a restrictive and preventive ordinance, or statute of God concerning things [that are] lawful (*ḥalāl*) and things [that are] unlawful (*ḥarām*)".[67] Islamic scholars vary in the ways they describe the term *ḥadd* technically. First, some scholars take into account whose rights have been violated and limit *ḥudūd* crimes to those with pre-established, immutable penalties prescribed in the Qur'ān or referred to by the Prophet's Sunna. The punishment for a *ḥudūd* crime, once it has been reported to the authorities, is mandatory and can neither be reduced nor increased, nor pardoned nor waived by anyone. In contrast, penalties for less serious *taʿzīr* crimes vary and can be left to the discretion of the *qāḍī* (judge) or *ḥākim* (ruler).[68] From this viewpoint, *qiṣāṣ* crimes, whose penalties have been predetermined in the Qur'ān or the Prophet's Sunna, could also be classified as *ḥudūd*. Doi enumerates the following seven *ḥudūd* crimes: namely, murder/manslaughter or other bodily injury (*qatl/jurḥ*); theft (*sariqa*); fornication or adultery (*zinā*); defamation (*qadhf*); apostasy (*ridda*); inebriation (*shurb al-khamr*); and highway robbery (*qaṭʿ al-ṭarīq*).[69] His categorization is compatible with al-Māwardī's definition of crimes and in line with the majority of classical jurists, except for the Ḥanafīs who exclude inebriation and robbery from their list of *ḥudūd* crimes.[70]

Second, other scholars regard *ḥadd* as penalties prescribed as the absolute right of God (*ḥaqq Allāh*), which therefore eliminates murder, manslaughter as well as bodily injury on the grounds that penalties for those crimes are retaliatory in kind (*qiṣāṣ*) or financial restitution (*diya*) and thus considered the right

64 Muḥammad b. ʿAbd al-Wāḥid b. Amīr al-Ḥājj Ibn al-Humām, *Fatḥ al-Qadīr Sharḥ al-Hidāya* (Cairo: al-Amiriyya Press, 1336/1917), 4:139–140.

65 al-Shawkānī, *Nayl al-Awṭār*, 7:118.

66 Baʿalbakkī, 455–456; and Ibn Manẓūr, 4:93.

67 Doi, *Sharīʿah*, 221.

68 *Ibid.*

69 *Ibid.*, 225.

70 al-Māwardī, *al-Aḥkām as-Sulṭāniyya*, 218–223; Ibn Rushd, 2:424–449; al-Shirazī, *al-Muhadhdhab*, 2:266–289; Muḥammad Ibn Abī Bakr Ibn al-Qayyim al-Jawziyya, *aṭ-Ṭuruq al-Ḥukmiyya*, 106–107; ʿAwda, 2:345, 1:105–107; and al-Kāsānī, 7:33–97.

of man (*ḥaqq al-ādamī*). Here murder and manslaughter are excluded because, in such cases, the victim's heirs can seek restitution through *diya* rather than retaliation in kind, in contrast to *ḥadd* penalties that are non-negotiable. However, even *ḥudūd* crimes such as slander and theft can be pardoned by the victims if they have not been reported to the authorities. Among the contemporary scholars endorsing this opinion are Abū Zahra and ʿAbd al-Qādir ʿAwda, who argue that *ḥadd*, rather than *qiṣāṣ*, *diya*, and *taʿzīr* punishments, are sanctioned primarily to honor the absolute right of God aimed at maintaining social justice. However, defining *ḥudūd* crimes as violations of God's right will result in the exclusion of many crimes mentioned in the *ḥudūd* category explained above. In other words, only a few crimes such as apostasy (*ridda*), illicit sexual intercourse (*zinā*) and consumption of alcohol (*shurb al-khamr*) will then be classified as an absolute right of God, although punishment for the latter is neither fixed in the Qurʾān nor its status consistent in the Sunna.

Therefore, the alternative way of assessing the meaning of the term *ḥadd* in the maxim "Fixed punishments should be averted in the case of doubt/suspicion" (*al-ḥudūd tusqaṭ bi-sh-shubhāt*) is to follow the classical definition, as maintained by Doi, which considers murder a *ḥudūd* rather than *qiṣāṣ* crime because the latter can be avoided in the face of doubt. Therefore *ḥudūd* crimes will include those also punishable by *qiṣāṣ* and *diya*, but not by *taʿzīr*. This is in line with al-Māwardī's classification of crimes as *ḥudūd* and *taʿzīr*.[71]

In this sub-maxim, the meaning of the term *ḥadd* generally appears to be less strict than that defined in the two perspectives discussed above. Moreover, in the face of doubt, all *ḥadd* punishments mentioned in the texts can be averted, regardless of whether they relate to the rights of God or man. Here one can define the term *ḥudūd* as "legally fixed punishments" (*ʿuqūbāt al-muqaddara sharʿan*) to distinguish it from non-fixed, namely discretionary (*taʿzīr*) or political (*siyāsa*) punishments. That is to say, in Islamic Law, any penalty ascribed to any crime can be averted when doubt is a factor at play, as will be illustrated below.

The sub-maxim under discussion which averts *ḥudūd* in the face of doubt covers all fixed punishments mentioned in the Qurʾān and Ḥadīth. Therefore, the verses in which God says, "This is my *ḥudūd* [directive]" (*tilka ḥudūd Allāhi*)[72] can be interpreted to cover all facets of fixed punishments, prescribed by God as preventive and protective measures for mankind. They should neither be altered nor influenced by worldly rulers. As stated above, one can argue, in

71 al-Māwardī, *al-Aḥkām as-Sulṭāniyya*, 220.

72 *Cf.*, Q. 2:187.

response to the opinion that *qiṣāṣ* can be commuted to *diya* by the victim's heirs, that such an exchange of penalties also constitutes *ḥadd* stipulated by God.

Having defined *ḥadd*, we will now examine the relationship between the terms doubt (*shubha*) in this sub-maxim and uncertainty (*shakk*) in the grand maxim under which this maxim is subsumed, to distinguish between these two words often translated simply as 'doubt'. The term *shakk* (uncertainty) has been defined as an antonym of *yaqīn* (certainty), and the verbs sharing its root (*shīn-kāʾ-kāʾ*) all refer to having doubts, misgivings or being skeptical about something. The verbal noun *shubha* (doubt) shares the same triliteral root (*shīn-bāʾ-hāʾ*) with the verbs *shabbiha* (passive form II, to be in doubt) and *ishtabaha* (form verb, to resemble one another or to be in doubt). Technically the term *shubha* refers to something whose status is ambiguous, in the sense that one is uncertain whether it is legitimate or true. Thus, in the case of uncertainty (*shakk*), there is no evidence that the crime was committed by the accused and, as such, punishment cannot be apportioned. In contrast, in the case of doubt (*shubha*), there is some indication that the crime was committed by the accused, but the evidence put forward to establish the allegation is untenable, or the motive for the crime is contentious and contestable.

Thus, *shubha* plays a vital role in Islamic criminology, wherein emphasis is placed on the need to prove beyond any iota of a doubt that a particular accusation is genuine, because any doubt suspected in litigation will be considered an impediment to the validity of the suit and so provide grounds as to why guilt cannot be established against the accused person. *Shubha* in Islamic Law refers to what appears to be proven, but, in fact, is not.[73]

Particularly in *ḥudūd* crimes it is important that *shubha* be given more consideration and that the accused be presumed innocent until proven otherwise. The compelling reason which underlies this statement is that some punishments, like the death penalty, that result from the commission of any *ḥudūd* crime are irreversible once they have been carried out. In other words, acknowledging the authenticity of doubt (*shubha*) can help avoid or commute *ḥadd* penalties in cases where the right of God is involved.[74] If for any legal reason bordering on doubt the law fails to establish that a crime has been committed, it is incumbent to identify whether the right of God is involved. In that case, there will be neither *ḥadd* nor compensation. When either the rights of God and man, or solely the right of man, are involved, *ḥadd* will be dropped

73 Ibn al-Humām, *Fatḥ al-Qadīr*, 4:140.

74 al-Sarakhsī, 9:151–156.

but compensation must be allotted. Islamic scholars coined the maxim "Doubt interdicts only infliction of *ḥadd* punishment, not due financial compensation" (*ash-shubha tamnaʿ wujūb al-ḥadd wa-lā tamnaʿ wujūb al-māl*),[75] which acknowledges the tremendous value of doubt in waiving *ḥadd* for the culprit without neglecting justice for the victim.

One may pose the question: Why is there a need for compensation when the accusation has been quashed by doubt? The answer is that, although the allegation is interdicted, *ḥadd* is dropped because it involves the right of God. Violation of God's right is open to forgiveness, especially when doubt is implicated. The involvement of man's right is undeniable because there is an element of truth in the case. For instance, if someone in possession of stolen goods claims that they were actually found elsewhere and are only being held for safekeeping, the individual would be exempted from *ḥadd*. However, the goods must be returned to the rightful owner. However, if the person holding the goods has made use of them, then he/she must pay compensation.

A similar situation would arise if a man sleeps with a woman to whom he is not legally married and then claims that the act was a mistake. If doubt (*shubha*) impedes the legal procedure, causing it to fail, then a value equivalent to a fair dower (*mahr al-mithli*) must be paid to the woman. The same applies to cases of homicide, for example, where it cannot be established whether the accused was intentionally guilty, the court will resort to the financial restitution, because "Doubt interdicts the obligation of *ḥadd* punishment, but not financial compensation" (*ash-shubha tamnaʿ wujūb al-ḥadd wa-lā tamnaʿ wujūb al-māl*).[76]

Normally theft (*sariqa*) belongs in the category of *ḥudūd* crimes, for which punishment has varied historically amongst the Schools of Islamic Jurisprudence. Stealing trivial objects or essentials for life (*e.g.*, bread) was originally permissible and, in Abū Ḥanīfa's opinion, should not attract a *ḥadd* penalty. According to him, doubt also plays a role in the prohibition of hunting animals or stealing water or other natural resources such as sand. The majority of scholars do not accept Abū Ḥanīfa's assumption, arguing that doubt (*shubha*) is not involved in those cases. In their opinion, if pilfering a so-called normally worthless item that has become sufficiently valuable (*niṣāb*) to warrant theft worth penalizing, or if water or animals are stolen from someone's possession, then a *ḥadd* penalty must be imposed.[77]

---

75 al-Kāsānī, 7:81.

76 *Ibid.*; Ibrāhīm Ibn ʿAlī Ibn Farhun, *Tabṣirat al-Ḥukkām fī Uṣūl al-Aqḍiyya wa-Manāhij al-Aḥkām* (Beirut: Dār al-Kutub al-ʿIlmiyya and Cairo: al-Amiriyya Press, 1301/1883), 2:119–125.

77 Ibn al-Humām, *Fatḥ al-Qadīr*, 4:327; al-Zarqānī, 95; and Ibn Qudāma, *al-Mughnī*, 10:247.

However, Abū Ḥanīfa does not always provide the most lenient perspective. In the case of adultery, for example, Mālik, al-Shāfiʿī and Ḥanbal assert that if a man finds a woman in his bed and has sexual intercourse with her, assuming that she is his wife, then *ḥadd* should not be accorded to him because doubt (*shubha*) is involved.[78] However, Abū Ḥanīfa refuted such a claim on the grounds that doubt was not in question because, although a man can sleep in a relative's bed (not a cousin), having sexual intercourse with a female relative is emphatically prohibited.[79] Consider also the examples in which an accused retracts his confession that was the only evidence available,[80] or in which witnesses withdraw their statements thus nullifying the only proof obtainable.

Although it can generally be said that the presence of doubt will commute if not overturn a *ḥadd* sentence, Schools of Jurisprudence vary in their classification and attempts to further refine justice in cases involving doubt. The Mālikī and Ḥanbalī Schools place doubt in one large category, while the Ḥanafī and Shāfiʿī Schools attempt to apply various categories. For example, the Ḥanafīs sub-divide doubt into three categories:

1. Doubt regarding actions (*shubha fī l-fiʿl*): when an individual does not know whether an act is/is not legal because there is neither explicit nor precise textual evidence on the issue. In these cases, the perpetrator who commits such an offence, but claims to have had no explicit proof, will not be punished with *ḥadd*. However, justice will be allotted on anyone who commits an offence while being aware of any evidence refuting its legality. One example is the act of sexual intercourse with an irrevocably divorced wife while she is still in her period of purification (*ʿidda*).[81]
2. Doubt regarding ownership (*shubha fī l-maḥall / shubhat al-milk*): where two texts appear seemingly contradictory, such as a verse that stipulates cutting off of a thief's hand as punishment for thievery, and a Ḥadīth which says that a father owns his son's property. Thus, if a father steals his son's property, he will not attract a *ḥadd* penalty because of the doubt inherent in the legitimacy or illegitimacy of the property.[82] The Ḥanafīs determinedly hold the view that *shubha fī l-maḥall* is applicable in any

78 Ibn Qudāma, *al-Mughnī*, 10:155.

79 Ibn al-Humām, *Fatḥ al-Qadīr*, 4:147.

80 Ibn Qudāma, *al-Mughnī*, 9:119; and Ibn Ḥazm, *al-Muḥalla*, 8:252. The fact that the Prophet did not want to punish Māʾiz instantly upon his confession shows that the Prophet forsaw potential doubt which could lead to averting *ḥadd* for Māʾiz.

81 al-Kāsānī, 7:37.

82 ʿAwda, 2:214.

case where there is "legitimate evidence that nullifies the invalidity of the act at issue".[83]

3. Doubt in contract (*shubha fī l-ʿaqd*): a view solely attributed to Abū Ḥanīfa and refuted by his disciples (Abū Yūsuf and Muḥammad al-Shaybānī). In this case, if a man has sexual intercourse with his *maḥārim* (relatives or in-laws as stipulated in Qurʾānic verse 4:23, and in various Ḥadīth), he should not be punished with *ḥadd.*

However, all these Ḥanafī proposals, including *shubha fī l-ʿaqd,* are rejected by the other Schools.[84] Al-Shāfiʿī sub-divides *shubha* into three categories:

1. Doubt regarding the [anatomical] site of the act (*shubha fī l-maḥall*): when a man has vaginal or anal sexual intercourse with his legitimate wife and while she is menstruating or fasting. These acts revolve around the place of the act in time. Although the man has the right to have intercourse with his wife, certain circumstances are not permitted.
2. Doubt regarding the perpetrator (*shubha fī l-fāʿil*): when a man was presented with a woman as his wife and with whom he had intercourse. Such a case will not attract a *ḥudūd* penalty because of his doubt (*shubha*) and ignorance (*jahl*) of the act. However, if he knows what he is doing then a *ḥadd* punishment will be meted out.[85]
3. Doubt regarding the legality/illegality of an act (*shubha fī l-jiha*): when there is a legal dispute among scholars on a particular issue. Marriage laws provide several examples. Ibn ʿAbbās, in contrast to the majority of scholars, at one time supported the legality of temporary marriage (*mutʿa*). Abū Ḥanīfa considered a marriage contract that was concluded without the consent of the bride's legal guardian (*walī*) permissible,[86] while Mālik agreed that a marriage contract could be drawn up without witnesses. In these cases, if the married couples engaged in sexual intercourse, they would not be held liable for adultery. Moreover, even if the couples believed that the act was prohibited, their actions would not be punishable because disagreement amongst the scholars had caused doubt (*shubha*).[87]

---

83 *Ibid.*, 2:214; al-Kāsānī, 7:37.

84 ʿAwda, 2:214; al-Kāsānī, 7:37.

85 Muḥammad b. Aḥmad al-Khatib al-Shiribīnī, *Mughnī al-Muḥtāj* (Beirut: Dār al-Fikr, n.d.), 4:160–170.

86 al-Kāsānī, 7:35.

87 ʿAwda, 2:213.

The disparity in the categorization of doubt (*shubha*) has legal implications as explained in each School's approach to the concept.

Certainty, Uncertainty and Means of Proof

There are many means of proof set out in Islamic criminal law. While some are substantial, such as eyewitness statements and confession, and considered authentic by scholars of Islamic jurisprudence, other means of proof are circumstantial and their acceptability is controversial depending on the nature of the case brought before the court of justice. There are two substantial means of proof in Islamic criminal Law that, for the purpose of this discussion, are testimony (*shahāda*) and confession (*iqrār*).

Evidence/Eyewitness Account: "The Burden of Proof is on the Claimant and the Oath is on the One Who Denies" (*al-bayyina ʿalā l-muddaʿī wa-l-yamīn ʿalā man ankar*)[88]

This sub-maxim is coded directly from a statement by Prophet Muḥammad. Its authenticity is unanimously agreed upon among the traditionalists.[89] The maxim is widely applicable in establishing whether a claim between litigant parties is genuine. According to this sub-maxim, the normal procedure for giving evidence before a court of justice is that the onus of proof is on the plaintiff to establish what he alleges to be the truth, while the oath is on the defendant who denies the claim. The mechanism of proof is to produce evidence (*bayyina*) as reflected in the first word of the maxim. Debate amongst Islamic scholars has been inconclusive as to the meaning of *bayyina* in this maxim. The majority of classical Islamic jurists, *i.e.*, the Ḥanafīs, Mālikīs, Shāfiʿīs and majority of Ḥanbalīs,[90] hold that the meaning of *bayyina* in the Ḥadīth from which the maxim is derived is restricted to witnesses alone. They argue that, in most Qurʾānic verses (*e.g.*, Q. 2:282 and 24:4) or Ḥadīths, the word 'witness' or *shahāda* is used where evidence is required. In one Ḥadīth Anas Ibn Mālik narrates the following: "The first case of *liʿān* [repudiation] that occurred in Islam was when Hilāl Ibn Umayya accused his wife in the presence of the Prophet of having committed illicit sexual intercourse with Sharik Ibn Samha. The Prophet said to him: "You have to produce evidence [*bayyina*] otherwise

88 *Majalla*, Article 76.

89 al-Tirmidhī, Ḥadīths Nos. 1342 and 1356; al-Daraquṭnī, Ḥadīth No. 9; Aḥmad b. Ḥusayn al-Bayhaqī, *as-Sunān al-Kubrā*, edited by Muḥammad A. ʿAta, (Makkah: Maktabat Dār al-Baz, 1994), Ḥadīth No. 11892; Ibn Mājah, Ḥadīth No. 2321; and al-Bukhārī, "*Bāb al-Bayyina ʿalā l-Muddaʿī*" in *Kitāb ash-Shahādat*.

90 al-Ramalī, 8:314; al-Shiribīnī, *Mughnī al-Muḥtāj*, 4:461; and al-Bahūtī.

you will receive a fixed [*ḥadd*] punishment on your back". He said: "O Prophet! When one of us sees a man having intercourse with his wife, should he go and seek four witnesses [*bayyina*]". But the Prophet insisted, saying: "You must produce evidence or you must receive a fixed [*ḥadd*] punishment on your back". Hilāl then said: "On Him who sent you with truth, I am speaking truth, may God send down something that will free my back from *ḥadd* punishment".[91] It is argued that the meaning of '*bayyina*' which the Prophet referred to in this Ḥadīth is 'witnesses' based on Qur'ānic verse 24:4 that states that four witnesses are required in the case of *zinā*.

However, Ibn Taymiyya, Ibn al-Qayyim al-Jawziyya, Ibn Farhun (d. 799/1397), Ibn Ḥajar al-ʿAsqalānī (d. 852/1449), as well as a host of contemporary Islamic scholars, affirm that the word *bayyina* in Islamic jurisprudence has a wider meaning than 'witness'. In their view, the word *bayyina* signifies any means that can be used to prove a claim; to restrict its meaning to two or four witnesses would undermine the connotation of the word. Ibn Qayyim al-Jawziyya asserts that the word *bayyina*, as expressed in Qur'ānic verses 6:57 and 57:25, does not only imply eyewitnesses in any case but also indicates proof and clear signs.[92] Accordingly, it is argued that the word *shahāda* (witness) is one of the means of proof or evidence (*bayyina*), and *bayyina* is a conclusive proof that clarifies truth.[93] In other words, the scope of *bayyina* (means of proof) is broader than that of *shahāda* (witness); while the latter is one type of *bayyina*, not all *bayyiya* are necessarily *shahāda*.[94]

From the foregoing discussion, it is safe to say that not limiting the meaning of *bayyina* in this context complies with the purpose of the Sharīʿa, namely, to establish justice. To give rights to their owners is one of the most visible ways of establishing justice. Of course, by extending the connotation of *bayyina* to include any other means of evidence such as signs, DNA, forensic evidence, and photography would clearly enhance the establishment of justice. However, if evidence is restricted to only eyewitnesses, it will pervert the course of justice and neglect many rights of men.

However, a critical evaluation of the arguments of those who wish to restrict *bayyina* to mean only eyewitnesses reveals that the Ḥadīth upon which their argumentation is based actually sides with the second opinion. In the

91 al-Bukhārī, *Kitāb at-Tafsīr*, Ḥadīth No. 4747; al-Ashʿath, Ḥadīth No. 2254; al-Tirmidhī, Ḥadīth No. 3179; and Ibn Mājah, Ḥadīth No. 2067.

92 Ibn al-Qayyim al-Jawziyya, *aṭ-Ṭuruq al-Ḥukmiyya*, 15.

93 Aḥmad al-Ḥuṣarī, *ʿIlm al-Qaḍāʾ wa-Adillat al-Ithbāt fī l-Fiqh al-Islāmī* (Beirut: Dār al-Kitāb al-ʿArabī, n.d.), 1:11.

94 Ibn al-Qayyim al-Jawziyya, *Iʿlām al-Muwaqqiʿīn*, 1:90; and Ibn Farhun, 1:161.

Ḥadīth, it is reported that the Angel Gabriel (Jibrīl) revealed to the Prophet the Qur'anic verses: "And for those who accuse their wives, but have no witness except themselves, let the testimony of one of them be four testimonies by God that he is one of those who speak the truth. And the fifth (oath will be) that the curse of God be upon him if he should be among the liars" (Q. 24:6–7). These two verses consider an oath of the accusation of adultery between a couple (*liʿān*) as evidence to prove that the plaintiff's claim is genuine and that the defendant is innocent. In addition, there were many ways in which claims had been proven during the life of the Prophet. It is reported that the Prophet had used *qasāma* (a legal procedure in which 50 people were asked to take an oath), *qiyāfa* (a system to establish the parenthood of a child),[95] and *qurʿa*, (drawing lots) as means of evidence to prove cases.[96] This intuitively indicates that a claim can be proved by any just means of evidence, be it conclusive or circumstantial, depending on the enormity and gravity of the matter. Of course, there are many means of evidence drawn upon in our contemporary age (such as photography, autopsy, forensics, and DNA) whose efficacy is more reliable than personal testimony that might be based on falsehood. Maḥmaṣṣānī remarks that, because of the unreliability of eyewitnesses in their testimony, the Islamic legal system has been undermined.[97]

The argument here is not to undermine the orthodox proofs. However, it is possible to say that means of proof (*bayyina*) could be restricted to eyewitnesses in cases that involve criminal acts, and stand as conclusive evidence if the requirements are fulfilled and more specifically so in cases that are solely the right of God. However, in any other criminal case in which the right of man is sought to be protected, eyewitnesses would be primarily sought, but if efforts to secure them prove unsuccessful, circumstantial evidence (*bayyina ẓarfīya*) could be resorted to as a secondary means of proof.

Testimony: "What is Established by Convincing, Just Evidence is as What is Established by an Eyewitness" (*ath-thābit bi-l-burhān ka-th-thābit bi-l-ʿiyān*)[98]

Testimony or *shahāda* is one of the conclusive means of evidence that proves claims in general and criminal liability in particular. The legality of *shahāda*

---

95 Not all Muslim jurists accept this method of proof. See al-Sarakhsī, 17:70, for more on this issue.

96 Saʿid b. Darwish al-Zaharani, *Tarāʾiq al-Ḥukm al-Muttafaq ʿalayhā wa-l-Mukhtalaf fīhā fī sh-Sharīʿa al-Islāmiyya*, 2nd edn. (Jeddah: Maktabat al-Sahaba, 1994), 29.

97 Maḥmaṣṣānī, 176.

98 *Majalla*, Article 75; Haydar, 1:65; and A. al-Zarqāʾ, *Sharḥ al-Qawāʿid al-Fiqhiyya*, 367.

is based on the Qur'ān, Sunna and scholarly consensus (*ijmāʿ*).[99] It is reported that a man from Ḥaḍramawt and a man from the tribe of Kinda submitted a dispute to the Prophet, who said: "Your two witnesses or your oath" (*shahidāk aw yamīnihi*).[100] This Ḥadīth supports the universally accepted use of testimony from the era of the Prophet.[101] The word 'witness' has many connotations in the Arabic language, amongst which are viewing (*muʿāyana*);[102] presence (*ḥuḍūr*, as in Q. 2:185); knowledge (*ʿilm*, as in Q. 3:18); swearing (*ḥalf*, as in Q. 63:1); and information (*ikhbār*).[103] In short, *shahāda* is the giving of truthful information for the purpose of substantiating a legal right before a court of law.[104] The majority of Islamic scholars pay attention to the articulation of the phrase "I bear witness" (*ashhad*) while other scholars, including Abū Ḥanīfa, Mālik, and apparently Aḥmād Ibn Ḥanbal, Ibn Taymiyya, and Ibn al-Qayyim, amongst others, do not consider the articulation of any specific word necessary to convey testimony.[105]

It is generally considered obligatory to stand as a witness in litigation involving the claims of men, and also in criminal cases that involve the right of God. However, one is not morally or legally obliged to give testimony, especially in the case of sexual intercourse, where it is often thought commendable neither to report nor to provide witnesses in such cases involving the right of God; *i.e.*, to conceal (*satara*) a Muslim's defect is better than to expose him. This is based on the case of Mā'iz when the Prophet said to Huzal: "Why not condone/cover him with your garment?" (*hallā satartah bi-ridā'ik?*)[106] The right of man, on

---

99 Q. 2:282–283, Q. 4:135, and Q. 65:1–2.

100 al-Bukhārī, Ḥadīth No. 2380; and Muslim, Ḥadīth No. 138.

101 al-Ramalī, 8:292; and Ibn Qudāma, *al-Mughnī*, 9:120.

102 See Sābiq, 3:426.

103 Aḥmad Ibrāhīm, *Ṭuruq al-Ithbāt fī sh-Sharīʿa l-Islāmiyya* (Cairo: al-Maṭbaʿat as-Salafiyya, n.d.), 28; and al-Zaharani, 34.

104 Ibn al-Humām, *Fatḥ al-Qadīr*, 3:364; and Ibn Farhun, 1:164.

105 al-Kāsānī, 6:273; Ibn al-Humām, *Fatḥ al-Qadīr*, 7:375; al-Dasūqī, *Hāshiyat ad-Dasūqī ʿalā sh-Sharḥ al-Kabīr*, edited by Muḥammad ʿUlaysh (Beirut: Dār al-Fikr, n.d.), 4:165; Ibn Farhun, 1:209; Ibrāhīm b. ʿAbdullāh b. Abī al-Dam, *Adab al-Qaḍā'* (*al-Manẓūmāt fī l-Aqḍiyya wa-l-Ḥukūmāt*), edited by Muḥammad M. al-Ruḥaylī, (Damascus: Dār al-Fikr, n.d.), 383; Ibn Qudāma, *al-Mughnī*, 9:216; and Ibn al-Qayyim al-Jawziyya, *aṭ-Ṭuruq al-Ḥuqmiyya*, 272–273.

106 Aḥmad b. Ḥanbal al-Shaybanī, *al-Musnad* (Cairo: Mu'assasat Qurtuba, n.d.), Ḥadīth No. 21940; al-Bayhaqī, No. Ḥadīth 16735. See also, Ibn Farhun, 1:176; ʿIzz al-Din ʿAbd al-Salam, *Qawāʿid al-Aḥkām fī Maṣāliḥ al-Anām* (Beirut: Dār al-Kutub al-ʿIlmiyya, n.d.), 1:160; and al-Shinqitī, 8:297.

the other hand, must be retrieved from the accused in order to protect people's properties.[107]

General conditions which have some bearing on the acceptability of eyewitness testimony are puberty, sanity, liberty, sight, faculty of speech, probity, trustworthiness, vigilance, precision, memory, and Islam.[108] In addition, some scholars opine that a testimony should be proclaimed in the courtroom in a specific language, although this view is opposed by the Mālikīs and several Shāfiʿīs.[109]

However, in criminal cases, in order to establish certainty and to remove any bit of doubt, certain conditions are stipulated for the acceptance of witnesses, depending on the nature of the crime. One condition that is controversial and has attracted the attention of human rights' activists around the world is the gender of witnesses. The majority of classical Islamic scholars, including the Ḥanafīs, are of the opinion that, in the case of *ḥadd* and *qiṣāṣ* crimes, witnesses should be restricted to men.[110] They argue that the Qurʾānic verse that allows women to bear witness in financial cases reasons that two women are deemed equivalent to one man because of their forgetfulness.[111] Introducing the testimony of women would necessitate recognition of doubt (*shubha*); in this way, *ḥadd* and *qiṣāṣ* punishments could be revoked by any credible reason for doubt. Thus, to accept a woman's testimony in such cases would cast doubt on the plaintiff's claim and perhaps render it invalid. Another reason put forward to justify the rejection of female witness in *ḥudūd* and *qiṣāṣ* cases is that women do not normally attend gatherings where such crimes occur. Lastly, one may resort to hearing a woman's testimony as a last option when there are too few men who can bear witness.[112] Thus, if women are not allowed to bear witness in cases of *ḥudūd* and *qiṣāṣ* crimes, claims may well be rendered in vain.

However, Ibn Ḥazm al-Ẓāhirī and a host of other scholars accept the testimony of women in all, including *ḥudūd* and *qiṣāṣ*, cases, arguing that because the Qurʾān has accepted their testimony in financial cases, no difference should be drawn for criminal offences. In response to the first opinion, it is

107 Ibn Farhun, 1:165.

108 al-Kāsānī, 6:266; al-Qarāfī, *Anwār al-Burūq*, 4:97; Ibn Qudāma, *al-Mughnī*, 9:164–165; Ibn Taymiyya, *Majmūʿ al-Fatāwā*, 35:409; and Ibn Rushd, 2:452.

109 al-Dardir, *ash-Sharḥ al-Kabīr* 4:164–165.

110 Yūsuf Ibn ʿAbdullāh Ibn ʿAbd al-Barr, *al-Kāfī fī Fiqh Ahl al-Madīna* (Beirut: Dār al-Kutub al-ʿIlmiyya, 1987), 2:906; Ibn Rushd, 2:448; Ibn Qudāma, *al-Mughnī*, 9:222; Ibn al-Humām, 7:369–370; and Ibn Nujaym, *al-Baḥr ar-Rāʾiq*, 7:62.

111 Q. 2:282.

112 al-Kāsānī, 6:268 and 279; al-Dardir, *ash-Sharḥ al-Kabīr*, 4:185–189; Ibn ʿAbd al-Barr, *al-Kāfī*, 2:906; Ibn Rushd, 2:448; and Ibn Qudāma, *al-Mughnī*, 4:222.

argued that, since the Qurʾān has accepted women's testimonies in financial cases—despite the concern about *shubha*—the acceptance of their testimonies in other cases is undeniable. Moreover, the Qurʾān does not completely nullify the acceptability of women's testimony but rather stipulates certain conditions: namely, that two women testify in lieu of one man, which is also applicable in *ḥudūd* and *qiṣāṣ* cases. In the case of a woman who was reported to have committed adultery (*zinā*), the Prophet said that if she admitted to it, then *ḥadd* should be inflicted upon her for her sin.[113] If the Prophet accepted her confession as evidence in a *ḥudūd* crime, then other women's testimonies should also be admissible.

As regards the excuse that women do not normally witness *ḥadd* offences, one can argue that the absence of women in public gatherings where crimes might likely occur was an accurate feature of an age long past. The truth is that nowadays modern women are exposed to all facets of life and it would be short-sighted to ignore or refuse their testimony on incidents about which they might be knowledgeable. Moreover, to say that a woman's testimony is fraught with doubt, and therefore should be dismissed, is simply untenable in the modern age. There are women who are very intelligent, have excellent memories and would excel in giving evidence. Having said that, the reason why the majority of classical Islamic jurists refuse the testimony of women in *ḥudūd* and *qiṣaṣ* cases is not meant to degrade their status but rather to protect both the rights of the accuser and accused. Because punishment for *ḥudūd* and *qiṣaṣ* crimes can be revoked where there is room for credible doubt, and because women have been described as forgetful, any litigant could make use of the element of doubt as an excuse to jeopardize the rights of his opponent.

This discussion concludes that, if the punishment for a crime involves the right of God and if the standard of evidence required is high in order to erase any shadow of doubt, then a woman's testimony will not be allowed because, from an Islamic legal point of view, it might cause any evidence to appear dubious, which would abate the case. Thus justice allotted to either the plaintiff or the defendant might be unfavorably distorted. However, if the case involves the right of man and evidence is needed to establish that right, then recourse to a woman's testimony is paramount.[114]

The number of witnesses required in criminal cases differs according to each crime committed. The comparative gravity of the crime necessitates the

113 al-Bukhārī, Ḥadīth Nos. 2190 and 2549; and Muslim, Ḥadīths Nos. 1697 and 1698.

114 al-Marghinani, *al-Hidāya*, 7:33–96; see also Baderin, 102–103, for other ways of interpreting the text which equates two women to one man in witness.

number of witnesses required, which ranges from one to four depending on the nature of the case.

Four Witnesses

Generally, there is an agreement among Muslim scholars that four male witnesses are required for the offence of adultery/fornication (*zinā*), based on Qur'ānic verses 4:15, 24:4, 13, and the prophetic Sunna, where it is reported that the Prophet said: "Present four witnesses or you receive *ḥadd* punishment on your back".[115] Ibn Qudāma reports that Muslims are in consensus that fewer than four witnesses in the case of adultery is not acceptable.[116] This requirement is held in order to set a higher degree of certainty in such a crime. However, the question regarding the number of witnesses required to testify in an adultery case established by the offender's confession (*iqrār*) must be addressed. Abū Ḥanīfa, Ibn Ḥazm, several Mālikīs, Shāfiʿīs, and one version of Ḥanbalī thought, all approve of two witnesses, based on the generally agreed upon number of witnesses in confessions. However, other Ḥanbalī writings and several Mālikīs and Shāfiʿīs opine that four witnesses are also required for confession. They argue that, in the case of *zinā*, if confession must be uttered four times before it can be accepted, then, by analogy, witnesses to confession should number four. Moreover, if a *ḥadd* punishment cannot be executed without four confessions, then the court cannot pronounce a crime *ḥadd* unless there are four witnesses to that confession.[117]

Two Witnesses

The majority of Islamic jurists have included additional crimes such as the wine-drinking, theft, brigandage, highway robbery, armed rebellion, apostasy, and cases of murder that lead to *qiṣāṣ*, to the list of cases that can be proven by the testimonies of only two witnesses who have fulfilled the aforementioned general requirements. This is the opinion of the Ḥanafī, Mālikī, Shāfiʿī and Ḥanbalī Schools.[118]

---

115 See al-Ashʿath, Ḥadīth No. 2254.

116 Ibn Qudāma, *al-Mughnī*, 9:148; and Ibn al-Qayyim al-Jawziyya, *aṭ-Ṭuruq al-Ḥukmiyya*, 126.

117 Ibn al-Qayyim al-Jawziyya, *aṭ-Ṭuruq al-Ḥukmiyya*, 127.

118 al-Kāsānī, 7:33–96; Ibn al-Humām, *Fatḥ al-Qadīr*, 7:370–372; Imām Mālik Ibn Anas, *al-Mudawwana al-Kubrā* (Beirut: Dār Sadir, 1975), 16:443; al-Zarqānī, 4:178; al-Shāfiʿī, *Kitāb al-Umm*, 6:16–19; and Ibn Qudāma, *al-Mughnī*, 8:230–236. See also Ibn Nujaym, *al-Baḥr ar-Rāʾiq*, 7:62 and 66; Ibn Juzayy al-Kalbī, 298; Ibn al-Humām, *Fatḥ al-Qadīr*, 7:369–370; al-Shawkānī, *Nayl al-Awṭār*, 7:181–183; and al-Bahūtī, 6:434.

The admissibility of two witnesses is based on the Qurʾān and Ḥadīths. The Qurʾān says: "and get two witnesses among your own men".[119] It is also reported that the Prophet said to the plaintiff in two litigations: "Provide your two witnesses or you take an oath" (*shāhidāk aw yamīnihi*).[120] In this category, the admission of female witnesses is contentious, based on the lack of consensus among scholars on the legality and admissibility of a woman's testimony in *ḥudūd* and *qiṣāṣ* offences. Accordingly, those who would permit women to testify in any case suggest that two women would be accepted in lieu of one man, in line with the Qurʾānic verse 2:282 that states: "one man and two women" (*...fa-in lam yakunā rajlayni fa-rajulun wa-amraʾatān*).[121] It is reported that Aʿtā Ibn Rabah and Hammad Ibn Sulayman accepted three male and two female witnesses in a crime of adultery.[122] In the case of murder punishable by *qiṣāṣ*, Ibn Ḥazm of the Ẓāhirī School allows the testimony of two trustworthy Muslim men, or one Muslim man with two women, or four women, arguing that such flexibility in the composition of witnesses is also acceptable in cases of financial compensation.[123]

The fundamental question in this provision is: Why should two women equal one man? Is there, in fact, any equality of rights in legal procedures, as professed by Islam? The fact is that as Islam acknowledges the equality of men and women as human beings, and ensures its enshrinement in all facets of human life, it does not, as Baderin observes, "advocate absolute equality of roles between them".[124] Baderin further maintains that the equality of men and women is recognized in Islam on the principle of "equal, but not equivalent".[125] It is also argued that, except in the case of contractual matters, where Islamic Law requires two women in lieu of one man, there is no other section in the text in which this restriction is mentioned. This indicates that female witnesses should not be conditioned to the provision made in contractual matters. El-Bahnassawi submits the following:

119 Q. 2:282, *cf.*, Q. 5:106 and Q. 65:2.

120 al-Bukhārī, Ḥadīth No. 2380; Muslim, Ḥadīth No. 138; and on criminal liability, al-Nasaʾī, *as-Sunān*, Ḥadīth No. 5992; al-Bayhaqī, Ḥadīth No. 20995, both also on financial litigation.

121 Q. 2:282.

122 Ibn Qudāma, *al-Mughnī*, 8:198–199.

123 Ibn Ḥazm, *al-Muḥalla*, 11:143. This opinion is ascribed to al-Awzaʿī (d. 157 AH), Sufyān al-Thawrī (d. 161 AH), and ʿAtaʾ (d. 114 AH); see al-Shawkānī, *Nayl al-Awṭār*, 7:182; Ibn al-Qudāma, *al-Mughnī*, 8:97–98, Ibn Qayyim al-Jawziyya, *aṭ-Ṭuruq al-Ḥukmiyya*, 133.

124 Baderin, 60.

125 *Ibid.* A similar view is echoed in Muhammad Qutb, *Islam: The Misunderstood Religion* (Dacca: Adhunik Prokashani, 1978), 129; and in Ismail R. al-Faruqi and Lois Ibsen al-Faruqi, *The Cultural Atlas of Islam* (New York: Macmillan, 1986), 150.

> It should be borne in mind that Islam attributed this differentiation between the sexes to their respective natural disposition, though it had acknowledged their creation from the same origin and essence. It is not indicative of woman's inferiority but touches directly on people's interest and the safeguarding of justice.[126]

In general, women are allowed to stand as witnesses in cases that involve bodily injuries not punishable with *qiṣāṣ*. According to Mālikī doctrine, women can bear witness in cases of non-intentional homicide and intentional bodily injury because both only incur pecuniary compensation (*arsh*). As such, if women testify with men in crimes of *munaqqila* (an injury whereby a bone is displaced) and *ma'mūma* (a head wound reaching the cerebral membrane), their testimonies will be accepted because the outcome of the punishment of the two commissions, with regard to their being intentional (*'amd*) or unintentional (*khaṭa'*) acts, is the same.[127] Thus, one man and two women are accepted in such crimes with testimonies that include the plaintiff's exculpatory oath.[128]

One Witness with Oath

Generally, the minimum standard requires two witnesses. However, because of the demand that justice be established, scholars advocate for at least one witness coupled with his oath (the nature of which is discussed below). There are two differing opinions on whether this standard should be accepted in judicial procedure. Islamic jurists unanimously agree that one witness and his oath is not acceptable in any case that is strictly *ḥudūd*, as this involves the right of God. However, Mālikīs, Shāfi'īs and Ḥanbalīs accept one witness and his oath[129] based on the opinion of Ibn 'Abbās, in which it is reported that the Prophet adjudicated with one witness and his oath.[130] However, Ḥanafīs maintain that one witness and his oath is inadmissible in any case: namely, this possibility has never been stated in the Qur'ān and the authentic relevant Ḥadīth would require that the defendant rather than the plaintiff take an oath.[131] The Ḥanafī

126 Salim El-Bahnassawi, *Women Between Islam and World Legislation* (Kuwait: Dār al-Qalam, 1985), 132. See also Abdur Rahman Doi, *Woman in Shari'ah* (London: Ta-Ha Publishers, 1989); and Lamya al-Faruqi, *Women, Muslim Society and Islam* (Indianapolis: American Trust Publications, 1987).

127 Ibn 'Abd al-Barr, *al-Kāfī*, 2:906–911.

128 Ibn Rushd, 2:453; and al-Qarāfī, *Anwār al-Burūq*, 4:87–91.

129 Ibn Farhun, 1:215; al-Qarāfī, *Anwār al-Burūq*, 4:146; al-Shiribīnī, *Mughnī al-Muḥtāj*, 4:443; and Ibn Qudāma, *al-Mughnī*, 9:151.

130 Muslim, Ḥadīth No. 1712; al-Ash'ath, Ḥadīth No. 3610.

131 al-Kāsānī, 6:225.

stand on this issue is problematic, however, since there is a sound Ḥadīth that indicates that one witness coupled with his oath can be accepted. An *uṣūl* principle allows the merging of texts that are thought to contradict each other, which would not imply an abrogation of the law but rather making available extra evidence.[132] Al-Qarāfī and Ibn Farhun of the Mālikī School enumerate cases in which one witness and his oath can be admitted. Some such cases involve pecuniary claims including theft (*sariqa*), usurpation (*ghaṣb*), confession (*iqrār*), warrants or 'sureties' (*wakāla*) and retaliation for bodily injuries (*qiṣāṣ*).[133]

An oath is of a simple nature and can be used in five situations. It offers one way to settle disputes between litigant parties and derives its legality from various Qur'ānic verses such as Q. 5:89 and Q. 2:77 and from prophetic Ḥadīths. For example, Ibn 'Abbās narrates that the Prophet stated: "If all people have given their claim [without evidence], some people might have claimed other people's properties, but the oath is on the defendant".[134] The five situations in which an oath can be applied are as follows:

1. as a defense for the accused in cases where the plaintiff has no evidence (*i.e.*, no witnesses);
2. to rectify claims (*da'wā*), as in an oath taken by the plaintiff with one or two male or two female witnesses;
3. by the plaintiff after the refusal (*nukūl*) of the defendant;
4. by the plaintiff after the presentation of all the evidence in order to finalize the judgment; and
5. by the defendant who has only circumstantial (*lawth*) rather than conclusive evidence, in a process called *qasāma*.[135]

The following can be said with regard to the first three conditions.

(1) Scholars have agreed unanimously upon the validity of the use of an oath in the first situation.

(2) The majority of Islamic jurists have debated the second procedure and support it in some matters, while the Ḥanafīs reject it, arguing that the Ḥadīth supporting its legality is weak.[136] However, the majority of scholars assert that

132 al-Amidi, 4:175.

133 al-Qarāfī, *Anwār al-Burūq*, 4:90; and Ibn Farhun, 1:215.

134 al-Bukhārī, Ḥadīth No. 2477.

135 Ibn Farhun, 1:147; and al-Zahrānī, 192.

136 al-Shawkānī, *Nayl al-Awṭār*, 9:191.

the Ḥadīth of Ibn ʿAbbās mentioned above that narrates the Prophet's judgment on one witness and his oath (of the plaintiff) is authentic, does not invalidate the normal procedure, but offers an additional way of establishing facts.[137]

(3) There is also contention between the majority of Islamic scholars and the Ḥanafīs regarding the third use of an oath; while it is sanctioned by the majority of scholars, the Ḥanafīs disallow it based on their argument for the second procedure mentioned above.[138] However, this procedure is only applicable in matters with testimony that clearly involve the right of man.

(4) After a long ongoing debate regarding the legality of taking an oath under the fourth situation, *i.e.*, by the plaintiff after he has presented two witnesses, jurists have concluded that this system is totally unacceptable for *ḥudūd* crimes that involve the absolute right of God. Therefore, in such cases, neither the plaintiff nor the defendant should be asked to take an oath.[139] However, a plaintiff would be asked to take an oath if there were any suspicious circumstances surrounding a claim involving the right of man: namely, if someone provides false evidence to substantiate his claim that property was stolen. It is reported that ʿAlī Ibn Abī Ṭālib asked a plaintiff to swear an oath beside his two witnesses. When the plaintiff refused, ʿAlī said: "I will not adjudicate to you for which you do not take an oath".[140] It is reported that Judge Shurayh asked a plaintiff to take an oath due to the dissemination of an allegation. When asked on what basis he had innovated such a procedure, the judge replied that he had to contrive new means for obtaining evidence for novel problems created by man.[141] Ibn Qayyim al-Jawziyya remarks that this procedure is not too dissimilar from the precept or spirit of the Sharīʿa, particularly in the case of probability of indictment.[142] However, no scholar will approve of such a procedure in cases, such as adultery and consumption of alcohol, involving *ḥudūd* or *qiṣāṣ* crimes, especially when the absolute right of God is involved. If someone retracts his confession, he will neither be punished nor asked to take an oath. Therefore, in cases where there is no confession, it would be preferable not to

137 *Ibid.*, 9:195; and Ibn Farhun, 1:215.

138 al-Shāfiʿī, *Kitāb al-Umm*, 6:241; Ibn Farhun, 1:154–155; and Ibn Qudāma, *al-Mughnī*, 9:235.

139 Ibn Qudāma, *al-Mughnī*, 9:238; al-Kāsānī, 6:226; al-Ghazālī, *al-Wajīz fī Fiqh ash-Shāfʿī*, 2:159; and Ibn Farhun, 1:157.

140 Ibn al-Qayyim al-Jawziyya, *aṭ-Ṭuruq al-Ḥukmiyya*, 113.

141 *Ibid.*

142 *Ibid.*

seek an oath,[143] except in monetary disputes where scholars disagree on an oath's legality.[144]

(5) The fifth situation involves *qasāma*, a method of proof also known during the era before the advent of Islam (*Jāhiliyya*). It is a process that necessitates the taking of multiple oaths to substantiate or refute claims of homicide that corroborate with circumstantial evidence (*bayyina ẓarfīya*).[145] In Islamic Law, the legitimacy of this practice rests on the authority of a Ḥadīth in which Sahl Ibn Abī Hathma narrates that the Prophet applied *qasāma* in the case of Huwaisa.[146] The Prophet said to the victim's relatives who accused their enemies of murder: "Would you take an oath that entitles you to the blood of your fellow?"[147] With some exceptions,[148] the majority of Islamic jurists, including the Ḥanafīs, Mālikīs, Shāfi'īs and Ḥanbalīs, approve the legality of this procedure in cases of murder where evidence is only circumstantial.[149] Antagonists contend that this procedure contradicts the well-established norms of the Islamic legal system that require a plaintiff to give evidence. They argue that *qasāma* is neither admissible nor equivalent to evidence that is required to prove a claim.[150] However, it can be said that *qasāma* does not provide conclusive evidence, and, although the Prophet used the process to adjudicate a case, it may not, in actuality, be an additional means of adjudication in Islamic Law. Furthermore, one cannot rule on a claim of homicide solely by means of *qasāma*, except in the case of *lawth* (*i.e.*, suspicious circumstantial evidence that questions whether the case is *bona fide*). Conversely, if *qasāma* proves effective in establishing justice between litigants—especially in matters involving the right of man—then there is no doubt that it is in the spirit of Islam to accept such a system.

---

143 Ibn Qudāma, *al-Mughnī*, 9:238.

144 *Ibid.*; and al-Zahrānī, 205.

145 al-'Asqalānī, *Fatḥ al-Bārī*, 7:156.

146 The Ḥadīth is famous as "Ḥadīth al-Huwayyisa and Muhayyisa" in which it is reported that two Anṣār (Muḥammad's patrons in Madina) were on their way to Khaybar. One of them, 'Abdullāh ibn Sahl, was killed by an unknown murderer. Muhayyisa claimed that the Jews were the murderers. See the full analysis of this story in Rudolph Peters, "Murder in Khaybar: Some Thoughts on the Origins of Qasāma Procedure in Islamic Law", *Islamic Law and Society*, 9/2 (2002).

147 al-Bukhārī, Ḥadīth No. 7192.

148 al-Shawkānī, *Nayl al-Awṭār*, 7:186.

149 al-Kāsānī, 7:286; Ibn Anas, 5:186–187; al-Shiribīnī, *Mughnī al-Muḥtāj*, 4:101; and al-Bahūtī, 6:74.

150 al-Zahrānī, 218.

The normal legal procedure before a judge is that the defendant must first prove that his case is genuine, while the accused is responsible for damages, according to the maxim "The burden of proof is on the claimant and the oath is on the one who denies" (*al-bayyina ʿalā l-muddaʿī wa-l-yamīn ʿalā man ankar*). However, if the accused denies all the charges, then he must take an oath to exculpate himself. However, certain circumstances will affect changes in the procedural *qasāma* system: *e.g.*, when a defendant refuses to take an oath, or when a plaintiff has no proof but only suspicions based on facts. For example, one can speak of *qasāma fī dimāʾ* (blood) when someone is found dead in the company of a hostile group of people, although no one is placed under arrest, or *qasāma fī l-amwāl* (financial, property) when armed robbers storm a house in the presence of witnesses who, however, fail to observe what was actually looted. Ibn Qayyim al-Jawziyya argues for the legality of the latter. Thus, if *qasāma* can help establish a homicide in the case of circumstantial evidence, then, it should also become an accepted means of proof for situations resembling the latter case, which is even more conclusive because witnesses can at least report the commission of an offence, although they have forgotten some details. Here, any means can be applied to substantiate whether the claim is genuine.[151]

Confession: "Confession [of Guilt] is Binding Proof Only on the Confessor" (*al-iqrār ḥujja qāṣira*),[152] and "One is Responsible for his Confession" (*al-marʾ muʾākhadh bi-iqrārihi*)[153]

Confession is one of the *prima facie* means to establish the liability of a criminal act, especially if the crime is for disclosure. In fact, it is believed to be the ultimate evidence for guilt.[154] A culprit is said to be innocent until proven guilty, beyond any reasonable doubt, of the alleged crime, *actori incumbit onus probandi*.[155] However, Islamic Law enacts the legality of confession in order to establish justice while, at the same time, balancing the rights of the defendant and offender. There are many cases in which evidence can be somewhat difficult or impossible to attainable. Such cases could involve both the rights of

151 Ibn al-Qayyim al-Jawziyya, *aṭ-Ṭuruq al-Ḥukmiyya*, 110–112.

152 Ibn Nujaym, *al-Ashbāh wa-n-Naẓāʾir*, 255; al-Sarakhsī, 4:225–226; *Majalla*, Article 78; and M. al-Zarqāʾ, *al-Madkhal*, 667.

153 *Majalla*, Article 79; Haydar, 1:70; al-ʿAsqalānī, *Fatḥ al-Bārī*, 8:476; A. al-Zarqāʾ, *Sharḥ*, 401; and similar codification in al-Suyūṭī, *al-Ashbāh*, 464.

154 Peter Mirfield, *Confessions* (London: Sweet and Maxwell, 1985), 49.

155 Islamic Law emphasizes this principle under the doctrine of *istiṣḥāb* (presumption of continuity). See Kamali, *Principles*, 297–309; and Baderin, 103.

God and man. When the right of God (*ḥaqq Allāh*) is concerned, confession may not be commendable as the right of God is based on forgiveness and pardon. However, when the right of man (*ḥaqq al-ādamī*) is involved, confession is seen as paramount and an indispensable means of proof, especially where evidence is deadlocked. Making a confession binds the confessor to his statement which can be retracted only when the absolute right of God is involved, such as in claims of adultery and consumption of alcohol, or when partly the rights of God and man are concerned, such as in claims of theft. Thus, the above-stated sub-maxims indicate that one is held legally responsible for one's confession and that confession stands as legally effective evidence that cannot be refuted in the rule of law.

The legality of confession is based on the Qur'ān,[156] Ḥadīth, scholarly consensus (*ijmāʿ*), and analogy (*qiyās*). It is reported that Mā'iz and Ghamidi confessed their adultery to the Prophet and punishments were inflicted on them on the basis of their confession.[157] There is no disagreement among Islamic scholars on the general acceptability and legality of confession. By analogy (*qiyās*), if witnesses can be accepted, then confession is yet more acceptable and reliable than a witness. It would be irrational (*ghayr maʿqūl*) for someone to confess and incriminate himself when knowing the severe consequence of that confession.[158] To eliminate any benefit of doubt and safeguard the validity of confession, Islam stipulates several conditions: namely, the confessor must have reached puberty, be sane, and of sound mind. Thus the confession of a minor, an insane person or someone who has been coerced is invalid. Moreover, the confessor must not be under suspicion and his statement of confession must be explicit. If someone confesses to adultery, the legal terms referring to adultery must be employed, such as "I had sexual intercourse with her" as opposed to "I slept with her," or, in the case of theft, "I stole the property of a certain person"[159] as opposed to "I took the property".

---

156 Q. 3:81, Q. 4:135, and Q. 9:102.

157 See note on the Ḥadīth of Mā'iz and Ghāmidī in Muḥammad b. ʿAbdullāh al-Naysābūrī, *al-Mustadrak ʿalā ṣ-Ṣaḥīḥayn*, edited by Muṣṭafā A. ʿAta (Beirut: Dār al-Kutub al-ʿIlmiyya, 1990), Ḥadīth No. 8077, 4:402.

158 al-Burnu, *Mawsūʿat al-Qawāʿid*, 2:227.

159 Ibn Qudāma, *al-Mughnī*, 5:149; al-Kāsānī, 7:222; al-Shiribīnī, *Muhgnī al-Muḥtāj*, 2:245; Aḥmad b. Muḥammad al-Sawī, *Bulghat as-Sālik li-Aqrab al-Masālik* (Cairo: Maktabat al-Bāb al-Ḥalabī, 1952), 2:176; al-Dardir, 3:397; ʿAbd al-Karīm Zaydān, *Niẓām al-Qaḍā' fī sh-Sharīʿa l-Islāmiyya* (Baghdad: Maṭbaʿat l-ʿAni, 1404/1983), 157; and al-Qayyim al-Jawziyya, *aṭ-Ṭuruq al-Ḥukmiyya*, 173.

Confession is defined linguistically and technically as a piece of information given by a person to state his involvement in an alleged offence.[160] This definition comprehends a civil right and criminal liability. By stating involvement in the offensive act, that person indicates he is liable for the consequence of the offence. By stating that a person's right is in his own hands indicates the liability to return the property. The nature of this evidence is the utmost proof possible before a court of law. However, many maxims related to confession have been discussed from varying points of view in different jurisprudence books, all of which could be summarized under a few headings.

As confession stands as evidence and a way of testimony in a court of law, it is assumed that the confessor is being truthful with regard to what actually happened. For that reason, he is bound by his own admission that is not transferable to any other accused. Take, for example, two or more people who are being accused of murder. At first all deny the charges; then later one of the accused comes forward, without any duress or coercion, and confesses his involvement in the crime, saying that the offence was actually committed by him and some other people. In such a case, his confession would be taken on his own account, so that the other co-accused would not be convicted by that confession until some other proof emerged to establish their involvement. However, if the offence is adultery, and he confesses his mutual involvement in it, he would be punished for both adultery/fornication (*zinā*) and defamation (*qadhf*) if at a later time his incrimination of the other individuals was proven untrue.

Condition Binding Acceptability of Confession: "Coercion Prevents the Validity of Confession" (al-ikrāh yamnaʿ ṣiḥḥat al-iqrār)[161]

It is generally acceptable that an honest confession (*iqrār*), made without force or under any other unusual condition, shall be accepted. However, the question arises about whether a confession made under coercion (*ikrāh*) or any other means of compulsion should be acceptable as proof in court. The opinions of scholars differ. The majority of jurists hold the view that confession should be made voluntarily, and any confession subject to coercion, duress

---

160 Muḥammad al-Rāzī, *Mukhtaṣar aṣ-Ṣiḥāḥ*, 529; al-Fayumī, *al-Miṣbāḥ al-Munīr*, 2:681; Muḥammad b. Yaʿqub al-Fayruzabādī, *al-Qāmūs al-Muḥīṭ* (Beirut: Mu'assasat ar-Risāla, 2005), 593; Ibn Farhun, 2:53, *cf.*, with English definitions of confession, see Fred Kaufman, *The Admissibility of Confession*, 3rd edn. (Toronto: Carswell Company, 1979), 4–5.

161 al-Sarakhsī, 24:83.

or other conditional forces is invalid.[162] This opinion is based on the Qur'ān, Ḥadīth, and analogy (*qiyās*).

In the Qur'ān God says: "Except under compulsion his heart remains firm in faith".[163] In his commentary, al-Shiribīnī canvasses that if an utterance made under compulsion is not regarded as the nullification of one's faith, then the same should be applied to confession made under coercion.[164] God also calls Muslims to testify, even if it is against yourselves: "Ye who believe! Stand firmly for justice, as witness to God even as against yourselves".[165] The words used in the verse 'witness [...] against yourselves' refer to confession. It is unanimously agreed upon among scholars that any false witness is unacceptable in establishing fact; thus a confession made under duress should not be taken under consideration as it could be false.[166]

In a Ḥadīth the Prophet says that "God will ignore what men think in their minds to do until they do it or talk about it, and also He will leave out of the reckoning man's acts under compulsion".[167] This Ḥadīth categorically dismisses any act committed out of compulsion. Thus, any confession made under duress shall not be accepted. From a logical perspective, confession is regarded as one of the valid forms of evidence that should not contain errors, if it is based on the natural will of the confessor. However, if coercion is a factor, there is a probability that the confessor might lie, which will not serve the purpose for which confession was intended.

However, a few jurists hold the view that confession should always be accepted. This is based on the fact that the woman whom Ḥāṭib bin Abī Balta'a sent to the pagans of Makkah with a letter was compelled and forced to produce the letter after her denial.[168] Against this latter opinion, it could be argued that the evidence that the woman carried a letter was a divine revelation from God to His messenger.

As already discussed in some detail above, in the Nigerian case concerning Safiyyatu, the first procedural error that led to her confession was that someone reported the occurrence to the police without including correct details, although concealment is recommended in such cases. The Court accepted the appellant's admission/confession without giving her the right of defense

162 Peters, *Crime and Punishment*, 9.

163 Q. 16:106.

164 al-Shiribīnī, *Mughnī al-Muḥtāj*, 2:240–241.

165 Q. 4:134.

166 al-Kāsānī, 7:223. See also, Fred E. Inbau and John E. Reid, *Criminal Interrogation and Confessions* (Baltimore: Williams and Wilkins, 1967), 143.

167 Ibn Mājah, Ḥadīth No. 2043; *cf.*, al-Bukhārī, Ḥadīth No. 4968.

168 al-Bukhari, Sahih, Hadith no. 6259; Muslim, Sahih, Hadith no. 2494.

or having witnesses present during the confession. The confession should not have been admissible by law as Safiyyatu claimed that she did not understand the charge against her. Moreover, if someone confesses to adultery, benefit of the doubt should be given, which did not occur in the case of Safiyyatu. Ibn 'Umar narrated that Prophet Muḥammad said: "Avoid these filthy things which God has forbidden, and if anyone commits any of them, he should conceal himself with God's most High Veil and turn to God in repentance".[169] Thus, interrogating someone about the crime of adultery is questionable because, during the Prophet's life, all adultery offences were punishable based on voluntary confession rather than on enforcement or imposition. It is reported on the authority of 'Imrān Ibn Ḥusain that a woman of the Juhaina tribe came to the Prophet when she was pregnant as a result of fornication, and said: "O God's messenger, I have committed something for which a prescribed punishment is due, so execute it on me". God's messenger called her guardian and said, "Treat her well and when she delivers, bring her to me". It is also reported in the Ḥadīth reported by Abū Hurayra that a man among a group of Muslims came to the Prophet in the mosque and called, "O God's messenger, I have committed adultery". The Prophet turned away from him. The man confessed to that four times and when four people witnessed his claim, the Prophet asked him, "Are you insane?" The man replied, "No," and then the Prophet asked him, "Have you been married before?" He replied, "Yes," and then the Prophet ordered him to be stoned.[170] From the two traditions, it is clear that, in such situations, it is the right of the confessor to be given the benefit of the doubt and it is the responsibility of the judge not to admit the confession in the first instance.

Retraction of Confession: "Retraction of Confession in Matter that involves Right of Man is not Allowed." (al-iqrār fī ḥuqūq al-ʿibād lā yaḥtamil ar-rujūʿ)[171]

Retraction of a confession is one of the interesting issues deliberated under the rule of confession in Islamic criminal law. It emphasizes the importance of establishing criminal justice in Islam to protect the rights of victims while, at the same time, preventing enforcement of a severe punishment on an innocent accused. In the realm of confession and its retraction, it is of fundament importance to identify the nature of the crime and the punishment accorded

169 al-ʿAsqalānī, *Bulūgh al-Marām*, Ḥadīth No. 1048.

170 al-Bukhārī, Ḥadīth No. 6747; and Muslim, Ḥadīth No. 1691.

171 al-Kāsānī, 7:209.

to it. Doing so will facilitate deciding whether retraction is or is not allowed, and, if so, then under what conditions.

By looking into the nature of the liability involved, crimes can be classified into three categories.

1. Crimes that only violate the right of man (*ḥaqq al-ādamī*), *e.g.*, as in murder (*qatl*). This kind of crime means that the victim or his relatives may pardon the culprit, and this pardon will be efficacious. Here the jurists unanimously agree that once a confession is made in such a sensitive case, the culprit has no right to retraction. Of course, if the confession is made through his own free will without any force and all requirements are met, thus, retraction is ineffective. This is because, if it were to be allowed, there would be a prejudice against the people's [the victim or his relatives] rights and justice would not be established.[172] For example, if someone confessed that he had killed someone and later retracted his confession, his retraction would not be heard because of the right of the individuals involved and the acceptability of retraction in such a situation would jeopardize criminal liability.
2. Crimes that only violate the right of God (*ḥaqq Allāh*), such as adultery (*zinā*) and intoxication (*shurb al-khamr*). There is disagreement among scholars on the acceptability of retraction in this category. Most scholars approve retraction of confession if the crimes only involve the violation of the right of God. They argue that when Mā'iz ibn Mālik came to the Prophet confessing his commission of adultery, the Prophet said to him: "Probably you only kissed [the woman] or winked or looked at her!" He replied, "No, O God's apostle!"[173] It can be inferred from the Prophet's question that he meant to give Mā'iz a chance to retract his confession.[174] When Mā'iz fled, was apprehended and then stoned to death, the Prophet was heard to say: "Why didn't you leave him? Perhaps he may repent and God will forgive him".[175] This comment from the Prophet denotes that repentance made after a confession also stands as a retraction. Because a retracted confession is a piece of information that involves both truth

172 *Ibid.*, 7:61; al-Ramalī, 7:431; Ibn Qudāma, *al-Mughnī*, 5:288; and al-Sarakhsī, 17:189.

173 al-Naysābūrī, Ḥadīth No. 8077, 4:402.

174 al-Kāsānī, 7:233; and al-Shiribīnī, *Mughnī al-Muḥtāj*, 4:150.

175 al-Nasa'ī, *as-Sunān*, Ḥadīth No. 7207; 'Abdullāh b. 'Abd al-Raḥman al-Dārimī, *al-Sunān*, edited by Fawwaz Aḥmad Zamalī and Khalīl al-Saba' al-'Alamī, (Beirut: Dār al-Kitāb al-'Arabī, 1407/1986), Ḥadīth No. 2318.

and falsehood, the contradiction raises doubt, and the principle is to avert a *ḥadd* punishment if doubt exists.[176] Ibn ʿAbd al-Barr reports that there is consensus among Islamic jurists on the invalidity of a confession or testimony that has been retracted in any *ḥadd* punishment.[177]

Another opinion of other scholars claims that when a crime only involves the violation of the right of God, then retraction is not accepted. They claim that if retraction is allowed, the Companion must have been ordered by the Prophet to pay *diya* compensation for the killing of Māʾiz. Thus, the absence of such judgment indicates that retracting a confession is not acceptable.[178] It is also reported by Abū Hurayra that a father accused a woman of committing adultery with his son. The Prophet said to Unays: "O Unays, go to this woman in the morning and if she makes a confession then stone her".[179] It is canvassed that if a retraction is accepted the Prophet must have explained that to Unays, as there is probability that the woman might want to retract her confession. If retraction is not allowed in crimes involving the right of man, then logically it should not be allowed in the crimes involving the right of God.[180]

However, it can be said that the argument for the latter opinion is by no means unacceptable, as in the first claim the Prophet must have asked them to pay *diya* compensation. However, the Prophet did not ask them because Māʾiz had not made clear his retraction and, as such, we cannot assume that his escape from punishment denotes his retraction. In the second claim, there is a probability that the Prophet did not tell him about the retraction as he might have known all the conditions relating to confession, including that of retraction. The last claim can be rebutted on the basis that the two rights are very different in principle. The right of God is based on forgiveness and remission, while the right of man is based on contention. Therefore, in the former case, one can escape punishment by means of repentance and forgiveness from God, while, in the latter case, an effort must be made to balance justice. Furthermore, one is not obliged to confess to any crime involving the right of God, as opposed

176 al-Sarakhsī, 9:49; al-Bahūtī, 6:85; and Ibn al-Humām, *Fatḥ al-Qadīr*, 5:408.

177 Yūsuf Ibn ʿAbdullāh Ibn ʿAbd al-Barr, *al-Istidhkār*, edited by Salim M. ʿAta, (Beirut: Dār al-Kutub al-ʿIlmiyya, 2000), 7:503.

178 Ibn Qudāma, *al-Mughnī*, 10:167.

179 al-Bukhārī, Ḥadīth No. 2190; and Muslim, Ḥadīth No. 1697.

180 al-Sarakhsī, 49.

to the right of man. However, to confess voluntarily to a crime that involves the right of man is highly recommended.[181]

In the case of Safiyyatu, it is argued that she should have been acquitted on the grounds that she retracted her confession. However, her retraction is said to have been made not by herself but by her legal representative, a fact that undermined her retraction. Moreover, the State counsel incorrectly argued that the retraction of a confession can only be made in the case of *qiṣāṣ*, according to Sections 166 and 188, (1), (2) of the SCPC. According to the above maxim, retraction is unacceptable in cases that involve the right of man; however, the case in question (fornication) involves the absolute right of God.

3. Crimes that violate both the rights of God and man. Due to disagreement on the legality of retracting confession in the category discussed above, there is a slight discrepancy as to whether retraction is allowed in crimes involving both the rights of God and man, which can be summarized as follows.

   If retraction is made in a crime involving both rights, the *ḥadd* punishment should be dropped because doubt (*shubha*) is embedded in it. But the right of man should be reclaimed from the confessor if it can be established that his confession was made when he was of sound mind, and that the confession was not extracted under duress. However, if an accusation of unchasteness is the crime, retraction stands as the reclamation of the accused's reputation and as a kind of *taʿzīr* punishment that can be accorded to the proclaimer of the defamation.[182]

Another important issue to round off the discussion on confession is that the effect of confession is only binding on the confessor. This means that if someone confesses to his own involvement as well as to that of another person, the effect would rest on the shoulders of the confessor alone, and not the co-accused. Evidence must stem from a confession made voluntarily, which obviously is not the case for the co-accused. Such would be the case for someone admitting to murder while claiming that another person was also involved. The consequence of his confession would only affect him alone, but not be forced upon the alleged co-accused, although the co-accused might be found guilty based on another source of evidence.[183]

---

181 al-Māwardī, ʿAlī b. Muḥammad, *al-Ḥāwī al-Kabīr* (Beirut: Dār al-Kutub al-ʿIlmiyya, 1999/1419) 13:210–211.

182 Ibrāhīm Muḥammad Ibn Mufliḥ, *al-Mubdiʿ Sharḥ al-Muqniʿ* (Beirut: Dār al-Maktab al-Islāmī, 1400/1979), 10:368; and al-Kāsānī, 7:232–234.

183 See Muhammad Waqar-ul-Haqq, *Islamic Criminal Laws* (*Hudood Laws & Rules with Up-to-Date Commentary*) (Lahore: Nadeem Law Book House, 1994), 152; and al-Burnu, *Mawsūʿat al-Qawāʿid*, 1:233.

This maxim (*i.e.*, "Retraction of Confession in Matter that involves Right of Man is not Allowed.") has been observed in the case of Safiyyatu and her co-accused, Yakubu Abubakar, in which the Upper Sharīʿa Court of Sokoto State of Nigeria turned down the alleged accusation of Safiyyatu that Yakubu was the one who impregnated her. Thus Yakubu was acquitted.[184] Although it could be argued that, since Safiyyatu (the prime accused) implicated another party in the same accusation, the authorities has the right to summon the co-accused and investigate the allegation thoroughly. Indeed, although the court did summon Yakubu regarding this allegation, which he denied, there is no doubt that the authorities failed to carry out a sufficiently thorough investigation not to convict Yakub but to find way of acquittal for the accused person (Safiyyatu).

Another way to approach the case to balance the equation is to regard the matter as involving doubt (*shubha*) which thus provides an opportunity to avert *ḥadd* punishment. As pointed out earlier, the crime of adultery by nature cannot be committed by one individual. This is one reason why the Qurʾān mentions both genders when prescribing the punishment, although it can be said that, during the Prophet's lifetime, a confessor of adultery was punished on his own accord without questioning his co-accused, which indicates that one individual can be punished for adultery. Of course, Māʿiz and al-Ghamidi were punished separately, and the Prophet need not question them individually as each had already voluntarily confessed and did not allege that anyone else was involved. Thus, their cases are quite different from that of Safiyyatu and Yakubu.

General Application of the Grand Maxim *al-Yaqīn lā Yazūl bi-sh-Shakk* and its Subsidiaries in Several Northern Nigerian Sharīʿa Criminal Law Cases

The implications of doubt, *shakk* and *shubah*, can be found in many discussions on criminal penalties and liabilities in Islamic literature. Although the approach of each School in applying a maxim may differ, some aspects are common to all. In the case of defamation (*qadhf*), for example, if a woman is falsely accused of being unchaste and denies the accusation but then refuses to take an oath before the court, she will not receive the prescribed *ḥadd*

184 Women's Aid Collective, *Safiyyatu's Case*, trans. Ibrahim Ladan (Enugu, Nigeria: Women's Aid Collective, 2003).

punishment for such a crime because the fundamental principle is the innocence of the accused.[185]

In the case of *Shalla and others v. State*, the accused persons were found guilty of murdering Abudullahi Alhaji Umaru, merely based on information that their victim had insulted the Prophet. The appellants (Shalla *et al.*), who lodged the appeal against the decision of the High Court of Kebbi State, had themselves not actually heard the alleged insults that the victim was supposed to have said against the Holy Prophet. In other words, it was uncertain what the appellants considered to be defamation of the Prophet before they assailed and murdered the man.[186] To emphasize the importance of certainty in Islamic criminal law, the learned Judges in the above case affirmed that:

> It is also a settled law that a provocative act or utterance offered or reported by one person cannot be a ground or jurisdiction (justification) for killing a third party (or person) who neither offered the act nor was heard to have uttered the alleged words against the accused person.[187]

Of course, it is a principle in Islamic Law that information spread against someone must be ascertained before legal action can be taken against him.[188]

If a group, rather than one person, steals someone's property, doubt (*shubha*) will nullify the call for a *ḥadd* punishment. In such cases, if each member of the group received a *ḥadd* punishment, an injustice would occur. If the value of the stolen property were shared equally among the thieves, each share would be less than the minimum value (*niṣāb*) of stolen property that is adjudged to attract *ḥadd* under the law. If one of the thieves were punished, then he would be a victim of injustice. This is the majority opinion, supported by Ibn Qudamah of the Ḥanbalī School, while other Ḥanbalīs hold the view that each thief should be punished with *ḥadd*.[189]

In most cases of theft (*sariqa*) judged under full implementation of the Sharīʿa in the Northern States of Nigeria, there was no uncertainty regarding the minimum value (*niṣāb*) for theft before the courts called for amputation of the culprits' hands. Take, for instance, the case of *Hashimu Galadima Maberaya* [complainant] *v. Abdul-Rahman Isahaka and two others* [defendants]. Here the total value of the goods the accused individuals allegedly stole

185 Ibn Qudamah, *al-Mughni*, 12:409.
186 Weekly Law Report of Nigeria, 30 August 2004, 47.
187 *Ibid.*, 51.
188 Quran 49:6.
189 Ibn Qudamah, *al-Mughnī; Ibid.*, 12:468.

was 12,328 Naira, which is equivalent to US$102. The value of gold at that time was $862.15, ¼ of which equaled $215.53. The exchange rate was $1 = N120. Thus the *niṣāb* for which one can be convicted of theft under Islamic Law would then be $215.53 × N120 = 25,863 Naira and 6 kobo. This calculation demonstrates that the total value of the stolen goods had not reached the *niṣāb* for one individual, much less for two individuals if the amount were to be divided. Moreover, the accused were imprisoned between 20 February and 6 July 2002 before their hands were subsequently amputated. Indeed, if doubt (*shubha*) had been taken into account and the value of the stolen goods thoroughly investigated, the hands of the accused might have been spared.[190]

In contrast, the case of *Jamilu Isaka* [complainant] *v. Abukakar Abdullahi Kaura* [defendant][191] reveals that showing the investigating officers where the stolen property was hidden away and then retrieving it constitutes an element of certainty that the accused person indeed intentionally committed the act of theft which is punishable under Islamic Law by amputation. However, what has not been ascertained in this case is whether the accused was tortured before his confession.

Undoubtedly a criminal investigation is necessary in this case because it involves the right of man. However, if the stolen goods are returned, is it still necessary to carry out the prescribed punishment? It could be said that all provisos for convicting the accused have been fulfilled: *i.e.*, the stolen goods were recovered from where the accused had hidden them, photographs were taken while the goods were being retrieved, two police officers testified to his confession during interrogation, and the *niṣāb* of the stolen property was N30,350, or equivalent to $252.91667. Thus, the judges convicted the accused person and his co-offender under the provision of Section 144 punishable under Section 145 of Zamfara State Sharīʿa Penal Code 1999 (ZSSPC 1999).

In the case of *Attorney General* (*Zamfara State*) *v. Surajo Mohammed,* there are similar flaws of irregularity, not only related to a disregard for the requirement of *niṣāb* but also for procedural error. Surajo Mohammed was accused of stealing a she-goat valued at only N2,200 by the first assessor and at only N1,800 by the second assessor.[192] The decision of the Upper Sharīʿa Court (USC) of

---

190 See for the details of the case, Zakariyah, *Applications of Legal Maxims*, Appendix 7. The same argument is observed in *Attorney General* (*Zamfara State*) *v. Ibrahim Suleiman.* The accused person is convicted of theft under Section 144 punishable under Section 145 of ZSSPC 1999. The total value reported to have been stolen was N21,000 equivalent to US$175, while the *niṣāb* was estimated as US$215.53.

191 See for the details of the case, Zakariyah, *Applications of Legal Maxims*, Appendix 2.

192 *Ibid.*, Appendix 4.

Gusau Zamfara State of Nigeria was taken to the Court of Appeals where it was learnt that the appellant was suffering from a mental ailment. In addition, his lawyer observed that criminal procedures were violated during his cross-examination. The counsel for the appellant submitted that the USC erred in law for not producing a witness for the statement of confession upon which the conviction was based. However, the respondent counsel rebuked the submission on the grounds that witness to confession only applied to civil not criminal matters as stated in the Mālikī Book of Islamic Jurisprudence.

Since the conviction was based only on a statement of confession, considered non-compliant with the rule of justice, one could suggest that the appeal should be granted in accordance with the traditional statement which thus states: "you should avoid executing judgement if there exists doubt no matter how minute".[193] Thanks to the Hons. Qāḍīs of the Sharīʿa Court of Appeal Gusau, Zamfara State, who vividly studied the argument of each party, concluded that there were irregularities in the USC procedures, and thus quashed its decision.

Furthermore, if two trustworthy men bear witness in court against an accused person, claiming that he robbed the plaintiff, and thereafter claim that they too were robbed by the same accused individual, their witness will not be accepted as they have become litigants in the case. The doubt (*shubha*) present in their case is that they have become suspect of enmity towards the accused. Moreover, in a case of murder where the corpse is found in an enemy's compound, and there is a witness but no confessor, *qasāma* (taking 50 oaths by the claimants) will be resorted to because of the suspicion (*shubha*) surrounding the case, even though the *qasāma* procedure contradicts the normal criminal procedure for taking an oath.

Some contemporary Islamic writers have suggested that modern methods of crime detection such as DNA, laboratory analysis, photography and sound recording could be used to establish criminal offences, instead of claiming *shubha*. They claim that those means are more reliable and efficient than verbal testimony.[194] One of the reasons on which this assertion is based is that the means for securing the objectives of Islamic Law are 'flexible and remain

---

193 See Zakariyah, *Applications of Legal Maxims*, Appendix 4, 6; *cf., Dahiru Gambo* [*Appellant*] *v. State* [*Respondent*] (*Kano*) where the value of the stolen property was valued at N3000, and the Upper Sharīʿa Court sentenced the accused to 2 years imprisonment and 50 lashes. However, the convicted individual appealed successfully against the judgement. See Zakariyah, *Applications of Legal Maxims*, Appendix 11.

194 Noorslawat, Sabtu, *The Basic Principle of Sharīʿa for the Enforcement of Hadd Punishment for Theft*, M.A. Thesis, (Birmingham UK: Birmingham University, 1977) 16–17.

open to consideration'. This hypothesis could be used in the cases of Amina Lawal, Safiyyatu Husseini and Bariya Magadisu. Since the crime of adultery can never be committed unilaterally, and the co-accused persons in the three cases denied their involvements in the allegation, it would be worthwhile to suggest that using modern evidence to ascertain the genuineness of the allegation, not to ascribe a *ḥadd* punishment on any of the accused but to free the helpless women. In Bariya's case, the learned Judges based their verdict on her confession and appearance of pregnancy.

First, one point of inquiry is whether pregnancy can be used to convict a single girl of fornication.[195] There is no convincing evidence to support the acceptance of pregnancy as reliable evidence for fornication. Among the different Schools of Jurisprudence, only the Mālikīs accept such circumstantial evidence as proof while others hold a contrary view.[196] Some reasons why pregnancy cannot be accepted as evidence are as follows. Pregnancy only proves evidence that intercourse has taken place but not that the woman has given her consent; she could have been raped while conscious or unconscious. She may be under the impression that a marriage contract is legitimate, even a temporary marriage contract that is deemed legal by some Shiʿites as reported to be the opinion of Ibn ʿAbbās.[197] She may not consider guidance as a condition for marriage, and thus have entered marriage without her legal guardian (*walī*). Perhaps she became pregnant without coitus; if a man's sperm enters the vagina by means other than through sexual intercourse, as debated on Newsline of the Nigerian Television Authority (NTA) on 18 March 2001 after a 10-year-old virgin was said to be pregnant.[198] All these reasons constitute an element of doubt (*shubha*) whereby pregnancy cannot be accepted as sole evidence to convict a woman of adultery or fornication.

Second, one might question whether in such cases the confession of an accused individual can be taken without allowing the right of retraction or providing the benefit of doubt. It is reported that the Prophet gave Māʿiz, as

---

195 Class Gender and the Political Economy of Sharīʿa ... online at: http://www.nigerdeltacongress.com/carticles/class%20gender%20and%20the%...03/05/04, p. 4 of 7.

196 Ibn Qudamah, *al-Mughī*, 10:192.

197 This opinion has been revoked by Ibn ʿAbbās and the latest opinion of him is prohibition. However, if sexual intercourse between a man and women occurs on the basis of legality of *mutʿa*, such action will not attract a prescribed *ḥadd* punishment. See al-Shinqīṭī, Muḥammad al-Amin bn Muḥammad al-Mukhtār, *Iḍwāʾ al-Bayān fī Īḍāḥ al-Qurʾān bi-l-Qurʾān*, (Beirut: Dār al-Fikr, 1995/1415), 1:129; Ibn Rushd, Muḥammad bn Aḥmad bn Muḥammad Aḥmad, *Bidāya al-Mujtahid wa Nihāyat al-Muqtaṣid*, (Cairo: Dār al-Ḥadīth, 2004/1425), 3:80.

198 Class Gender and the Political Economy of Sharīʿa, p. 5 of 7.

well as al-Ghamidi, the chance to retract their confessions when both came to him confessing their acts of adultery. Throughout the Bariya case, at no point did the judges systematically give her the benefit of doubt or introduce her right of retraction as did the Prophet for the two Companions.

Third, if the co-accused denies his involvement in the alleged crime, should Bariya alone be convicted based on two pieces of evidence, knowing that a single individual cannot commit such a crime. To this, it could be said that during the life of the Prophet, there were some instances that single individuals were punished for adulterous acts. The bottom line is that it is possible to convict a single person on the grounds of valid evidence among which is confession. However, it is alleged that if an element of doubt has crept into the procedure by which the confession was deduced, the verdict is considered invalid.

In Safiyyatu's case, one of the reasons given by her counsels was that the actual date, time and location where the offence was committed were not stated in the court procedure. This as well as other legal procedural errors cast gnawing doubt on the credibility of the verdict.[199] Also, the issue of acceptability of pregnancy as evidence to convict an accused is contestable and tainted with doubt. Even in the Mālikī School of Thought, one may conceive pregnancy as lasting for 7 years; thus, in this regard, Safiyyatu might have conceived her pregnancy while she was still legally married to her former husband. There was no evidence to prove otherwise before the court handed down its judgment.[200] In other words, it is possible that the baby to whom Safiyyatu gave birth could have been fathered by her former husband. All these elements constitute what the Sharīʿa terms as *shubha* which must be considered in averting a *ḥadd* punishment. In *Aminal Lawal v. State*, there is contention whether retraction of a confession made by the accused/defendant representative is acceptable. It is reported that the representative of Amina Lawal retracted her confession at the Upper Sharīʿa Court Funtua. However, this retraction was dismissed on the grounds that it was made not by the accused/appellant. This disagreement will lead us to inquire into the *locus standi* of a legal representative and his action, and to investigate whether retraction can be made even at the last minute before execution of the sentence. With regard to the latter, one can infer from the words of the Prophet ("why not leave him, perhaps, he may repent") when Māʿiz was chased by his executors that retraction of confession in such a case (adultery) is acceptable. With regard to the former, legal representatives act as if they were the individual concerned, and restricting the acceptability of retraction of a confession to the accused alone will undermine the

199 Yawuri, 196.

200 Peters, *Re-Islamization*, 236.

essence of legal representation. Albeit, as a result of arguments imbedded in the basis of Amina's conviction, it could be suggested that the judges needed to be cognizant of the objective of Islamic Law in this particular case and consider the allegation as doubtful and the *ḥadd* punishment as nullified.[201]

Furthermore, the legal procedure followed in Amina's case also casts doubt (*shubha*) on the credibility of the allegation. In the response of the Sharīʿa Court of Appeal Kastina, the learned Judge poses some credible questions to discredit this allegation: Why did these policemen, who witnessed an offence being committed before their very eyes, fail to arrest the accused until after 11 months (namely, information contained in the filed case stated that the two accused cohabited for 11 months)? Notwithstanding the policemen's knowledge that Amina and Yahaya committed the alleged offence for a period spanning 11 months did the accusers catch them in the actual act (*zina*) or were they informed?[202] It is remarkable to state that doubt may be created in an admission where the admission has lost any of its validity.

In Islamic criminal law and its procedures it is important to call for witnesses in cases where a confessional statement is the sole evidence in convicting the accused. This is referred to in *Isiya and others v. State*[203] where the USC relied on their confession. When the accused persons denied the confession, the evidence induced from it was nullified on the basis that the Upper Shari'a Court (USC) failed to call for witnesses during the trial as required by law. In rejecting the USC decision, the learned Judges are reported to have said: "Conviction of an accused cannot stand without the testimony of just witnesses." Not only this inconsistency in what was written in the Court's procedural book (p. 5, §14),[204] it casts doubt on the evidence relied upon in convicting the accused persons.

Conclusion

Legal maxims regarding certainty and doubt, as well as their related sub-maxims, are of immense importance in Islamic criminal law. Indeed, they are the core element by which criminal justice can be achieved. In this chapter, the grand maxim and its related sub-maxims have been given extensive treatment. The central message in all our discussions is that human beings are assumed

201 NNLR, 498.

202 *Ibid.*, 498–499.

203 See for the details of the case, Zakariyah, *Applications of Legal Maxims*, Appendix 1.

204 *Ibid.*

innocent of any accusation until proven otherwise by means of rigorous evidence. Any allegation that lacks the support of credible evidence shall not be entertained, and any iota of doubt plunged into evidence will render it invalid. Confession, as one type of substantial evidence, can be considered valid inasmuch as the confessor has not retracted it, especially where the nature of the crime is *ḥudūd* and solely involves the absolute right of God, which is based on forgiveness. However, certainty may be difficult to attain in all cases; thus where a case involves the right of man, it is espoused that circumstantial evidence should be sought in order to regain the rights of the victim involved.

No singular, all-encompassing definition exists among Islamic Law scholars for what constitutes circumstantial evidence. However, it can be said that any circumstantial evidence, such as photographs, fingerprints, tape recordings, confidential documents, and DNA, can be used in a number of criminal cases to support substantive evidence that lacks the necessary legal requirements.

It is a fundamental principle that the use of circumstantial evidence is unacceptable in any *ḥudūd* crime, which can be pardoned if not yet reported to the authorities, because the absolute right of God based on forgiveness are involved. However, in crimes that are partly the rights of God and man, circumstantial evidence can be used to establish the right of man. If the legal consequence is mainly pecuniary, such as *diya*, circumstantial evidence can be used inasmuch as the plaintiff can present substantial evidence that needs to be elevated to a higher requirement. However, if the legal consequence is punitive, as in the case of theft, defamation/slanderous accusations and even retaliatory penalties—according to Ḥanafīs, but contrary to the majority view—then circumstantial evidence cannot be used for fixed punishments. In other words, circumstantial evidence cannot be used to inflict *ḥadd* and *qiṣāṣ* punishments, although it can be used to award discretionary *taʿzīr* penalties.

Another burning issue surrounding the admittance of circumstantial evidence concerns the appearance of pregnancy. It is reported that ʿUmar Ibn al-Khaṭṭāb affirmed that pregnancy is one of the yardsticks for convicting an unmarried woman of adultery. In his documented reports he states: "I fear if time passes and one said, 'we do not see stoning [to death] in the Book of God' and consequently they will go astray by abolishing this obligation revealed by God. Lo! Indeed, stoning [to death] is a right [of God] on anyone who committed adultery and he/she is married-before (*muḥsin*) if there is evidence (*bayyina*) or pregnancy [appeared] or confession established".[205] Remarking on this assertive opinion, al-Suyūṭī said: "Using the appearance of pregnancy as a factor for determining the adulterous status of a woman is attributed to

205 al-Bukhārī, Ḥadīth Nos. 6441 and 6829.

ʿUmar and adopted by Mālik".[206] This is contrary to the opinion held by the majority of Islamic scholars, including the Ḥanafīs, Shāfiʿīs and Ḥanbalīs, because it is not necessarily the case that once a woman becomes impregnated through sexual intercourse that it be deemed adultery. She could have become pregnant through artificial insemination, or by other means known to the modern age. In fact, the woman could have been sexually abused or raped while she slept. In all of these cases, there is agreement that a woman cannot be awarded a *ḥadd* punishment because of the doubt (*shubha*) involved; as a principle, *ḥudūd* should be averted in the face of doubt.[207] A woman is said to have been brought before ʿUmar accused of adultery because she was pregnant while unmarried. When she explained that she had been raped while asleep, she was therefore acquitted. In another story, when a woman was brought before ʿUmar for the same reason and explained that she had been coerced, she was acquitted.[208] This is the reason why criticism has been heaped on the judgment of the Upper Sharīʿa Courts of the Sokoto and Kastina States of Nigeria, in which Safiyyatu and Amina were convicted of adultery because they appeared pregnant while not legally married.

To sum up the stance of Islamic scholars on acceptable evidence, it is clear that evidence is not only restricted to witnesses, as perceived by the majority of Islamic scholars. It is also the case that bearing witness by any suitable means to establish justice among litigants can be deemed as evidence. In general, the testimonies of women are not acceptable in crimes that are solely the right of God because women are often assumed, *inter alia*, not to frequent such locations where crimes take place. Regarding these rights, concealment of the wrongdoing and admonition of the wrongdoer is encouraged. In any criminal case in which women are allowed to bear witness, textual evidence prescribes that two women are equivalent to one man. However, in cases where male witnesses are unavailable, a woman's evidence is admissible in corroboration with other circumstantial evidence.

It is a debatable point among classical and contemporary Islamic scholars whether circumstantial evidence and modern investigative technology can be used in Islamic Law in general, and in Islamic criminal law in particular. The majority of Islamic scholars approve any circumstantial evidence that is sought to establish justice in general,[209] as opposed to Ibn Nujaym and al-Ramalī

206 al-Shinqitī, 5:319–321.

207 *Ibid.*; and al-Tirmidhī, Ḥadīth No. 1456.

208 al-Shinqitī, 5:392.

209 ʿAlī b. Khalīl al-Ṭarāblusī, *Muʿīn al-Ḥukkām fī-mā Yataraddad bayna l-Khaṣimayn min al-Aḥkām* (Cairo: Maṭbaʿat al-Bāb l-Ḥalabī, 1393/1973), 166; Muḥammad Amin Ibn ʿUmar

(d. 1004/1596) who opine that circumstantial evidence is not admissible.[210] It is argued in support of the acceptability of circumstantial evidence that, at times, circumstantial evidence could be stronger than traditional substantive evidence. Such an example could be the case where four witnesses claim that adultery was committed but the woman was eventually proven to be chaste. There might also be stronger evidence proving the claims of the witnesses to be false. In that case, circumstantial evidence will render the claim moot.[211]

Generally speaking, there are cases where it becomes necessary to resort to circumstantial evidence, such as all human rights cases claiming to be divested from the owner or cases where aggression is meted out unjustly to human beings. In such cases, it is deemed paramount to resort to circumstantial evidence in the absence of substantive evidence, or in corroboration with it, because the intention of the Sharīʿa is to establish justice among mankind by any means possible. However, some cases do not necessarily require such investigation: namely, any case involving an absolute right of God, such as adultery or consumption of alcohol. The use of circumstantial evidence is generally acceptable in cases of civil liability, in claims of rights and in cases of discretionary penalties (*taʿzīrāt*), where the use of fingerprints, autopsies, DNA, photographs, and audio recordings have become established. The use of these modern technologies are permissible in cases where punishment need not be averted by means of doubt.[212]

Most cases brought before a court of law in the Northern Nigeria Sharīʿa saga between 1999 and 2007 exhibit many noticeable flaws in the legal proceedings, particularly prominent in all cases of adultery and theft included in

---

Ibn ʿĀbidīn, *Ḥāshiyat Ibn ʿĀbidīn* or *Radd al-Muḥtār ʿalā d-Durar al-Mukhtār* (Beirut: Dār al-Fikr, 2000), 5:354; Ibn Farhun, 2:93; al-Qarāfī, *Anwār al-Burūq*, 4:167; Ibn ʿAbd al-Salam, 2:107; Ibn al-Qayyim al-Jawziyya, *aṭ-Ṭuruq al-Ḥukmiyya*, 4; and Ibn al-Qayyim al-Jawziyya, *Iʿlām al-Muwaqqiʿīn*, 1:103.

210 Ibn Nujaym, *al-Ashbāh wa-n-Naẓāʾir*, 248.

211 al-Zahrānī, 341. See also Ibn Farhun, 2:93; Ibn al-Qayyim al-Jawziyya, *aṭ-Ṭuruq al-Ḥukmiyya*, 26 and 83–84.

212 For further references on witness, oath, and circumstantial evidence, see Taha Jabir al-Alwani, "Judiciary and Rights of the Accused in Islamic Criminal Law", in Tahir Mahmood (ed.), *Criminal Law in Islam and the Muslim World: A Comparative Perspective* (New Delhi: Institute of Objective Studies, 1996), 256–263; M. Cherif Bassiouni *et al.* (eds.), *Islamic Criminal Law and Procedure: An Introduction* (Westport, CT: Praeger, 1988); Ibn al-Qayyim al-Jawziyya, *aṭ-Ṭuruq al-Ḥukmiyya*, 218; al-Māwardī, *al-Aḥkām as-Sulṭāniyya*, 69–73; A.M. ʿAwad, "The Rights of the Accused Under Islamic Criminal Procedure", in M. Cherif Bassiouni (ed.), *The Islamic Criminal Justice System* (New York: Oceana Publications, 1982), 91–107; Baderin, 97; and Peters, *Crime and Punishment*, 12–19.

this chapter. One can observe that the rule of certainty in all ramifications has been undermined, *i.e.*, perhaps as a result of the lack of experience that judges exhibit in the Courts of First Instances (Lower and Upper Sharīʿa Courts) or perhaps due to the influence of political undertones. Thus we wish to suggest that, in cases involving *ḥudūd* crimes, proper steps must be followed to guarantee that the Sharīʿa is not made a target for criticism.

CHAPTER 5

Legal Maxim regarding Hardship and Facility: "Hardship Begets Facility" (*al-Mashaqqa Tajlib at-Taysīr*)*

Hardship and Facility in Islamic Criminal Law

One of the beauties of Islamic Law is its recognition of the fallibility of human beings in carrying out their spiritual and mundane activities. Moreover, it comprehends the difficulties they will face in achieving both their spiritual and mundane objectives. Thus, Islamic Law endorses the breach of certain rules in cases of dire necessity. The maxim which establishes this approval and is supported by sound evidence from the Qur'ān, Ḥadīth, and scholarly consensus (*ijmāʿ*) is "Hardship begets facility" (*al-mashaqqa tajlib at-taysīr*).

Definition and Interpretation of the Legal Maxim *al-Mashaqqa Tajlib at-Taysīr*

The maxim "Hardship begets facility" is one of the basic general maxims agreed upon amongst Islamic jurists. It is applicable to almost all issues and branches of Islamic jurisprudence. Because of the important role it plays in Islamic Law, it is now being recognized as a fundamental maxim,[1] used as a legal concession in the Sharīʿa for any recognized hardship (*mashaqqa*). Thus, it serves the purpose of Islamic Law to alleviate or remove burdens that people may face in exercising the religious rites.[2]

The origin of the maxim is derived from an in-depth study of the Islamic textual injunctions of removing hardship (*rafʿ al-ḥaraj*). It is clearly stated in many Qur'ānic verses and traditional texts that Islam enjoins facility and leniency in any case that leads to difficulty. A Qur'ānic verse states: "God intends for you ease, and He does not want to make things difficult for you",[3] adding

---

* al-Suyūṭī, *al-Ashbāh*, 76; Ibn Nujaym, *al-Ashbāh wa-n-Naẓā'ir*, 89; and al-Zarkhashī *al-Manthūr*, 3:169; al-Zarqa, A., Sharh, 157; Al-Burnu, al-Wajiz, 26.

1 al-Shāṭibī, 2:136–156; al-Suyūṭī, *al-Ashbāh*, 76; Ibn Nujaym, *al-Ashbāh wa-n-Naẓā'ir*, 89; and al-Zarkhashī *al-Manthūr*, 3:169–170.

2 Ibn Nujaym, *al-Ashbāh wa-n-Naẓā'ir*, 89–90.

3 Q. 2:185.

 | DOI 10.1163/9789004304871_006

in other verses, "and [He] has not laid upon you in religion any hardship"[4] and "God wishes to lighten [the burden] for you; and man was created weak".[5] Many other verses suggest that Muslims can find their way out of any difficulty.[6] Although they differ in context, these verses impart the same implications; namely, that God will ease difficulty and hardship whenever it exists as well as make humans understand that what is virtuous and legal is commensurate with their own moral responsibility. Thus, in fact, there is nothing in Islamic Law that surpasses the human capacity to accomplish.[7] The Prophet is reported to have said: "Religion is very easy and whoever overburdens himself in his religion will not be able to continue in that way".[8]

Conversely, of course, some of the legislation in Islamic criminology may appear difficult and severe for mankind to endure, but that is not sufficient reason to brand them as 'barbaric' or 'relics of antiquity'. Just because we may derive great pleasure from many of our daily activities, such as eating, drinking, having intercourse with one's spouse, we may not intuit the proportion of hardships (*mashaqqa*) lurking beneath the surface of what appears normal or ordinary.[9]

The relevance of this maxim to Islamic criminal justice lies in the fact that, although committing certain crimes such as illicit sexual intercourse (*zinā*) or intentional homicide (*qatl ʿamd*) is never permitted, other crimes such as theft (*sariqa*) and consumption of alcohol (*shurb al-khamr*) or forbidden foodstuffs can be justified under dire, extenuating circumstances. Nevertheless, if a fundamental rule is broken due to dire necessity (*ḍarūra*), and the right of man (*ḥaqq al-ādamī*) is involved, then restitution is recommended. Events that occurred during ʿUmar Ibn Khaṭṭāb's rule provide a vivid proof that rules can be breached in dire circumstances. It is reported that ʿUmar suspended *ḥadd* punishment for theft during a period of famine in Medina.[10] The crime was neither legalized nor 'fiscalized', but the severe punishment for a *ḥudūd* crime was waived or reduced temporarily, depending on the perpetrator's circumstances, in order to alleviate the hardship of starvation.

Most of the verses that stand as legal evidence for the breach of rules during a period of hardship are related to the consumption of forbidden (*ḥarām*)

---

4 Q. 22:78.

5 Q. 4:28.

6 *Cf.*, Q. 5:7 and Q. 2:286.

7 al-Shāṭibī, 2:119.

8 al-Bukhārī, *Kitāb al-Imān*, Ḥadīth No. 39.

9 al-Shāṭibī, 2:425 and 434.

10 Ahmed al-Raysuni, *Nazariyyah al-Maqasid ʿind al-Imam al-Shatibi*, Saudi Arabia, al-Dar al-ʾAlamiyyah lil-Kutub al-Islami, 1992/1412, 333; al-Hafnawi, al-Shubhat, 292,

foodstuffs, although this leniency is not exclusively restricted to food. Al-Jaṣṣāṣ (d. 370/980) remarks that if the wisdom behind allowing prohibited things is meant to spare a life under dismal conditions, then this wisdom is relevant for all forms of prohibited matters and the ruling (*ḥukm*) must hold for all cases of existing necessity.[11] Therefore, the maxim implies that for any obligation under Islamic Law which might cause hardship and inconvenience in some cases, the Sharīʿa provides facility (*taysīr*) for such hardship.

There are two kinds of hardship (*mashaqqa*) envisaged in human activities. The first is hardship caused by man's natural limitations. Such hardships, which do not pose a threat to life and limb, are not facilitated. In other words, they are the inexorable and inevitable hardships that man must undergo just by living. This type of hardship is inseparable from acts of devotion (*ʿibāda*) and compulsory to endure from an Islamic point of view, like striving to acquire spiritual reward or seek knowledge, or like performing one's prayer while standing or fasting during hot weather. The second type of hardship is that which extends beyond man's capacity and varies from one person to another.[12] The hardships recognized in this second category can claim lives or inflict permanent damage or disabilities on the human body.[13]

Hardships Recognized in Islamic Law and Their Facilities

It is noted that all facilities provided in Islamic Law are based on this maxim. Al-Suyūṭī refers all of the legally approved facilities in Islamic Law to seven reasons,[14] each of which is applicable to some matter in Islamic jurisprudence.

Journey

Journeys (*safar*) can be fraught with hardship that must be facilitated when schedules, such as the number of prayer cycles (*rakaʿāt*), are disrupted and havoc played with the traveler's ability to adhere to religious duties. In such cases, one's prayers normally consisting of four *rakaʿāt* might be reduced

11 al-Jaṣṣāṣ, 1:129.

12 al-Nadawī, 428; ʿUmar b. Muḥammad al-Khabbāzī, *al-Mughnī fī Uṣul al-Fiqh*, edited by Muḥammad Muzhar Baqa, (Makkah: Umm al-Qura University Press, 1403/1982), 225.

13 al-Suyūṭī, *al-Ashbāh*, 80.

14 The seven reasons are *ṣafar* (journey), *maraḍ* (illness), *ikrāh* (coercion), *nisyān* (forgetfulness), *jahl* (ignorance), *naqṣ* (defect/disability) and *ʿusr wa-ʿumūm al-balwā* (difficulty and general necessity). As *nisyān* and *jahl* have been treated under the maxim of intention and action, only the remaining five will be mentioned here.

to two perhaps the noon (*ẓuhr*), afternoon (*ʿaṣr*), and night (*ʿishāʾ*) prayers. Therefore, the law must sometimes turn a blind eye, so to speak, to allow travelers to break their fast in Ramadan, or to wipe wet hands over their socks instead of washing their feet during ablution, or to miss the communal Friday prayer obligatory for men (*jumuʿa*), or to eat meat from an animal slaughtered in an unlawful (*ḥarām*) manner.

Such leniency is hardly applicable in Islamic criminal theory. Indeed, no traveler will enjoy leniency if he commits a *qiṣāṣ* crime that attracts a retaliatory punishment. No one, either at home or abroad, is allowed to kill a fellow human being, as the texts that prohibit murder give no exception to the rule. If a traveler encounters the hardship of starvation or attack by thugs, he cannot ward off that hardship by sacrificing a member of the group. Moreover, if a boat is sinking, it is not acceptable to jettison a fellow passenger to guarantee the safety of the others onboard. For such actions, everyone involved in the criminal act must pay adequate compensation (*diya*).[15]

However, if a traveler finds himself in dire straits while on his journey, he will be allowed to consume alcohol, eat forbidden food, or use other people's belongings without their consent, under legal concession (*rukhṣa*). In such cases, the individual will neither be accused nor charged with committing religious offences or criminal acts, if he has acted in good faith and within the limits allowed him. Where his offence has involved a right of man, it will be standard procedure for the offender to pay compensation for damages incurred as the legal maxim teaches us: "Necessity does not invalidate the right of others" (*al-iḍṭirār lā yubṭil ḥaqq al-ghayr*).[16] In contrast, violation of the right of God in times of hardship (*mashaqqa*) will attract no penalty because God forgives and pardons human errors.

However, life is complex and we must question: Can legal concessions be extended to include serious crimes such as fornication (*zinā*) and false accusation (*qadhf*). Neither classical nor contemporary Islamic jurists have suggested that such acts are permissible. However, if a woman is on a journey and wants to marry without a parent or legal relative present to stand as custodian (*walī*) as required by law, she will be allowed to request that a male co-traveler stand in as *walī*. Thus, any sexual intercourse taking place between the couple would not be considered adulterous (*zinā*). In response to this issue, al-Shāfiʿī responded in agreement: "When a matter becomes difficult, its rule becomes expanded" (*idha ḍāq al-amr ittasaʿ*).[17]

15 Al-Suyuti, al-Ashbah, 77.

16 Ibn Rajab, *al-Qawāʿid*, 36; *Majalla*, Article 33; and M. al-Zarqāʾ, *al-Madkhal*, §602.

17 Ibn Nujaym, *al-Ashbāh wa-n-Naẓāʾir*, 84; and al-Suyūṭī, *al-Ashbāh*, 83.

Illness

If someone is ailing (*maraḍ*), the number of religious rites can be reduced, suspended or replaced by alternative rites for reasons of health. These facilities include performing ablution with sand in lieu of water, particularly if foul water could cause severe damage or exacerbate the illness; leaving congregational prayers; or breaking or foregoing a period of fasting. Here one can pay penitence for one's omissions upon regaining full health, for example, by giving an elderly person sustainable food for each day missed. Other possible concessions might entail performing the major (*ḥajj*) and minor (*ʿumra*) pilgrimages by proxy or, according to some Schools, disregarding the issue of gender during medical examinations.[18] In a classical example, the opinion of scholars is still inconclusive regarding the use of medicinal alcohol. While some Ḥanafīs approve its use for healing during dire situations, others scholar disagree.[19] Such situations are all covered by such leniency.[20]

In Islamic criminal law, using illness as an excuse to commit a crime holds little credibility, although this can sometimes be an impediment in criminal cases. In fact, a murder conviction can be averted if the accused is judged to be 'criminally insane'. However, such claims have to be verified by experts to ensure that the rights of victims are not jeopardized.

Coercion

The Arabic word *ikrāh* literally means coercion or a compelling force that drives someone to do what he would not ordinarily do.[21] Coercion has been recognized as a legal reason to justify the commission of offences or the omission of obligatory duties. In Islamic criminal law, the effect of coercion is a subject of controversy, especially in crimes involving the right of man. In crimes that warrant retaliation (*qiṣāṣ*) in kind, coercion is not considered a convincing excuse for instigating injury or murder. Thus, if someone is coerced (*mukrah*) to commit murder, and then does the killing, both he as primary active agent as well as the coercer (*mukrih*) would be executed in line with *qiṣāṣ*. The majority of Islamic scholars assert that the individual who is coerced will be held responsible for committing murder if he could have chosen

18 Ibn Nujaym, *al-Ashbāh wa-n-Naẓā'ir*, 84. In this case, maximum precautions must be taken guarantee that no offence will be committed. Thus, if a male doctor must inspect a woman's private areas, it is recommended that either her husband or her male relative be present.

19 Ibn Nujaym, *al-Ashbāh wa-n-Naẓā'ir*, 75.

20 al-Suyūṭī, *al-Ashbāh*, 77.

21 al-Bahūtī, 4:1631–1632.

otherwise and that the coercer, or motor behind the killing, should also be held responsible.[22] This is because no life is considered more valuable than another. Abū Ḥanīfa maintains that the person coerced should be accorded a *taʿzīr* rather than *qiṣāṣ* penalty while the coercer should be held responsible for the crime. He based his argument on the fact that the person coerced was forced to act against his will; like a puppet in the hands of a puppeteer, he became simply a tool used for the killing.[23] These views are based on a situation where the purpose of coercion is completed (*ikrāh tāmm*). However, if coercion is only meant to be a threat (*ikrāh ghayr muljī*), there will be no doubt that full responsibility for the murder will rest upon the actual killer (who was supposedly coerced). In cases where someone coerced actually destroys another person's property, whether coercion is or is not complete, both the active agent and the coercer, or only the coercer, will be held responsible for damages.[24]

However, in certain *ḥudūd* crimes, coercion can result in acquittal even though legal rules have been violated. For instance, if a woman claims to have been raped or sexually abused under duress, she will be acquitted of adultery in light of Qur'ānic verse 24:33, which states that a woman has not sinned when compelled to commit this crime.[25] If she claims that she consented to escape punishment, then there will be sufficient reason to treat the case as clouded by doubt (*shubha*) based on the legal maxim: "Fixed [*ḥadd*] punishment should be averted in the face of doubt" (*al-ḥudūd tudraʾ bi-sh-shubhāt*).

Despite the legal ruling that commutes *ḥadd* in the face of doubt, the Mālikīs do not completely accept this premise. Rather they assert that a woman's claim of coercion should be substantiated by convincing evidence, such as screaming or struggling while being raped, or by traces of blood on her body attesting to mutilation of her vagina.[26] It is reasonable to assume that rape would more likely be committed in a secluded rather than public place. Thus, several modern means of detection, such as DNA, should be used to confirm the claim and to establish the right of the raped women. However, if the accused man rejects the authenticity of the modern technique to establish the accusation of rape, his rejection could reduced the punishment of *ḥadd* to *taʿzīr*

22 Ibn Qudāma, *al-Mughnī*, 8:266–267; and al-Suyūṭī, *al-Ashbāh*, 13.

23 al-Kāsānī, 7:177; and Ibn al-Humām, *Fatḥ al-Qadīr*, 7:307.

24 al-Bahūtī, 4:639; Ibn Rajab, *al-Qawāʿid*, 309; and al-Suyūṭī, *al-Ashbāh*, 134.

25 Ibn Qudāma, *al-Mughnī*, 9:59–60.

26 Ibn Qudāma quoted the Mālikī view in *al-Mughnī*, 9:79. It appears that the reliable Mālikī view is to accept the woman's claim. The reservation mostly concerns the claim of a slave girl; see al-Qarāfī, *ad-Dakhīra*, 12:59; and Ibn ʿAbd al-Barr, *al-Kāfī*, 2:1074.

(discretionary).[27] On the other hand, if the man himself claims to have been raped by the woman, Ḥanafīs jurists still consider the claim valid and the man should be acquitted for committing adultery. They argue that the claim of coercion has rendered the case dubious, and, according to the Ḥadīth, *ḥadd* should be averted in the face of doubt.[28] However, the Mālikīs and Ḥanbalīs maintain that men cannot be the victim of rape because such an act would not have occurred without their choosing or desire.[29] This view is ill-conceived as there are many occasions in which men can become the victims of rape, particularly in the modern age. The general mentality, perhaps a relic from an older generation, tends to believe that a woman cannot take advantage of a man sexually; however, recent history has proven otherwise. In the case of *Debbie Lane [offender] v* Scottish *CSC*, the Sheriff observed that a "prison-based sex offender program had been designed for men". As such, he sentenced Lane to 100 hours of community service instead of sending her to prison for sexually harassing a 13-year-old boy.[30] This mentality has been criticized by Alayne Frankson-Wallece, a UN prosecutor:

> It is too naïve to suggest that a woman cannot be the perpetrator of acts of sexual violence against a man. Further, that women have not and do not take sexual advantage of men in situations where the question of consent has been nullified by the operative circumstances [...] Similarly,

---

27 See Azman Mohd Noor, "Punishment for Rape in Islamic Law", *Malayan Law Journal* 5 (2009); Azman Mohd Noor and Ahmad Basri Ibrahim, "The Rights of a Rape Victim in Islamic Law", *IIUM Law Journal* 16/1 (2008): 65–83. Regarding the recent debate on the admissibility of modern means of proof featured in rape cases in Pakistan, see the article "DNA Evidence Inadmissible in Rape Cases, Says Pakistan", *Legal Monitor Worldwide (Jordan)*, 31 May 2013, News 1. See http://tribune.com.pk/story/556392/rape-cases-dna-tests-not-admissible-as-main-evidence-cii-front-page/ (last accessed: 31 March 2014).

28 Ḥadīths remit *ḥadd* from Muslims as much as possible, because if a judge were to err when executing a punishment, this would be far more acceptable than making an error when enforcing the penalty.

29 Ibn Qudāma, *al-Mughnī*, 6:187.

30 Reported in *Scottish Metro*, 8 March 2007, 11. The same mentality is enshrined in most world legislations; see *Priya Patel v Justices Arijit Pasayat and S.H. Kapadia*. The honorable justices refer to Section 375 of the IPC which emphatically states that "rape can be committed only by a man". Thus Priya was acquitted of the charge of gang rape on this basis. See "Woman Can't Be Prosecuted on Gang Rape Charge: Court", *The Hindu*, 14 July 2006; http://www.thehindu.com/todays-paper/tp-national/woman-cant-be-prosecuted-on-gang-rape-charge-court/article3104565.ece (accessed: 11 March 2014).

> an act of rape, in the sense of non-consensual sexual intercourse, can be committed by woman against woman and man against man.[31]

The honorable prosecutor's comments on the issue present the need for reform to change such an outlook.

Coercion (*ikrāh*) can also necessitate a violation of the right of God inasmuch as the coerced is of sound mind and firm faith. The Qur'ān states that anyone coerced into uttering a statement of disbelief in Islam will not suffer God's wrath, "except him who is forced thereto and his heart is at rest with faith".[32] Thus, if someone is compelled to revoke Islam, *i.e.*, the crime of apostasy (*ridda*), they will neither be considered an apostate nor be punished. The same applies to the act of drinking alcohol (*shurb al-khamr*). If someone is compelled to confess, the confession will not be admitted in a court of law.[33]

Defect or Disability

Human defects or disabilities (*naqṣ*) attract leniency, such as not imposing religious or legal responsibilities on an insane (*majnūn*) person.[34] Thus, if someone commits a crime due to their disability or natural defect, such as insanity, they will not be adjudged as perpetrator of a *ḥudūd* or *qiṣāṣ* offence. The above also applies to children. In the case of adultery (*zinā*), defamation (*qadhf*), drinking alcohol (*shurb al-khamr*), etc., the offender will not be accused of committing a *ḥudūd* crime; however, a minor may be given a discretionary (*taʿzīr*) penalty as reprimand and warning should the act reoccur in the future. The proportional punishment commensurate with the gravity of the offence is left to the authorities to decide. Although *qiṣāṣ* cannot be issued to a minor (*ṭifl*) or insane (*majnūn*) individual who commits a murder, however, financial restitution (*diya*) must be paid to the victim's relatives by the *ʿāqila* (blood relatives or supporters of the culprit).[35] However, women are excluded from this group of relatives because gender is also a factor for which leniency can be sought.

---

31 See Desmond Allen, "Women Can Rape Men, Says Female Judge", *Jamaica Observer*, 6 March 2007; https://www.jamaicaobserver.com/news/119959_Women-can-rape-men-says-female-judge (accessed: 11 March 2014).

32 Q. 16:106.

33 See Ch. 3, Section 'Coercion' for details on the effect of *ikrāh* in Islamic criminal law.

34 al-Suyūṭī, *al-Ashbāh*, 80; al-Burnu, *al-Wajīz*, 228; and Wahba Muṣṭafā al-Zuhaylī, *al-Qawāʿid al-Fiqhiyya wa-Taṭbīqātuhā fī l-Madhāhib al-Arbaʿa* (Damascus: Dār al-Fikr, 2006), 1:266.

35 The group of people who are responsible for supporting the culprit in the case of murder, especially the culprit's kin. See Powers, 172.

For example, women are not required under Islamic Law to participate in paying financial restitution for a relative who has committed murder, regardless of whether the crime involves an unintentional killing (*qatl khaṭaʾ*) by an adult, or an intentional killing (*qatl ʿamd*) by a child or someone criminally insane.[36]

Difficulty and General Necessity

The phrase *al-ʿusr wa-ʿumūm al-balwā* demonstrates that the broad use of facilitation is included under general necessity (*ʿumūm al-balwā*) and insurmountable difficulty (*ʿusr*). Islamic Law recognizes that life by nature is fraught with ups and downs. Provision is made for situations where there is pressing hardship (*mashaqqa*) or where man may have to omit a religious practice (*ʿibādāt*) or commit an illicit act to surmount enormous difficulties. This legal concession (*rukhṣa*) is covered by the grand maxim concerning hardship (*mashaqqa*) of which difficulty (*ʿusr*) and general necessity (*ʿumūm al-balwā*) are among the causes. Caution should be exercised to ensure that this provision is restricted to what is permitted under the law. Al-Burnu observes that *ʿusr* and *ʿumūm al-balwā* are only taken into consideration when no further clarification can be found in texts.[37] Of course, to make a law effective, some restrictions must be imposed on the use of concessions. What we sometimes consider to be difficult may vary widely from one situation to another. Taking this into account, 'general necessity' helps to expand the context which applies to mankind in general.

Much of the legislation enacted in Islam law, whether derived from direct texts or implied meanings, is based on concession.[38] In criminal law, a male doctor may examine the intimate areas of a woman's body if there is no alternative. A man may ask to see his proposed bride before deciding to agree on the marriage.[39] Imām Abū Ḥanīfa extensively expands upon the use of this facility to permit a girl to marry without her custodian (*walī*), or without fulfilling the condition of trustworthiness (*ʿadāla*) of the witnesses.[40] In addition, the Ḥanafis, as opposed to scholars from other Schools (*madhāhib*), do not

36 A. al-Zarqāʾ, *Sharḥ*, 161.
37 al-Burnu, *al-Wajīz*, 228.
38 *Ibid.*
39 Ibn Nujaym, *al-Ashbāh wa-n-Naẓāʾir*, 80.
40 *Ibid.*

stipulate any specific marriage formula during consummation of the marriage, expressly to prevent any allegation of adultery.[41]

Furthermore, in difficult situations, which is the bedrock of necessity (*ḍarūra*), a woman's testimony (*shahāda*) can be admitted in matters where it would traditionally be excluded, such as when someone accused of raping a chaste girl denies the accusation and claims that he only caressed her. Here, a woman's testimony regarding the girl's virginity will be given due consideration, although other circumstantial evidence may be admissible to strengthen her testimony and make the case potentially more tenable in a court of law.

In all cases where the breach of rules in Islamic criminal law is officially permitted, concessions range from abolishment, reduction, substitution and advancement, to deferment and alteration of the punishment.[42] In the case of *qiṣāṣ* crimes, retaliatory penalties for criminal offences can be reduced, commuted, substituted, altered or abolished. Thus, if someone takes a life by mistake, *qiṣāṣ* can be annulled by a pardon (*ʿafw*) or substituted by financial restitution (*diya*) from the victim's relative as deemed acceptable and in tandem with the Qurʾānic verse: "Whoever forgives his brother of any [of the punishment] shall follow it with kindness".[43]

Nature of Necessary Harm or Hardship

Ḍarūrāt is the plural noun of *ḍarūra* or *ḍarar*, which means unavoidable injury, hardship and harm. *Ḍarar* is precisely the opposite of benefit (*nafʿ*). The normative word *muḍṭarr*, meaning someone forced or compelled to commit an act that he neither wishes nor is capable of doing,[44] is derived from the same root (*ḍād–rāʾ–rāʾ*) as *ḍarar*. In other words, someone who sustains an injury that forces him to behave strangely or try to avoid injury is a so-called *muḍṭarr* (one under compulsion).[45] Furthermore, *ḍarar* can also refer to a situation whereby someone has reached a limit and will apparently die or nearly succumb if he fails to take that which is prohibited.[46]

---

41 *Ibid.*

42 al-Suyūṭī, *al-Ashbāh*, 82.

43 Q. 2:178; Ibn Nujaym, *al-Ashbāh wa-n-Naẓāʾir*; ʿAwda, 1:774; and Ibn Qudāma, *al-Mughnī*, 8:352.

44 Ibn al-ʿArabī, *Aḥkām al-Qurʾān*, 1:55.

45 *Ibid.*

46 al-Zarkashī, *al-Manthūr*, 2:319.

Moreover, *ḍarar* is a way to preserve lives from being lost or badly injured.[47] Such definitions have been criticized for being too narrow and restricted to preserving life alone, whereas 'necessity' is a much more extensive concept. According to contemporary Islamic scholars, *ḍarar* (necessity) is defined as "a compelling situation where one has to commit an illegal act" to preserve the five fundamental necessities,[48] which are life (*nafs*), religion (*dīn*), intellect or knowledge (*ʿaql*), offspring/lineage (*nasl*), and wealth/property (*māl*).

The disparity between the classical and contemporary definitions of *ḍarar* is that the classical state of necessity is restricted to the preservation of life, which contemporary Islamic jurists say must also include the four other states of necessity stated in their definition above. The excuse often given for this restriction in the classical definition is either that it defines necessity only in the context of the discussion, or that *ḍarar* (necessity) is usually discussed in the Qurʾān in connection with the issue of starvation.[49] This is not to say that the scholars of Islamic Law were ignorant of the fact that the state of necessity goes beyond preserving life alone. Many classical Islamic jurists have discussed the state of necessity in a wider scope than defined in the Qurʾānic context, such as in the various books by al-Ghazālī (d. 505/1111) in which he includes all five categories of necessity.[50]

Several controversial issues, *e.g.*, the act of committing illicit sexual intercourse in the face of harm/difficulty (*ḍarar*) due to starvation, surround the use of the maxim in question in Islamic criminal cases. For instance, can a destitute woman whose life is in danger commit an illicit sexual act with a man who uses that act as a condition for helping her? It is reported that ʿUmar Ibn al-Khaṭṭāb pardoned a woman who committed adultery under a similar circumstance.[51] However, neither classical nor contemporary Islamic

47 al-Dardir, *ash-Sharḥ al-Kabīr*, 2:183; and Ibn Qudāma, *al-Mughnī*, 8:595.

48 Haydar, 1:38; M. al-Zarqāʾ, *al-Madkhal*, 2:997; and al-Zuhaylī, *Naẓariyyat aḍ-Ḍarūra ash-Sharʿiyyah Muqāranah maʿa l-Qānūn al-Waḍaʿī*, 4th edn. (Beirut: Muʾassasah ar-Risāla, 1405/1985), 67–68.

49 Mansour al-Mutairi, *Necessity in Islamic Law*, unpublished Ph.D. Thesis (Edinburgh: Edinburgh University, 1997), 13.

50 al-Ghazālī, *al-Mustaṣfā*, 1:174. In addition to al-Ghazālī, a host of classical Islamic scholars, to a lesser or greater extent, have discussed this topic and included all five as paramount necessities to be preserved. See al-ʿAynī, 2:85.

51 See Ahmed Elashhab, *The Criminal Liability in Islamic Law* (Tripoli: The World Islamic Call Society, 1994), 185–186. Elashhab quotes Ahmed Fathi Bahnasi on page 257. According to the report, a woman was brought to ʿUmar, having been accused of committing adultery "because she was thirsty and saw a shepherd, who refused to give her a drink till she committed adultery, and she did". ʿUmar consulted people to decide whether he should penalise her (by stoning). ʿAlī said: (")This woman was (is) in case of necessity and (she)

scholars approve of this practice. Although this is a possible scenario, allowing such an excuse could open the door to illicit practices (*fasād*). Moreover, there certainly could be ways other than *zinā* to remedy such a situation. A woman enmeshed in such dire straights (*ḍarūrah quṣwā*) could seek a job or request help from the government. At worst, she might be able to take out a loan, even if she had to pay interest (*ribā*) under the principle of the lesser of two evils (*akhaff aḍ-ḍararīna*). All such avenues could be exploited instead of committing such a grave offence.[52]

Another contemporary issue concerning the application of this maxim in criminal law is the question whether a pregnant woman should be allowed to terminate her pregnancy in light of critical or life-threatening difficulties. Modern scholars have questioned the right to terminate in cases referring. The position of the law states that termination of pregnancy is prohibited if it takes place after 120 days of gestation.[53] However, before this period, a pregnancy may be terminated on condition that the mother's health is not endangered. Moreover, using an invalid excuse for terminating a pregnancy is unacceptable in Islam.

Rules of Necessity and Conditions for Leniency

Many maxims, in one way or another, form subsidiaries of the basic general maxim. While some of them explain or expand upon the basic general maxim, others provide conditions for leniency (*taysīr*). In this section, we shall discuss some of these maxims in light of their relevance to criminal offences in Islamic Law.[54]

---

should be released. (And) Omar released her". If the report is true it may be accepted as *ijmā'* of the *ṣaḥāba*, which at the time was considered evidence, as discussed in *uṣūl*. It is possible to accept it under necessity but the question remains: does preserving her life supersede her act of adultery? This will be referred to in the hierarchy of preserving the five necessities.

52 See Izzu al-Din, Abdul 'Azeez bn Abdul al-Salam, *Qawaid al-Ahkam fi Masalih al-Anam*, Cairo: Maktaba al-Kulliyyat al-Azhar, 1991/1414, 99. The author insisted that not excuse for committing act of zina even under the pretext of darura.

53 al-Burnu, *al-Wajīz*, 240. This is because after that period the fetus has developed into a completely formed human being, and therefore terminating the pregnancy at that stage is considered to be a grave sin. See Q. 17:41; al-Bukhārī, *Kitāb Bad' al-Khalq*, Ḥadīth No. 3036; and Muslim, *Kitāb al-Qadr*, Ḥadīth No. 2643.

54 There is no consistency in the classification of these maxims. Some maxims mentioned here are classified under the grand maxim discussed in Ch. 6 because of the correlation between these two grand maxims in terms of the issues relevant to both of them. This

"Whenever the Circle of an Affair Narrows, it is Widened, and Whenever it Widens, it is Narrowed" (idhā ḍāq al-amr ittasaʿ wa-idhā ittasaʿ ḍāq)[55]

This sub-maxim is a further explanation of the grand maxim and indicates that facility should not be abused. The two phrases in this subsidiary maxim are closely intertwined and emphasize how the grand maxim might also be applied. The summary of this maxim states that, if there is an apparent hardship (*mashaqqa*) in any matter, there should also be facility (*taysīr*) for it. The elimination of hardship should reverse the matter to its original rule. As A. al-Zarqā' states: "If necessity and hardship cause facility, the facility should be enjoyed until the condition changes; then one should revert to the normal rule".[56]

Al-Shāfiʿī has been credited with the coinage of the maxim for a woman who had lost her guardian (*walī*) while on a journey. When she asked the scholar if she could appoint another man to be her *walī*, al-Shāfiʿī agreed: "because if the circle of the matter narrows, it is widened [by an easement]". This indicates that one of the aims of Islamic Law is to make things easy for its adherents and to make them avail of the concessions for facility (*taysīr*) when they encounter difficulty.[57] The second part of the maxim concerning the extent to which a breach of rules can be legally accepted under the banner of necessity will be dealt with after the next subsidiary maxim.

For instance, it is clearly expressed in Qur'ānic verses 4:101–103 that, in the wake of hardships during war, Muslims are allowed to shorten their obligatory prayers, so that four pillars of prayer (*rakaʿāt*) can be reduced to two. However, after war has ended, prayers should be performed as normal.[58] It is also reported that the Prophet prohibited the storage of meat sacrificed for the *Aḍḥā* festival for more than three days because of the villagers coming to visit the people of Medina. However, when festivities ended, the citizens were allowed to store meat for a longer period of time.[59]

---

author sees al-Burnu's classification as sensible and applicable to my needs in this book. *Cf.*, al-Burnu, *al-Wajīz*, 230–250; and Ibn Nujaym, *al-Ashbāh wa-n-Naẓā'ir*, 77–84.

55 al-Suyūṭī, *al-Ashbāh*, 83: and Ibn Nujaym *al-Ashbāh wa-n-Naẓā'ir*, 84. The *Majalla* mentions the first part of the maxim in Article 18. See also A. al-Zarqā', *Sharḥ*, 165; M. al-Zarqā', *al-Madkhal*, §599; and al-Burnu, *al-Wajīz*, 230.

56 A. al-Zarqā', *Sharḥ*, 163; and al-Burnu, *al-Wajīz*, 230.

57 M. al-Zarqā', *al-Madkhal*, §599; and al-Burnu, *al-Wajīz*, 230.

58 Q. 4:101–103.

59 Muslim, Ḥadīth No. 1971; al-Ashʿath, Ḥadīth Nos. 2812 and 2813; al-Nasa'ī, Ḥadīth No. 2032.

It can be deduced from the Qurʾānic verse and prophetic tradition referred to above that it is in the spirit of Islamic Law to provide facilitation for the masses when faced with any difficulty in their daily activities or legislation. Although the references mentioned above are particular to certain issues in Islamic jurisprudence, their applications are not restricted to those issues because "Consideration is given to the generality of the word, not the peculiarity of the cause [of revelation]" (*al-ʿibra bi-ʿumūm al-lafẓ lā bi-khuṣūṣ as-sabab*).[60] Those references form the basis for the legality of ensuring facility for the public good; once the difficulty ceases, lawful practice returns to the status quo.[61]

"Necessities Render prohibited Things Lawful" (aḍ-ḍarūrāt tubīḥ al-maḥẓūrāt)[62]

This sub-maxim is itself a broad principle, in spite of its being classified under the grand maxim, and popular maxim among jurists. Its interpretation differs slightly from that of the grand maxim in question. However, its popularity, together with the grand maxim, is related to the fact that they derive their sources from the Qurʾānic verse: "He [God] hath explained to you in detail what is forbidden to you except under compulsion of necessity".[63]

When man is faced with dire necessity, he is allowed to use what is forbidden until he secures a permissible opportunity. Broadly speaking, 'necessity' as recognized by the Sharīʿa can be categorized as follows:

1. Necessity that can change the legal status of an action from prohibited (*maḥẓūr*) to permissible (*mubāḥa*), such as eating normally forbidden carrion and pork, when fearing starvation;
2. Necessity that cannot change the rule (*ḥukm*) but can be carried out when the condition warrants, such as taking someone's property without permission. This is allowed, provided that the owner of the property suffers less hardship than the perpetrator had he not acted. However,

---

60 al-Shinqitī, 2:302, 360; Abū Hayyan Muḥammad b. Yūsuf al-Andalusi, *al-Baḥr al-Muḥīt fī t-Tafsīr*, edited by ʿAdil Aḥmad, (Beirut: Dār al-Kutub al-ʿIlmiyya, 1993), 3:505; Shihāb al-Dīn al-Ālūsī, *Rūḥ al-Maʿānī* (Beirut: Dār Iḥyāʾ at-Turāth al-ʿArabī, n.d.), 6:120–122; al-Ghazālī, *al-Mustaṣfā*, 1:236; Muhammad b. ʿAbdullah b. Bahadir al-Zarkashī, *al-Baḥr al-Muḥīṭ fī Uṣūl al-Fiqh*, (Beirut: Dār al-Kutub al-ʿIlmiyyah 2000/1421) 2:367.

61 al-Burnu, *al-Wajīz*, 232.

62 al-Suyūtī, *al-Ashbāh wa-n-Naẓāʾir*, 84; Ibn Nujaym, *al-Ashbāh wa-n-Naẓāʾir*, 85; *Majalla*, Article 21; A. al-Zarqāʾ, *Sharḥ*, 185; and al-Burnu, *al-Wajīz*, 234.

63 Q. 6:119, 140; Q. 5:3; Q. 2:173.

compensation must be given to the owner of the property because the principle of "Necessity does not invalidate the rights of others" (*al-iḍṭirār lā yubṭil ḥaqq al-ghayr*).[64]

3. Necessity that is neither recognized in Islam nor granted facilitation is, *e.g.*, the killing of a fellow Muslim under the pretext of compulsion, or the act of adultery under the pretext of sexual passion. Offences falling under this category cannot be legally justified.[65]

The attention given to this maxim by both classical and contemporary Islamic scholars should not be underestimated. What remains controversial is the question whether it is a subsidiary of the grand maxim "*al-mashaqqa tajlib at-taysīr*" or of the grand maxim "*aḍ-ḍarar yuzāl*". This quandary, which will be discussed later, arises from the fact that *ḍarūra* in this maxim can be used interchangeably with *mashaqqa* and *ḍarar*. To classical Islamic jurists, the maxim of *aḍ-ḍarūra* is a sub-division of the maxim *lā ḍarar*, while the maxims *lā ḍarar* and *al-mashaqqa* are synonymous, or "*mutadākhil wa muttaḥid*" (interwoven and concordant). However, al-Burnu affirms that there is no unity between the two legal maxims but rather that they are interwoven. He observes that the legal maxim *aḍ-ḍarūrā* emerged to affirm the legality of facilitation (*taysīr*) in the face of difficulty. Thus, it is appropriate to consider it as a 'sister' of the maxim *al-mashaqqa*.[66]

On the other hand, *lā ḍarar* or *aḍ-ḍarar* is an independent maxim, which explains the need for eliminating any harm (*ḍarar*) posed by someone against another. Although al-Burnu recognizes the interchangeability of the two grand maxims, he asserts that one maxim focuses on general difficulty (*ḍarar*) encountered by mankind, while the other concentrates on the prohibition of initiating or inflicting greater harm (*ḍirār*) on another individual.[67] Therefore, the maxim *al-mashaqqa* and its 'sisters' are more applicable to the facility provided for ordinary difficulties rather than difficulties beyond our control. For example, difficulties caused by disability are not necessarily caused by human beings, whereas the maxim of *aḍ-ḍarar yuzāl* is specific to any hardship caused by human transgression affecting a person's life, body or property.

Although their existence is present in both maxims, the reasons or causes for these difficulties differ. The effect of the maxim *aḍ-ḍarūra* in both cases is that the elimination of that hardship or harm is legal if and when the

---

64 M. Al-Zarqa, 213; al-Burnu, al-Wajiz, 244.

65 al-Burnu, *al-Wajīz*, 236–237.

66 Al-Burnu, ibid.

67 *Ibid.*, 234.

individual observes and adheres to all the prescribed conditions laid down for the elimination of that hardship. Thus someone is allowed to drink alcohol during hardship (*mashaqqa*), provided there is nothing else to drink, and someone may have to kill or injure a burglar in the defense of his property and family under the maxim of eliminating harm (*ḍarar*).

"What is Permitted by Virtue of Necessity Should be Estimated According to its Quantity" (mā ubīḥa li-ḍ-ḍarūrāt yuqaddar bi-qadarihā),[68] *or "Necessity is Estimated According to Its Quantity"* (aḍ-ḍarūra tuqaddar bi-qadarihā)[69]

These two maxims are phrased differently but denote the same meaning. The former was coined by classical Islamic jurists, while the latter has been rephrased by modern jurists. The two maxims are set as conditions and restrictions to regulate the use of the provision of facility (*taysīr*) in the case of necessity. As mentioned above, the Qur'ān has categorically stated that the only acceptable excuse for breaking rules is reasonable and genuine necessity: *i.e.*, "without willful disobedience, or transgressing due limits" (*ghayra bāghin wa-lā 'ādin*).[70] Thus, any facility given should be minimized, as some people may abuse the facility under the pretext of necessity. This is an indication that he who abuses the chance will be guilty of disobedience.

The yardstick for determining the proportion of facility to grant under the pretext of necessity is what is recognized by the law, namely, the five necessities of religion (*dīn*), life (*nafs*), offspring/lineage (*nasl*), wealth/property (*māl*), intellect (*'aql*) and what would be required to safeguard them.[71] However, it is also worth remembering that the amount of what is prohibited to protect these five necessities is relative. What is deemed to be a sustainable portion for one individual may not be sustainable for another. Under the proportionality of necessity, when someone is allowed to drink or eat a prohibited substance it must not be used in excess because "Necessity is estimated according to its quantity" (*aḍ-ḍarūra tuqaddar bi-qadarihā*). Moreover, while someone may not steal a large quantity of flour on the grounds of necessity, the same would

68 al-Suyūṭī, *al-Ashbāh*, 84; and Ibn Nujaym, *al-Ashbāh wa-n-Naẓā'ir*, 86.

69 *Majalla*, Article 22; M. al-Zarqā', *al-Madkhal*, §601; and al-Burnu, *al-Wajīz*, 239.

70 *Cf.*, Q. 2:173, Q. 6:145, and Q. 16:115.

71 See al-Ghazālī, *al-Mustaṣfā*, 1:139–140; Muḥammad Muslehuddin, *Philosophy of Islamic Law and The Orientalists: A Comparative Study of Islamic Legal Systems* (Lahore: Islamic Publications, 1980), 163.

not apply to someone who steals a loaf of bread because of extreme hunger. Stealing the flour is neither allowed nor legally justifiable because the robbery went beyond the limit of necessity, while stealing a loaf of bread is excusable under the rule of necessity.[72]

Where conditions warrant that the law would be breached, there must be a mechanism in place to block the occurrence of evil. For example, if a male doctor has to step in for an absent midwife, a female assistant should be with him under the rule of "blocking of evil" (*sadd adh-dharīʿah*). Failure to have a female assistant present in such a situation could lead to a criminal offence in Islam that attracts a discretionary punishment. The same applies when a male, rather than female, doctor must examine the more intimate areas of a female patient's body. This however should not be unduly exploited.

"What is Permissible by Virtue of Excuse Becomes Invalid With the Expiration of the Excuse" **(mā jāz li-ʿudhur baṭala bi-zawālihi)**[73]

This maxim is similar to the above but its focus is on the duration of the license to break the rules. The duration set for the expiration of the reprieve granted to break the law in the face of necessity is until that hardship (*mashaqqa*) or the cause (*ʿilla*) of the hardship disappears. The phrase used in Qurʾānic verses on the permissibility of prohibited things in the face of necessity is "neither craving nor transgressing" and, as such, has placed a clear limitation on the exploitation of the provision. Thus, this indicates, as al-Rāzī (d. 604/1209) states: "If the reason for the permission contained in the verses legalizing a violation of rules ceases to exist, the permission is no more".[74] Thus, if one is given facility to drink alcohol in the wake of thirst, or to eat forbidden meat in the wake of starvation, then at the point when thirst or starvation ceases to exist the law returns to its *status quo*, and what is forbidden will again be liable for punishment. This is because the necessity to alter the law to avoid excessive hardship and punishment is gone, and according to a legal maxim that regulates this issue is: "What is permissible by virtue of excuse becomes invalid with the expiration of the excuse" (*mā jāz li-ʿudhur baṭala bi-zawālihi*).

---

72 Maḥmaṣṣānī, 155.

73 al-Suyūṭī, *al-Ashbāh*, 85; Ibn Nujaym, *al-Ashbāh wa-n-Naẓāʾir*, 86; and *Majalla*, Article 23.

74 Muḥammad b. ʿUmar Fakhr al-Dīn al-Rāzī, *at-Tafsīr al-Kabīr* (Beirut: Dār al-Kutub al-ʿIlmiyya, n.d.), 2:13.

"Need, Whether of Public or Private in Nature, is Considered a Necessity" (al-ḥāja tunazzil manzilat aḍ-ḍarūra, ʿāmma kānat aw khāṣṣa)[75]

The previous sub-maxims concern necessity, while this maxim includes any other need, be it personal or public. Thus, *ḥāja* is a need that is pressing to a lesser degree than necessity (*ḍarūra*). Ibn Qayyim al-Jawziyya, in an attempt to draw a demarcation between *ḍarūra* and *ḥāja*, opined that *ḥāja* is when what is prohibited as a preventive measure (*sadd adh-dharīʿa*) becomes permissible for the public interest, while what is prohibited with definite purpose can only be permissible by virtue of necessity.[76] However, according to the maxim in question, *ḥāja* is regarded as *ḍarūra* in some circumstances.[77] Exceptions or facilitation can be considered in three situational categories:

1. Necessity (*ḍarūra*), a situation where a person is allowed the violate the law and commit an unlawful act, because if he failed to act then his life, dignity, religion, offspring, and property would be endangered.[78]
2. Need (*ḥāja*), a situation whereby a person could encounter less difficulty or hardship if he failed to commit an unlawful act, although his life would not be in danger. Committing an unlawful act would ward off difficulty.
3. Luxury (*kamāliyya* or *taḥsīniyya*), a situation in which a person seeks something excessive to maximize enjoyment in his life. For example, in Islamic criminal law, looking at a foreign woman (with sexual desire) outside one's own family is prohibited in order to complement the preservation of offspring and the enforcement of that law.[79]

The first and second categories are the rights protected by Islam and the facilities enacted to achieve this. The last category, however, is not subject to discussion. Simply put, if a law is broken in order to enhance a life of luxury, the perpetrator will be subjected to criminal charges.

---

75 al-Suyūṭī, *al-Ashbāh*, 88; Ibn Nujaym *al-Ashbāh wa-n-Naẓāʾir*, 91; *Majalla*, Article 32; and al-Burnu, *al-Wajīz*, 242.

76 Ibn al-Qayyim al-Jawziyya, *Iʿlām*, 3:119.

77 *Cf.*, al-Shāṭibī, 2:8, al-Ghazālī, *al-Mustaṣfā*, 2:481; al-Amidi, 3:393–396; and al-Rāzī, *at-Tafsīr*, 2:578.

78 Haydar, 1:38; M. al-Zarqāʾ, *al-Madkhal*, 2:997; and Wahba Mustafa al-Zuhayli, *Naẓariyyat aḍ-Ḍarūra ash-Sharʿiyya*, 67–68.

79 al-Shāṭibī, 2:12.

When considering *ḥāja* as a supportive element of necessity, if a situation becomes problematic, either publicly or privately, easements can be given to facilitate the situation. The only marked difference between *ḥāja* and *ḍarūra* is that, in the case of the latter, the commission of an unlawful act to prevent envisaged damage or injury is obligatory, whereas, in the former, one can choose not to prevent it. Here it is pertinent to remark that, in cases of necessity or need, a person is not allowed to choose what will harm and endanger his life, or affect any other preserved rights to life, even in the case of worship. al-Shāṭibī stresses that "it is not the right of a capable person to inflict on himself strenuous and harsh burdens by doing exhausting deeds. But he should aim to perform legitimate deeds in order to be rewarded".[80] Choosing a difficult deed that could be injurious to life in order to draw nearer to God is not part of religion. Ibn ʿAbd al-Salām observes that such strenuous deeds are not considered as a glorification of God and that engaging in one renders the act non-rewardable.[81]

Preservation of Rights: "Necessity Does Not Invalidate the Rights of Others" (*al-iḍṭirār lā yubṭil ḥaqq al-ghayr*)[82]

Another measure designed to curb the abusive use of the provision of facility is the protection of people's rights, as mentioned earlier. Despite the fact that someone is allowed to damage or use another person's property when necessity prevails, provided that said damage would not result in equal or greater harm for the owner of the goods, Islamic Law does not divest the rights of individuals. The Qur'ān categorically denounces all ways of taking people's property illegally.[83] Whether the reason for breaching the rules relates to a natural (*samāwī*) hardship, such as starvation or in defense of one's rights, or to an unnatural (*ghayr samāwī*) cause, such as uttering an abusive word under compulsion where an individual is absolutely unable to choose between options, the rights of the individual(s) affected are always protected under Islamic Law.

80 *Ibid.*, 2: 119; and Ibn ʿAbd al-Salam, *Qawāʿid al-Aḥkām*, 30.

81 Ibn ʿAbd al-Salam, *Ibid.*, 30.

82 Ibn Rajab, *al-Qawāʿid*, 26; *Majalla*, Article 33; M. al-Zarqāʾ, *al-Madkhal*, §602; and al-Burnu, *al-Wajīz*, 44.

83 Q. 4:2, 29; and Q. 2:188.

The Prophet is reported to have said: "It is unlawful to take the property of a Muslim without his express consent".[84] Thus, in cases where someone in dire need makes off with another person's belongings in order to save himself, the majority of Islamic scholars agree that it is incumbent on offender, or his guardian, or the government's treasury if he is indigent, to reimburse the owner for the value of the property lost.

The only waiver given to the perpetrator is that he can plead not guilty of stealing. Yet, the owner's rights must be indemnified because absconding with his property would deprive him of his rightful ownership which would contradict a fundamental principle of Islamic justice. Divesting people of their belongings without any restitution, even if the reason is to save a life, would amount to eliminating harm with harm, which is antithetical to the spirit of Islamic Law.[85]

General Application of the Grand Maxim *al-Mashaqqa Tajlib at-Taysīr* and its Subsidiaries in Several Northern Nigerian Sharīʿa Criminal Law Cases

As discussed earlier, under the maxim of giving hardship provision of facility, illness and general necessity among others are factors that warrant facility for the perpetrator in Islamic criminal law. In some cases, these factors have been undermined when adjudicated under the full implementation of the Sharīʿa in Northern Nigeria. Take, for instance, the case of *Abukakar Abdullahi Kaura* [defendant] *v. Jamilu Isaka B/Magagi* [complainant], where the Upper Sharīʿa Court K/Namoda found the defendant guilty of theft (*sariqa*). It was reported that, on 20 November 2000 at about 3:30 am, the said accused broke into a shop belonging to the complainant and stole clothes worth N30,350. However, in this case, it was observed that the accused should have been given a lesser punishment (*taʿzīr*) instead of amputation of his right hand, as decided by the court, because of his dire circumstances. He explained before the court that he was an ex-prisoner and a family man without means of support. Perhaps he might have been suffering from a mental illness as well resulting from his long

---

84 *Cf.*, Muslim, "*Kitāb al-Imān*", Ḥadīth No. 108; and Muḥammad Shams al-Ḥaqq al-al-ʿAẓīmabādī, *ʿAwn al-Maʿbūd Sharḥ Sunān Abī Dāwūd, Bāb fī ṣ-Ṣulḥ*, 2nd edn. (Beirut: Dār al-Kutub al-ʿIlmiyya, 1995), 9:373–374.

85 al-Burnu, *al-Wajīz*, 244.

imprisonment. All these factors constitute what could be termed 'hardship' that warrants facility under Islamic criminal law.[86]

Similarly, in the case of *Commissioner of Police* [Zamfara State as complainant] *v. Buba Bello Jangebe* [defendant], facility given for ignorance of the fact of law was undermined. The accused was convicted for stealing a cow during the earlier years after re-introduction of Islamic penal law in Northern Nigeria. On 21 February 2000, Jangebe was charged for conspiracy and stealing a cow belonging to Dan Mande Matuna. It is astonishing that the accused was arrested by a vigilante group rather than by the owner of the cow. Moreover, it was police officer Shafi Garba who took him to court for the crime instead of the cow's owner. If theft is a crime concerning the right of man, it is legally inappropriate for the accused to be charged since no one had complained that the cow had gone missing. However, if theft is a crime attributed to the absolute right of God, then the property need not be returned and perhaps punishment could have been avoided. However, while scrutinizing the case, it was not clear how it has been viewed.

My observation is that, since the case was one of the first to be tried under the new, fully implemented Islamic penal law, there were irregularities in the legal procedures from the outset, which accounted for many erroneous judgments. Moreover, it was claimed that the herdsman was ignorant of the fact of the law, which is one of the factors that renders punishment of offences of that nature abated. In addition, no adequate infrastructure was in place to enlighten the public as to the severity of the punishment resulting from confession to such crimes. At that particular point in time, before re-enforcement of the Sharīʿa, poverty was rampant in the society at large, which could serve as justification for the claim of necessity leading to the commission of theft. Had the souls of mankind been sanctified before the introduction of penal codes, Jangebe and people like him might not have succumbed to such a disruptive attitude.[87]

In the same vein, the factors of ignorance of the fact and details of the law of adultery could be argued in the cases of Aminal Lawal, Safiyyatu Hussaini and Bariya Magadisu. Here, there was an absence of facility given for ignorance. It could be argued that since the convicted women were villagers, it is possible that they were ignorant of what constitutes the term *zinā* as well as their rights

86 See for details, Zakariyah, *Applications of Legal Maxims*, Appendix 2.

87 See for details of the case, Zakariyah, *Applications of Legal Maxims, Appendix* 8; and Opeloye, Muhib O., *The Sustainability of Shariah in a Pluralistic and Democratic Nigeria*, 5th Faculty of Arts Guest Lecture Series, (Lagos State University, 24 August 2005).

to retract their confessions. While adultery and fornication are unequivocally denounced in Islam, there is no suggestion whatsoever that women are permitted to commit *zinā* under the pretext of harm (*ḍarar*). However, there must be full compliance with the standard rules laid down for prosecuting and convicting any accused person of such an offense.

Conclusion

This chapter has explained the stand Islamic Law takes in considering hardship, which states that facility must be provided for mankind. Moreover, those factors that necessitate giving facility as well as their application in criminal cases have been enunciated. Here emphasis has been on the facility for redemption, not only for the victim but also for the culprit in any dire situation.

A victim's rights can never be negated in vain because "Necessity does not invalidate the rights of others" (*al-iḍṭirār lā yubṭil ḥaqq al-ghayr*). However, if a person's rights are violated because of necessity (*ḍarūra*), generally the perpetrator will not be punished under the provision "Necessities render illicit things lawful" (*aḍ-ḍarūrāt tubīḥ al-maḥẓūrāt*). However, any excessive use of this provision will warrant that blame be laid upon the perpetrator because "Necessity is estimated according to its quantity" (*aḍ-ḍarūra tuqaddar bi-qadarihā*). While there are three categories of provisions aimed to facilitate human life, *viz* necessity (*ḍarūra*), needs (*ḥāja*) and luxury (*kamāliyya* or *taḥsīniyya*), the second category relates to the level of necessity for both individuals and the public because at times both necessity and need are inseparable.

CHAPTER 6

Legal Maxim regarding Elimination of Harm: "No Injury/Harm Shall Be Inflicted or Reciprocated" (*Lā Ḍarar wa-lā Ḍirār*)*

Prohibition and Elimination of Harm (*Ḍarar*)

The fourth basic general maxim, which is directly lifted from the Ḥadīth of the Prophet, deals with the prohibition of harm and injury and elimination of hardship as defined in Chapter 5. This maxim encompasses many subjects in Islamic Law and is widely applicable to any matter relating to the occurrence, avoidance, and elimination of harm in obligatory duties. Of course, the rules of Islamic jurisprudence are laid down to attract benefits and to eliminate hardship,[1] in order to protect the five necessities of life recognized by Islam: religion (*dīn*), life (*nafs*), offspring/lineage (*nasl*), wealth/property (*māl*) and intellect (*ʿaql*).[2] The maxim emphasizes the purposes of the Sharīʿa (*maqāṣid ash-sharīʿa*) and their actualization and realization by way of deterrents (*zajr*) or preventive measures (*sadd adh-dharīʿa*), or minimization of their occurrence.[3]

Definition and Interpretation of the Maxim *Lā Ḍarar wa-lā Ḍirār*

Some Muslim scholars prefer to coin the maxim as "Harm should be eliminated" (*aḍ-ḍarar yuzāl*), citing "No harm shall be inflicted or reciprocated" (*lā ḍarar wa-lā ḍirār*) as evidence for the legality of the maxim.[4] Others code the Ḥadīth as a grand maxim with other subsidiary maxims.[5] The reason for this, according to al-Burnu, is that the Ḥadīth encompasses all ways of inflicting harm (*ḍarar*), whether by transgression or in reciprocation. And in fact,

* al-Shatibi, *al-Muwafaqat*, 2:72, 3:55, 61; al-Suyuti, *al-Ashbah*, 83; Ibn Nujaym, *al-Ashbah*, 72; M. Al-Zarqa, 165; al-Burnu, *al-Wajiz*, 26.

1 al-Nadawī, 287.

2 al-Shāṭibī *al-Muwafaqat*, 1:31.

3 Ibn al-Najjār, *Sharḥ al-Kawkab al-Munīr*, 4:443–444.

4 al-Suyūṭī, *al-Ashbāh*, 83; and Ibn Nujaym, *al-Ashbāh wa-n-Naẓāʾir*, 85.

5 *Cf.*, *Majalla*, Article 19; A. al-Zarqāʾ, *Sharḥ*, 165; M. al-Zarqāʾ, *al-Madkhal*, 586; and al-Burnu, *al-Wajīz*, 251.

 DOI 10.1163/9789004304871_007

using the Ḥadīth as a maxim strengthens its status.[6] In his comment on the Ḥadīth that forms the basis for the maxim, al-Shāṭibī says that, although the Ḥadīth is not as sound as others, it embodies all kinds of harm that are prohibited in Islam.[7] A. al-Zarqā᾽ distinguishes between the two maxims, as "the maxim stated by the tradition of the Prophet stands as a prohibition of inflicting *ḍarar* and the other one indicates that if *ḍarar* occurs for one reason or another, it should be removed".[8] Presented thus, the two maxims do appear characteristically distinct.

Preventing harm is a fundamental principle (*aṣl*) generally agreed upon and widely applied in Islamic jurisprudence, as it has its roots firmly in Qur᾽ānic injunctions and in the traditions of the Prophet. God in the Qur᾽ān states: "no mother shall be treated unfairly [caused harm] on account of her child, nor father on account of his child",[9] and prohibits giving property to an infant who cannot manage his affairs in order not to cause harm to afflict him in the future as he might destroy the property before attaining puberty.[10] Instructions for distributing inheritance require that "no loss [harm] is caused to any one".[11] It is also reported that a landowner came to the Prophet complaining about another man who had planted a tree on his property, thus harming the land. Because of this, the Prophet asked the man to pay compensation to the landowner or give him the tree as a gift. The planter refused both options, so the Prophet asked the landowner to destroy the tree, and told its owner: "You are harming someone".[12]

This maxim has been interpreted in different ways. Some scholars interpret the two words as synonyms, asserting that the latter (*ḍirār*) is nothing more than an emphasis on the former (*ḍarar*), while other scholars hold that the two words have different meanings because "Establishing a new norm is better than emphasizing an existing one" (*at-ta᾽sīs aw-lā min at-ta᾽kīd*).[13] However, there is no unique interpretation given to either word. The most common interpretation states that the word *ḍarar* means inflicting harm on another person who has not caused you harm, while *ḍirār* means inflicting

6 al-Burnu, *al-Wajīz*, 251.
7 al-Shāṭibī 3:185.
8 A. al-Zarqā᾽, *Sharḥ*, 166.
9 Q. 2:233.
10 Q. 4:5.
11 Q. 4:12.
12 al-Ash'ath, 15:321–322; Ibn Taymiyya, *Majmūʿ al-Fatāwā*, 4:479 and 28:104; Ibrāhīm Muḥammad Ibn Mufliḥ, *al-Furūʿ*, edited by Abū al-Zahra Hazim (Beirut: Dār al-Kutub al-ʿIlmiyya, 1418/1997), 4:219.
13 al-Suyuti, al-Ashbah, 135; M. al-Zarqa, 165.

harm, beyond what is legally acceptable, on another person who could have caused you harm.[14] Ibn ʿAbd al-Barr (d. 463/1071) in his *Tamhīd* gives an interesting distinction between the two words: "*Ḍarar* is harm inflicted on another and from which the perpetrator derives benefit [*manāfiʿ*], while *ḍirār* is harm inflicted on another from which no one benefits".[15]

Drawing on these different interpretations, two ways of inflicting harm (*ḍarar*) can be inferred: namely, either with or without any reason or legal justification. Pointless, legally unjustifiable harm can be further categorized in one of two ways: *i.e.*, (1) *ḍarar* can refer to harm that is in no way beneficial, that Islam deems utterly abhorrent, that is more severe than an intentional transgression stemming from a whim or caprice, such as random killing whose perpetrators deserve prosecution; or (2) *ḍarar* can refer to an act that benefits the perpetrator, that is not considered criminal but which nevertheless demands the financial restitution (*diya*) to the victim, such as when someone starts a bonfire in his garden to clear out rubbish but accidentally harms a neighbor when the fire spreads, despite having taken every precaution. However, when someone is harmed due to a perpetrator's negligence (*ihmāl*), then the act will be considered a criminal offense and prosecution will attract a discretionary *taʿzīr* assignment.

Even when reasons for having caused harmful acts can be legally justified, as in the case of fixed (*ḥadd*) punishments, the law provides measures to deter other malicious crimes. The harm incurred and its punishment pursuant to the law depends upon the type of crime: *i.e.*, the death penalty (*itlāf nafs*) for intentional homicide (*qatl ʿamd*) and banditry (*ḥirāba*); stoning to death (*rajm*) for adultery (*zinā*) committed by a married individual; amputation (*qaṭʿ*) of hands for theft (*sariqa*); and flogging (*jald*) for fornication (*zinā*) committed by an unmarried individual, for drinking alcohol (*shurb al-khamr*), and for the defamation (*qadhf*) of a chaste person. The implementation of such fixed punishments also causes harm and results in severe injury if not death. However, despite there being a margin of injury in all the fixed punishments (*ḥudūd*) in Islamic criminal law, this injury is not recognized as a reason to eliminated punishments that are meant to be preventive measures (*sadd adh-dharīʿa*) required by the Sharīʿa in order to protect citizens from harmful, vicious deeds.

Thus, to interpret the words *wa-lā ḍirār* as "and no harm in reciprocation" could be misleading, because punishing an offender for his crime could arguably come under the prohibition of reciprocation. However, penalizing offenders as a deterrent to decrease or prevent harmful incidents would provide

14 al-Hamawi, 118; and al-Burnu, *al-Wajīz*, 252.

15 Ibn ʿAbd al-Barr, *at-Tamhīd*, 20:158.

greater benefits than allowing them to go unpunished (*i.e.*, an attitude of permissibility towards an offence is more harmful than punishing an offender). While no legal system will exempt an offender from rightful punishment, there will be discrepancies in the degree or severity of punishments accorded. Guaranteeing the safety of the public at large is the government's paramount task. That is why Islamic Law, seeking to benefit both public and private interests, enacts appropriate measures to punish offenders as a deterrent to prevent further criminal acts against society.

An individual who initiates an injurious act that causes harm deserves punishment. Although some jurists subscribe to the interpretation "and no reciprocal harm" for the traditional maxim *wa-lā ḍirār*, punishing crime does not contradict the rules laid down to protect the masses, for the following reasons. First, no one should take the law into one's own hands and inflict injury on another person as revenge for harm suffered. That is why Islam advocates recourse to authority.[16] Second, anyone who poses a threat to the general public deserves no protection; the Prophet states: "A transgressor has no rights" (*laysa li-ʿirq ẓālim ḥaqq*).[17] Third, Islam sometimes (a) recommends settlement through the payment of blood money (*diya*) in lieu of retaliation in kind (as in Q. 2:178); (b) encourages forgiveness for the crime of defamation (*qadhf*) (as in Q. 24:22); and recommends concealment of errors in any situation that would attract a *ḥadd* punishment if reported to the authorities (as in the prophetic Ḥadīth).[18] This philosophy does not contradict the necessity of bringing wrongdoers to justice, particularly in cases related to the right of God where there is room for forgiveness if the offence is concealed. Even if the wrongdoer is subsequently punished, it may serve as expiation.[19]

Be that as it may, on the basis of this maxim, according to various interpretations, harm can be prevented in three ways. First, while an individual should always attempt to escape harm, if avoidance seems impossible, then the other should not be harmed in one's attempt to allay the situation. Second, if someone has been harmed in any way, revenge should not exceed the degree of the original harm. Third, someone may legally attempt to avert an anticipated harm, but subject to the first two conditions just stated. Taking into consideration the ways in which harm or injury can be averted will definitely serve the purpose of justice intended by the Sharīʿa for resolving disputes.

16 Quran 4:59 and 83.
17 al-Tirmidhī, Ḥadīth No. 1394; and al-Ashʿath, Ḥadīth No. 3073.
18 al-Bukhārī, Ḥadīth No. 2310; Ibn Mājah, Ḥadīth No. 2544; and al-Ashʿath, Ḥadīth No. 4893.
19 M. al-Zarqāʾ, *al-Madkhal*, 586; and al-Burnu, *al-Wajīz*, 255.

Related Maxims

"Injury Should be Removed" (aḍ-ḍarar yuzāl)[20]

While the basic general maxim discussed above prohibits unjustified harm against fellow human beings, this maxim addresses the position of the law when harm has occurred. Intuitively we realize that not every human being adheres to rules; thus, whether a single individual or the public at large is threatened, the law requires that the cause of harm be eliminated.[21] For instance, if a house is built too near to a public path that could endanger passers-by, or affect neighbors, the government has the authority to demolish it.[22] All legislation enacted to facilitate the smooth running of people's lives is included in this maxim. Once harm (*ḍarar*) has occurred, then it must be eliminated within the limits of the law. However, during the process of carrying out the law, certain conditions must be observed, which is the focus of the following maxims.

"Harm Should be Prevented as Much as Possible" (aḍ-ḍarar yudfaʿ bi-qadr al-imkān)[23]

One fundamental principle of Islamic Law states that any means to prevent the occurrence of harm (*ḍarar*) should be sought because it is better to prevent than to alleviate harm. Legally it is preferable to eliminate harm without causing further trouble, but should that prove difficult then the secondary harm must be proportionate to the original offence. It is worth observing that the maxim under consideration differs from the sub-maxim: "Necessity is estimated according to its quantity" (*aḍ-ḍarūra tuqaddar bi-qadarihā*).[24] While the latter is particular for the measure of allowance given for eliminating natural difficulties, the maxim we will deal with here relates to the degree of freedom allowed for someone trying to eliminate harm caused by another person. As indicated in this maxim, one can either attempt to prevent the first occurrence of harm or to prevent further occurrences thereafter.

Measures put in place to prevent the occurrence of harm should be in accordance with the principle of public interest (*maṣāliḥ ʿāmma*) that conforms

20 al-Suyūṭī, *al-Ashbāh*, 83.

21 *Ibid.*; Ibn Nujaym, *al-Ashbāh wa-n-Naẓāʾir*, 85; *Majalla*, Article 20; and al-Hamawi, 1:37.

22 al-Burnu, *al-Wajīz*, 258.

23 *Majalla*, Article 31; M. al-Zarqāʾ, *al-Madkhal*, 587; and al-Burnu, *al-Wajīz*, 256.

24 See page 151.

to the spirit of Islam.[25] Evidence that typifies this can be found in a Qurʾānic directive[26] telling Muslim leaders to fortify themselves with any means of power in order to prevent harm caused by an enemy. To that end, all preventative measures to thwart crime must be sought both by the state and its citizens.

This maxim is widely applicable to many matters involving both the occurrence as well as the elimination of harm or danger. Based on this maxim, someone may defend himself against any aggression that could endanger his life or inflict damage to his body or property. During the process of defending oneself, any injury suffered by the aggressor would not be considered a criminal act as long as it was proportionate to the aggressor's potential for causing injury. For example, when someone has just cause to fend off an intruder who has forcibly entered his home and threatened his household, he will be exempted from punishment or paying compensation for vigorously defending his hearth. It is reported that the Prophet said: "Whoever draws a sword on Muslims, his blood has become legal [target]" (*man shahar ʿalā l-muslimīn sayfan fa-qad aṭallah damah*).[27] Thus anyone committing a violent and dangerous act (*muḍirr*, causing *ḍarar*) against another human being should not be surprised if the potential victim chooses to defend himself, even if that brings harm to the aggressor. The same applies to victims of attempted rape; if a woman prevents being raped by killing the would-be rapist, then she will not be convicted of murder based on the rule that harm should be prevented. Although it might be said that killing is a more heinous crime than rape, in fact rape comprises two moral dangers: namely, adultery/fornication (*zinā*) and the possible spread of outrage (*baghi*), and the forceful violation of another person's rights. Islamic Law will not offer protection to an individual who willingly commits such acts.[28]

As we have already said, it is more advantageous to prevent the occurrence of harm, rather than having to cope with its aftermath, in accordance with Islamic Law. The Qurʾān warns: "O ye who believe! Avoid being overly suspicious",[29] yet it is apparent that leaving a suspect unchecked may trigger grave danger to society. Thus, in the face of a highly probable, grave danger to the public at large, it is in the interests of Islamic Law to take appropriate measures, even if minor rights must be infringed upon. Many examples of practices

---

25 al-Burnu, *al-Wajīz*, 256.

26 Q. 4:71 and 102, and Q. 8:60.

27 Shaykhzadah, 4:320, Ibn Humam, *Fathul qadir*, 10:232, al-Murghinani, *al-Hidayah, fi sharh bidaya al-mubtadi*, Beirut, Dar I'hya' al-Turath al-Arabi, n.d. 4:448.

28 al-Tirmidhī, Ḥadīth Nos. 1394 and 1396; al-Ashʿath, Ḥadīth No. 3073.

29 Q. 49:12.

in contemporary law enforcement echo this principle. For instance, the use of Closed-Circuit Television (CCTV) to measure the speed of vehicles can prevent the occurrence of road accidents that could cost lives; detaining alleged criminals can also be justified under this maxim. While one may claim that such measures constitute justice, on one hand, but restrict personal liberty, on the other hand, one must also remember that a perpetrator (*i.e.*, the criminal) violates a fundamental principle of Islamic Law.

We can also infer from Qurʾānic verse 49:12 that being suspicious may be considered immoral, thus pragmatically presupposing that an individual may be innocent. It is reported that Ḥāṭib Ibn Abī Baltaʿa, a Companion of the Prophet, asked a woman to take a letter to his relative in Makkah in which he divulged the Muslims' plan to conquer the city. The Prophet sent ʿAlī Ibn Abī Ṭālib, Zubayr and al-Miqdād to intercept the woman and retrieve the letter. When they met her along the road, they searched her thoroughly until the letter was retrieved.[30] Thus one can infer from this story that it is possible to search a highly suspicious individual. However, in this case, perhaps the woman's involvement should not have been considered suspicious because the Prophet was inspired by Ḥāṭib's letter.

If one can justify an investigation in order to dispel suspicion or thwart a potentially harmful situation, the measure should be proportionate to justify the use of such a fundamental principle in Islamic Law. However, if the allegation proves false, the rights of the accused must be protected, *e.g.*, by compensating the accused if the government rather than a single individual was in error. Furthermore, if the allegation would have resulted in a *ḥadd* punishment, the accuser must be punished either by applying the prescribed *ḥadd* punishment or by obliging him to compensate the accused if punishment is impossible due to other legal impediments.[31]

Under no condition will Islam recommend that a person be held suspect or accused of a crime that is the absolute right of God which is open to forgiveness and pardon. This by no means suggests that Islamic Law turns a blind eye to sins but rather that it protects an individual's right to privacy. The Prophet is reported to have said: "Whoever commits a sin [against a right of God] should keep it secret to himself. If he discloses it, we will impose the fixed [*ḥadd*] punishment of God on him".[32] At the same time, Islam condemns any evil act and denounces the spread of malice. Thus, if someone is suspected of exploiting

---

30 al-Bukhārī, Ḥadīth No. 6540.

31 al-Nawawī, *Sharḥ Ṣaḥīḥ Muslim*, 11:207; Baderin, 109–110; and see al-Alwani, 256–263.

32 Mālik b. Anas b. Mālik, *al-Muwaṭṭa*, (Beirut: Dār 'Ihyā' al-Turāth al-ʿArabī, 1985/1406), 2:747; Ḥadīth No. 37, 4:146; and al-Bayhaqī, 8:326.

women for the purpose of prostitution, or if someone's breath reeks of alcohol, or if screaming is heard from inside a house suggesting an incident of rape or murder, then it is acceptable to report such a suspicious abnormal occurrence to the appropriate authorities in order to prevent a crime.[33]

> ***"Greater Harm Should be Prevented by Committing a Lesser Injury"* (aḍ-ḍarar al-ashadd yuzāl bi-ḍ-ḍarar al-akhaff),[34] *or "The Lesser of Two Evils or Injuries Should be Chosen"* (yukhtār ahwan ash-sharrayn aw akhaff aḍ-ḍararayn),[35] *or "If Two Evils Clash, the Greater Should be Prevented by Committing the Lesser"* (idhā taʿāraḍat mafsadatān rūʿiya aʿẓamahumā ḍararan bi-irtikāb akhaffihumā)[36]**

The three maxims quoted above are identical in connotation and point to the same rule. As already indicated, because harm may not be reciprocal, the only legal way to eliminate harm in the face of necessity is to consider which is the lesser of two evils. Thus the active agent is legally bound to choose the lesser harm to avoid the greater evil. That which is prohibited therefore becomes permissible in dangerous situations, provided that neither excessive nor disproportionate damage occurs.[37] Qurʾānic verse 2:217 unequivocally states:

> They ask you concerning fighting in the sacred month. Say, fighting therein is a great [transgression] but a greater [transgression] with God is to prevent mankind from following the way of God; to disbelieve in Him, to prevent access to the sacred mosque and to drive out its inhabitants and oppression is worse than killing.

This Qurʾānic verse originated as a refutation of the claim of Makkah pagans that Muslims had violated their sacred month by fighting. However, the Qurʾān draws a comparison between the offensive act of fighting during the sacred month and the acts of persecution and oppression, concluding that violation of the sacred month is a lesser offence.[38]

33 al-Māwardī, *al-Aḥkām as-Sulṭāniyya*, 314.

34 Ibn Nujaym, *al-Ashbāh wa-n-Naẓāʾir*, 88; and *Majalla*, Article 28.

35 *Majalla*, Article 29.

36 al-Suyūṭī, *al-Ashbāh*, 87; Ibn Nujaym, *al-Ashbāh wa-n-Naẓāʾir*, 89; *Majalla*, Article 28; and Ibn Rajab, *al-Qawāʿid*, 112.

37 Ibn Nujaym, *al-Ashbāh wa-n-Naẓāʾir*, 89; al-Atāsī and al-Atāsī, 1:68; and Haydar, 1:36.

38 al-Mutairi, 66.

From the above, one can deduced that if someone is coerced to choose between drinking alcohol or committing adultery, then, according to this maxim, for a number of reasons consumption of alcohol would be the lesser crime and attract a milder punishment than adultery. Moreover, drinking alcohol does not violate the right of man, in contrast to adultery that violates both the rights of the victim as well as of the offender who was coerced to act. This example applies to any criminal act prohibited in Islam. However, one can also argue that an individual may commit an even greater crime under the influence of alcohol. However, the commission of a greater crime remains uncertain, whereas being coerced into choosing between two unavoidable evils poses an immediate quandary.

Another example demonstrates the relevance of choosing a lesser evil (*ḍarar al-akhaff*), that personal property in the form of heavy luggage may be tossed overboard into the sea to save the lives on a sinking ship. However, the owners of the discarded luggage must be compensated for their loss of property, because necessity does not invalidate one's rights.[39] In contrast, a group of travelers facing starvation may not kill a member of their group, which would constitute a criminal offence; the lives of all members of the group are equally valuable, as stated in *Regina v Dudley and Stephens*,[40] and *U.S. v Holmes, 1 Wallace Junior 1*.[41]

One might question whether, under duress, it would be better to jump from a great height to an inevitable death or to choose death at the hands of the coercer. Does the nature of inflicted harm differ according to the deed? While there is no consensus among scholars, Abū Ḥanīfa suggests that both situations are equally fraught with harm. Abū Yūsuf, one of the companions of Abu Hanifa, asserts that opting to jump to one's death would constitute active suicide or a sin greater that passive surrender to murder.[42] The latter opinion is deemed to be in line with the objectives (*maqāṣid ash-sharīʿa*) of Islamic Law. Therefore, the legal liability for an act depends on the circumstances involved.[43] In case of murder, the killer is declared legally liable, unlike situations where the cause of death, be it suicide or indirect homicide, is difficult to establish.

If in the face of hardship, someone must commit a prohibited act to safeguard a fundamental principle preserved in Islam, it is important that he gives preference to a less evil act. For example, while paying the enemy ransom for a Muslim held captive is permissible, leaving the Muslim captive is a grave

39 *Ibid.*, 56; and al-Burnu, *al-Wajīz*, 261.

40 Maḥmaṣṣānī, 158.

41 *Ibid.*

42 Ibn Nujaym, *al-Ashbāh wa-n-Naẓāʾir*, 90.

43 *Ibid.*; and al-Burnu, *al-Wajīz*, 262.

error because the enemy might violate his rights. A surgeon is permitted to carry out a Caesarian section when a woman experiences difficulties during natural childbirth. Risk to the infant left in the womb is far greater than risk of injury resulting from surgery. Although surgery may endanger the lives of both mother and baby, it is probable that the surgery will prove successful. In contrast, it is uncertain whether the mother will eventually be able to deliver naturally without medical assistance.[44]

The above maxim can also be applied in a different way. If a pregnant woman is told that both twins in her womb will die if the life of one twin is not terminated before her pregnancy reaches full term, she may decide not to consent to termination because every life is equally valuable. In any case, the woman would not be held responsible for withholding her consent if both twins died.[45] However, if the woman is told that her pregnancy must be aborted or her own life will be endangered, opinions vary about what measures may be taken. The bone of contention is whether saving the mother's life is preferred to that of the unborn baby, or whether both lives are equally valuable. The sensitivity of this issue lies in the fact that Islam denounces all ways of ending a life, including that of a fetus once it has been adjudged as living.[46] Logically, however, preservation of a known, existing, active life (the mother) is preferred to saving the life of a yet unknown, still developing fetus. However, one harmful deed cannot eliminate another wrong.

"Personal Injury Should be Incurred to Prevent General Injury" (yutaḥammal aḍ-ḍarar al-khāṣṣ li-dafʿ ḍarar ʿāmm)[47]

Islamic Law gives preference to safeguarding public over personal or individual benefits. The generality and particularity of injury depends upon the number of people affected if harm is eliminated or crime committed. The purpose of the Sharīʿa is to protect the five fundamental principles or necessities of life. Thus, when a conflict arises as to which of these necessities should be first protected, a choice must be made on the basis of quantity. For instance, the government can confiscate an individual property, which indeed poses a

44 al-Burnu, *al-Wajīz*, 261.

45 A. al-Zarqāʾ, *Sharḥ*, 196. Giving mothers the choice of selecting "unwanted pregnancy" is emphasized in the CEDAW Committee (Convention on the Elimination of All Forms of Discrimination Against Women). See Sarah Joseph, Jenny Schultz, and Melissa Castan, *The International Covenant on Civil and Political Rights: Cases, Materials, and Commentary* (Oxford: Oxford University Press, 2000), 137. This is contrary to the Islamic view that prohibits abortion after a certain period of gestation. See Omran, 8–9; and Baderin, 74.

46 Abdel R. Omran, *Family Planning in the Legacy of Islam* (London: Routledge, 1992), 8–9. Baderin, *International Human Rights and Islamic Law*, pp. 74–75.

47 Ibn Nujaym, *al-Ashbāh wa-n-Naẓāʾir*, 87; *Majalla*, Article 26; and Haydar, 1:36.

threat, in order to protect the general public from its detrimental effects. Under such circumstances, compensation will be awarded to the individual owner as remedy.

Furthermore, the maxim can be applied to the legality of prohibiting all *ḥudūd crimes* and retaliatory (*qiṣāṣ*) acts, which endanger the public's safety. For instance, a severe punishment is prescribed for adultery and fornication (*zinā*), not only for the reasons already discussed herein regarding the crime, but also to prevent prostitution and the spread of communicable diseases such as HIV that could eventually proliferate and infect millions of people. Thus, punishing an individual who commits such a crime, if proven, is preferable to endangering public health.[48]

The same applies to legislation on retaliation, which is drawn up to prevent murder and the spread of enmity among mankind. It also encompasses any restriction deemed expedient by the government to protect the public interest, even if individual rights will be violated. Thus, the government can declare certain acts or the consumption of particular products illegal if they threaten to harm the public. In this regard, cigarettes could be banned to protect public health, although there is no precise or affirmative prohibition against smoking in Islamic Law. Thus, if someone violated a ban placed on smoking, he would receive a discretionary (*taʿzīr*) penalty as stipulated in the legislation.

"Preventing Evil is Better Than Attracting Benefits" **(darʾ al-mafāsid aw-lā min jalb al-maṣāliḥ)**[49]

The previous maxim focused on situations in which a choice must be made between conflicting evils. However, this maxim deals with the question of preference in situations where both benefits (*maṣlaḥ*) and dangers (*mafsada*) exist. According to the maxim in question, preference is given to warding off evil over the acquisition of benefits. Qurʾānic verse 2:219 states the reason for the prohibition of alcohol as follows:

> If they ask you [O Muḥammad] concerning alcoholic drink and gambling, say: "In them is a great sin, and [some] benefits for men, but the sin of them is greater than their benefit . . .".

48 Sābiq, 2:402.

49 al-Suyūṭī, *al-Ashbāh*, 78; Ibn Nujaym, *al-Ashbāh wa-n-Naẓāʾir*, 90; *Majalla*, Article 30; al-Zarkashī, *al-Manthūr*, 1:348; *Majalla*, Article 46; al-Qarāfī, *Anwār al-Burūq*, 4:369; and al-Shāṭibī, 3:190.

yas'alūnaka 'ani l-khamri wa-l-maysiri qul fīhimā ithmun kabirun wa-manafi'u li-n-nāsi wa-ithmuhumā akbaru min naf'ihimā...

This verse stands as evidence that, if there are evils (*ithm*) and benefits (*manāfi'*), the evil should be obviated by not seeking the benefit, except where the benefit is greater than the evil. This is because the verse explains that sin (*ithm*) is greater than benefits (*manāfi'*).[50] Ibn Taymiyya sheds light on this maxim when he says that, if an injury or benefit were in conflict, then the best one must be upheld. In other words, if securing a benefit or preventing an injury is in conflict with a similar benefit or injury, the more beneficial must be sought between the two opposing benefits and the less injurious must be sought between the two opposing injuries,[51] using criteria from the Sharī'a.

Islam attaches more importance to what is prohibited (*manhiyāt*) than to what is required (*ma'mūrāt*). In the words of the Prophet: "If I ask you to do something, do of it as much as you can, but if I forbid you something, you should refrain from it".[52] Based on the prophetic text, it is highly recommended to avoid committing evil at the expense of acquiring benefits.

***"If a Prohibitive Injunction Contradicts What is Permissible, the Prohibition is Given Preference Over the Permissible Unless the Permissible [Benefit] is of Greater Importance"* (idhā ta'āraḍ al-māni' wa-l-muqtaḍī yuqaddim al-māni' illā idhā kān al-muqtaḍā a'ẓam),[53] *or "If the Lawful and Unlawful Coincide, Preference Will be Given to Maintaining Prohibition"* (idhā ijtama' al-ḥalāl wa-l-ḥarām aw al-mubīḥ wa-l-muḥarrim ghullib al-ḥarām)[54]**

Similar maxims to the one discussed above are the maxims of preference between obligation and recommendation. The aim of the maxims here is to examine imperative statements in the texts in contrast to the negative instruction. When someone encounters a situation where a textual directive is difficult to obey, then what yardstick should he use to measure which conflicting order should be followed? For example, one text might forbid the consumption of alcohol while another text deems it permissible in the face of necessity. The preference is to heed the text that prohibits the act, except, as mentioned

50 al-Burnu, *al-Wajīz*, 275.

51 Ibn Taymiyya, *Majmū' al-Fatāwā*, 23:343; 'Awda, 1:575 and 707.

52 al-Bukhārī, Ḥadīth No. 6858; and Muslim Ḥadīth No. 1337.

53 al-Zarkashī, *al-Manthūr*, 1:348; *Majalla*, Article 46; and M. al-Zarqā', *al-Madkhal*, §595.

54 al-Zarkashī, *al-Manthūr*, 1:125; al-Suyūṭī, *al-Ashbāh*, 105; and Ibn Nujaym, *al-Ashbāh wa-n-Naẓā'ir*, 109.

above, when in dire need. In fact, the maxim reflects the value of precaution in Islamic Law. One is not allowed to exploit excessively any provision given in exceptional circumstances, and should err on the side of conservative behavior. In this regard, Islam forbids merchants to trade in any prohibited substance such as alcohol, harmful drugs, and so on, although they would benefit financially in doing so.[55] However, because there is a text prohibiting their consumption, it is not permitted to opt for the advantages of profitable trade over regard for the prohibitive text. The same applies when a man cannot identify which among several women would be a legitimate bride to marry. Here, as a measure of precaution, it would be in his best interests to forego his rights and not marry any of the women. Because there is a textual directive prohibiting marriage with certain women,[56] a man should exercise caution before marrying someone whose identity is unknown to him.[57]

However, these maxims are not universally applicable because there are situations where more benefits can be derived if prohibition is given preference over recommendation. For example, if someone's property consists of both legal and illegal elements, the owner can still make use of them if the legal proportion outweighs what is illegal. If the man were to forfeit all his property, then he could find himself in dire straights. However, as said before, Islam offers facility when necessity demands. Having said that, it is recommended that one takes full precaution to make his or her dealings legal.[58]

With regard to lying, based on the Ḥadīth of the Prophet, a person is allowed to tell a lie to settle a dispute between two litigants. Someone cannot be branded deceitful or a habitual liar (*kadhdhāb*) for telling two parties different stories, if his aim is to settle a dispute.[59]

General Application of the Grand Maxim *Lā Ḍarar wa-lā Ḍirār* and its Subsidiaries in Several Northern Nigerian Sharīʿa Criminal Law Cases

Islam denounces any unnecessary infliction of harm and injury and prohibits any unjust affliction of punishment or penalties on mankind. As an overall objective, Islam also strives to eliminate the occurrence of harm (*ḍarar*), whether as a result of aggressive behavior or as a reciprocal response. With

55 Q. 2:275.
56 Q. 4:22–24.
57 al-Burnu, *al-Wajīz*, 267.
58 *Ibid.*
59 al-Bukhārī, *Kitāb aṣ-Ṣulḥ*, Ḥadīth No. 2546; Muslim, *Kitāb al-Birr*, Ḥadīth No. 2605.

this in mind, some of the cases adjudicated in Northern Nigeria during the re-enforcement of the fully implemented Sharīʿa will be subject to criticism.

The case of *Attorney General of Zamfara State* [complainant] *v. Lawal Akwata R/Doruwa* [defendant][60] could be considered as having inflicted unnecessary harm on the defendant, considering the literal meaning and source of the maxim "No harm shall be inflicted or reciprocated" (*lā ḍarar wa-lā ḍirār*). Here the prosecutor was not directly involved in the dispute. The victim had forgiven the accused perpetrator and, in fact, had not himself initiate a case against him. Rather it was Lawali Sani Dauda on behalf of the Commissioner for Justice, Attorney General of Zamfara State, that lodged the complaint. At the end of the trial, the Upper Sharīʿa Court found the accused guilty and sentenced him to 6 months in prison or payment of N10,000 (equivalent to $83.33). However, imprisoning the accused for such a petty offence is simply inflicting harm unjustly.[61]

Similarly, in the case of *Hashimu Galadima Maberaya* [complainant] *v. Abdul-Rahman Isahaka and two others* [defendants], it was observed that the total value allegedly stolen by the accused individuals was N12,328 (equivalent to $102). Imprisoning the accused between 20 February and 6 July 2002 before subsequent amputation of their hands is not commensurate with their offence. Thus the punishments handed down are considered unjust.[62]

In another case, after Bariya Magadisu admitted to having had sexual intercourse out of wedlock with a man, she was thereafter accused of *qadhf* or defamation because she did not have evidence to prove the allegation. As traditionally required under Islamic Law for *zinā* and *qadhf*, there were no eyewitnesses to substantiate the accusations against her, both of which demanded severe penalties. Such a case accentuates the important role DNA testing can play to provide essential evidence and eliminate doubt. Thus DNA evidence would not only have overturned her conviction for adultery (*zinā*) and defamation (*qadhf*) but would also have helped dispel the harmful effects she would have suffered as a result of such allegations. Determining the right of man (*ḥaqq al-ādamī*) attached to this case as well as upholding justice for all mankind is the objective of Islam Law.

When there is a contradiction between that which is certain (*yaqīn*) and that which is apparent (*ẓāhir*), such as the appearance of pregnancy or the absence of four eyewitness accounts in the case of adultery, it will be in the best interest of Islam to establish whose right is involved in the case. If there is no allegation of rape, the higher proof will be accepted; that is, four

60 See page 78.

61 See Zakariyah, *Applications of Legal Maxims*, Appendix 6.

62 *Ibid.*, Appendix 7.

eyewitnesses in order to eliminate the threat of harm (*ḍarar*) if a *ḥadd* punishment is wrongly executed. Therefore this author finds that considering a pregnancy in cases of adultery to establish a *ḥadd* punishment is less important under Islamic Law, since the crime concerns the absolute right of God (*ḥaqq al-Allāh*), not man.

Moreover, investigating cases such as adultery (*zinā*), consumption of alcoholic (*shurb al-khamr*) and apostasy (*ridda*)—when not committed publicly—can be considered as infringing on human rights since those offences do not affect mankind directly. In other words, any crime that does not directly involve human rights should not be subject to investigation, which would entail inflicting undue harm (*ḍarar*) on the accused. In *Bariya v. Zamfara police, Safiyyatu v. Sokoto State*, and *Amina Lawal v. Kastina*, the ways in which these cases were reported are considered to have been an intrusion on the rights of the accused, which has caused them personal harm.[63]

It can be argued that challenging the pregnancy of Amina Lawal is an act of inflicting unwarranted harm on her since even the Mālikī School of Jurisprudence has established that "a woman may carry a pregnancy for 5 years before delivery".[64] Thus, Amina Lawal divorced her former husband less than 5 years earlier, which still provides her with some benefit of doubt.

Conclusion

This chapter has elucidated Islam's stand on the prohibition and elimination of harm whether through aggression or reciprocation thereof. A set rule in Islam states that in order to eliminate harm two major conditions must be satisfied: namely, harm must not be inflicted to remove harm but greater harm may be avoided by committing a lesser offense. However, if harm is inherent in both acts, and of an equal magnitude, then one should consider the structure: a prohibitive injunction should be given preference over and above an injunction that permits an act. This is in accordance to the maxim "If a prohibitive injunction contradicts what is permissible, the prohibition is given preference over the permissible unless the permissible [benefit] is of greater importance" (*idhā taʿāraḍ al-māniʿ wa-l-muqtaḍī yuqaddim al-māniʿ illā idhā kān al-muqtaḍā aʿẓam*). An established principle in Islamic Law states: "Preventing evil is better than acquiring benefits" (*darʾ al-mafāsid aw-lā min jalb al-maṣāliḥ*).

---

63 See the submission of Safiyyatu Husaini's counsel in Zakariyah, *Applications of Legal Maxims*, Appendix 10, 14; see also Peters, *Re-Islamization*, 241.

64 See NNLR 2003, 496.

CHAPTER 7

Legal Maxim of Custom: "Custom is Authoritative" (*al-ʿĀda Muḥakkama*)*

Custom in Islamic Criminal Law

Customs or societal norms are recognized in Islamic Law as an authority upon which judgments can be based. All major books on Islamic jurisprudence recognize *ʿāda* (manners, habits, indigenous traditions) and *ʿurf* (customs) as sources of Islamic Law.[1] The recourse to custom dates back to the time of Prophet Muḥammad, followed by the era of his Companions (*aṣḥāb*) and Followers (*tābiʿūn*, after his demise). Many cases were reported in which rulings were based on popular customs.[2] Mālik Ibn Anas (d. 179/795) considered the customs of the people of Medina (*ʿamal ahl il-madina*) as a source of Islamic Law whenever there was dispute in making law.[3] Moreover, al-Shāfiʿī had no option but to change the points of view he held in Iraq because of the different customs and circumstances he encountered when in Egypt.[4] It is undeniable that all civilized legal systems in our modern era consider the authoritativeness of custom (*ʿāda* and *ʿurf*) as also recognized in Islamic jurisprudence.[5]

The Arabic word *ʿāda* is derived from the triliteral Arabic root (*ʿayn-wāw-dāl*) and etymologically linked to the verb meaning 'to return'. The word denotes the customs, manners, and habits to which people constantly return time and again.[6] *ʿĀda* is defined as practices that have become deeply rooted in a culture through their recurrence, that have been accepted by people of sound nature,[7]

---

* al-Suyuti, al-Ashbah, 89; Ibn Nujaym, al-Ashbah, 79; M. al-Zarqa, 219; al-Burnu, al-Wajiz, 26.

1 Ibn al-Qayyim al-Jawziyya, *aṭ-Ṭuruq al-Ḥukmiyya*, 101; al-Nadawī, 301; and al-Atāsī and al-Atāsī, 1:78.

2 See al-ʿAynī, 12:16.

3 al-Ghazālī, *al-Mustaṣfā*, 1:187; Abū Muḥammad ʿAlī b. Aḥmad Ibn Ḥazm, *al-Iḥkām fī Uṣūl al-Aḥkām* (Cairo: Dār al-Ḥadīth, 1404/1983), 2:552; and Ibn Qudāma, *Rawḍat an-Nāẓir*, 2:479–480.

4 Abū Zahra, 128; Khallaf, *ʿIlm Uṣūl al-Fiqh*, 90; and Kamali, *Principles*, 361.

5 M. al-Zarqāʾ, *al-Madkhal*, 1:132.

6 al-Aṣfahānī, 302.

7 M. al-Zarqāʾ, *al-Madkhal*, 2:838.

 | DOI 10.1163/9789004304871_008

or that are recurrent but based on neither rhyme nor reason.[8] The noun *'urf* is said to be synonymous with *'āda*, both in definition and concept,[9] and derived from the triliteral root (*'ayn-rā'-fā'*) for the verb *'arafa*, which means 'to know'.[10] It is technically defined as "what is established in life from reason and acceptable by sound natural disposition".[11] M. al-Zarqā', in his effort to distinguish between *'āda* and *'urf*, describes *'urf* as "the behavior of a group of people in their saying and doings".[12] From this, *'urf* can be viewed as narrower in scope than *'āda*, because it refers to only the customs of a group while *'āda* also refers to the customs of particular individuals. In other words, all *'urf* is *'āda*, but not all *'āda* is *'urf*.[13]

As expressed above, the use of the terms *'āda* and *'urf* is controversial although one can say categorically that they are often interchangeable.[14] Ibn 'Ābidīn (d. 1252/1836) remarks that a habit is derived from frequency and recurrence because it is practiced frequently and in succession.[15] It has become well known and entrenched in the hearts and minds of individuals who accept it without any logical connection or factual evidence as a customary fact. *'Āda* and *'urf* imply the same meaning despite their conceptual distinctions.[16] It is also important to state that for *'urf* to be accepted and applied in Islam, it must be of sound nature, because Islam cannot accommodate all customs contradicts the divine texts and deviates from the spirit of the law.[17]

Attributing the force of law to custom is inevitable in Islamic Law owing to its nature of universal applicability, as the norms of ethnic groups and social sub-groups differ considerably. Moreover, because custom is intuitively rooted in people's lives and utterances, the need to consider popular customs is inevitable. Thus, a judge must have recourse to the customs of people before giving a conclusive verdict in any case of litigation.

---

8 Aḥmad Fahmī Abū Sanna, *al-'Urf wa-l-'Āda fī Ra'y al-Fuqahā'* (n.p., 1992), 8; and al-Jurjānī, 149.

9 al-Burnu, *al-Wajīz*, 276.

10 al-Fayruzabadi, 3:179; and Ibn Manẓūr, 9:239.

11 al-Jurjānī, 154.

12 M. al-Zarqā', *al-Madkhal*, 1:131.

13 Mohammad Akram Laldin, *The Theory and Application of* 'Urf *in Islamic Law*, Ph.D. Dissertation (Edinburgh: University of Edinburgh Press, 1995), 22.

14 al-Burnu, *al-Wajīz*, 276.

15 Ibn 'Ābidīn, *Ḥāshiyat Ibn 'Ābidīn*, 2:114.

16 *Ibid.*

17 Muḥammad M. al-Shalābī, *Uṣūl al-Fiqh al-Islāmī* (Beirut: Dār al-Nahda al-'Arabiyya li-t-Tiba'a wa-n-Nashr wa-t-Tawzi', 1986), 323; and al-Sarakhsī, 16:62.

Evidence of the Use of Custom in Islamic Law

Many Islamic jurists recognize *ʿāda* and *ʿurf* as supportive sources of Islamic Law.[18] The justification for the legality of *ʿāda* can be traced to texts, although there is no direct use of the term *ʿāda* in the Qurʾān. However, there are derivative statements providing the basis for the recognition of custom. Various places in the Qurʾān and Ḥadīths suggest the use of custom. In Qurʾānic verse 7:199, God enjoins three things among which is *ʿurf* (literally, 'that which is good'). According to Ibn al-ʿArabī (d. 543/1148), the meanings of *ʿurf* in this verse indicate what is meant in this context.[19] There are four interpretations given to the meaning of *ʿurf* in the verse: namely, that it is synonymous with kindness (*maʿrūf*); that it means there is 'no god except God'; that it signifies anything known (*maʿrifa*) to be part of religion; that it entails anything good, not rejected by the people, and endorsed by the Sharīʿa.[20] Al-Qurṭubī further explains the relevance of the word in the verse to the meaning in question, saying: "*ʿurf*, *maʿrūf* and *maʿrifa* is anything that is good, approved by reason, and acceptable by mankind".[21] M. al-Zarqāʾ maintains that the word *ʿurf* in this verse forms the proof for the legality of *ʿurf* in this context, because the customary practice of people is normally good, reasonable and accepted.[22] In Qurʾānic verse 4:19 the word *maʿrūf*, which is the passive particle of *ʿurf*, is used to indicate the authority of custom and culture in the Islamic legal framework. Ibn Kathir (d. 774/1373), in his commentary on this verse, includes that here *maʿrūf* refers to a custom of any good character that is reasonable and acceptable.[23] In this regard, al-Nadawī also says that the above verse shows that God enjoins both husband and wife to live together and give one another their due right based on their custom and culture; this certainly differs among nations and peoples.[24] In another verse, custom is referred to the amount that a man must spend for the mother of his child (Q. 2:233). This indicates that custom and popular practice is the yardstick for innumerable Islamic Laws. Another example of the legality of *ʿurf* is the following Qurʾānic verse 24:58:

---

18 al-Shalābī, *Uṣūl al-Fiqh al-Islāmī*, 323.

19 Ibn al-ʿArabī, *Aḥkām al-Qurʾān*, 2:823.

20 ʿAbdullāh b. Muslim Ibn Qutayba, *Taʾwīl Mushkil al-Qurʾān*, 3rd edn. (Beirut: Dār al-Kutub al-ʿIlmiyya, n.d.), 4.

21 al-Qurṭubī, 7:344. The same opinion is expressed by al-Qarāfī. (See al-Qarāfī, *Anwār al-Burūq*, 3:149; and Abū Sanna, *al-ʿUrf wa-l-ʿĀda*, 29.

22 M. al-Zarqāʾ, *al-Madkhal*, 1:137; and Kamali, *Principles*, 37.

23 Abū al-Fidaʾ Ismāʿīl Ibn Kathir, *Tafsīr al-Qurʾān al-ʿAẓīm* (Beirut: Dār al-Fikr, 1401/1980), 1:466.

24 al-Nadawī, *al-Qawāʿid al-Fiqhiyya*, 294.

> O you who have believed, let those whom your right hands possess and those who have not [yet] reached puberty among you ask permission of you [before entering] at three times: before the dawn prayer and when you put aside your clothing [for rest] at noon and after the night prayer. [These are] three times of privacy for you …

From this verse one might infer that, in centuries past, those three periods of time (morning, midday and night) were when people undressed. Intuitively, the ruling is based on the popular custom of a culture. Thus, when customs in another country differ, or manners and practices change through the progression of time, then rules should also be allowed to evolve.[25]

In many prophetic traditions, considerations were given to customs. The *res* adjudication of custom can be found, for example, in the case of Bara' Ibn 'Azib who came to the Prophet and asked about a camel that had entered and destroyed a garden. The Prophet replied:

> The safety of the property is to be borne by the owner of the property during the day and the safety of the animal is to be borne by the owner of the animal during the night.[26]

From this narration, the jurists could conclude that the owner of the animal would only be liable for damages to the property during the night. This ruling is based on the existing custom at that time when animals were allowed to roam the land freely during the day to look for sustenance.[27] Ibn Najjar remarks that this Ḥadīth is the most logical and best proof ever provided for taking *ʿāda* into consideration in Islamic Law.[28]

Undoubtedly, Islam allows rulings to be based on custom, whenever there is no explicit text addressing the issue at hand, or where the text sets no precise limit regarding its application, or where there is no agreement on the interpretation of the text.[29] This is evident in the advice given to a woman

---

25 *Ibid.*, 297; and al-Qurṭubī, 12:304.

26 al-Nasaʾī, Ḥadīth No. 5785; al-Ashʿath, Ḥadīth No. 3570; al-Bayhaqī, Ḥadīth No. 17461, 342; al-Daraquṭnī, Ḥadīth No. 217, 3:155; and Aḥmad al-Shaybānī, Ḥadīth No. 18629.

27 Ibn 'Abd al-Barr, *at-Tamhīd*, 11:89; al-ʿAzīmabādī, 9:350; Muḥammad Ibn Ismāʿīl al-Ṣanʿānī, *Subl as-Salām*, edited by Muḥammad al-Khawli, 4th edn., (Beirut: Dār Iḥyāʾ al-Turāth al-ʿArabī, 1379/1959), 3:264.

28 Ibn al-Najjār, 4:40.

29 al-Shalābī, 324–325; Ibn al-Najjār, 4:452–453.

by the Prophet when she asked about the inconsistency of her menstruation. The Prophet referred her to the custom of her fellow women or to what she was accustomed before the onset of the inconsistency.[30] In another directive Ḥadīth, although of controversial authenticity, it is reported that the Prophet said: "What the Muslims deem good is good in the sight of God".[31] Regarding its authenticity, some scholars state that the Ḥadīth is *mawqūf* because the chain (*isnād*) of narrations stops with a Companion and not with the Prophet.[32] Whatever may be the status of the Ḥadīth, its implication confirms the authority of *ʿāda* and *ʿurf* in Islamic Law because the Prophet's trusted Companions, who were classified as 'rightly guided ones', would not be expected to invoke something that contradicted the authoritative texts, and in doing so undermine their status.[33]

Furthermore, based on scholarly consensus (*ijmāʿ*), both classical and contemporary Islamic scholars have established the legality of *ʿurf* and *ʿāda* as important resources for solving problems that arise in Islamic Law.[34] Moreover, the formulation of maxims related to *ʿāda* by those scholars is an indication of consensus with respect to the authority and legality of *ʿāda* and *urf*.[35] There are many ways in which customs can be admitted as authoritative in Islamic Law among are:

1. Going by the principle that what has been established by virtue of custom is like that which has been established in texts, for issues for which explicit evidence cannot be found in primary Sharīʿa sources;[36]
2. Specifying the meaning of a text, or restricting an absolute meaning (of a text);[37] and
3. Settling disputes among people on matters pre-dominated by *ʿurf*.[38]

---

30 al-Shawkānī, *Nayl al-Awṭār*, 1:341.

31 Aḥmad al-Shaybānī, 1:379; and al-ʿAynī, 23:266.

32 al-Amidi, 4:166; Ibn Ḥazm, *al-Iḥkām*, 6:194; and al-Suyūṭī, *al-Ashbāh*, 89.

33 See al-Burnu's comment on the Ḥadīth, al-Burnu, *al-Wajiz*, 270–271.

34 Kamali, *Principles*, 372; and Zaydān, *al-Wajīz*, 254.

35 *Cf.*, al-Ramalī, 8:42; Ibn ʿĀbidīn, 6:423; Haydar, 1:40; and al-Dasūqī, *Ḥāshiyat ad-Dasūqī*, 2:4.

36 *Majalla*, Article 45.

37 al-Sayyid Ṣāliḥ ʿAwad, *Aṭhar al-ʿUrf fī t-Tashrīʿ al-Islāmī* (Cairo: Jamiʿat al-Azhar, 1997), 348–367; and M. al-Zarqāʾ, *al-Madkhal*, 893.

38 al-Shalābī, 326.

Relevant Maxims Related to Custom

"People's Practice is Authoritative and Should be Reckoned With" (istiʿmāl an-nās ḥujja yajib al-ʿamal bi-hā)[39]

Generally, the law must take into consideration the custom and practices of people in any matter that is not detailed, or whose verdict is based on the *ʿurf* and *ʿāda* of the people who use them. In regulating to which extent *ʿurf* can be applied in Islamic Law, jurists have unanimously agreed that, if custom contradicts the explicit Qurʾānic or Ḥadīth texts (*naṣṣ*), then customary rule will not be enforceable.[40] In other words, custom is not applied when there is clear text addressing the issue at hand. However, the relevance of the above sub-maxim is to broaden the authoritative scope of custom in Islamic Law. Moreover, this maxim also includes all sorts of *ʿurf*, whether general (*ʿāmm*) or individual (*fardī*), practical (*ʿamalī*) or verbal (*qawlī*). Islamic jurists unanimously agree that if a custom is general, meaning that it is not restricted to a particular group of people or a particular place in time, it can be used to indicate the meaning of texts and is not subject to analogy, such as a custom still in practice since the Prophet's era.[41] One example might be a contract for manufacture (*istiṣnāʿ*), which, although it contradicts the general Islamic principle on contracts, is allowed because it is a popular custom known since the beginning of Islam.[42]

Despite the seeming consensus on *ʿurf* / *ʿāda*, scholars disagree as to the effect of individual customs (*ʿāda fardiyya*), *i.e.*, practices known to a particular region, profession or set of experts, or Islamic legal terms derived from general language to specify a text.[43] The majority of Islamic jurists, including those from the Ḥanafī and Shāfiʿī Schools, consider individual custom neither appropriate nor generally applicable.[44] In other words, individual customs and practices (*urf*) cannot form the basis for textual exegeses or general principles of Islamic Law. An individual custom from one particular region cannot be given

---

39 Ibn Rajab, *al-Qawāʿid*, 121–122; *Majalla*, Article 37; M. al-Zarqāʾ, *al-Madkhal*, 60; and al-Burnu, *al-Wajīz*, 292.

40 al-Shalābī, 324; and Kamali, *Principles*, 373.

41 al-Shalābī, 324; and al-Burnu, *al-Wajīz*, 277.

42 al-Burnu, *al-Wajīz*, 277.

43 *Ibid.*, 278.

44 *Ibid.*, 292.

preference or undermine other individual customs.[45] However, if it has been asserted that an individual custom is valid to determine the connotation of a text, then its use should be restricted to the people who practice that custom; the resulting rule will not be binding on people from other regions where other customs prevail.

"What is Known by Virtue of Custom is as a Stipulated Condition" (al-maʿrūf ʿurfan ka-l-mashrūṭ sharṭan),[46] *and "What is Stipulated by Virtue of Custom is Like What is Stipulated by Text"* (at-taʿyīn bi-l-ʿurf ka-t-taʿyīn bi-n-naṣṣ)[47]

The two foregoing sub-maxims consider *ʿurf* a measure for determining the conditions binding human activities and engagements with other people who practice the same custom, even if those conditions are not stipulated at the time. For example, if a visitor eats his host's food, he will not be charged for theft, if it is a known custom that a visitor has the right to utilize his host's goods without permission. In some places, it is customary that a woman's dowry is divided or suspended until a future time known to the couple; this condition is generally acceptable even when not expressly mentioned during the marriage.[48] Thus, if an inhabitant of that region marries without paying the full dowry, his marriage will still be valid and neither he nor his wife will be considered adulterous.

However, the Ḥanafīs consider that practical or physical custom, if general, are capable of specifying textual meanings, in contrast to the majority of Muslim jurists who do not endorse *ʿurf* unless it is verbal.[49] For example, if a host foregoes the customary practice and forbids his guest to use his telephone, but the visitor uses it nevertheless, then the visitor would be guilty of breaching the condition of hospitality and would be liable to pay compensation.

---

45 *Ibid.*, 279; and al-Zarkashī, *al-Manṯūr*, 2:362.

46 Ibn Nujaym, *al-Ashbāh wa-n-Naẓāʾir*, 99; *Majalla*, Article 43; and al-Burnu, *al-Wajīz*, 306.

47 *Majalla*, Article 45; M. al-Zarqāʾ, *al-Madkhal*, 612; and al-Burnu, al-*Wajīz*, 306.

48 Sābiq, 2:159–166.

49 al-Burnu, *al-Wajīz*, 280.

***"Real Meaning Shall be Set Aside on the Strength of the Meaning Established by Custom"* (al-ḥaqīqa tutrak bi-dalālat al-ʿāda),[50] *and "A Written Document is Like an Expression"* (al-kitāb ka-l-khiṭāb),[51] *and "A Recognized Sign of a Deaf-Mute is Like an Explicit Expression"* (al-ishāra l-maʿhūdali l-akhras ka-l-bayān bi-l-lisān)[52]**

These sub-maxims address verbal practice (*ʿurf qawlī*), which is a conventional term used among a group of people to communicate specific meaning intuitively understood without any need for linguistic expression.[53] The sub-maxim "Real meaning shall be set aside on the strength of the meaning of the custom" indicates that, if there is contradiction between the vernacular and *ʿurf*, preference will be given to the indicative customary meaning. An apt example is the use of the monetary terms *dirham* and *dinār* today, as opposed to their use in the distant past; these modern currencies borrow only their name (not their value) from the ancient currencies. Similarly, if a phrase is considered offensive in one social context but not in another, and someone accustomed to the latter context uses the phrase in the former, he can be charged with defamation owing to the context in which he uses the phrase.

The sub-maxim "A written document is like an expression" considers that the effects of written and spoken texts are equivalent. Since verbal *ʿurf* is considered tenable in a court of law, it stands to reason that those who, for one reason or another, are incapable of expressing their thoughts verbally are entitled to present written texts. In fact, this consideration is paramount in the legal system. Before a written document can be legally tenable, it should be clearly written, and the handwriting of the presenter should be recognizable.[54] Thus, if one writes a statement deemed to be insulting or offensive, even if such a person is a deaf-mute, his writing will be admitted as evidence that he has committed an offence.

The sub-maxim "A recognized sign of a deaf-mute is like an explicit expression" specifically addresses what we refer to as 'sign language' or 'signing' or the manual communication used by mutes, which stands as a clear verbal statement[55] through which justice can be established in human activities. The

---

50 *Ibid.*, 299.

51 Ibn Nujaym, *al-Ashbāh wa-n-Naẓā'ir*, 339; and *Majalla*, Article 69; *cf.* al-Suyūṭī, *al-Ashbāh*, 308.

52 al-Burnu, *al-Wajīz*, 280; A. al-Zarqā', *Sharḥ al-Qawā'id*, 351; *Majalla*, Article 70.

53 al-Burnu, *al-Wajīz*, 281.

54 al-Atāsī and al-Atāsī, 1:190; and al-Burnu, *al-Wajīz*, 302.

55 Ibn Qudāma, *al-Mughnī*, 12:259–260.

way in which a mute chooses to express himself, whether in writing or by signing, is legally valid: namely, whether in confession (*iqrār*), testimony (*shahāda*), contracts (*ʿaqd*), swearing (*ḥalf*), defamation (*qadhf*), apostasy (*ridda*), and so forth.[56] However, sign language or signing is not given effect in cases involving the absolute right of God because of the likelihood of doubt (*shubha*). Recall the maxim that says "Fixed [*ḥadd*] punishment should be averted in the face of doubt" (*al-ḥudūd tudraʾ bi-sh-shubhāt*). Thus, if a mute claims or gives witness that someone else has committed a crime that constitutes *ḥadd*, punishment will not be awarded because of the provision that *ḥudūd* should be averted in the face of doubt. Islamic scholars disagree on the acceptability of signing in the case of defamation of chastity. Abū Ḥanīfa and a version of Ḥanbal's thought opine that if a mute commits defamation, his act will not be regarded as a *ḥudūd* offence since it is not explicit, and *ḥadd* will not be inflicted on the person accused by the mute until someone who can speak aloud clearly gives witness confirming the accusation.[57] However, if a mute is under accusation, and his sign language is recognized as indicating the offence, the defamation will be considered an accusation because a mute cannot claim doubt (*shubha*), and because defamation (*qadhf*), according to Abū Ḥanīfa, is an absolute right of God (*ḥaqq Allāh*).[58] For Mālik, al-Shāfiʿī and one viewpoint from the Ḥanbal School, *qadhf* is a right of man, and, as such, an accused mute is punishable when there is a sufficient number of witnesses to convict him.[59]

Conditions Binding the Enforcement of Custom

As already mentioned, before a custom can be deemed acceptable, it must be endorsed by people of reasonably good and sound behavior. Other conditions must also be met before custom can be considered authoritative and acceptable as a source of Islamic Law. The sub-maxims that follow provide conditions to regulate the enforcement of custom.

---

56 This is the general view of the majority of Muslim jurists. See al-Bahūtī, 5:392; Ibn Qudāma, *al-Mughnī*; and al-Ḥaṭṭāb, 6:154.

57 al-Sarakhsī, 16:133; and Haydar, 1:63.

58 al-Atāsī and al-Atāsī, 1:193–198; and al-Burnu *al-Wajīz*, 304.

59 al-Shinqitī, 3:409; and al-Burnu, *al-Wajīz*, 304–305.

> ***"Custom is Enforced Where There is no Legal Detail"* (inna al-ʿāda taḥkum fī-mā lā ḍabṭ lah sharʿan),[60] *"Custom is Considered Only When it is Regularly Occurring and Prevailing"* (innamā tuʿtabar al-ʿāda idhā ʿiṭṭaradat aw ghalabat),[61] *"Consideration is Given Only to a Prevailing, Widespread, Non-Sporadic Custom"* (al-ʿibra li-l-ghālib ash-shāʾiʿ lā n-nādir),[62] *"No Consideration is Given for an Emergency Custom"* (lā ʿibra bi-l-ʿurf aṭ-ṭāriʾ)[63]**

These four sub-maxims have been coined to serve as conditions that must be considered before custom can be authoritatively enforced. These conditions are: that the custom does not contradict authoritative texts; that the custom is prevalent; that the custom is known to the public who uses it; and that the custom is continuously practiced. The non-controversial condition set for the legality of *ʿāda* and *ʿurf* is that there should be no contradiction between it and the explicit texts. However, there are many ways in which *ʿāda* and *ʿurf* can contradict texts, or rulings, established through texts:

1. If *ʿāda* or *ʿurf* is contradictory in any way: such as would be the practice of nudity or not adequately covering the body in some parts of the world; the practice of engaging in usury (*ribā*) by most banks worldwide; the manufacture and consumption of alcoholic drinks; and the legality of prostitution in some countries. All such *ʿādāt* and *aʿrāf* (pl. for *ʿāda* and *ʿurf*, respectively) are vehemently prohibited in Islamic countries. If an individual commits any of the above acts in a setting where Islamic Law is implemented, he will be punished for having committed a sinful act.
2. If *ʿāda* or *ʿurf* contradicts, *e.g.*, a general text or the ruling derived from it through the means of.
3. If there is a text whose ruling is based on *ʿāda* and *ʿurf*: some scholars opine that such a text can be set aside in favor of *ʿurf* if the *ʿurf* has changed,[64] while others believe that it cannot be changed.[65]

---

60 al-Zarkashī, *al-Manṯūr*, 2:356, and al-Burnu, *al-Wajīz*, 282.

61 al-Suyūṭī, *al-Ashbāh*, 92; Ibn Nujaym, *al-Ashbāh wa-n-Naẓāʾir*, 99; *Majalla*, Articles 41–42; M. al-Zarqāʾ, *al-Madkhal*, 606–607; and al-Burnu, *al-Wajīz*, 295.

62 *Majalla*, Article 42; M. al-Zarqāʾ, *al-Madkhal*, 607; and al-Burnu, *al-Wajīz*, 295.

63 al-Burnu, *al-Wajīz*, 297; and Ibn Nujaym, *al-Ashbāh wa-n-Naẓāʾir*, 101; *cf.*, al-Suyūṭī, *al-Ashbāh*, 92.

64 Ibn Qudāma, *al-Mughnī*, 2:66; and Ibn Mufliḥ, 4:157.

65 See Ibn Qudāma, *al-Mughnī*, 2:64; and al-Ramalī, 3:417.

4. If *ʿurf* contradicts issues that have been established by independent scholarly reasoning (*ijtihād*), the verdict based on *ijtihād* will be changed in accordance with the change in custom.[66]

Another way in which *ʿurf* can contradict a text is when the textual language—not necessarily the entire text—contradicts the vernacular. In other words, if a customary connotation differs from a word in a textual sense, one should consider whether the written word has no legal effect, and in that case the use of *ʿurf* will supersede. This is applicable in the swearing of oaths where the vernacular of the person taking an oath will be given consideration in a court of law.[67]

The three other conditions that can be inferred from the last three maxims mentioned above are namely: continuity (*ʿiṭṭirād*), predominance (*ghalāba*), and prevalence (*shuyūʿ*) of the custom. Before a custom can be considered authoritative, three conditions must be fulfilled.[68] An enforced custom must be continuously in use and enjoy widespread practice. If it is a common ongoing tribal custom to delay dowry payment until a particular time, then this custom will be upheld and the marriage not considered invalid (*nikāḥ bāṭil*), nor their cohabitation rendered adulterous. An exception is the case where a woman or her guardian requests a different arrangement. Thus if marriage or sexual intercourse occurs before the newly specified condition is met, then the marriage will be invalid and the couple legally punishable for adultery. Also, before a custom can be considered binding, it should be predominant and prevailing, that is, the custom must be well known to the majority of people affected by it.[69]

The essence of these conditions lies in the fact that a custom may be general (*ʿāmm*) and prevailing, although not practiced by the majority of people. The prevalent nature of the custom may not be admitted when the law passes judgment.[70] In contrast, if a custom is neither prevalent nor predominant, but rather specific (*khāṣṣ*), common and recurrent among certain people or professionals, it may be given consideration when there is dispute among the individuals concerned. For instance, if someone is accused of an act considered an offence in one location but not in another, it will be difficult to determine

66 This issue will be elaborated under the maxim *lā yunkar taghayyur al-aḥkām bi-taghayyur al-azmān.*

67 al-Burnu, al-*Wajīz*, 287.

68 *Ibid.*, 295–296.

69 al-Suyūṭī, *al-Ashbāh*, 92–93.

70 al-Burnu, *al-Wajīz*, 296.

a legal ruling, in the sense that the judge will face the dilemma whether to consider the norm of the accused or custom of the accuser. By and large, these conditions are set to achieve justice among litigants on issues that are based on *ʿurf*.

The importance of continuity of custom resounds in the case of offences committed in the past but brought to court after a considerable lapse of time. If the accused admits that he committed the crime in accordance with a former custom that is no longer in practice, he will be judged on the basis of the earlier, no longer present (or lack thereof) custom.[71] If, for example, someone admits to having stolen 100 pounds 20 years earlier, his admission of guilt will provoke a punishment based on the value of the pound at the time he committed the crime. This is because no effect is given to intermittent custom.

In summary, the custom and culture of a people determine the nature of crimes not stipulated in legal texts. Some such customs include punishments, which are usually discretionary, that are legislated to deal with criminal offences in order to safeguard the public. This is the situation when texts predetermine the punishment but leave it to custom to determine the legal requirements to be met before such acts can be deemed criminal and appropriate punishments meted out. As Baber Johansen observes, custom determines the equivalent of the amount the Sunna assigns to *diya* payments. Thus, what is considered to be the monetary equivalent of 100 camels in one country may be different in another country.[72] In *ḥudūd* crimes, custom (*ʿāda*) determines whether adultery has been committed in cases where the dowry or marriage ceremony is delayed or suspended or in cases where one of the requirements for a marriage contract (*ʿaqd nikāḥ*) has not been fulfilled. A similar consideration applies in the crime of defamation, as verbal custom (*ʿurf qawlī*) determines the offence of defamation, as well as apostasy. Finally, customary practices and traditions (*ʿurf / ʿāda*) can be used to determine the type of discretionary punishment to be awarded to an accused whose offence cannot be substantiated with a prescribed punishment.[73]

71 *Ibid.*, 297–298.

72 Baber Johansen, "Legal Literature and the Problem of Change: The Case of the Land Rent", *Islam and Public Law: Classical and Contemporary Studies*, edited by Chibli Mallat (London: Graham and Trotman, 1993), 29–47; Wael B. Hallaq, *Authority, Continuity and Change in Islamic Law*, (Cambridge, UK: Cambridge University Press, 2005), 166.

73 See Zakariyah, "Custom and Society", 90.

Effect of Changes in Time and Custom on Fixed Punishments

Islamic Law is said to be universal. One of the dimensions of its universality is that it is both flexible and rigid. Its flexibility lies in the fact that some of its rulings can be altered according to changes in time, place, circumstances and culture, namely, if such rulings were initially enacted on the custom and culture of past generations.[74] Its rigidity lies in the fact that some of its rulings cannot be altered, rendered ineffective. In other words, such rulings have been fixed and ordained, with consideration being given to their robustness in all circumstances. One unresolved controversy among orthodox Islamic Schools and reformists is whether rulings can be changed, regardless of whether they are fixed or deduced from Islamic legal texts. If so, can customs or changes in custom also affect the law?

"It is Undeniable That Rules Change as Times Change" (lā yunkar taghayyur al-aḥkām bi-taghayyur al-azmān)[75]

These questions surround the codification of the maxim in question, which first appeared in Article 39 of the *Majalla* in the Ottoman Empire, in the form quoted above. However, as discussed below, some interpreters have inserted the phrase "custom or personal opinion" (*al-ʿurfiyya aw al-ijtihādiyya*) to protect it from criticism.[76]

The maxim regarding alteration of rules according to changes in time and circumstance has faced criticism from different perspectives because of the loss in codification of the maxim as will be explained shortly. Muslehuddin is one critic who states that the maxim cannot be taken at face value.[77] He argues that any rule derived from the Qurʾān and sound Ḥadīths or deducted by analogy based on the two primary sources are everlasting.[78] He further explains that, if laws based on the aforementioned sources are subject to change, then "the law would have ceased to exist long ago".[79] Based on this hypothesis, no change would be allowed for rulings derived from Qurʾānic and Ḥadīth texts.[80]

---

74 Kamali, *Principles*, xxii and 255; and al-Shalābī.

75 *Majalla*, Article 39; Haydar, 1:43; Fakhr al-Dīn al-Zaylaʿī, *Tabyīn al-Ḥaqāʾiq Sharḥ Kanz ad-Daqāʾiq* (Cairo: Dār al-Kutub al-Islāmiyya, 1313/1895), 1:140; A. al-Zarqāʾ, *Sharḥ*, 227–229; al-Nadawī, 158; and al-Burnu, *al-Wajīz*, 310.

76 Haydar; al-Shalābī; and al-Burnu, *al-Wajīz*, 311.

77 Muslehuddin, *Philosophy*, 176.

78 *Ibid.*

79 *Ibid.*

80 *Ibid.*

To some extent, what Muslehuddin has said is a fact that cannot be enfeebled. However, we have seen that some rulings derived from the Qur'ān and Ḥadīth have been subjected to change as new circumstances (time, location, customs) have occurred. Apt examples to illustrate this point are found in Qur'ānic verse 24:58 and in a prophetic Ḥadīth, respectively:

> O you who have believed, let those whom your right hands possess and those who have not [yet] reached puberty among you ask permission of you [before entering] at three times:...[81]

> It is the responsibility of the owners of properties to take care of them in the day and the responsibility of the owners of animals to restitute for what their animals destroy in the night.[82]

However, if custom, or times have changed or if one nation rules differently with what has been established in both the Qur'ānic and Ḥadīth textual sources, can such rulings be changed? According to Saeed Ramadan in his book *Ḍawābiṭ al-Maṣlaḥ*[83] and Muslehuddin in *The Philosophy of Islamic Law*,[84] any ruling that can be changed is restricted to custom. However, neither of these authors accepts that customary rulings can be derived from the Qur'ān or Ḥadīths or by analogy based on both sources. At one point, Muslehuddin asserts that Islamic Law cannot be altered although it possesses an amazing capacity to accommodate change.[85] He further argues that changes in rules can only be met on the basis of the rule of necessity and need.[86]

By and large, taking the above sub-maxim at face value may create the impression that all rulings in Islamic Law can be altered. Nevertheless, what is certain is that, because the conditions, needs, and circumstances affecting mankind are not static, the laws governing their lives should therefore also be dynamic. Rulings must be made compatible with the phenomena of life. Having said that, Islamic texts emphasize that the religion of Islam has

81 Q. 24:58.

82 Ibn Mājah, Ḥadīth No. 2332; al-Ash'ath, Ḥadīth No. 3569; and Mālik, *al-Muwaṭṭa'*, Ḥadīth No. 677.

83 Said Ramadan al-Buti, *Ḍawābiṭ al-Maṣlaḥa fī sh-Sharī'a al-Islāmiyya*, 411–413, quoted by Muslehuddin, *Philosophy*, 172–176.

84 Muslehuddin, *Ibid.*

85 *Ibid.*, 242–243.

86 *Ibid.*, 243.

been completed and perfected[87] and affirm that God's revelation left nothing unexplained.[88] If this is indeed the case, why must rulings be changed?

In order to strike a balance between support for and opposition to changes, it is important to state that some rulings that have been explicitly ordained cannot be altered and include, for example, the number of lashes due for *ḥadd* punishments of adultery or false accusations that an innocent person is immoral or unchaste, and so on. Such rulings cannot be changed under any circumstance because of what has been mentioned and because the reason for the prescribed number is not mentioned and cannot be rationalized (*ghayr maʿqūla al-maʿnā*).[89]

However, other rulings can be subjected to changes in time and circumstance. According to Ibn al-Qayyim al-Jawziyya "Commandments [*aḥkām*, pl. for *ḥukm*] are of two types: one type that does not change from one state [...] regardless of time, location or the independent reasoning [*ijtihād*] of four Imāms, and another type that changes according to time, location and circumstances".[90] The rulings that change according to time and circumstance are either based on custom and culture (*ʿāda* and *ʿurf*) or based on *ijtihād*.

Rulings Based on Custom

If an enacted ruling is based on custom (*ʿurf*), then that ruling can be altered when the custom changes. To quote al-Qarāfī (d. 684/1285): "Anything in the Sharīʿa attributed to customs, its ruling changes when the custom changes to a new one" (*kullu mā huwa fī sh-sharīʿa yattabiʿ al-ʿawāʾid yataghayyar al-ḥukm fī-hi ʿinda taghayyur al-ʿāda ilā mā yaqtaḍīh al-ʿāda al-mutajaddida*).[91] In other words, if a textual ruling is based on a customary value, that ruling can be changed. Thus, it will be appropriate to reconstruct the sub-maxim to affect the above assertion by adding the adjectives 'customary' (*ʿurfiyya*) or 'personal exertion' (*ijtihādiyya*) to the maxim. That is to say: "The changing of rulings based on customs or personal opinion due to changes in times/circumstances cannot be denied" (*lā yunkar taghayyur al-aḥkām al-ʿurfiyya aw al-ijtihādiyya bi-taghayyur al-azmān*).[92] Of course, it is emphatically stated in *Durar al-Ḥukkām Sharḥ al-Majalla* that the meaning of the maxim with regard

---

87 Q. 5:3.

88 Q. 6:38.

89 al-Burnu, *al-Wajīz*, 282–283 and 301–311.

90 Muḥammad al-Zarʿī, *Ighāthat al-Lahfāt*, edited by Muḥammad Ḥāmid al-Faqī, (Beirut: Dār al-Maʿrifa, 1975), 1:330–331.

91 Quoted in al-Shalābī; See a similar statement in al-Burnu, *al-Wajiz*, 283.

92 See al-Nadawī's observation, as opposed to that of al-Burnu, *al-Wajīz*, 311.

to the alteration of rulings is peculiar to those based on *ʿurf* and *ʿāda*, but "firm rules based on the text shall not be changed".[93] This provision guards against misuse of the maxim.

The reason why rulings based on customs and culture must change as time passes is that needs of people vary with time. A law constructed to be static will impose hardship (*mashaqqa*) and constraint. One classical example given in books to illustrate the effect of this maxim is that, in the past, inspecting a model of a house was considered sufficient and equal to viewing the actual house before buying it. In the past, houses were generally built in the same way, while today houses are constructed in different ways, making it imperative to view the house and its particular property in its entirety before purchase. Other examples are the imposition of compensation on the usurper of an orphan's property, or closing mosques for fear of thieves.[94]

It is worth noting that to preserve the divine nature of the Qurʾān and the authority of Ḥadīth, and to curtail the possibility of that divine rulings are radically altered, legal texts categorized as unambiguous rulings (*muḥkamāt*) should not be supplanted by the customs and culture of a people. However, in several instances rules have been changed legally in Islamic Law as an interim measure in cases of necessity and need resulting from hardship and difficulty, such as when ʿUmar Ibn al-Khaṭṭāb suspended punishment for theft during the time of drought.[95]

Rulings Based on Personal Exertion

Rulings established by personal exertion and reasoning (*ijtihād*) can also be changed, regardless of whether they have been deduced directly or indirectly from the texts. For example, what constitutes prohibited wine is a subject of debate between the Ḥanafīs and the majority of Islamic jurists (*fuqahāʾ*). The Ḥanafīs hold that prohibited wine refers to wine brewed from grapes; thus, no amount of wine from fermented grapes can be consumed while drinking non-intoxicating amounts of wine obtained from other fermented materials is allowed. In contrast, the majority of Islamic scholars maintain that all types of potentially intoxicating drinks are prohibited, taking into account the general implication of the Qurʾānic verse that prohibits intoxicants and the Ḥadīth that prohibits all intoxicants.[96]

---

93 Haydar, 1:43.

94 *Ibid.*; al-Zaylaʿī, 1:140; and al-ʿAsqalānī, 2:450.

95 Kamali, *Principles*, 325.

96 Reference to Qur'an 5:90 and the prophetic Ḥadīth reported by Ibn Mājahthat says "Any intoxicant is forbidden" (*kull muskirin ḥarām*); Ibn Mājah, *Sunān*, Ḥadīth No. 2340, 3:107.

Islamic scholars employ personal exertion and reasoning (*ijtihād*) to arrive at verdicts, which might or might not enjoy consensus (*ijmāʿ*). If there is consensus based on *ijtihād* but the cause (*ʿilla*) upon which *ijtihād* is based is no longer effective or needs to be changed, those rulings must also be changed.[97] For example, ʿUmar ibn al-Khaṭṭāb initiated the payment of blood money (*diya*) due to a culprit from the public treasury (*dīwān*), which was contrary to the practice during the times of the Prophet and Abū Bakr when *diya* was paid by the culprit's heir (*ʿāqila*). ʿUmar's practice became the consensus because he opined that the reason why the *ʿāqila* was held responsible for paying blood money could also be achieved through the public treasury. More importantly, if the payment of *diya* is restricted to only the *ʿāqila*, the benefits of the *diya* for the family of the victim may be compromised due to procrastination of disbursement.[98] Rulings may also be based on the personal exertion and reasoning (*ijtihād*) of Islamic scholars extrapolated from the purpose of the Sharīʿa.

In the field of Islamic criminal law, there are ways, such as those already mentioned above, whereby rulings can be changed to suit the needs of the public. Indeed, a large segment of punishments in Islamic Law are left to the discretion of the authorities in accordance with variations in time and place, in recognition of the fact that Islamic criminal jurisprudence acknowledges such changes and provides leverage to accommodate them. Discretionary (*taʿzīr*) punishments vary in suitability according to time, place and circumstance. However, the bone of contention is whether a substantive law, such as a fixed number of lashes or stoning to death, can be substituted by another form of punishment, such as imprisonment in lieu of lashes, due to changes in time and circumstance. All Islamic scholars have affirmed unanimously that no substantive punishments can be eradicated or changed.[99] Nevertheless, while it is said that ʿUmar ibn al-Khaṭṭāb's moratorium on punishing theft during periods of drought[100] was based on necessity, it was the people's behavior towards the uncustomary and dire circumstances at that time which necessitated the change.

It is worth emphasizing that the maxim at hand was first introduced in the Ottoman *Majalla*.[101] This forms the basis for the criticism of innovation

97 See a lengthy discussion on the validity and legality of *ijtihād* in Kamali, *Principles*, 471–497.

98 This is the Ḥanafī view. However, there are other opinions regarding the use of *dīwān* for the *diya*; see al-Sarakhsī, 27:124–125; Zuhayli, *al-Fiqh al-Islāmī*, 6:322–323.

99 *Ibid.*, 310–311; and al-Nadawī, 158.

100 Kamali, *Principles*, 325.

101 Peters, *Crime and Punishment*, 69–74.

in Islam and systematic derogation of the Divine Law to suit the whim and caprice of the Ottoman regime.[102] It is reported in the Ottoman Criminal Code (OCC) that instead of flogging, a fine should be imposed, as in Articles 20 and 67:

> If [a person] kisses [another] person's son or approaches him on his way and addresses [indecent words] to him, [the *qāḍī*] shall chastise [him] severely and a fine of one *akce* shall be collected for each stroke.
>
> If [a person] steals a purse or a turban or towels, unless his hand is to be cut off, the *cadi* [*qāḍī*] shall chastise [him] and a fine of one *akce* shall be collected for [every] stroke [or one *akce* shall be collected for each stroke].[103]

The above suggests that the Sharīʿa has been derogated and fiscalized. However, from Articles 20 and 67 mentioned above, one can infer that their purpose does not support this claim. Rather, as Peters observes about Article 67, it is meant to "regulate a case in which a person has stolen, but cannot be sentenced to the fixed punishment for theft" and to legislate for any other offences that the Sharīʿa does not specify punishment for.[104] The OCC Article 67 includes a condition that unless the charge against the convicted person can be proven, a *taʿzīr* instead of *ḥadd* punishment shall be inflicted. This removes the misconception that any Islamic regime can twist the fixed Islamic Law. The fact that Islamic fixed penalties were rarely enforced during that regime is not a reason to suggest that *ḥadd* punishments were abolished or that they had become superannuated and outdated. The truth is that they were and remain active and suitable for all generations, even though there are rules and conditions set to protect both claimants and defendants.

In addition to the rulings that can be changed in Islamic criminal law, Islamic legal procedure provides room for change as time, place and circumstances change.[105] Many instances have been recorded in Islamic history when legal procedures were not fixed. Take, for instance, the creation of prisons at the time of ʿUmar ibn al-Khaṭṭāb, which was not in practice during the lives of the Prophet and Abū Bakr. Furthermore, the reformation of prisons in

102 *Ibid.*

103 *Ibid.*, 74.

104 *Ibid.*, 72 and 74.

105 See Baderin, 34, 46 and 98.

Islamic history has drastically changed with the dictates of time and circumstances. Also, keeping civil records by registering births, marriages, deaths, etc., is now approved under Islamic Law because of changes in the circumstances and mentality of people. All such inventions have no substantive textual evidence but are rather legal procedures that complement the substantive rulings in Islamic Law.[106]

General Application of the Grand Maxim *al-ʿĀda Muḥakkama* and its Subsidiaries in Several Northern Nigerian Sharīʿa Criminal Law Cases

In Islamic criminal law, if an accused believes that, according to the custom of the land, s/he is permitted to take a certain amount of goods from the host's property without committing an offensive act, then the accused will not be convicted for a criminal act. In *Isiya and Others* [*appellants*] *v. State* [*Zamfara respondent*], the appellants believed that they had been given free access to the accuser's house. This is one of the arguments put forward in the Court of Appeal before the appeal was granted.[107] In a different case, it was argued that since Safiyyatu Huseini spoke Hausa, a language customarily spoken by people in north Nigeria, it was the responsibility of the court to explain the meaning of *zinā: i.e.*, what the term for adultery/fornication entailed, the legal ramifications of committing such an offence, and how the Sharīʿa penal code rules on such issues. In other words, since Safiyyatu did not speak Arabic, in order to justify the validity of the verdict, the term needed to be interpreted into customary language.[108] However, this opinion was rebutted by the co-judge in *Amina v. State* where it was remarked that the term *zinā* is "no longer an Arabic word. It is basically a Hausa word. As such, Hausa people have no suitable word other than this".[109] Of course, the word *zinā* has been localized and it could be quite difficult to prove that Muslims do not know the connotation of the term. However, one could also argue that, while the literal meaning is generally known, legal specifications and ramifications may still be unfamiliar to the vast majority of Muslims in Nigeria.

---

106 For further reading see al-Zuhayli, *al-Qawāʿid al-Fiqhiyya*, 353.

107 See Zakariyah, *Applications of Legal Maxims*, Appendix 1.

108 *Ibid.*, Appendix 10, 24.

109 See NNLR, 2003, 513.

In Amina Lawal's case, it was assumed that Amina found sexual intercourse with Yakubu acceptable,[110] based on the false impression that custom allowed it because, before the Sharīʿa penal code was fully implemented, the *modus operandi* had been to give consent before the culmination of a proper marriage.[111]

Conclusion

From the above discussion, it is clear that Islamic Law considers custom authoritative in criminal law. This is because the law deals with society, and society is dynamic rather than static. Custom has been given consideration since the period of the Prophet Muḥammad, and there are some rulings in Islamic Law based on custom enacted by the Qurʾān or Sunna of the Prophet. Intuitively we know that, if those customs change over time and place, the rulings attached to them will also change. This is not to say that Islamic Law is entirely mutable. Of course, any fixed rulings cannot be altered, as they have nothing to do with custom, as in the number of lashes given to a convicted adulterer or the punishment of theft established with proof. The only way in which fixed punishments appear to change is when they are abandoned due to a legal technicality, such as doubt in the accusation or in the face of necessity.

110 Her co-accused who later denied the accusation and was discharged on unfounded evidence to convict him.

111 See Yawuri, 197.

CHAPTER 8

Conclusion

Summary

Chapter 1 opens this book with an examination of the roots of Islamic Law, as a subject that developed gradually through the emergence of the four Sunni and the Shiite Schools of Islamic Jurisprudence (*madhāhib*). The primary sources of Islamic Law during the first half of the era of Islam were the Qurʾān and the Prophet's Sunna. This does not mean that other sources were not resorted to but most scholars relied directly on the original texts.

Adhering to the literal meanings in the two primary sources (Qurʾān and Ḥadīth) proved challenging to the idea of universality in Islamic Law, however. Thus the scholars of Islamic jurisprudence (*fiqh*) took recourse to other generally approved sources of knowledge such as consensus (*ijmāʿ*) and analogy (*qiyās*) based on and derived from the two textual sources. Moreover, the demand to solve novel issues spurred the emergence of other concepts through extrapolation of the aims and objectives of Islamic Law, such as juristic preference (*istiḥsān*) and public interest (*maṣāliḥ al-mursala*).

The development of the science of Islamic jurisprudence (*uṣūl al-fiqh*), which brought about the creation of many new technical terms, as well as the later solidification of Islamic legal maxims, are additional hallmarks of the intellectuality of early Islamic scholars. Such technical apparatus were undoubtedly essential legal problem-solving tools that also helped unify the scattered thoughts of different Schools in their various literatures.

Chapter 2 discusses extensively the nitty-gritty of the concept of Islamic legal maxims (*al-qawāʿid al-fiqhiyya*) and analyzes its historical development, legality, roles, and importance. It is asserted that, although *al-qawāʿid al-fiqhiyya* have been defined in various ways by many classical and medieval scholars and their successors, no link between their definitions and the core role of the subject matter appeared until recently when both Kamali and Mawil posited that *al-qawāʿid al-fiqhiyya* are to serve the overall objectives (*maqāṣid ash-sharīʿa*) of Islamic Law. This insight has created new dimensions regarding how legal maxims might be applied to novel contemporary issues, without deserting divine texts, and still fostering the tenets of Islamic Law. During the course of the discussion, it is established that the science of *al-qawāʿid al-fiqhiyya* is

 | DOI 10.1163/9789004304871_009

an independent subject, as opposed to part of the science of jurisprudence (*uṣūl al-fiqh*), as some describe it. Other terms and subject matter occasionally confused with *al-qawāʿid al-fiqhiyya* are *inter alia* '*ḍābit*' (controllers or topical legal maxims) and '*naẓariyya*' (style of writing on a particular topic of jurisprudence). Although occasionally used synonymously with *qāʿida*, the *ḍābit* is said to be less applicable to some issues in Islamic jurisprudence as it is actually a principle meant to control a particular subject, as opposed to the term *qāʿida*, which is a rule applicable to many, if not all, subjects and issues in Islamic jurisprudence. The cardinal difference between *naẓariyya* and *qāʿida* is that *qawāʿid* are coined in precise phraseology and their particulars need not be detailed, whereas *naẓariyya* is a relatively new style of writing detailing a particular theme (topic) in Islamic jurisprudence.

Furthermore, Chapter 2 outlines the emergence and development of *al-qawāʿid al-fiqhiyya*, and reveals that they went through three stages (primitive, florescence and mature) before becoming an established discipline. During the primitive stage, expressions attributed to the Prophet or his Companions were neither treated as independent maxims nor recorded as such, although some later developed into maxims. Rather, *qawāʿid* were only memorized by Islamic scholars. The second landmark stage saw widespread dogmatism (*taqlīd*), or following one School of Thought blindly, while the spirit of *ijtihād* (legal reasoning through personal exertion) was on the brink of extinction. Thus the subject of *al-qawāʿid al-fiqhiyya* was enshrined and relevant literature sprang up in different dimensions. The final stage consolidates the efforts of the two preceding stages with standardization of the subject matter. Although it is claimed that study of the subject matter has reached its peak, there are, however, many empty pockets for knowledge that could be filled by studying the subject academically and empirically. While the Ottoman *Civil Code* (*Majalla l-Aḥkam al-ʿAdliyya*) appears to be an empirical study on the subject, it lacks an academic protocol.

Chapter 2 also enumerates the sources, categories, roles and importance of Islamic legal maxims. Their sources are the Qurʾān, Ḥadīths, scholarly consensus (*ijmāʿ*) and expressions by *mujtahidūn* (scholars who have attained the ability to conduct *ijtihād* and *qiyās*). Having various sources from which legal maxims are derived necessitates utilizing different categorizations, *viz*: the grand general maxims (*al-qawāʿid al-fiqhiyya l-kulliyya*), independent general maxims (*al-qawāʿid al-fiqhiyya l-mustaqilla*), and topical legal maxims (*ḍawābiṭ*). We contend that the topical legal maxims could be classified as legal maxims subsumed under both grand general and general independent maxims as opposed to the prevailing idea of separating them. It is also asserted that the more sources explored to codify legal maxims, the more powerful and encompassing the maxims will become. It is further established that any maxim derived from the Qur'ān and Ḥadīths is regarded as authoritative despite its possible limitation in scope.

Lastly, in Chapter 2, the role and importance of Islamic legal maxims are firmly stressed. Islamic scholars unanimously agree that Islamic legal maxims play a vital role in grasping many issues scattered throughout the books of jurisprudence and aid judges to comprehend the basic tenets of Islamic Law on any contentious issue. However, whether legal maxims can be used as primary evidence when giving verdicts in a court case conducted under standards of Islamic Law has long been an issue generating heated debate. We submit that, if a legal maxim is derived directly or indirectly from the texts (*i.e.*, the Qur'ān and authentic Ḥadīths), or from sound consensus or complete analogy, there is no doubt that such a maxim is sufficient to be used as basis for judgment.

Chapters 3 to 7 constitute the central part of this book, as they each explore one grand general maxim and its relevant sub-maxims, and provide ample examples of their application.

Chapter 3 emphasizes the importance that Islamic criminal law attaches to the assessment of the intention of an accused before passing a verdict and awarding an appropriate punishment. The first grand legal maxim discussed is the corroboration of intention (*niyya*) with action (*ʿamal*). If an accused were to be punished unlawfully, punishment might cause irreparable damage, and failure to consider intention in Islamic criminal law could lead to injustice being perpetrated against the innocent. Evidence of intentionality in Islamic criminal law ranges from overt expressed utterances of perpetrators in forms of confession, defamation, or blasphemy to physical objects used for committing a crime. With regard to overt expression, there is need for further clarification to ensure straightforward and grammatically clear statements; problems might arise if the language used to express a criminal act is ambiguous. In such cases, determining the commission of a *ḥudūd* or *qiṣāṣ* crime would also become a matter of controversy.

The question whether the nature of an object can provide proof of criminal intent raises questions, since the object mentioned in the prophetic Ḥadīth was limited to the meaning of 'stick' the issue of extension of the scope of tools to include other modern means of killing, such as chemical weapons, guns, and missiles is discussed. Because Muslims believe that Islam is a universal religion, its applicable law should accommodate all means of killing since the aim and the result are the same. This will be the case especially in retaliatory (*qiṣāṣ*) crimes to guarantee justice to victims and their relatives. Not only the rights of victims and their relatives must be protected; Islamic Law also considers the rights of the accused.

Chapter 4 discusses an assortment of maxims that cast doubt onto criminal offences and provide exceptions such as ignorance (*jahl*), duress (*ikrāh*), forgetfulness (*nisyān*), etc. It is affirmatively propounded that certainty (*yaqīn*) cannot be overruled by uncertainty (*shakk*) or doubt (*shubha*). In the doctrines of scholars of *fiqh* and *uṣūl*, certainty is considered a strong proof while doubt is weakness in evidence. Although scholars of *fiqh* attempt to elevate the category 'probability' (*ẓann*) to the level of certainty, it is unlikely that certainty can be obtained in all cases. Probability cannot be accepted as substantive evidence in criminal cases which involve the absolute right of God because *ḥadd* punishments can be of an irrevocable nature.

In criminal cases where there is contradiction between the principle of certainty (*yaqīn*) and that which is apparent (*zāhir*), the apparent should be relied on because it is closer to justice and the spirit of Islamic Law. The principle of certainty should be upheld until the facts prove otherwise. This elucidates the maxim referred to as *actori incumbit onus probandi*, or the principle of presumption of continuity (*iṭṭirād*). That is why it is in line with natural justice to ascribe criminal acts to their nearest point in time. Under the rule of certainty, there is an unresolved issue concerning the originality of things; are they originally permitted or prohibited? The opinions of Islamic scholars are threefold: something is permissible (*mubāḥ*), prohibited (*ḥarām*), or suspended (*tawaqquf*). The relevance of this issue is to identify what is certain but not incriminating. If it is accepted that the fundamental principle (*aṣl*) is that things are originally permissible, then it follows that the commission or omission of any act other than the one explicitly prohibited or made compulsory by texts would not be criminalized.

Doubt (*shubha*) is also said to be another mechanism to diminish the strength of *ḥadd* punishments, as the maxim states: "*Ḥudūd* punishment should be averted in the face of doubt" (*al-ḥudūd tudraʾ bi-sh-shubhāt*). It is argued in this text that not only predetermined (*ḥadd*) but retaliatory (*qiṣāṣ*) punishments might be averted in the face of doubt because both can have a serious damaging effect on the alleged culprit. One is assumed to be innocent of any accusation until proven otherwise. Any allegation that lacks credible evidence shall not be entertained. Any iota of doubt plunged into evidence shall render such evidence invalid. However, it may be difficult to attain certainty in all cases; thus, when a case involves the rights of an individual, it is espoused that circumstantial evidence should be sought in order to regain the right of the person involved.

Chapter 5 details Islam's stand on considering hardship (*mashaqqa*) as *raison d'être* in creating facility (*taysīr*) for human beings. This chapter enunciates not only those factors that necessitate giving facility but also demonstrates how these factors can be utilized in criminal cases. Here we emphasize that, in any dire situation, facility is provided to redeem the rights not only of the victim but also the culprit. A victim's rights will never be in vain because "Necessity does not invalidate the right of others" (*al-iḍṭirār lā yubṭil ḥaqq al-ghayr*). However, if another person's right is violated because of necessity (*ḍarūra*), then the perpetrator will generally not be punished under the provision "Necessities render illicit things lawful" (*aḍ-ḍarūrāt tubīḥ al-maḥẓūrāt*). However, any excessive use of this provision will necessitate incriminating the perpetrator because "Necessity is estimated according to its quantity" (*aḍ-ḍarūra tuqaddar bi-qadarihā*). While there are three categories of provisions aimed at facilitating the lives of human beings, *viz.* necessity, need and luxury, 'need' is graded at the level of necessity for both the individual and the public at large because at times they are inseparable.

Chapter 6 elucidates the position of Islam on the prohibition and elimination of harm (*ḍarar*) whether in terms of initial or reciprocal aggression. It is a settled rule in Islam that harm must be removed, and in doing so two major conditions must be observed: harm must not be removed by its like, and greater harm can be prevented by committing a lesser offense. However, if the element harm is equally prevalent in both choices, one should look to legal maxims to help decide one's preference. Take, for example, the maxim "If a prohibitive injunction contradicts what is permissible, the prohibition is given preference over the permissible unless the permissible [benefit] is of greater importance" (*idhā taʿāraḍ al-māniʿ wa-l-muqtaḍī yuqaddam al-māniʿ*). In Islamic Law, it is an established principle that "Preventing evils is better than acquiring benefits" (*dar' al-mafāsid aw-lā min jalb al-maṣāliḥ*).

Chapter 7 explains the legality of custom in the Islamic legal system and how it affects the way legal rulings change according to time and circumstance. Here we discuss that the custom given to authority could be practical (*ʿamalī*) or verbal (*qawlī*), and several maxims are explored to this effect. In either case, whether a custom is practical or verbal, certain conditions must be met before custom can be given significant effect: namely, the custom must not contradict explicit texts, must enjoy regular occurrence, and must be prevalent.

The application of the maxims studied throughout this book depicts several criminal cases worthy of critical review in light of Islamic legal maxims (*al-qawāʿid al-fiqhiyya*). Our finding has revealed that, due to the void or lack of correlation between legal maxim theory and its relevance to the objectives of the Sharīʿa (*maqāṣid ash-sharīʿa*), there are massive failures of observation of justice in delivering judgments in Islamic criminal law. Moreover, some Muslim jurists and judges have a scanty knowledge of the science of Islamic legal maxims or find their meaning and relevance obscure. This has contributed to irregularities and/or miscarriage of justice in a number of cases brought before Sharīʿa courts. Thus, the five grand legal maxims treated in this book pose the question of whether the overall objectives of the Sharīʿa were observed in the criminal procedures of cases brought before courts in those states that implement the Sharīʿa.

Recommendations

In writing this book, critical analysis, observations and evaluations have been made. There is a need for intertextualizing and hyper-texualizing the concepts and the contexts of Islamic texts in order to bring about a comprehensive codification which will cater for the novel issues of the present as well as later generations. It is time to depart from stringent adherence to one specific School of Jurisprudence by adopting a system of legal pluralism whereby several juristic views can be merged by means of the new concept of *talfīq* or principles selected from different Schools on a specific topic (*takhayyur*) for pragmatic purposes. Both *talfīq* and *takhayyur* incorporate a broad range of strategies required to deal with the sensitive issues that may arise in any state adopting full implementation of the Sharīʿa.

There is a need for highly qualified Islamic jurists in Islamic Sharīʿa courts and legislative assemblies. There is also a need to appoint dynamic, broad-minded jurists who can view issues in a wide-ranging context. This should help reduce the level of criticism about the suitability of Islamic Law to the modern age. There are many ways to achieve criminal justice in Islamic Law, equally applicable today as in the past:

1. Application of legal maxims which are based on the tenets and overall objectives of Islamic Law;
2. Evaluation of the socio-economic status of the accused prior to conviction; and
3. Evaluation of the socio-political context of the accusation to determine both the benefit and the evil underlying the prosecution of the accused as exemplified by the Prophet.

The five basic legal maxims summon Islamic criminal jurists and judges to establish the overall objectives of the Sharīʿa in a quest for justice in each criminal case because the ultimate goal of Islamic Law is to "promote the benevolent nature of Islam, especially where the reasoning for such [...] is commensurate with prevalent needs of social justice and human well-being".[1] However, much work is still needed to encourage the implementation of Islamic legal maxims. Literature on this subject matter is lacking in the English language, and even available translations exhibit disparities and deficiencies in translation. Thus, it would be generally advantageous to standardize the translations of Islamic legal maxims.

There is also a need for better, more consistent application of Islamic legal maxims to fields other than criminal law, such as family law, political law and commercial law. We must acknowledge the efforts of al-Sawwat and al-Nadawī, who both have written books on the application of legal maxims in Islamic family law and Islamic transaction law respectively. However, their books do not enjoy wide readership because they are written in Arabic and they do not take contemporary issues into consideration. Thus this lacuna of literature addressing contemporary issues in English begs to be filled.

In addition to filling scholarly gaps, the practical application of Islamic legal maxims could also be improved. In many Islamic countries that implement full or partial Islamic Law, there is a need to consider the overall objectives of Islamic Law in dealing with some sensitive issues. One way to achieve this is to inter-textualize the evidence in Islamic Law to extrapolate the wisdom of Islam and its overall objectives in legislation. Undoubtedly, Islamic legal maxims share some of these features, and undermining their usefulness would be equivalent to ignoring valuable tools available to help achieve this noble goal.

Nigeria provides a neat case study demonstrating the need for judicial responsibility aided by appropriate, informed implementation of the Sharīʿa. The Nigerian Sharīʿa Council needs to establish different judiciary arms as a system of checks and balances. Justice can be achieved through judicial professionalism and qualified judges. It is expected that professional and qualified judges "demonstrate a clear rational perspective of issues based on evidence placed before them and not to be biased by emotions and zealousness".[2] These different judiciary arms would, to some extent, help curb miscarriages of justice and block blind criticism of the legal system of the states.

As we have seen through detailed analysis of cases judged in the states implementing full Sharīʿa law in northern Nigeria, some cases were quashed when brought before the appeal courts. Had the defendants not sought to apply to the Court of Appeal, they would have been unjustly punished. It is an established rule in Islamic Law that a judge, who delivers a verdict based

1 Baderin, 220.

2 *Ibid.*, 224.

on the dictates of his personal independent reasoning, should be rewarded. If, however, his judgment is subsequently proved to be wrong and, as a consequence, impinges on the right of man, any injured party should be awarded compensation by the government who employed the judge. This would ensure that, while a judge would not be held accountable because of his human fallibility, miscarriage of justice would be mitigated by recompensating the victim for this grave error.

Equally, Sharīʿa-implementing states need to ensure that all infrastructures are put in place before embarking upon full implementation, not only to ensure that the law will be applied responsibly but also to avoid criticism and garner praise. This could be realized by observing examples of the Prophet's practice and strategy in transmitting the Sharīʿa through different stages. The social welfare of a country's citizenry is paramount to minimizing criminality. As Sanusi notes, critics of the Sharīʿa point out that in the absence of any change in the "material living conditions of the masses of the population [...] all appearances of change are cosmetic".[3] To justify the execution of criminal convictions, there must be an extension of justice to government officials. If Islamic states allow malpractice in public office, such as turning a blind eye to the embezzlement of public funds by government officials, then undoubtedly criticism of the Sharīʿa will spread worldwide.

Human rights organizations and human rights activists should understand that, while a miscarriage of justice might occur in some cases, human beings are not infallible and their actions inevitably far from perfection. This does not imply that criticism is unwanted because constructive critique based on good intentions can indeed help rectify imperfections in the law and its application. Allowing an imperfection to prevail in the mistaken belief that there is no way to redress it is intolerable.

The negativity expressed during discussions on Muslim legal codes for punishments for crimes such as adultery, theft, etc., and the undermining approach of "cultural relativism" towards Islamic doctrines will stand as obstacles blocking the admittance of any constructive criticism voiced by opponents of the Sharīʿa. As Sanusi observes, such negative descriptions "are considered value-judgments reflecting certain elements of cultural arrogance and unacceptable claims of superiority [...] [which make] dialogue difficult if not impossible".[4] I am not *esprit de corps* with those who try to use the Sharīʿa as a political

---

3 S. Lamido Sanusi, "The West and the Rest: Reflections on the Intercultural Dialogue about Shariʿah", in Philip Ostien, Jamila Nasir, and Franz Kogelmann (eds.), *Comparative Perspectives on Shariʿah in Nigeria*, (Ibadan: Spectrum Books), 255.

4 *Ibid.*, 262.

weapon to destabilize any country, but I do believe that, in some criminal cases, miscarriages of justice did occur in the first judgments of the Lower Sharīʿa Courts in Nigeria. If we are ever to get a clear picture of what is really going on in Nigeria as well as in other countries that implement the Sharīʿa, political vendettas and journalistic smearing need to be set aside when criticizing any element of Islamic Law.

It is the sincere intention of the author that this book, with its comprehensive articulation on the concept 'Islamic legal maxims', will undoubtedly assist present-day Muslim jurists to relate the application of Islamic criminal law in the Muslim world with the one vital factor most blatantly missing, namely, the overall objectives of the Sharīʿa.

Glossary of Arabic Terms

Aḍḥā	festival celebrated on the 10th of *Dhū al-Hijja* (Islamic calendar)
aḥkām ash-sharʿ	pertaining to legal rulings derived from specific evidence
ahl al-ḥadīth	scholars who adhere to Ḥadīths
ahl al-raʾy	scholars who adhere to rationalization
akhaff aḍ-ḍararīna	lesser of two evils
amr (pl. *umūr*)	a matter, issue or act
arsh	pecuniary compensation
aṣl	fundamental concept / principle
ʿāda (pl. *ʿādāt*)	custom / manner / habit (see *ʿurf*)
qawlī	verbal practice
ʿamalī	customary practice
fardiyya	regional / professional / expert practice
ʿadāla	trustworthiness
ʿafw	pardon
ʿamal (pl. *aʿmāl*)	action / custom / practice
ʿamal / ʿurf ahl al-Madina	custom / practice of the people of Medina
ʿamd	premeditated intent, purpose, *mens rea* (see *qaṣd janāʾī*)
ʿāmid	intentional perpetrator
ʿāqila	blood relatives / supporters
ʿarafa	to know (see *ʿurf*)
ʿaṣr	afternoon, as in prayer
baghī	treason against a just leader, outrage / injustice
batr	amputation
bayyina	clear proof, evidence
bayyina ẓarfīya	circumstantial evidence
bulūgh	puberty
daʿwā (pl. *daʿāwā*)	claim
dīn	religion
diwān	public treasury
diya	blood money,
mughallaẓ	extra blood money
dunyāwiyya	related to mankind's day-to-day activities
dhukūriyya	masculinity
ḍaʿīf	weak, as in a Ḥadīth chain of transmission

 | DOI 10.1163/9789004304871_010

ḍābiṭ (pl. *ḍawābiṭ*)	controller, maxim governing a particular subject
ḍarar	harm / injury / abuse
ḍarūra (pl. *ḍarūrāt*)	necessity
quṣwā	dire necessity
ḍawābiṭ al-fiqhiyya	controllers or topical maxims
ḍirār	inflicted harm beyond limits of legality, without benefit
fajr	morning prayer
faqiha	verb to know
fāqih (pl. *fuqahā'*)	qualified Islamic scholars
fasād	illicit practices
fatwā (pl. *fatawā'*)	religious verdict
fiqh	Islamic jurisprudence
ghalaba	predominance
ghalabat aẓ-ẓann	probable certainty
ghālib aktharī	preponderant majority rule
ghaṣb	usurpation
ghayr maʿqūla l-maʿnā	irrational
ghayr samāwī	unnatural cause
ḥadd (pl. *ḥudūd*)	serious or capital crimes with predetermined punishments
Ḥadīth (pl. *aḥadīth*)	corpus of sayings, deeds and teachings of the Prophet
ḥāja	need less pressing than necessity
ḥajj	major pilgrimage
ḥākim	ruler
ḥalāl	lawful
ḥalf	swearing
ḥaqīqa	denotes the original meaning given to a word
lughawiyya	linguistic meaning
ḥarām	prohibited
ḥayāt	life
ḥirāba	banditry, armed robbery
ḥudūd	predetermined mandatory punishments
Allāh	predetermined mandatory punishments, absolute right of God
ḥuḍūr	presence
ḥukm	rule
aghlabī	preponderant rule
ghālib aktharī	preponderant majority rule

ḥuqūq (sg: *ḥaqq*)	rights
al-ādamī	right of man
Allāh	absolute right of God
humūm al-balwā	general necessity
iḍṭirād	continuity
ijmāʿ	scholarly consensus
ijtihād	personal independent reasoning
ijtihādiyya	related to personal exertion
ightiṣāb	rape
ikhbār	information
ikhtilāf al-mawjib	difference in the cause
ihmāl	negligence
ikrāh	coercion
ghayr muljī	incomplete coercion
muljī	complete coercion
tāmm	complete coercion
iljāʾ	compulsion
iqrār	confession
isnād	authoritative chain of Ḥadīth narration
istiḥsān	juristic preference
istiṣnāʿ	manufacturing contract
itlāf nafs	capital punishment
ʿibāda	acts of worship
ʿidda	woman's period of purification after divorce
ʿilla	cause, *ratio legis*
ʿilm	knowledge
ʿishāʾ	night, as in prayer
jahl	ignorance
jald	flogging
jawāmiʿ al-kalim	Prophet's inclusive expressions
jins wāḥid	one group
jumuʿa	communal Friday prayer obligatory for men
junūn	insanity
kadhdhāb	deceitful, habitual liar
kamāliyya	complement / embellishment / luxury (see *taḥsīniyya*)
khāṣṣ	personal / individual
khaṭaʾ	error, unintentional

khulṭ	financial transaction, as in trade
kullī muṭṭarid	consistent general rule
lafẓ (pl. *alfāẓ*)	expressions, wording
lawth	circumstantial evidence
liʿān	repudiation
maʾmūma	head wound reaching the cerebral membrane
maʾmūrāt	commanded
madhhab (pl. *madhāhib*)	Islamic School of Jurisprudence
madrasāt ahl al-kalām	dialectical schools of thought
mafsada	dangers
mahr al-mithl	fair dower
maḥẓūra	fundamentally prohibited
maʿnan (pl. *maʿānin*)	meaning, connotation
maʿrūf	kindness
Majalla al-Aḥkām al-ʿAdliyya	Civil Code
majāz	metaphorical or other meaning
majnūn	insane
makrūh	detestable
manāfiʿ	benefits
manhiyāt	prohibited
mansūk	abrogated
maqṣad (pl. *maqāṣid*)	purpose, objectives, will
maqāṣid ash-sharīʿa	overall objectives of the Sharīʿa
maqṣūd al-ʿiqāb	purpose of punishment
maraḍ	illness
maṣlaḥ	benefits
maṣāliḥ al-mursala	public interest
mashaqqa	hardship
mawqūf	broken chain of Ḥadīth narrations
muʿāmalāt	transactions, social affairs
muʿāyana	viewing
mubāḥa	fundamentally permissible
mubāshir	direct cause of a crime
muḍirr	injurious, causing harm
muḍṭarr	compelled, injured person behaving strangely, poor / destitute
muḥkam	ambiguity
muḥkamāt	unambiguous rulings

muḥsin	someone previously married
maḥẓūr	prohibited
mujtahidūn	the learned Muslims Jurisconsults
mukallaf	person of sound mind / a legally liable person
mukhṭiʾ	unintentional perpetrator
mukrah	person who is coerced
mukrih	person who coerces
munaqqila	an injury whereby a bone is displaced
muqʿad	sick person unable to change locations
muqayyad	restricted
mursal	incomplete chain of Ḥadīth transmitters
mustaḥabb	desirable
mutasabbib	indirect agent of a crime
mutʿa	temporary marriage
muthbit	one who makes the claim
muttasil	Ḥadīth attributed directly to the Prophet
muṭlaq	unrestricted
nafī	exile
naqṣ	defect or disability
naskh	abrogation
naṣṣ	Qurʾānic / Ḥadīth text
naum	sleep
naẓar	reason aimed at attaining particular knowledge
naẓariyya	theory, style of writing detailing a particular topic in Islamic jurisprudence
al-fiqhiyya	theory of Islamic jurisprudence / *fiqh*
al-ʿāmma	general theories
al-ʿaqd	theory of contract
al-iqrār	theory of confession
al-ithbāt	theory of evidence
al-ʿurf	theory of customs / traditions
nikāḥ bāṭil	invalid marriage
nisyān	oblivion, forgetfulness
niṣāb	minimum value for theft
niyya	intention
nukūl	defendant's refusal to take oath
qadhf	defamation of character, accusation of being unchaste
qāḍī	judge

qaḍiyya	proposition / theorem
qaʿīdat ar-rajul	pillar of the man, married woman
qiyāfa	system to establish a child's parenthood
qasāma	legal procedure to establish a homicidal crime
fī dimāʾ	bloody crime
fī l-amwāl	financial or property crime
qaṣd janāʾī mens rea	(see *ʿamd*)
wāḥid	one intention / purpose
qatl ʿamd	intentional murder
qatl khaṭaʾ	unintentional murder
qaṭʿ al-ṭarīq	highway robbery
qawad	retaliation
qawāʿid (sg. *qāʿida*)	legal maxims
ʿāmma	general maxims
al-fiqhiyya	Islamic legal maxims
al-kulliyya	basic general legal maxims
al-kulliyya al-mustaqilla	independent general legal maxims
al-milkiyya	maxims of ownership
khāṣṣa	specific legal maxims
uṣūliyya	maxims related to principles of Islamic jurisprudence
qiṣāṣ	crimes against God and man, retaliation in kind
qiyāfa	system to establish parenthood
qiyās	analogical deduction
qurʿa	drawing lots
raʾy	rationalization based on personal opinion
rafʿal-ḥaraj	removing hardship
rajm	stoning to death
rakaʿāt	prayer cycles
ribā	usury
ridda	apostasy
rukhṣa	legal concession
sadd adh-dharīʿa	prevention of evil
safar	journey
samāwī	natural, as in cause
sariqa	theft
satara	to conceal
siyāsa	politics

Sunna	prophetic tradition
ṣaḥāba (*aṣḥāb*)	Companions of the Prophet
ṣalāt	prayers
shabiha / ishtabaha	to resemble another thing
shahāda	testimony, statement, witness
shāhid al-ʿayn	eyewitness
shakk	doubt as in uncertainty / suspicion
sharaʿ	verb to legislate
Sharīʿa (*Sharīʿa*)	lit., path to be followed, way to the source
shibh ʿamd	quasi-intention
shurb al-khamr	consumption of alcohol
shubha	doubt
fī l-jiha	doubt regarding legality / illegality of an act
fī l-ʿaqd	doubt in the contract
fī l-fāʿil	doubt in the perpetrator
fī l-fiʿl	doubt in the action
fī l-maḥall or *l-milk*	doubt of ownership
shuyūʿ	prevalence of the custom
tābiʿūn	Followers of the Prophet, born after his demise
tadākhul	integration
taḍilla	forgetfulness
taḥsīniyya	complement / embellishment / luxury (see *kamāliyya*)
takhayyur	selection of rules from different Schools of Law
talfīq	merging parts of rules from various Schools
taqlīd	blind imitation, dogmatic adherence to a particular School
tawaqquf	cessation
taysīr	easement / facility
taʿzīr	crimes against man with variable discretionary punishments
ṭahāra	cleanliness
ṭalāq bāʾin	complete or irrevocable divorce
ṭifl (pl. *aṭfāl*)	child
ukhrāwiyya	rules that guide religious rites
umma	global community
ʿumra	minor pilgrimage
ʿumūm al-balwā	general necessity
ʿuqūbāt ash-sharʿiyya	Islamic punishments
muqaddara sharʿan	legally fixed punishments

ʿurf (pl. *aʿārf*)	custom / practice
ʿāmm	general custom
khāṣṣa	particular / individual custom
qawlī	verbal custom
ʿurfiyya	related to the customary norm
ʿusr	difficulty
uṣūl al-fiqh	science of Islamic jurisprudence
wahm	illusion
wājib	obligatory
wakāla	warrants or sureties
walī	legal guardian
wujūb	obligation
yamīn (pl. *aymān*)	oath
yaqīn	certainty
zajr	deterrent
zinā	adultery, illicit sexual relations
ẓāhir	apparent
ẓann	probability
ẓuhr	noon, as in prayer

List of Maxims

 | DOI 10.1163/9789004304871_011

42. *al-Mashaqqa tajlib at-taysīr* (Hardship begets facility) 23, 50, 53, 136
43. *an-Nātij aw-lā min al-ʿārif* (The producer [of something] is more entitled to its profit than the claimant [of the ownership]) 26
44. *ar-Rukhaṣ lā yata ʾaddā mawāḍiʾihā* (Facilities should not be taken beyond their premises) 27
45. *ash-Shubha tamnaʿ wujūb al-ḥadd wa-lā tamnaʿ wujūb al-māl* (Doubt interdicts only infliction of *ḥadd* punishment, not due financial compensation) 102
46. *at-Tābiʿ tābiʿ* (The accessory shares the same rule of the root) 57
47. *at-Taṣarruf ʿalā r-raʿiyya manūṭ bi-l-maṣlaḥa* (Governance should be in the public interest) 54
48. *at-Ta ʾsīs aw-lā min at-ta ʾkīd* (Establishing a new norm is better than emphasizing an existing one) 43
49. *at-Taʿyīn bi-l-ʿurf ka-t-taʿyīn bi-n-naṣṣ* (What is stipulated by virtue of custom is like what is stipulated by text) 179
50. *at-Taʿzīr ilā l-imām ʿalā qadr ʿaẓam al-jurm wa-ṣigharh* (It is left to the leader/judge to decide an appropriate discretionary punishment considering the proportionate [nature] of the offence) 18n90, 27, 55
51. *ath-Thābit bi-l-burhān ka-th-thābit bi-l-ʿiyān* (What is established by convincing, just evidence is as what is established by an eyewitness) 107
52. *al-Umūr bi-maqāṣidihā* (Matters shall be judged by their objectives) 23, 42, 46, 53, 60, 62
53. *al-Yaqīn lā yazūl bi-sh-shakk* (Certainty cannot be overruled by doubt) 42, 53, 80, 84
54. *Darʾ al-mafāsid aw-lā min jalb al-maṣāliḥ* (Preventing evil is better than acquiring benefits) 168, 172
55. *Hal al-aymān mabniyya ʿalā l-ʿurf* (Is oath based on custom?) 74
56. *Hal al-ʿibra li-l-maqāṣid wa-l-maʿānī aw li-l-alfāẓ wa-l-mabānī* (Should effect be given to purpose and meanings or the words and forms?) 73
57. *Idhā ḍāq al-amr ittasaʿ wa-idhā ittasaʿ ḍāq* (Whenever the circle of an affair narrows, it is widened, and whenever it widens, it is narrowed) 148
58. *Idhā ḍāq al-amr ittasaʿ* (When a matter becomes difficult, its rule becomes expanded) 139
59. *Idhā ijtamaʿ al-ḥalāl wa-l-ḥarām aw al-mubīḥ wa-l-muḥarrim ghullib al-ḥarām* (If the lawful and unlawful coincide, preference will be given to maintaining prohibition) 169
60. *Idhā ijtamaʿ al-mubāshir wa-l-mutasabbib, yuḍāf al-ḥukm ilā l-mubāshir* (In the presence of the direct author of an act and the person who is the causer, the direct author is responsible therefore) 88
61. *Idhā taʿāraḍ al-māniʿ wa-l-muqtaḍī yuqaddim al-māniʿ illā idhā kān al-muqtaḍā aʿẓam* (If a prohibitive injunction contradicts what is permissible, the prohibition is given preference over the permissible unless the permissible [benefit] is of greater importance) 169, 172, 197

62. *Idhā taʿāraḍat mafsadatān rūʿiya aʿẓamahumā ḍararan bi-irtikāb akhaffihumā* (If two evils clash, the greater should be prevented by committing the lesser) 165
63. *Iʿmāl al-kalām aw-lā min ihmālih* (A word should be construed as having some meaning, rather than disregarded) 20, 53
64. *Inna l-ʿāda taḥkum fī-mā lā ḍabṭ lah sharʿan* (Custom is enforced where there is no legal detail) 182
65. *Inna li-ṣāḥib al-ḥaqq maqāl* (Indeed, the owner of the right has a say) 25
66. *Innamā tuʿtabar al-ʿāda idhā ʿiṭṭaradat aw ghalabat* (Custom is considered only when it is regularly occurring and prevailing) 46, 182
67. *Ishārah al-maʾhūdah li-l-akharas ka-l-bayān bi-l-lisān* (An identifiable sign from a person who is mute is like a declaration with the tongue)
68. *Istiʿmāl an-nās ḥujja yajib al-ʿamal bi-hā* (People's practice is authoritative and should be reckoned with) 45, 178
69. *Kullu muskirin ḥarām* (Any intoxicant is forbidden) 49, 188n96
70. *Kullu shayʾin fī-l-qurʾān aw, aw, fa-huwa mukhayyar* (In the Qurʾān, every injunction in which many things are joined together with the conjunctive particle 'or' [Arabic: *aw*] is an indication that a free choice is allowed among these things) 26
71. *Lā ḍarar wa-lā ḍirār* (No harm shall be inflicted or reciprocated) 23, 25, 49, 158, 171
72. *Lā ʿibra bi-l-ʿurf aṭ-ṭāriʾ* (No consideration is given for an emergency custom) 182
73. *Lā yujmaʿ al-ajr wa-ḍ-ḍamān* (Wage and responsibility cannot be combined) 27
74. *Lā yunkar taghayyur al-aḥkām bi-taghayyur al-azmān* (It is undeniable that rules [based on *ʿurf*] change with time) 45–46
75. *Lā yunkar taghayyur al-aḥkām al-ʿurfiyya aw al-ijtihādiyya bi-taghayyur al-azmān* (The changing of rulings based on customs or personal opinion due to changes in times/circumstances cannot be denied) 183n66, 187
76. *Lā yunsab ilā sākit qawlu qāʾil wa-lā ʿamal ʿāmil, innamā yunsab ilā kullin qawlihi wa-ʿamalihi* (No statement or action should be imputed to someone who is silent, but a statement and action should be imputed to the one who made the statement or carried out the action) 27, 51
77. *Lā yunsab li-sākit qawlun* (No statement is imputed to someone who keeps silent)
78. *Lā yunzaʿ shayʾun min yaddi aḥadin illā bi-ḥaqq thābit maʿrūf* (Nothing should be stripped from someone without legal right) 27
79. *Laysa li-ʿirq ẓālim ḥaqq* (A transgressor/unjust root has no right) 161
80. *Laysa li-l-imām an yakhruj shayʾan min yaddi aḥadin illā bi-ḥaqqin thābit maʿarūf* (It is not the right of the leader/judge to take away someone's property without an established and well-known right) 18n90, 27

81. *Mā askara kathīruhu, fa-qalīluhu ḥarām* (Any substance whose large quantity intoxicates is also prohibited in small quantities) 25
82. *Māʿalā l-muḥsinīn min sabīl* (No ground [of complaint] can there be against the good-doers) 48
83. *Mā ḥaruma istiʿmāluhu ḥaruma ittikhādhuhu* (When its use is forbidden, its possession is also forbidden) 54
84. *Mā jāz li-ʿudhur baṭala bi-zawālihi* (What is permissible by virtue of excuse becomes invalid with the expiration of the excuse) 152
85. *Mā thabat bi-l-yaqīn lā yazāl bi-sh-shakk* (Whatever is established by certainty cannot be removed by doubt) 80
86. *Mā ubīḥa li-ḍ-ḍarūrāt yuqaddar bi-qadarihā* (What is permitted by virtue of necessity should be estimated according to its quantity) 151
87. *Man qāsam ar-ribḥ fa-lā ḍamān ʿalayhi* (A profit shareholder is not held responsible for loss) 26
88. *Man sharaṭ ʿalā nafsihi ṭāʾiʿan ghayr mukrah fa-huwa ʿalayhi* (He who willingly gives a condition binding himself without compulsion shall be held responsible for it) 26
89. *Min qawāʿid ash-shariʿa al-kulliyya annahu lā wājib maʿa ʿajz wa-lā ḥarām maʿa ḍarūra* (Among the general legal maxims [of Islamic Law is that] there is no obligation in the face of incapability and there is no prohibition in the face of necessity) 30
90. *Yuḍāf al-amr ilā aqrab al-waqt* (A matter is attributed to the time closest to the event) 95
91. *Yukhtār ahwan ash-sharrayn aw akhaff aḍ-ḍararayn* (The lesser of two evils or injuries should be chosen) 165
92. *Yutaḥammal aḍ-ḍarar al-khāṣṣ li-dafʿ ḍarar ʿāmm* (Personal injury should be incurred to prevent general injury) 167

Bibliography

al-ʿAbdarī, Muḥammad Ibn Yūsuf. *al-Tāj wa-l-Iklīl li-Mukhtaṣar al-Khalīl.* 2nd edn. Beirut: Dār al-Fikr, 1398/1977.

Abdel Haleem, Muhammed, Adel Omar Sharif, and Kate Daniels. *Criminal Justice in Islam: Judicial Procedure in the Shariʿa.* London: I.B. Tauris, 2003.

Abū Sanna, Aḥmad Fahmī. *Naẓariyyat al-ʿĀmma li-l-Muʿāmalāt fī sh-Sharīʿa l-Islāmiyya.* Cairo: Dār at-Taʾlīf, 1965.

———. *ʿUrf wa-l-ʿĀda fī Raʾy al-Fuqahāʾ.* n.p., 1992.

Abu Sulayman, Abdul Hamid. *Towards an Islamic Theory of International Relations: New Directions for Islamic Methodology and Thought.* Herndon, VA: International Institute of Islamic Thought, 1993.

Abū Zahra, Muḥammad. *Uṣūl al-Fiqh.* Cairo: Dār al-Fikr al-ʿArabī, n.d.

———. *al-Jarima wa l-ʿUquba fī l-Fiqh al-Islāmī.* Cairo: Dār al-Fikr al-ʿArabī, 1998.

Ahmad, Ali. "Amina Lawal's Ordeal: Getting Past the Impasse". *Nigeria World,* 7 October 2003. http://nigeriaworld.com/articles/2003/oct/072.html (accessed: 23 February 2007).

Akintola, Ishaq. *Shariʿah in Nigeria: An Eschatological Desideratum.* Ijebu-Ode, Nigeria: Shebiotimo Publications, 2001.

Allen, Desmond. "Women Can Rape Men, Says Female Judge". *Jamaica Observer,* 6 March 2007; https://www.jamaicaobserver.com/news/119959_Women-can-rape-men-says-female-judge (accessed: 11 March 2014).

al-Ālūsī, Shihāb al-Dīn. *Rūḥ al-Maʿānī.* Beirut: Dār Iḥyāʾ at-Turāth al-ʿArabī, n.d.

al-Alwani, Taha Jabir. "Judiciary and Rights of the Accused in Islamic Criminal Law", in *Criminal Law in Islam and the Muslim World: A Comparative Perspective.* Edited by Tahir Mahmood. New Delhi: Institute of Objective Studies, 1996.

al-Amidī, ʿAlī Ibn Muḥammad. *al-Iḥkām fī Uṣūl al-Aḥkām,* 2nd edn. Edited by Sayyid al-Jumaylī. Beirut: Dār al-Kitāb al-ʿArabī, 1986.

al-Amiri, Rashed Saud. *Legal Maxims in Islamic Jurisprudence: Their History, Character and Significance.* Ph.D. Dissertation. Birmingham, UK: Birmingham University, 2003.

al-Andalusī, Abū Hayyan Muḥammad b. Yūsuf. *al-Baḥr al-Muḥīt fī t-Tafsīr.* Edited by ʿAdil Aḥmad. Beirut: Dār al-Kutub al-ʿIlmiyya, 1993.

Anderson, J.N.D. "The Legal Tradition", in *Islam in Africa.* Edited by James Kritzeck and William H. Lewis. New York: Van Nostrand Reinhold, 1969.

———. *Islamic Law in Africa.* London: Frank Cass, 1978.

al-Aṣfahānī, Rāghib. *al-Mufradāt fī Gharīb al-Qurʾān.* Edited by Muḥammad Sayyid Kaylānī. Lebanon: Dār al-Maʿrifa, n.d.

al-Ashqar, ʿUmar Sulaymān. *ash-Sharīʿa l-Ilāhiyya lā l-Qawānīn al-Jāhiliyya.* Kuwait: Dār al-Daʿwa, 1983.

al-ʿAsqalānī, Aḥmad b. Alī b. Ḥajar. *Bulūgh al-Marām*, with translation. Riyadh: Dār as-Salām Publications, 1996.

———. *Fatḥ al-Bārī Sharḥ Ṣaḥīḥ al-Bukhārī*. Edited by Muḥibb al-Dīn al-Khaṭīb. Beirut: Dār al-Maʿrifa, n.d.

al-Atāsī, Khalid and Muḥammad Ṭāhir al-Atāsī. *Sharḥ Majallat al-Aḥkām al-ʿAdliyya*. Damascus: Hams Press, 1349/1930.

el-Awa, Mohamed S. *Punishment in Islamic Law*. Plainfield, IL: American Trust Publications, 2000.

ʿAwad, A.M. "The Rights of the Accused Under Islamic Criminal Procedure", in *The Islamic Criminal Justice System*. Edited by M. Cherif Bassiouni. New York: Oceana Publications, 1982.

ʿAwad, al-Sayyid Ṣāliḥ. *Aṭhar al-ʿUrf fī t-Tashrīʿ al-Islāmī*. Cairo: Jamiʿat al-Azhar, 1997.

ʿAwda, ʿAbd al-Qādir. *at-Tashrīʿ al-Jināʾī l-Islāmī Muqāranan bi-l-Qānūn al-Waḍaʿī*, 13th edn. Beirut: Muʾassasat ar-Risāla, 1995.

al-ʿAynī, Aḥmad. *ʿUmdat al-Qārī*. Beirut: Dār Iḥyāʾ at-Turāth al-ʿArabī, n.d.

al-Azharī, Ṣāliḥ ʿAbd al-Samiʿ al-Abīh. *at-Thamar ad-Dānī, Sharḥ Risālat al-Qayrawānī*. Cairo: Maktabat wa-Maṭbaʿat Muḥammad ʿAlī Ṣabīḥ wa-Awladuhu, 1948.

al-ʿAzīmabādī, Muḥammad Shams al-Ḥaqq. *ʿAwn al-Maʿbūd Sharḥ Sunān Abī Dāwūd*. 2nd edn. Beirut: Dār al-Kutub al-ʿIlmiyya, 1995.

Baʿalbakī, Munīr al-Dīn. *al-Mawrid: A Modern Arabic-English Dictionary*. 8th edn. Beirut: Dār al-ʿIlm li-l-Malayin, 1997.

Baderin, Mashood A. *International Human Rights and Islamic Law*. Oxford: Oxford University Press, 2005.

———., *et al. Islam and Human Rights Advocacy for Social Change in Local Contexts*. New Delhi: Global Media Publications, 2006.

al-Baghdādī, Ghanim b. Muḥammad. *Mujmaʿ al-Ḍamānāt*. Beirut: ʿAlam al-Kutub, 1987.

el-Bahnassawi, Salim. *Women Between Islam and World Legislation*. Kuwait: Dār al-Qalam, 1985.

al-Bahūtī, Manṣūr b. Yūnus. *Kashshāf al-Qināʿ ʿan Matn al-Iqnāʿ*. Edited by Hilāl Musilihi Hilāl. Beirut: Dār al-Fikr, 1982.

al-Bannānī, ʿAbd al-Raḥman b. Jad Allāh. *Hāshiyat al-Bannānī ʿalā Sharḥ al-Jalāl al-Muhallā ʿalā Jamʿ al-Jawāmiʿ*. Cairo: ʿĪsā al-Bab al-Ḥalabī Press, n.d.

al-Barr, Ibn ʿAbd, and Yūsuf Ibn ʿAbdullāh. *al-Istidhkār: at-Tamhīd li-mā fī l-Muwaṭṭaʾ min al-Māʿānī wa-l-Asānīd*. Edited by Muṣṭafā Aḥmad al-ʿAlawī. Morocco: Ministry of Endowment and Islamic Affairs, 1967.

———. *al-Istidhkār: al-Kāfī fī Fiqh Ahl al-Madīna*. Beirut: Dār al-Kutub al-ʿIlmiyya, 1987.

———. *al-Istidhkār*. Edited by Salim M. ʿAta. Beirut: Dār al-Kutub al-ʿIlmiyya, 2000.

Bassiouni, M. Cherif, Editor. *The Islamic Criminal Justice System*. New York: Oceana Publications, 1982.

———, *et al.* Editors. *Islamic Criminal Law and Procedure: An Introduction*. Westport, CT: Praeger, 1988.

al-Bayhaqī, Aḥmad b. Ḥusayn. *as-Sunān al-Kubrā*. Edited by Muḥammad A. ʿAta. Makkah: Maktabat Dār al-Baz, 1994.

Bello, Iysa A. *The Medieval Islamic Controversy Between Philosophy and Orthodoxy:* Ijmāʿ *and Taʾwīl in the Conflict Between al-Ghazālī and Ibn Rushd*. Leiden/New York: Brill, 1989.

———. "The development of *Ijmaʿ* in Islamic Jurisprudence", in *Perspectives in Islamic Law and Jurisprudence*. Edited by M. Oloyede Abdul-Rahmon. Ibadan: National Association of Muslim Law Students, 2001.

Bello, Justice Muhammed. "Keynote Address at the National Seminar on *Shari'a*", in *Understanding Shari'a in Nigeria*. Edited by A.M. Yakubu, A.M. Kani, and I. Junaid. Ibadan: Spectrum Books Limited, 2000.

al-Btoush, Amin M. Sallam al-Manasyeh. *The Question of Abrogation* (Naskh) *in the Qurʾān*. Karak: Deanship of Research and Graduate Studies, Mu'tah University, 1994.

al-Burnu, Muḥammad Siddiq Aḥmad. *al-Wajīz fī Īḍāḥ al-Qawāʿid al-Fiqhiyya al-Kulliyya*. 5th edn. Beirut: Mu'assasat ar-Risāla, 2002.

———. *Mawsūʿat al-Qawāʿid al-Fiqhiyya*. n.p., 2003.

Burton, John. *The Sources of Islamic Law: Islamic Theories of Abrogation*. Edinburgh: Edinburgh University Press, 1990.

Coulson, Neil J. *History of Islamic Law*. Edinburgh: Edinburgh University Press, 1964.

———. *Succession in the Muslim Family*. Cambridge: Cambridge University Press, 1971.

al-Dabūsī, Abū Zayd. *Taʾsīs an-Naẓar*. Cairo: Maṭbaʿat al-Imām, n.d.

al-Dam, Ibrāhīm b. ʿAbdullāh b. Abī. *Adab al-Qaḍāʾ* (*al-Manẓūmāt fī l-Aqḍiyya wa-l-Ḥukūmāt*). Edited by Muḥammad M. al-Ruḥaylī. Damascus: Dār al-Fikr, n.d.

al-Daraquṭnī, ʿAlī b. ʿUmar. *as-Sunān*. Edited by al-Sayyid ʿAbdullāh Hāshim al-Madanī. Beirut: Dār al-Maʿrifa, 1966.

al-Dardir, Aḥmad. *ash-Sharḥ al-Kabīr*, in Muḥammad ʿArafa al-Dasūqī, *Ḥāshiyat ad-Dasūqī ʿalā sh-Sharḥ al-Kabīr*. Edited by Muḥammad ʿUlaysh. Beirut: Dār al-Fikr, n.d.

al-Dārimī, ʿAbdullāh b. ʿAbd al-Raḥman. *as-Sunān*. Edited by Fawwaz Aḥmad Zamalī and Khalīl al-Sabaʿ al-ʿAlamī. Beirut: Dār al-Kitāb al-ʿArabī, 1407/1986.

al-Dasūqī, Muḥammad ʿArafa. *Ḥāshiyat ad-Dasūqī ʿalā as-Sharḥ al-Kabīr*. Edited by Muḥammad ʿUlaysh. Beirut: Dār al-Fikr, n.d.

Doi, Abdur Rahman. *Non-Muslims Under Shariʿah* (*Islamic Law*). London: Ta-Ha Publishers, 1983/1997.

———. *Sharīʿah: Islamic Law*. London: Ta-Ha Publishers, 1984.

———. *Women in Shariʿah*. London: Ta-Ha Publishers, 1989.

Dutton, Yasin. *The Origins of Islamic Law: The Qurʾān, the Muwaṭṭaʾ and Madinan ʿAmal*. Richmond, Surrey, UK: Curzon Press, 1999.

Elashhab, Ahmed. *The Criminal Liability in Islamic Law*. Tripoli: The World Islamic Call Society, 1994.

Elgariani, Fawzy Shaban. Al-Qawāʿid al-Fiqhiyyah (*Islamic Legal Maxims*)*: Concepts, Functions, History, Classifications and Application to Contemporary Medical Issues*. Ph.D. Dissertation. Exeter: University of Exeter Press, 2012.

Emanuel, Lazar. *Latin for Lawyers: The Language of the Law*. Larchmont, NY: Emanuel Publishing, 1999.

Faruki, Kemal A. Ijmāʿ *and the Gate of* Ijtihād. Karachi: Gateway Publications, 1954.

al-Faruqi Ismail R. and Lois Ibsen al-Faruqi. *The Cultural Atlas of Islam*. New York: MacMillan, 1986.

al-Faruqi, Lamya. *Women, Muslim Society, and Islam*. Indianapolis: American Trust Publications, 1987.

al-Fayruzabadi, Muḥammad b. Yaʿqub. *al-Qāmūs al-Muḥīṭ*. Beirut: Muʾassasat ar-Risāla, 2005.

al-Fayumī, Aḥmad b. Muḥammad. *al-Miṣbāḥ al-Munīr fī Gharīb ash-Sharḥ al-Kabīr*. Beirut: Maktabat Lubnān, 1987.

Ferguson, Peter W. *Crimes Against the Person*. Edinburgh: Butterworths, 1990.

Gaiya, Musa A.B. "Commentary", in *Comparative Perspectives on Shariʿah in Nigeria*. Edited by Philip Ostien, Jamila Nasir, and Franz Kogelmann. Ibadan: Spectrum Books, 2005.

al-Ghazālī, Abū Ḥāmid Muḥammad. *al-Mustaṣfā min ʿIlm al-Uṣūl*. 3rd edn. Beirut: Dār Iḥyāʾ at-Turāth al-ʿArabī and Muʾassasat at-Tarikh al-ʿArabī, 1993.

———. *al-Wasīṭ fī al-Madhhab*. Edited by Aḥmad Mahmood and Muḥammad Thamir. Cairo: Dār al-Salām, 1997.

al-Hafnāwī, Manṣūr Muḥammad Manṣūr. *ash-Shubhāt wa-Aṭharuhā fī l-ʿUqūbat al-Jināʾiyya fī l-Fiqh al-Islāmī Muqāranan bi-l-Qānūn*. Cairo: Maṭbaʿat al-Amana, 1986.

Hallaq, Wael B. "The Logic of Legal Reasoning in Religious and Non-Religious Cultures: The Case of Islamic Law and the Common Law", *Cleveland State Law Review* 34 (1985–1986).

———. "Was al-Shāfiʿī the Architect of Islamic Jurisprudence?", *International Journal of Middle East Studies* 25/4 (Nov. 1993): 587–605.

———. *A History of Islamic Legal Theories: An Introduction to* Sunnī Uṣūl al-Fiqh. Cambridge: Cambridge University Press, 1997.

———. *Authority, Continuity and Change in Islamic Law*. Cambridge: Cambridge University Press, 2001.

———. *Sharīʿa: Theory, Practice, Transformations*. Cambridge: Cambridge University Press, 2009.

al-Ḥamawī, Aḥmad b. Muḥammad. *Ghamz ʿUyūn al-Baṣāʾir Sharḥ al-Ashbāh wa-n-Naẓāʾir*. Beirut: Dār al-Kutub al-ʿIlmiyya, 1405/1985.

Haneef, Sayed Sikanadar Shah. "Modern Means of Proof: Legal Basis for its Accommodation in Islamic Law". *Arab Law Quarterly* 20/4 (2006): 334–364.

Hasan, Ahmad. *The Early Development of Islamic Jurisprudence*. Islamabad: Islamic Research Institute, 1970.

———. *The Doctrine of* Ijmāʿ *in Islam*. Islamabad: Islamic Research Institute, 1978.

———. *Analogical Reasoning in Islamic Jurisprudence: A Study of the Juridical Principle of* Qiyās. Islamabad: Islamic Research Institute, 1986.

al-Ḥaṭṭāb, Muḥammad b. ʿAbd al-Raḥman. *Mawāhib al-Jalīl fī Sharḥ Mukhtaṣar Khalīl*. Beirut: Dār al-Maʿrifa, 1398/1977.

Haydar, ʿAlī. *Durar al-Ḥukkām fī Sharḥ Majallat al-Aḥkām*. Edited by Fahmī al-Ḥusaynī. Beirut: Dār al-Kutub al-ʿIlmiyya, n.d.

al-Haythamī, ʿAlī. *Mawārid al-Ẓamān*. Edited by Muḥammad ʿAbd al-Razzāq. Beirut: Dār al-Kutub al-ʿIlmiyya, n.d.

Human Rights Watch. *"Political Shariʿa"? Human Rights and Islamic Law in Northern Nigeria*. New York: Human Rights Watch, 22 September 2004.

al-Ḥuṣarī, Aḥmad. *ʿIlm al-Qaḍāʾ wa-Adillat al-Ithbāt fī l-Fiqh al-Islāmī*. Beirut: Dār al-Kitāb al-ʿArabī, n.d.

Ibn ʿĀbidīn, Muḥammad Amin Ibn ʿUmar. *Ḥāshiyat Ibn ʿĀbidīn* or *Radd al-Mukhtār ʿalā d-Durar al-Mukhtār*. Beirut: Dār al-Fikr, 2000.

Ibn Anas, al-Imām Mālik. *al-Mudawwana al-Kubrā*. Beirut: Dār Sadir, 1975.

Ibn al-ʿArabī, Abū Bakr Muḥammad b. ʿAbdullāh. *Aḥkām al-Qurʾān*. Edited by Muḥammad ʿAta. Beirut: Dār al-Fikr, n.d.

———. *al-Maḥṣūl fī ʿIlm al-Uṣūl*. Edited by Ḥusayn ʿAlī al-Yadri. Amman: Dār al-Bayāriq, 1999.

Ibn al-Ashʿath, Abū Dāwūd Sulaymān, Aḥmad Fahmī. *al-Sunān*. Cairo: Maṭbaʿat as-Saʿada, 1950.

Ibn Ḍūyān, Ibrāhīm b. Muḥammad. *Manār as-Sabīl fī Sharḥ ad-Dalīl ʿalā madhhab al-Imām Aḥmad ibn Ḥanbal*. Edited by ʿIsam al-Qalaji. Riyadh: Maktabat al-Muʿārif, n.d.

Ibn Farhun, Ibrāhīm Ibn ʿAlī. *Tabṣirat al-Ḥukkām fī Uṣūl al-Aqḍiyya wa-Manāhij al-Aḥkām*. Beirut: Dār al-Kutub al-ʿIlmiyya and Cairo: al-Amīriyya Press, 1301/1883.

Ibn Ḥazm, Abū Muḥammad ʿAlī b. Aḥmad. *al-Iḥkām fī Uṣūl al-Aḥkām*. Cairo: Dār al-Ḥadīth, 1404/1983.

———. *al-Muḥallā bi-l-Āthār*. Beirut: Dār al-Afāq al-Jadīda, n.d.

Ibn Ḥibbān, Muḥammad al-Bustānī. *Ṣaḥīḥ Ibn Ḥibbān*. 2nd edn. Edited by Shuʿayb al-Arnaʾut. Beirut: Muʾassasat ar-Risāla, 1993.

Ibn al-Humām, Muḥammad b. ʿAbd al-Wāḥid b. Amīr al-Ḥājj. *Fatḥ al-Qadīr Sharḥ al-Hidāya*. Cairo: al-Amīriyya Press, 1336/1917.

———. *at-Taqrīr wa-t-Taḥbīr*. Beirut: Dār al-Fikr, 1996.

Ibn Ibrāhīm, Abū Yūsuf Yaʿqub. *Kitāb al-Kharāj*. Cairo: al-Maṭbaʿat as-Salafiyya wa-Maktabatuhā, 1397/1976.

Ibn Juzayy al-Kalbī, Muḥammad b. Muḥammad b. Aḥmad. *al-Qawānīn al-Fiqhiyya*. Beirut: Dār al-Qalam, 1977.

Ibn Kathir, Abū al-Fida' Ismāʿīl. *Tafsīr al-Qur'ān al-ʿAẓīm*. Beirut: Dār al-Fikr, 1401/1980.

Ibn Mājah, Muḥammad b. Yazīd. *as-Sunān*. Edited by Muhammad Fu'ad ʿAbd al-Baqi. Beirut: Dār al-Fikr, n.d.

Ibn Maʿjuz, Muḥammad. *Wasā'il al-Ithbāt fī l-Fiqh al-Islāmī*. Beirut: Dār al-Bayda, 1984.

Ibn Manẓūr, Muḥammad b. Makram. *Lisān al-ʿArab*. Edited by Amin Muhammad ʿAbd al-Wahhab and Muḥammad Sadiq al-ʿUbayd. Beirut: Dār Iḥyā' at-Turāth al-ʿArabī and Mu'assasat al-Ṭārikh al-ʿArabī, 1997.

Ibn Mufliḥ, Ibrāhīm Muḥammad. *al-Mubdiʿ Sharḥ al-Muqniʿ*. Beirut: Dār al-Maktab al-Islamī, 1400/1979.

———. *al-Furūʿ*. Edited by Abū al-Zahra Hazim. Beirut: Dār al-Kutub al-ʿIlmiyya, 1418/1997.

Ibn al-Najjār, Muḥammad b. Aḥmad al-Futūḥī. *Sharḥ al-Kawkab al-Munīr*. Edited by Muḥammad al-Zuhaylī and Nazih Hummad. Riyadh: Maktabat al-ʿUbaykan, 1418/1997.

Ibn Nujaym, Zayn al-ʿĀbidīn Ibn Ibrāhīm. *al-Baḥr ar-Rā'iq*. 2nd edn. Beirut: Dār al-Maʿrifa, n.d.

———. *al-Ashbāh wa-n-Naẓā'ir ʿalā Madhhab Abī Ḥanīfa l-Nuʿmān*. Beirut: Dār al-Kutub al-ʿIlmiyya, 1993.

Ibn al-Qayyim al-Jawziyya, Muḥammad Ibn Abī Bakr. *Iʿlām al-Muwaqqiʿīn ʿan Rabb al-ʿĀlamīn*. Edited by Ṭāhā ʿAbd al-Ra'ūf. Beirut: Dār al-Jil, 1973.

———. *aṭ-Ṭuruq al-Ḥukmiyya*. n.p.: Maktaba Dār al-Bayan, n.d.

Ibn Qudāma, ʿAbdullāh b. Aḥmad. *Rawḍat an-Nāẓir wa-Jannat al-Munāẓir*. Edited by ʿAbd al-ʿAziz ʿAbd al-Raḥman al-Saʿid. 2nd edn. Riyadh: Imām Ibn Saud University, 1399/1978.

———. *al-Mudhnī*. Edited by ʿAbdullāh al-Turkī and ʿAbd al-Fattah al-Hilu. Riyadh: Dār ʿAlam al-Kutub, 1999.

Ibn Qutayba, ʿAbdullāh b. Muslim. *Ta'wīl Mushkil al-Qur'ān*. 3rd edn. Beirut: Dār al-Kutub al-ʿIlmiyya, n.d.

Ibn Rajab, Abū al-Faraj ʿAbd al-Raḥman b. Shihāb al-Dīn. *al-Qawāʿid fī l-Fiqh al-Islāmī*. Beirut: Dār al-Kutub al-ʿIlmiyya, 1992.

———. *Jāmiʿ al-ʿUlūm wa-l-Ḥikam*. Edited by Shuʿayb al-Arna'ut and Ibrāhīm Bajis. Beirut: Mu'assasat ar-Risāla, 1997.

Ibn Rushd, Muḥammad b. Aḥmad. *Bidāyat al-Mujtahid wa-Nihāyat al-Muqtaṣid*. Beirut: Dār al-Fikr, n.d.

Ibn Taymiyya, Aḥmad b. ʿAbd al-Ḥalīm al-Ḥarrānī. *al-Muḥarrir fī l-Fiqh*. 2nd edn. Riyadh: Dār al-Maʿārif, 1404/1983.

———. *Majmūʿ al-Fatāwā*. Medina: Mujammaʿ al-Mālik Fahd li-t-Tabaʿ al-Maṣḥaf al-Sharīf, 1995.

Ibn Ibrāhīm, Abū Yūsuf Yaʿqub, *Kitāb al-Kharāj*, 6th edn. (Cairo: al-Maṭbaʿat as-Salafiyya wa-Maktabatuhā, 1397/1976).

Ibrahim, Saeed Hassan, and Nasir b. Ibrahim Mehemeed. "Basic Principles of Criminal Procedure Under Islamic Shariʿah", in *Criminal Justice in Islam: Judicial Procedure in the Shariʿa*. Edited by Muhammad Abdel Haleem, Adel Omar Sharif, and Ian Edge. London: I.B. Tauris, 2003, 17–34.

Inbau, Fred E. and John E. Reid. *Criminal Interrogation and Confessions*. Baltimore: Williams and Wilkins, 1967.

Izzi Dien, Mawil. *Islamic Law: From Historical Foundations to Contemporary Practice*. Notre Dame: University of Notre Dame Press, 2004.

al-Jaṣṣāṣ, Aḥmad b. ʿAlī. *Aḥkām al-Qurʾān*. Edited by Muḥammad Ṣādiq al-Qamḥāwī. Beirut: Dār Iḥyāʾ at-Turāth al-ʿArabī, 1985.

Johansen, Baber. "Legal Literature and the Problem of Change: The Case of the Land Rent" in *Islam and Public Law: Classical and Contemporary Studies*. Edited by Chibli Mallat. London: Graham and Trotman, 1993.

Jowitt, Earl and Clifford Walsh. *Jowitt's Dictionary of English Law*. London: Sweet and Maxwell, 1977.

al-Jurjānī, ʿAlī b. Muḥammad. *Kitāb at-Taʿrīfāt*. Beirut: Dār al-Kutub al-ʿIlmiyya, 1983.

Kamali, Muhammad Hashim. Istiḥsān: (*Juristic Preference*) *and its Application to Contemporary Issues*. Jeddah: Islamic Research and Training Institute, Islamic Development Bank, 1997.

———. "*Qawaʾid al-Fiqh*: The Legal Maxims of Islamic Law", *Journal of the Association of Muslim Lawyers* 3/2 (October 1998); http://www.aml.org.uk/cms/assets/Uploads/journals/3.2/Kamali-Qawaid-al-Fiqh.pdf (accessed: 21 June 2006).

———. *Principles of Islamic Jurisprudence*. 2nd edn. Kuala Lumpur: Ilmiah Publishers, 2000.

———. "*Istiḥsān* and the Renewal of Islamic Law", *Islamic Studies* 43/4 (2004): 561–581.

Kamali, Mohammad Hashim. *An Introduction to Shariah*. Kuala Lumpur: Ilmiah Publishers, 2006.

al-Karkhī, ʿUbaydallah b. al-Ḥusayn, *Uṣūl al-Karkhī*. Cairo: Maṭbaʿat al-Imām, n.d.

al-Kāsānī, ʿAlāʾ l-Dīn Abī Bakr b. Masʿūd. *Badāʾiʿ aṣ-Ṣanāʾiʿ fī Tartīb ash-Sharāʾiʿ*. Beirut: Dār al-Kutub al-ʿIlmiyya, 1997.

Kaufman, Fred. *The Admissibility of Confession*. 3rd edn. Toronto: Carswell Company, 1979.

Kayadibi, Saim. *Doctrine of* Istiḥsān (*Juristic Preference*) *in Islamic Law*. Ph.D. Dissertation. Durham, UK: University of Durham Press, 2007.

Kelly, Michael J. "Islam and International Law: A Brief (In)Compatibility Study", *Pace International Law Review Online Companion*, (1 March 2010): 1–31.

al-Khabbāzī, ʿUmar b. Muḥammad. *al-Mughnī fī Uṣūl al-Fiqh*. Edited by Muḥammad Muẓhar Baqā. Makkah: Umm al-Qura University Press, 1403/1982.

Khadduri, Majid. *The Islamic Conception of Justice*. Baltimore: John Hopkins University Press, 1984.

Khaleel, Muhammad. "The Islamic Law Maxims". *Journal of Islamic Studies* 44/2 (2005): 191–207.

Khalīl, Ibn Isāq. *Mukhtaṣar al-Khiraqī*. Edited by Aḥmad Harakat. Beirut: Dār al-Fikr, 1415/1994.

Khan, M.M. *Islamic Law and Criminology*. New Delhi: Discovery Publishing House, 2011.

Ladan, Muhammad Tawfiq. *A Handbook on Sharia Implementation in Northern Nigeria: Women and Children's Rights Focus*. Kaduna, Nigeria: League of Democratic Women (LEADS-Nigeria), 2005.

Laldin, Mohammad Akram. *The Theory and Application of* ʿUrf *in Islamic Law*. Ph.D. Dissertation. Edinburgh: University of Edinburgh Press, 1995.

Lowry, Joseph E. "The Reception of al-Shāfiʿī's Concept of *Amr* and *Nahy* in the Thought of His Student al-Muzani", in *Law and Education in Medieval Islam: Studies in Memory of Professor George Makdisi*. Edited by Joseph E. Lowry, Devin Stewart, and Shawkat M. Toorawa. Cambridge, UK: Gibb Memorial Trust, 2004.

al-Maḥallī, Jalāluddīn Muḥammad b. Aḥmad. *Sharḥ al-Waraqāt fī Uṣūl al-Fiqh*. Palestine: al-Quds University, 1999.

Maḥmaṣṣānī, Ṣubḥī R. *Falsafat at-Tashrīʿ fī l-Islām*. Translated by Farhat J. Ziadeh. Kuala Lumpur: Open Press, 2000.

Mahmood, Tahir, Editor. *Criminal Law in Islam and the Muslim World: A Comparative Perspective*. New Delhi: Institute of Objective Studies, 1996.

Makdisi, George. "The Juridical Theology of Shāfiʿī Origins and Significance of *Uṣūl al-Fiqh*". *Studia Islamica* 59 (1984): 5–47.

Mālik b. Anas b. Mālik, *al-Muwaṭṭa*. Beirut: Dār ʿIhyāʾ al-Turāth al-ʿArabī, 1406/1985.

Malik, Sayed H.A. "Shariʿah: A Legal System and a Way of Life", in *Perspectives in Islamic Law and Jurisprudence*. Edited by Abdul-Rahmon M. Oloyede. Ibadan: National Association for Muslim Law Students, 2001.

al-Manawī, Muḥammad ʿAbd al-Raʾuf. *Fayḍ al-Qadīr Sharḥ al-Jāmiʿ as-Saghīr*. 2nd edn. Beirut: Dār al-Maʿrifa, 1972.

al-Māwardī, ʿAlī b. Muḥammad. *al-Aḥkām as-Sulṭāniyya wa-l-Wilāya ad-Dīniyya*. Beirut: Dār al-Kutub al-ʿIlmiyya, n.d.

———. *al-Ḥāwī al-Kabīr*. Beirut: Dār al-Kutub al-ʿIlmiyya, 1419/1999.

Mawdūdī, Abū al-Aʿlā. *Towards Understanding Islam*. Indianapolis: Islamic Teaching Center, 1970.

Messick, Brinkley. "Indexing the Self: Intent and Expression in Islamic Legal acts", in *Islamic Law and Society*. Edited by David S. Powers. Leiden: Brill, 2001.

al-Mirdāwī, ʿAlī b. Sulaymān. *al-Inṣāf fī Maʿrifat ar-Rājiḥ min al-Khilāf*. Edited by ʿAbdullāh al-Turkī. Cairo: Dār Ḥajar, 1995.

Mirfield, Peter. *Confessions*. London: Sweet and Maxwell, 1985.

al-Munāwī, Muḥammad ʿAbd al-Raʾuf. *Fayḍ al-Qadīr Sharḥ al-Jāmiʿ as-Saghīr*, vol. 5, 2nd edn. Beirut: Dār al-Maʿrifa li-t-Tibaʿ, 1391/1972.

Muslehuddin, Muḥammad. *Islamic Jurisprudence and the Rule of Necessity and Need*. Islamabad: Islamic Research Institute, 1980.

———. *Philosophy of Islamic Law and The Orientalists (A Comparative Study of Islamic Legal Systems)*. Lahore: Islamic Publications, 1980.

al-Mutairi, Mansour. *Necessity in Islamic Law*. Unpublished Ph.D. Thesis. Edinburgh: University of Edinburgh, 1997.

an-Naʿim, Abdullahi Ahmed. "The Future of Shari'a and the Debate in Northern Nigeria", in *Comparative Perspectives on Shariʿah in Nigeria*. Edited by Philip Ostien, Jamila Nasir, and Franz Kogelmann. Ibadan: Spectrum Books, 2005.

———. *Islam and the Secular State*. Cambridge, MA: Harvard University Press, 2008.

al-Nadawī, ʿAlī Aḥmad. *al-Qawāʿid al-Fiqhiyya: Mafhūmuhā, Nashʾatuhā, Taṭawwuruhā, Dirāsatuhā, Muʾallafātuhā, Adillatuhā, Muhimmatuhā, Taṭbīquhā*. 2nd edn. Damascus: Dār al-Qalam, 1998.

al-Nafrāwī, Aḥmad. *al-Fawākih ad-Dawānī*. Beirut: Dār al-Fikr, 1995.

al-Nasaʾī, Aḥmad Ibn Shuʿayb. "Bāb Shibh al-ʿAmd" *of* "Kitāb al-Qasāma" *in* as-Sunan. Edited by ʿAbd al-Ghaffar Sulaymān and Sayyid Kasrawi. Beirut: Dār al-Kutub al-ʿIlmiyya, 1991.

al-Nawawī, Yaḥyā b. Sharif. *al-Majmūʿ Sharḥ al-Muhadhdhab*. Beirut: Dār al-Fikr, 1997.

———. *Sharḥ Ṣaḥīḥ Muslim*. 2nd edn. Beirut: Dār Iḥyāʾ at-Turāth al-ʿArabī, 1392/1972.

al-Naysābūrī, Muḥammad b. ʿAbdullāh. *al-Mustadrak ʿalā ṣ-Ṣaḥīḥayn*. Edited by Muṣṭafā A. ʿAta. Beirut: Dār al-Kutub al-ʿIlmiyya, 1990.

Nielsen, Jørgen S. "Introduction", in *Shariʿa as Discourse: Legal Traditions and the Encounter with Europe*, Edited by Jørgen S. Nielsen and Christoffersen Lisbet. Farnham, Surrey, UK: Ash, 2010.

Noor, Azman Mohd. "Punishment for Rape in Islamic Law", *Malayan Law Journal* 5 (2009).

Noor, Azman Mohd, and Ahmad Basri Ibrahim. "The Rights of a Rape Victim in Islamic Law", *IIUM Law Journal* 16/1 (2008): 65–83.

Noorslawat, Sabtu. *The Basic Principle of Shariʿa for the Enforcement of Hadd Punishment for Theft*. MA Thesis. Birmingham, UK: University of Birmingham Press, 1977.

Nyazee, Imran Ahsan Khan. *General Principles of Criminal Law: Islamic and Western*. Islamabad: International Islamic Univerisity, Shariʿah Academy, 2007.

Okpu, Ugbana. *Ethnic Minority Problems in Nigerian Politics: 1960–1965*. Stockholm: Almqvist & Wilksell International, 1977.

Omran, Abdel R. *Family Planning in the Legacy of Islam*. London: Routledge, 1992.

Opeloye, Muhib O. *The Sustainability of Shariʿah in a Pluralistic and Democratic Nigeria*. Presentation at the 5th Faculty of Arts Guest Lecture Series, Lagos State University, Lagos, Nigeria, 24 August 2005.

Opwis, Felicitas. Maṣlaḥa *and the Purpose of the Law: Islamic Discourse on Legal Change from the 4th/10th to 8th/14th Century*. Leiden: Brill, 2010.

Ostien, Philip. "An Opportunity Missed by Nigeria's Christians: The Sharia Debate of 1976–78 Revisited", in *Muslim–Christian Relations in Africa, Islam in Africa*, 5. Edited by Benjamin Soares. Leiden and Boston: Brill, 2005, 221–255.

Peters, Rudolph. "Murder in Khaybar: Some Thoughts on the Origins of Qasāma Procedure in Islamic Law". *Islamic Law and Society* 9/2 (2002): 132–167.

———. *Islamic Criminal Law in Nigeria*. Ibadan: Spectrum Books Limited, 2003.

———. "The Re-Islamization of Criminal Law in Northern Nigeria and the Judiciary: The Safiyyatu Hussaini Case", in *Dispensing Justice in Islam: Qadis and Their Judgments*. Edited by Muhammad Khalid Masud, Rudolph Peters, and David S. Powers. Leiden: Brill, 2005.

———. *Crime and Punishment in Islamic Law: Theory and Practice from the Sixteenth to Twenty-First Century*. Cambridge: Cambridge University Press, 2006.

Powers, Paul R. "Intent in Islamic Law: Motive and Meaning in Medieval Sunnī Fiqh". Edited by Ruud Peters and Bernard Weiss. *Studies in Islamic Law and Society* 25. Leiden: Brill, 2005.

Qadir, Anwar A. *Islamic Jurisprudence in the Modern World*. Delhi: Taj Company, 1986.

Qaliʿajī, Muḥammad Rawwas and Ḥāmid S. Qunaybī. *Muʿjam Lughat al-Fuqahāʾ*. Beirut: Dār an-Nafaes, 1985.

al-Qarāfī, Aḥmad b. Idrīs. *al-Amniyya fī Idrāk an-Niyya*. Beirut: Dār al-Kutub al-ʿIlmiyya, 1984.

———. *adh-Dhakhīra*. Edited by Muḥammad Ḥājjī. Beirut: Dār al-Gharb al-Islāmī, 1994.

———. *Anwār al-Burūq fī Anwāʾ al-Furūq*. Edited by Khalīl al-Manṣūr. Beirut: Dār al-Kutub al-ʿIlmiyya, 1998.

Quadri, Yasir A. *Shariah: The Islamic Way of Life*. Ogun State, Nigeria: Shebotimo Publication, 2000.

al-Qurṭubī, Muḥammad b. Aḥmad. *al-Jāmʿ li-Aḥkām al-Qurʾān*. Cairo: Dār al-Kutub al-Miṣriyya, 1936.

Qutb, Muhammad. *Islam: The Misunderstood Religion*. Dacca: Adhunik Prokashani, 1978.

Quṭb, Sayyid. *Fī Ẓilāl al-Qurʾān*. Beirut: Dār ash-Shurūq, 1982.

Rabb, Intisar. *Doubt's Benefit: Legal Maxims in Islamic Law 7th–16th Centuries*. Ph.D. Dissertation. Princeton: Princeton University Press, 2009.

Rabb, Intisar A., "Reasonable doubt" in Islamic Law, The Yale Journal of International Law, 2015, vol. 40:41.

Ramadan, Said. *Islamic Law: Its Scope and Equity*, London: Macmillan, 1970.

Ramadan, Tariq. *Islam, the West and the Challenges of Modernity*. Leicester: The Islamic Foundation, 2001.

———. "An International Call for Moratorium on Corporal Punishment, Stoning and the Death Penalty in the Islamic World". 5 April 2005; http://tariqramadan.com/blog/2005/04/05/an-international-call-for-moratorium-on-corporal-punishment-stoning-and-the-death-penalty-in-the-islamic-world/ (accessed: 16 February 2014).

al-Ramalī, Shams al-Dīn Muḥammad. *Nihāyat al-Muḥtāj ilā Sharḥ al-Minhāj*. Beirut: Dār al-Fikr, 1984.

al-Raysuni, Ahmed, *Nazariyyah al-Maqasid "ind al-Imam al-Shatibi,* (Saudi Arabia, al-Dar al-ʾAlamiyyah lil-Kutub al-Islami), 1992/1412.

al-Rāzī, Aḥmad b. Faris. *Muʿjam Maqāyīs al-Lūgha*. Edited by ʿAbd al-Salam M. Harun. Beirut: Dār Iḥyāʾ al-Kutub al-ʿArabiyya, n.d.

al-Rāzī, Muḥammad b. Abī Bakr ʿAbd al-Qadir. *Mukhtār al-Ṣiḥāḥ*. Edited by Muḥammad Khatir. Beirut: Maktabat Lubnān, 1995.

al-Rāzī, Muḥammad b. Ḥusayn. *al-Maḥṣūl fī ʿIlm al-Uṣūl*. Edited by Ṭāhā J. al-ʿAlawānī. Riyadh: Muḥammad Ibn Saud University, 1400/1979.

al-Rāzī, Muḥammad b. ʿUmar Fakhr al-Dīn. *at-Tafsīr al-Kabīr*. Beirut: Dār al-Kutub al-ʿIlmiyya, n.d.

Sābiq, Sayyid. *Fiqh as-Sunna*. Cairo: Dār al-Fath li-l-ʿIlām al-Arabī, 1425/2004.

al-Salam, Ibn ʿAbd, and ʿIzz al-Dīn. *Qawāʿid al-Aḥkām fī Maṣāliḥ al-Anām*. Beirut: Dār al-Kutub al-ʿIlmiyya, n.d.

Salama, Maʾamoun M. "General Principles of Criminal Evidence in Islamic Jurisprudence", in *The Islamic Criminal Justice System*. Edited by M. Cherif Bassiouni. New York: Oceana Publications, 1982.

al-Saleh, Osman. "The Right of the Individual to Personal Security in Islam", in *The Islamic Criminal Justice System*. Edited by M. Cherif Bassiouni. New York: Oceana Publications, 1982.

al-Ṣanʿānī, ʿAbd al-Razzāq b. Humām. *Muṣannaf ʿAbd al-Razzāq*. Edited by Ḥabīb al-Raḥmān al-Aʿẓamī. Beirut: Maṭabiʿ Dār al-Qalam, n.d.

al-Ṣanʿānī, Muḥammad Ibn Ismāʿīl. *Subl al-Salām*. Edited by Muḥammad al-Khawlī. 4th edn. Beirut: Dār Iḥyāʾ at-Turāth al-ʿArabī, 1379/1959.

Sanusi, S. Lamido. "The West and the Rest: Reflections on the Intercultural Dialogue about Shariʿah", in *Comparative Perspectives on Shariʿah in Nigeria*. Edited by Philip

Ostien, Jamila Nasir, and Franz Kogelmann. Ibadan: Spectrum Books, 2005, 255–274.

al-Sarakhsī, Muḥammad b. Aḥmad. *al-Mabsūṭ*. Beirut: Dār al-Maʿrifa, 1986.

al-Sawī, Aḥmad b. Muḥammad. *Bulghat as-Sālik li-Aqrab al-Masālik*. Cairo: Maktabat al-Bāb al-Ḥalabī, 1952.

al-Sawwat, Muḥammad b. ʿAbdullāh. *al-Qawāʿid wa-ḍ-Ḍawābiṭ al-Fiqhiyya ʿInd Ibn Taymiyya fī Fiqh al-Usra*. Taʾif: Dār al-Bayān al-Ḥadītha, 2001.

Schacht, Joseph. *An Introduction to Islamic Law*. Oxford: Oxford University Press, 1964.

———. *The Origin of Muhammadan Jurisprudence*. Oxford: Oxford University Press, 1950.

Shabana, Ayman. *Custom in Islamic Law and Legal Theory*. New York: Palgrave Macmillan, 2010.

Shabbir, Mohammad. *Outlines of Criminal Law and Justice in Islam*. Selangor, Malaysia: International Law Book Services, 2002.

al-Shāfiʿī, Muḥammad b. Idrīs. *Kitāb al-Umm*. Beirut: Dār al-Maʿrifa, 1381/1961.

———. *ar-Risāla fī Uṣūl al-Fiqh* (*Treatise on the Foundations of Islamic Jurisprudence*), trans. Majid Khadduri, 2nd edn. Cambridge, UK: Islamic Texts Society, 1987.

al-Shalābī, Muḥammad M. *Uṣūl al-Fiqh al-Islāmī*. Beirut: Dār al-Nahda al-ʿArabiyya li-t-Tibaʿa wa-n-Nashr wa-t-Tawziʿ, 1986.

al-Shaltūt, Maḥmūd. *al-Islām*. Cairo: Maṭbaʿat al-Azhar, 1959.

Shariah Penal Code Law of Zamfara State of Nigeria. Zaria, Nigeria: Gasikiya Corporation Limited. 15 June 2000, vol. 3.

al-Shāṭibī, Abū Isḥāq Ibrāhīm b. Mūsā. *al-Muwāfaqāt fī Uṣūl ash-Shariʿa*. Edited by ʿAbdullāh Darraz. Beirut: Dār al-Maʿrifa, 1975.

al-Shawkānī, Muḥammad b. ʿAlī. *Nayl al-Awṭār*. Beirut: Dār al-Jil, 1973.

———. *Irshād al-Fuḥūl ilā Taḥqīq al-Ḥaqq min ʿIlm al-Uṣūl*. Edited by Muḥammad Saʿid al-Badrī. Beirut: Dār al-Fikr, 1992.

al-Shaybānī, Aḥmad b. Ḥanbal. *al-Musnad*. Cairo: Muʾassasat Qurtuba, n.d.

al-Shaybānī, Muḥammad b. al-Ḥasan. *Kitāb al-Aṣl*. Edited by Abū al-Wafaʾ al-Afghani. Hyderabad: Maṭbaʿat Dār al-Maʿārif al-ʿUthmāniyya, n.d.

Shaykhzadah, ʿAbd al-Raḥman b. Muḥammad. *Majmaʿ al-Anhar*. Beirut: Dār al-Kutub al-ʿIlmiyya, 1998.

Shehaby, Nabil. "*ʿIlla* and *Qiyās* in Early Islamic Theory", *Journal of the American Oriental Society* 102/1 (1982).

al-Shinqitī, Muḥammad al-Amin. *Aḍwāʾ al-Bayān*. Beirut: Dār al-Fikr, 1995.

al-Shirazī, Abū Isḥāq Ibrāhīm b. ʿAlī. *al-Muhadhdhab fī Fiqh al-Imām al-Shāfiʿī*. Beirut: Dār al-Fikr, n.d.

———. *al-Lamʿ fī Uṣūl al-Fiqh*. Beirut: Dār al-Kutub al-ʿIlmiyya, 1985.

al-Shiribīnī, Muḥammad b. Aḥmad al-Khaṭīb. *al-Iqnāʿ fī Ḥall Alfāẓ Abī Shujāʿ*. Cairo: Dār al-Maʿārif, n.d.

———. *Mughnī al-Muḥtāj ilā Maʿrifat Maʿānī Alfāẓ al-Minhāj*. Beirut: Dār al-Fikr, n.d.

Siddiqi, Muhammad Iqbal. *The Penal Law of Islam*. New Delhi: International Islamic Publishers, 1994.

al-Suyūṭī, ʿAbd al-Raḥman b. Abū Bakr. *al-Ashbāh wa-n-Naẓāʾir fī l-Naḥw*. Edited by Ṭāhā ʿAbd al-Raʾuf. Cairo: Sharkat al-Tibaʿa al-Faniyya al-Muttaḥida, 1975.

———. *al-Ashbāh wa-n-Naẓāʾir*. Beirut: Dār al-Kutub al-ʿIlmiyya, 1983.

———. *al-Durr al-Manthūr fī l-Tafsīr al-Maʾthūr*. Beirut: Dār al-Fikr, 1993.

Tabatabai, Hossein M. *An Introduction to Shiʿi Law: A Bibliographical Study*. London: Ithaca Press, 1984.

al-Ṭarāblusī, Ali b. Khalīl. *Muʿīn al-Ḥukkām fī-mā Yataraddad bayna l-Khaṣimayn min al-Aḥkām*. Cairo: Maṭbaʿat al-Bāb al-Ḥalabī, 1393/1973.

al-Tirmidhī, Muḥammad b. ʿĪsā. *Sunān al-Tirmidhī* or *al-Jāmiʿ aṣ-Ṣaghīr*. Edited by Bashashar ʿAwad Maʿruf. Beirut: Dār al-Gharb al-Islāmī, 1998.

Turner, James William Cecil and A.L. Armitage. *Cases on Criminal Law*. 3rd edn. Cambridge: Cambridge University Press, 1964.

Tyser, Charles R., D.G. Demetriades, and Ismail Haqqi Effendi, trans. *The Mejelle: Being an English Translation of* Majallah-el-Ahkam-i-Adliya *and a Complete Code on Islamic Civil Law*. Lahore: All Pakistan Legal Decisions, 1967.

United Nations General Assembly. *International Covenant on Civil and Political Rights*. 16 December 1966; http://www.ohchr.org/en/professionalinterest/pages/ccpr.aspx (accessed: 1 March 2014).

Walker, David M. *The Oxford Companion to Law*. Oxford: Oxford University Press, 1980.

Waqar-ul-Haq, Muhammad. *Islamic Criminal Laws* (*Hudood Laws & Rules with Up-to-Date Commentary*). Lahore: Nadeem Law Book House, 1994.

Weeramantry, Christopher G. *Islamic Jurisprudence: An International Perspective*, 2nd edn. Kuala Lumpur: The Other Press, 2001.

"Woman Can't Be Prosecuted on Gang Rape Charge: Court, *The Hindu*, 14 July 2006; http://www.thehindu.com/todays-paper/tp-national/woman-cant-be-prosecuted-on-gang-rape-charge-court/article3104565.ece (accessed: 11 March 2014).

Women's Aid Collective. *Safiyyatu's Case*. Trans. Ibrahim Ladan. Enugu, Nigeria: Women's Aid Collective, 2003.

Yawuri, Aliyu Musa. "Issues in Defending Safiyyatu Husseini and Amina Lawal", in *Sharia Penal and Family Laws in Nigeria and in the Muslim World: Rights Based Approach*. Edited by Jibrin Ibrahim. Zaria, Nigeria: Ahmadu Bello University Press Limited, 2004.

al-Zahrānī, Saʿid b. Darwish. *Tarāʾiq al-Ḥukm al-Muttafaq ʿalayhā wa-l-Mukhtalaf fīhā fī sh-Sharīʿa l-Islāmiyya*. 2nd edn. Jeddah: Maktabat al-Sahaba, 1994.

Zakariyah, Luqman. *Applications of Legal Maxims in Islamic Criminal Law with Special Reference to Shariah Law in Northern Nigeria* (*1999–2007*). PhD Thesis, Lampeter, UK, University of Wales, 2009.

———. "Custom and Society in Islamic Criminal Law: A Critical Appraisal of the Maxim *'al-Ādah Muḥakkamah'* (Custom is Authoritative) and its Sisters in Islamic Legal Procedures", *Arab Law Quarterly* 26/1 (2012): 75–97.

———. "Islamic Legal Maxims for Attainment of *Maqasid-ash-Shari'ah* in Criminal Law: Reflections on the Implications for Muslim Women in the Tension between Shari'ah and Western Law", in *Women in Islam: Reflections on Historical and Contemporary Research*. Edited by Terence Lovat. New York: Springer, 2012.

———. "Sharī'ah Values for Modern Societies: Analysis of Contents and Contexts", in *The Routledge International Handbook of Education, Religion and Values*. Edited by James Arthur and Terence Lovat. New York: Routledge, 2013.

al-Zamakhsharī, Maḥmūd b. 'Umar. *al-Kashshāf*. Edited. 'Abd al-Razzāq al-Mahdi. Beirut: Dār Iḥyā' at-Turāth al-'Arabī, n.d.

al-Zanjānī, Maḥmūd b. Aḥmad. *al-Tamhīd fī Takhrīj al-Furū' 'alā l-Uṣūl*. Edited by Muḥammad Adib Ṣāliḥ. 2nd edn. Beirut: Mu'assasat ar-Risāla, 1398/1977.

al-Zār'i, Muḥammad. *Ighāthat al-Lahfāt*. Edited by Muḥammad Ḥāmid al-Faqī. Beirut: Dār al-Ma'rifa, 1975.

al-Zarkashī, Muḥammad Ibn Bahādir. *al-Baḥr al-Muḥīṭ fī Uṣūl al-Fiqh*. Beirut: Dār al-Kutub al-'Ilmiyya, 1421/2000.

al-Zarkashī, Muḥammad Ibn Bahā' al-Dīn. *al-Manthūr fī l-Qawā'id*. 2nd edn. Edited by Taysir F.A. Maḥmūd. Kuwait: Ministry of Endowment and Islamic Affairs, 1405/1984.

al-Zarqā', Aḥmad b. Muḥammad. *Sharḥ al-Qawā'id al-Fiqhiyya*. 4th edn. Damascus: Dār al-Qalam, 1996.

al-Zarqā', Mustafa Aḥmad. *al-Madkhal al-Fiqhī al-'Āmm*. Damascus: Maṭba'at Jami'a, 1983.

al-Zarqānī, Muḥammad b. 'Abd al-Bāqī. *Sharḥ al-Muwaṭṭa'*. Beirut: Dār al-Kutub al-'Ilmiyya, 1990.

Zaydān, 'Abd al-Karīm. *Niẓām al-Qaḍā' fī sh-Sharī'a l-Islāmiyya*. Baghdad: Maṭba'at al-'Ani, 1404/1983.

———. *al-Wajīz fī Sharḥ al-Qawā'id al-Fiqhiyya fī sh-Sharī'a al-Islāmiyya*. Beirut: Mu'assasat ar-Risāla, 1997.

al-Zayla'ī, Fakhr al-Dīn. *Tabyīn al-Ḥaqā'iq Sharḥ Kanz ad-Daqā'iq*. Cairo: Dār al-Kutub al-Islāmiyya, 1313/1905.

al-Zuhaylī, Wahbah Muṣṭafā. *Naẓariyyat aḍ-Ḍarūra ash-Shar'iyyah Muqāranah ma'a l-Qānūn al-Waḍa'ī*, 4th edn. Beirut: Mu'assasah al-Risāla, 1405/1985.

———. *al-Qawā'id al-Fiqhiyya wa-Taṭbīqātuhā fī l-Madhāhib al-Arba'a*. Damascus: Dār al-Fikr, 2006.

Index